HOLT

HIGH SCHOOL HANDBOOK

2

John E. Warriner

HOLT, RINEHART AND WINSTON
Harcourt Brace & Company

Austin • New York • Orlando • Chicago • Atlanta
San Francisco • Boston • Dallas • Toronto • London

Author

John E. Warriner developed the organizational structure upon which *Holt High School Handbook 2* is based. He was the author of *English Composition and Grammar* and coauthor of *Elements of Writing*. He coauthored the *English Workshop* series, was general editor of the *Composition: Models and Exercises* series, and was editor of *Short Stories: Characters in Conflict*. He taught English for thirty-two years in junior and senior high school and college.

Critical Readers

Grateful acknowledgment is made to the following critical readers, who reviewed pre-publication materials for this book:

Charlotte H. Geyer
Former Language Arts
    Director
Seminole County, Florida

Nancy Light
Clarence High School
Clarence, New York

Belinda Manard
McKinley High School
Canton, Ohio

Faye Nelson
Northeast High School
Greensboro, North Carolina

Mark Sweeney
Marblehead High School
Marblehead, Massachusetts

Acknowledgments: See pages 630–632, which are an extension of the copyright page.

Printed in the United States of America

ISBN 0-03-094639-5

2 3 4 5 6   039   96 95 94 93

Contents in Brief

Table of Contents

▶ CHAPTER 4   **USING PRONOUNS**   185

Case Forms of Pronouns; Special Problems; Clear Reference

▶ CHAPTER 5   **USING MODIFIERS**   212

Forms and Uses of Adjectives and Adverbs; Comparison; Placement of Modifiers

■■■ *Part Three*

PHRASES, CLAUSES, SENTENCES   236

▶ CHAPTER 6 **PHRASES**   238

Kinds of Phrases and Their Functions

▶ CHAPTER 7 **CLAUSES**   261

The Functions of Clauses

▶ CHAPTER 8 SENTENCE STRUCTURE 277

Subjects, Predicates, Complements; Types of Sentences

▶ CHAPTER 13 **PUNCTUATION** 406

Other Marks of Punctuation

▶ CHAPTER 14 **SPELLING AND VOCABULARY** 438

Improving Your Spelling and Vocabulary; Forming New Words; Choosing the Appropriate Word

■■■■■ *Part Five*

COMPOSITION 466

CHAPTER 15 THE WRITING PROCESS 468

CHAPTER 16 PARAGRAPH AND COMPOSITION STRUCTURE 489

PART ONE

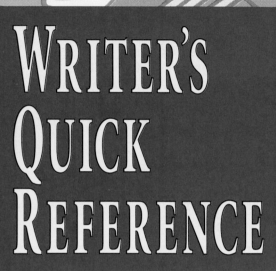

WRITER'S
QUICK
REFERENCE

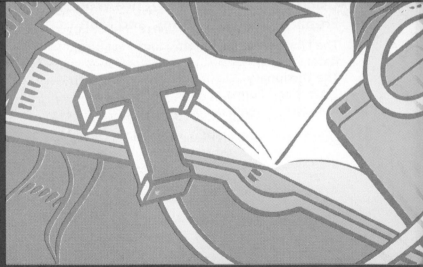

The **Writer's Quick Reference** is an alphabetical list of special terms and expressions with definitions, explanations, and examples. When you encounter a grammar or usage problem in the revising or proofreading stage of your writing, look for help in this section first. You may find all you need to know right here. But if you need more information, the **Writer's Quick Reference** will show you where in the book to turn for a fuller explanation. If you don't find what you are looking for in the **Writer's Quick Reference**, turn to the index on page 610.

You'll notice that some examples in this section are labeled *standard*, *nonstandard*, *formal*, or *informal*. The label *standard* or *formal* identifies usage that is appropriate in serious writing and speaking (such as in compositions and speeches). The label *informal* indicates standard English that is generally appropriate in conversation and in everyday writing such as personal letters. The label *nonstandard* identifies usage that does not follow the guidelines of standard English usage.

A

a, an These indefinite articles refer to one of the members of a general group. Use *a* before words beginning with consonant sounds, including the sounds *w* and *y*. Use *an* before words beginning with vowel sounds. Before a numeral or before a letter or an acronym, use *a* or *an* according to the way the numeral, letter, or acronym is pronounced.

EXAMPLES
- **A** unique solar calendar on **a** hillside in northwestern New Mexico was built by **an** ancient people of the Southwest, the Anasazi.
- Not **a** one of us has ever received **an** invitation to **a** young-people's party that required wearing **a** white tie.
- **A** 1992 survey showed that having **an** 800 number greatly increased business.
- On his term paper, Gary got **an** A for content and **a** B for manuscript style.
- The reporter was unable to confirm that the woman assisting the police investigators was **an** FBI agent.
- Uncle Leon claims to have seen **a** UFO when he was driving home from work.

abbreviation An abbreviation is a shortened form of a word or phrase. See pages 380–381 and 586–596.

EXAMPLE
- **Dr.** Frank **R.** Kling, **Jr.,** will deliver the keynote speech at 8:00 **P.M.**

abstract noun An abstract noun names a feeling, an idea, or a quality. See pages 88–89.

EXAMPLE
- According to our survey, the **qualities** that people value most in a friend are **kindness, generosity, humor,** and **trustworthiness.**

accept, except *Accept* is a verb meaning "to receive." *Except* may be either a verb or a preposition. As a verb, *except* means "to leave out." As a preposition, *except* means "excluding."

EXAMPLES ▪ I will **accept** another yearbook assignment.
▪ Should the military services **except** women from combat duty? [verb]
▪ She has typed everything **except** her Works Cited list. [preposition]

access, excess As a noun, *access* means "admittance" or "outburst." As a verb, it means "to gain admittance to." As a noun, *excess* means "an amount or quantity greater than usual or necessary." As an adjective, it means "extra; surplus."

EXAMPLES ▪ During construction, **access** to the mall is available only from Ridge Road. [noun]
▪ The speaker in "God's World" by Edna St. Vincent Millay expresses an **access** of joy brought on by the beauty of an autumn day. [noun]
▪ Beginning September 1, patrons of the county's branch libraries will be able to **access** the main library's computerized card catalog. [verb]
▪ This year's wheat harvest yielded an **excess** of three bushels per acre over last year's harvest. [noun]
▪ Many area restaurants donate their **excess** food to local food banks. [adjective]

accidentally, accidently The correct form is *accidentally*.

acronym An acronym is a word formed from the first (or first few) letters of a series of words. Periods are not used with acronyms. If there is any possibility that your readers will not recognize what the acronym stands for, add the complete term in parentheses after your first use of the acronym. See pages 588–589.

EXAMPLES ▪ Janell and I went **scuba** diving last weekend.
[*Scuba* is an acronym for self-contained underwater breathing apparatus.]

■ How many medical uses of **lasers** can you name? [*Laser* is an acronym for light amplification by stimulated emission of radiation.]

■ Developed in the late 1950s, **COBOL** (common business-oriented language) was the first commercial programming language.

action verb   An action verb expresses physical or mental activity. See pages 100–101.

EXAMPLE   ■ I **think** that Nathan **has** already **fed** the dog.

active voice   A verb is in the active voice when it expresses an action done *by* its subject. See pages 170–171.

EXAMPLE   ■ This assembly line **moves** truck chassis to the different work stations.

adapt, adopt   *Adapt* means "to change or adjust something in order to make it fit or to make it suitable." *Adopt* means "to take something and make it one's own."

EXAMPLES   ■ The movie was **adapted** from a best-selling novel.

■ For this production, the star **adopted** a German accent.

A.D., B.C.   *A.D.* is the abbreviation for the Latin phrase *Anno Domini,* meaning "in the year of the Lord." It is used with dates in the Christian era. *B.C.* is the abbreviation for "before Christ." It is used for dates before the Christian era. See pages 592–593.

EXAMPLES   ■ Julius Caesar was assassinated in 44 **B.C.**

■ Under the Gupta dynasty (**A.D.** 320–467), Hinduism flourished in India.

adjective   An adjective modifies a noun or a pronoun. See pages 95–100 and 214–215.

EXAMPLES   ■ Janice likes **the big, fluffy, gray** kitten, but I prefer **the little orange** one.

adjective clause   An adjective clause is a subordinate clause that modifies a noun or a pronoun. See pages 265–267.

EXAMPLE   ■ The poet **who wrote "The Love Song of J. Alfred Prufrock"** is T. S. Eliot.

adjective phrase An adjective phrase is a prepositional phrase that modifies a noun or a pronoun. See page 242.

EXAMPLE ▪ The orchids **from Mr. Connally's greenhouse** are more colorful than any others **in this flower show.**

adopt See **adapt, adopt.**

adverb An adverb modifies a verb, an adjective, or another adverb. See pages 104–106 and 216–218.

EXAMPLE ▪ **Sometimes,** when she's feeling **particularly** creative and energetic, Keiko will paint **very late** at night.

adverb clause An adverb clause is a subordinate clause that modifies a verb, an adjective, or an adverb. See pages 270–273.

EXAMPLE ▪ I can't go to the movies **until I finish my homework.**

adverb phrase An adverb phrase is a prepositional phrase that modifies a verb, an adjective, or an adverb. See pages 242–243.

EXAMPLE ▪ **In the game's final seconds,** Vijay slammed the ball **through the hoop.**

adverse, averse *Adverse* means "opposing" or "harmful." *Averse* means "unwilling."

EXAMPLES ▪ Exhausted from struggling against **adverse** currents, the canoers welcomed the rest stop.
▪ Smoking has **adverse** effects on health.
▪ In August Wilson's play *The Piano Lesson,* Berniece is **averse** to selling the piano because it represents her heritage.

advice, advise *Advice* is a noun meaning "opinion about what to do in a situation." *Advise* is a verb meaning "to offer an opinion to; recommend."

EXAMPLES ▪ The media specialist gave us **advice** about potential sources for our research papers.
▪ He **advised** us not to overlook sources other than print materials.

WRITER'S QUICK REFERENCE

affect, effect   *Affect* is a verb meaning "to influence." As a verb, *effect* means "to bring about or accomplish." As a noun, *effect* means "the result [of an action]."

EXAMPLES   ▪ Decisions of the United States Supreme Court **affect** the lives of many people.
▪ Some of the decisions **effect** great social change. [verb]
▪ In history class, did you learn about the far-reaching **effects** of the *Brown* v. *Board of Education of Topeka* decision? [noun]

aggravate   *Aggravate* means "to make more serious or troublesome." Informally, it is commonly used for "annoy" or "irritate."

INFORMAL   Their constant gossiping really aggravates me.

FORMAL   In her journal, Sarah Kemble Knight describes how the onset of darkness **aggravated** the discomforts of her 1704 journey from Boston to New York.

agreement   Agreement is the correspondence, or match, between grammatical forms, specifically a verb and its subject or a pronoun and its antecedent. See **Chapter 2: Agreement.**

EXAMPLES   ▪ **Reuben** and **Bill are preparing** a report on Poe's short story "The Masque of the Red Death." [subject-verb agreement]
▪ **They** have finished gathering **their** information, and now **each** of them is drafting **his** half of the report. [pronoun-antecedent agreement]

ahold of, a hold of   *Ahold of* is used informally for "a hold, or grasp, of." Avoid it in formal speaking and writing. Instead, use **a hold of.**

INFORMAL   How did you get ahold of the company's application form?

FORMAL   In Alice Walker's short story "Everyday Use," Dee (Wangero) recoils when her sister Maggie tries to take **a hold of** the quilts their grandmother made.

ain't *Ain't* is nonstandard. Avoid it in formal speaking and in all writing other than dialogue.

all ready, already *All ready* means "all prepared." Use it if you can substitute *ready* alone without changing the meaning of the sentence. *Already* is an adverb meaning "prior to a specified point in time" or "even now."

EXAMPLES ■ Are you **all ready** for the exam?
         ■ We have **already** studied the chapter on common usage problems.

all right *All right* means "satisfactory," "unhurt; safe," "correct," or, in reply to a question or to preface a remark, "yes." *Alright* is a misspelling.

EXAMPLES ■ Yehuda Amichai, in "Laments on the War Dead," compares love to a night light that gives a sleeping infant the sense that everything is **all right.**
         ■ **All right,** all those in favor of the motion say "Aye."

all the farther, all the faster These expressions are used informally in some parts of the United States. In formal situations, use *as far as* or *as fast as.*

INFORMAL   The first act was all the farther we had read in *A Raisin in the Sun.*
  FORMAL   The first act was **as far as** we had read in *A Raisin in the Sun.*

all together, altogether *All together* means "everyone in the same place." Use it if you can substitute *together* alone without changing the meaning of the sentence. *Altogether* is an adverb meaning "entirely."

EXAMPLES ■ My sister is flying in from Boston so that my family will be **all together** for the Thanksgiving holiday.
         ■ The president is **altogether** opposed to the bill.

allusion, illusion An *allusion* is an indirect reference to something. An *illusion* is a mistaken idea or a misleading appearance.

WRITER'S QUICK REFERENCE

EXAMPLES ▪ Flannery O'Connor makes numerous biblical **allusions** in her stories.
▪ **Illusions** of success haunt Willy Loman in *Death of a Salesman.*
▪ Makeup can be used to create an **illusion.**

almost, most Avoid using the clipped (shortened) form *most* for *almost* in all writing other than dialogue.

EXAMPLE ▪ **Almost** [*not* Most] everyone in class was saddened by the outcome of Ferdowsi's story of Sohráb and Rostám in the *Shahname.*

a lot With the article *a, lot* may be used as a noun or as an adverb. In its noun use, the expression means "a large number or amount." In its adverb use, it means "a great deal; very much." Both uses are informal; avoid them in formal speaking and writing situations. *Alot* is a misspelling of the phrase in either use.

EXAMPLES ▪ **A lot** of my friends work part time. [noun]
▪ The bus was **a lot** later than usual. [adverb]

already See **all ready, already.**

altar, alter *Altar* is a noun meaning "a table or stand at which religious rites are performed." *Alter* is a verb meaning "to change."

EXAMPLES ▪ This is the **altar** used in the Communion service.
▪ Do not **alter** your plans on my account.

altogether See **all together, altogether.**

alumni, alumnae *Alumni* (ə lum´nī) is the plural of *alumnus* (a male graduate). *Alumnae* (ə lum´nē) is the plural of *alumna* (a female graduate). As a group, the graduates of a coeducational school are usually called *alumni.*

EXAMPLES ▪ Each year the **alumni** who played on the football team provide two scholarships.
▪ Did the administration ask the **alumnae** how they felt about admitting men to the school?
▪ Men and women from the first graduating class attended the **alumni** reunion.

ambiguous reference   An ambiguous reference occurs when a pronoun can refer to either of two antecedents. See pages 205–206.

AMBIGUOUS   Karen told Sue that she had been nominated for class president. [Who had been nominated: *Karen* or *Sue*?]

CLEAR   "I've been nominated for class president," Karen told Sue.

CLEAR   "You've been nominated for class president," Karen told Sue.

among   See **between, among.**

amount of, number of   Use *amount of* to refer to a singular word. Use *number of* to refer to a plural word. See also **Number,** page 120.

EXAMPLES   ■ A large **amount of** work is done in the library. [*Amount of* refers to the singular word *work.*]

■ A large **number of** books have been checked out of the library. [*Number of* refers to the plural word *books.*]

A.M., P.M.   The abbreviation *A.M.* stands for the Latin phrase *ante meridiem,* meaning "before noon." It is used to designate times from midnight to noon. The abbreviation *P.M.* stands for the Latin phrase *post meridiem,* meaning "after noon." It is used to designate times from noon to midnight. Use *A.M.* and *P.M.* with numerals only. See pages 593–594.

EXAMPLE   ■ Coach said that the bus would leave at 8:00 A.M. sharp.

an   See **a, an.**

and, but   Writers sometimes choose to begin a sentence with *and* or *but* for a particular stylistic effect. Many authorities on usage agree that to begin a sentence with *and* or *or* is perfectly acceptable. In general, however, avoid beginning a sentence with *and* or *but* in your writing for school unless you've discussed this point of usage with your teacher.

and etc.   The abbreviation *etc.* stands for the Latin words *et cetera,* meaning "and others" or "and so forth." Consequently, *and* should not be used before *etc.*

EXAMPLE
■ We are studying twentieth-century American novelists: Ernest Hemingway, Margaret Walker, Jean Toomer, Pearl Buck, **etc.** [*not* and etc.]

and/or   Avoid using this confusing construction. Decide which alternative, *and* or *or,* expresses what you mean, and use it alone.

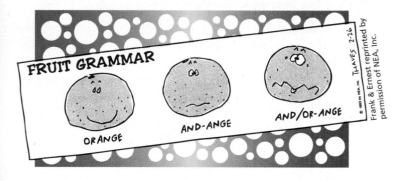

and which, and who   The expressions *and which,* and *and who* should be used only when a *which* or a *who* clause precedes them in the sentence.

NONSTANDARD   At the state livestock show, Jesse plans to show his prize-winning heifer and which he has raised from a calf.

STANDARD   At the state livestock show, Jesse plans to show his heifer, **which** is a prizewinner **and which** he raised from a calf.

STANDARD   At the state livestock show, Jesse plans to show his prizewinning heifer, **which** he raised from a calf.

anecdote, antidote   An *anecdote* is a short, entertaining account of an occurrence, usually a personal or biographical one. In a piece of writing, an *anecdote* may be used to support a main idea. See page 492. An *antidote* is a remedy to counteract a poison or, by extension of that meaning, anything that works against an unwanted condition.

EXAMPLES
- Chinese philosophers often use **anecdotes** to impart truths about human experience.
- Poison control centers are staffed by people who are knowledgeable about **antidotes** for various poisons.
- Owning a pet can be an effective **antidote** for loneliness.

antecedent   An antecedent is the word that a pronoun stands for. See pages 90 and 133–140.

EXAMPLE
- **Jim** showed **Kara** and **Luisa** the portrait **he** had painted of **them**. [*Jim* is the antecedent of *he*. *Kara* and *Luisa* are the antecedents of *them*.]

antidote   See **anecdote, antidote.**

anxious, eager   Although both *anxious* and *eager* mean "desiring greatly," *anxious* suggests some uneasiness over the outcome.

EXAMPLES
- The narrator of Joaquim Maria Machado de Assis's story "A Canary's Ideas" describes how **anxious** he was to find the escaped bird.
- Tamisha is **eager** to show us her vacation photographs.

any more, anymore   In the expression *any more, any* is an adverb modifying the adjective *more*. Used together, the two words specify a quantity. *Anymore* is an adverb meaning "now; nowadays." It is generally used only in negative constructions. In some parts of the country, however, it is used in positive constructions as well.

FORMAL   Do you know **any more** Caddo folk tales in which Coyote's actions affect human society?

FORMAL   Kam Shing doesn't work at the record store **anymore**.

INFORMAL   It's hard to find black-and-white TV sets **anymore**.

any one, anyone   In the expression *any one, any* is an adjective modifying the pronoun *one*. Used together, the two words specify one member of a group. *Anyone* is a pronoun meaning "one person, no matter which." Often, pronunciation provides a clue to the meaning you intend.

EXAMPLES   ■ **Any one** of you could win the poetry contest. [stress on *one*]
           ■ **Anyone** who finishes the test early may go to the media center. [stress on *any*]

anyways, anywheres   Omit the final *s* from these words and others like them (*everywheres, nowheres, somewheres*).

EXAMPLES   ■ I couldn't take both band and art **anyway** [*not* anyways].
           ■ Are your grandparents going camping **anywhere** [*not* anywheres] this summer?

appositive   An appositive is a noun or a pronoun placed beside another noun or pronoun to identify or explain it. See pages 256–257.

EXAMPLE   ■ The British writer **Saki** was born in Burma, now called the Union of Myanmar. [*Saki* identifies the noun *writer.*]

appositive phrase   An appositive phrase consists of an appositive and its modifiers. See pages 257–258.

EXAMPLE   ■ Saki, **the pseudonym of H. H. Munro,** was the name of a cup-bearer in Omar Khayyám's *Rubáiyát.* [The prepositional phrase *of H. H. Munro* modifies the appositive *pseudonym.*]

appraise, apprise   *Appraise* means "to decide the value of." *Apprise* means "to notify."

EXAMPLE   ■ The coin dealer will **appraise** my coin collection and **apprise** me of its value.

apt, liable, likely   Both *apt* and *liable* are informally used as equivalents of *likely*. In formal usage, however, the three terms are not interchangeable. *Apt* suggests a natural inclination or tendency, while *likely* suggests probability. *Liable* suggests exposure to something undesirable, including legal action.

EXAMPLES   ■ Dad's **apt** to worry when I'm late.
           ■ Do you think the Bears are **likely** to win the division title this year?
           ■ Renters are **liable** for any damage caused by their pets.

article *A, an,* and *the,* the most frequently used adjectives, are articles. See page 97.

as See **like, as.**

as if See **like, as if.**

assistance, assistants *Assistance* is help; *assistants* are those who help.

EXAMPLE ■ For **assistance** with the items in this display case, ask one of the sales **assistants.**

at Avoid using *at* after a construction beginning with *where.*

NONSTANDARD Where is the Crow Canyon Archaeological Center at?

STANDARD **Where** is the Crow Canyon Archaeological Center?

at this point in time, at this moment in time Both of these phrases are redundant. Instead, use *at this time* or *now.*

EXAMPLE ■ The people of Africa can **now** [*not* at this point in time] hear oral performers on radio and television as well as at public gatherings.

author Avoid using *author* as a verb; use *write* instead.

EXAMPLE ■ Santha Rama Rau **wrote** [*not* authored] her first book, *Home to India,* while she was an undergraduate at Wellesley College in Massachusetts.

averse See **adverse, averse.**

a while, awhile *While* is a noun meaning "a period of time." Used with the article *a,* it may stand alone or serve as the object of a preposition. *Awhile* is an adverb meaning "for a short time."

EXAMPLES ■ It's been quite **a while** since we saw you. [noun]
■ The enchiladas will be ready in **a while.** [noun; object of the preposition *in*]
■ Let's sit here **awhile.** [adverb]

B

backward, backwards Use either *backward* or *backwards* as an adverb. Use *backward* only as an adjective.

EXAMPLES
- The Hebrew story of Noah and the Flood relates how Shem and Japheth walked **backward** [*or* **backwards**] to avoid seeing their father's nakedness. [adverb]
- The cat stalked away without even a **backward** glance at the dog. [adjective]

bad, badly *Bad* is an adjective. *Badly* is an adverb. In standard English, only the adjective form should follow a sense verb, such as *feel, see, hear, taste,* or *smell,* or other linking verb.

NONSTANDARD   If the meat smells badly, don't eat it.
STANDARD   If the meat smells **bad,** don't eat it.

NOTE   Although the expression *feel badly* has become acceptable in informal situations, use *feel bad* in formal speaking and writing.

bare, bear As an adjective, *bare* means "without the customary covering, equipment, or supplies" or "without tools or weapons." As a verb, it means "to uncover." As a verb, *bear* means "to carry or possess," "to produce," or "to endure." As a noun, it means "a large, heavy mammal with shaggy fur and a very short tail." See also **born, borne.**

EXAMPLES
- We can tell when the woman upstairs is home by the sound of her heels on the **bare** floors. [adjective]
- Lifting a huge rock with his **bare** hands, Theseus finds a sword and a pair of sandals left by his father, Aegeus, the king of Athens. [adjective]
- The newspaper's investigative reporters **bared** appalling conditions at several migrant camps. [verb]
- In the Cheyenne myth "How the World Was Made," Maheo decides that Grandmother Earth should begin to **bear** life. [verb]

- Please turn your radio down; I can't **bear** the noise any longer. [verb]
- The quarry in William Faulkner's story "The **Bear"** is the elusive Big Ben. [noun]

base, bass As a noun, *base* means "foundation" or "headquarters." As an adjective, it means "having or showing little or no honor, courage, or decency" or "of comparatively low worth." As a noun, *bass* (pronounced $b\bar{a}s$) means "a low, deep sound or tone, as of a voice or an instrument" or "an instrument or musical part for such a tone." As an adjective, it means "of, for, or having the range of a bass." Pronounced *bas,* the noun *bass* is the name of various families of fishes.

EXAMPLES
- The speaker in Percy Bysshe Shelley's poem "Ozymandias" quotes the ironic inscription on the **base** of the tyrant's shattered monument. [noun]
- Eight days after Hurricane Andrew, the president announced that Homestead Air Force **Base** in South Florida would be rebuilt. [noun]
- Having neglected to write a thank-you note, the child was scolded for her **base** ingratitude. [adjective]
- Bronze is a **base** metal; gold is a precious one. [adjective]
- A **bass** well known for his interpretations of spirituals, Paul Robeson also starred in Broadway plays and Hollywood films. [noun]
- A bassoon is a double-reed **bass** woodwind with a long, curved stem attached to the mouthpiece. [adjective]
- Last weekend, Hannah caught a three-pound **bass** at Coe's Landing. [noun]

bazaar, bizarre *Bazaar* is a noun meaning "a market or street of shops and stalls" or "a sale of various items." *Bizarre* is an adjective meaning "grotesque" or "marked by extreme contrasts or inconsistencies."

EXAMPLES
- After his mother dies, the title character of Ssu-ma Ch'ien's biographical story "Nieh

Cheng" has second thoughts about earning his living as a butcher in the **bazaar.**
- Elena wrote a poem about the **bizarre** dream she had last night.

B.C. See **A.D., B.C.**

bear See **bare, bear.**

because In formal situations, do not use the construction *reason . . . because.* Instead, use *reason . . . that.*

INFORMAL	The reason for the eclipse is because the moon has come between the earth and the sun.
FORMAL	The **reason** for the eclipse is **that** the moon has come between the earth and the sun. [This sentence can also be rephrased entirely to be more concise: *The eclipse is caused by the moon's coming between the earth and the sun.*]

being as, being that Avoid using either of these expressions for *since* or *because.*

EXAMPLE	- **Because** [*not* Being as] Ms. Ribas is a gemologist, she may know the value of these gemstones.

beside, besides *Beside* is a preposition meaning "by the side of" or "next to." *Besides* may be used as either a preposition or an adverb. As a preposition, *besides* means "in addition to" or "other than." As an adverb, it means "moreover."

EXAMPLES	- He set the plate of sandwiches **beside** the bowl of fruit punch. [preposition]
	- **Besides** fringe benefits, the job offered a high salary. [preposition]
	- No one **besides** Lurleen wanted to go to the mall. [preposition]
	- I'm not in the mood to go shopping; **besides,** I have an English test tomorrow. [adverb]

between, among Use *between* when referring to only two items or to more than two when each item is being compared individually to each of the others.

EXAMPLES ▪ The money from the sale of the property was divided **between** Sasha and Antonio.
▪ Don't you know the difference **between** a simile, a metaphor, and an analogy? [*Between* is used because each figure of speech is compared individually to each of the others; in other words, the figures of speech are compared two at a time.]

Use *among* when you are referring to more than two items and are not considering each item in relation to each other item individually.

EXAMPLE ▪ The money from the sale of the property was divided **among** the four relatives.

bizarre See **bazaar, bizarre.**

board, bored   As a noun, *board* means "a flat piece of wood" or "a group of people who guide an organization." As a verb, it means "to cover with flat pieces of wood," "to receive meals, or room and meals, for pay," or "to get on [a ship, bus, plane, etc.]." *Bored* is the past participle of the verb *bore.* Used as a past-tense verb, it means "drilled," or "failed to interest." Used as an adjective, it means "uninterested."

EXAMPLES ▪ One of the **boards** on the deck needs replacing. [noun]
▪ When is the next meeting of the hospital's **board** of directors? [noun]
▪ Fortunately, we had time to **board** up the windows before the hurricane hit. [verb]
▪ Jesse will **board** with his former neighbors, the Franklins, while he attends Grambling State University. [verb]
▪ In one medieval play about the biblical Flood, Noah's wife refuses to **board** the ark and has to be carried on. [verb]
▪ To make an abacus for her younger sister, Yoshi first **bored** a hole in each of the wooden beads. [verb]
▪ I like the movie's soundtrack, but the plot **bored** me. [verb]

- How can they be **bored** by their own home movies? [adjective]

born, borne   *Born* means "given birth." *Borne* means "carried; endured."

EXAMPLES   ■ Ynes Mexia was **born** in Washington, D.C.
■ They have **borne** their troubles better than we thought they would.

borrow, lend   *Borrow* means "to take [something] temporarily." *Lend* means "to give [something] temporarily." Its principal parts are *lend, (is) lending, lent, (have) lent.*

EXAMPLES   ■ Ben **borrowed** a copy of William Least Heat-Moon's book *PrairyErth* from Mr. Platero.
■ He never forgets to return the books people have **lent** him. [verb]

   Loan, a noun in formal language, is sometimes used in place of *lend* in informal speech.

borrow off, borrow from   Avoid using *borrow off* in writing. Instead, use *borrow from.*

EXAMPLE ■ Do you have a pen I could **borrow from** [*not* borrow off] you?

brake, break As a verb, *brake* means "to slow down or stop." As a noun, it means "a device for slowing down or stopping." As a verb, *break* means "to cause to come apart; to shatter." As a noun, it means "a fracture."

EXAMPLES ■ He **braked** the car and swerved to avoid hitting the child. [verb]
■ An automobile **brake** will overheat if used too often. [noun]
■ If you're not careful, you'll **break** the mirror. [verb]
■ The **break** in the bone will heal in about six weeks. [noun]

bring, take *Bring* means "to come carrying something." *Take* means "to go carrying something."

EXAMPLES ■ I'll **bring** my Wynton Marsalis tapes when I come over.
■ Please **take** the model of the Globe Theater to the library.
■ You may **take** my softball glove to school today, but please **bring** it home this afternoon.

bust, busted Avoid using these words as verbs. Use a f of *break* or *burst,* depending on the meaning.

EXAMPLES ■ One of the headlights on the van is bro[not busted].
■ A pipe in the apartment above ours b [not busted].

but See **and, but.**

but, only See **double negative.**

but that, but what In formal situations, a *that* or *but what* after negative expressions s or *did not know.* Instead, use *that* alone.

INFORMAL I have no doubt but that [o be here soon.
FORMAL I have no doubt **that** they'

buy, by, bye As a verb, *buy* means "to purchase." As a noun, it means "something purchased or purchasable." As a preposition, *by* introduces a prepositional phrase ending with a noun. Its meaning depends on the relationship it expresses between the phrase and the noun or verb the phrase modifies. As an adverb, *by* means "near." *Bye* is sometimes also used informally in speech as a clipped (shortened) form of the interjection *goodbye,* meaning "farewell."

EXAMPLES ■ Not until 1766, when he was twenty-one, was Olaudah Equiano able to **buy** his freedom from slavery. [verb]
        ■ Those plantains were a good **buy**. [noun]
        ■ Did you know that the old song "Smile" was written **by** Charlie Chaplin? [preposition introducing the adverb phrase *by Charlie Chaplin,* which modifies *was written*]
        ■ Please stand **by;** we are experiencing technical difficulties with the audio. [adverb]
        ■ Waving wildly, the children yelled, "**Bye,** Grandma!" [interjection]

C

can, may Use *can* to express ability. Use *may* to express possibility. See page 166.

EXAMPLES ■ **Can** you play chess? [ability]
        ■ Josie **may** join us later. [possibility]

To express permission, *may* is used in formal situations and *can* is used in informal situations.

FORMAL   **May** I ride with you?
INFORMAL   **Can** I ride with you?

can't hardly, can't scarcely See **double negative.**

cannot (can't) help but In formal writing, avoid using *but* and the base form of a verb after the expression *cannot (can't) help.* Instead, use a gerund alone.

NONSTANDARD	I can't help but tap my foot when I hear mariachi music.
STANDARD	I can't help **tapping** my foot when I hear mariachi music.

capital, capitol As a noun, *capital* means "a city or town that is the seat of a government or the center of an industry" or "money or property owned by or used in a business." As an adjective, it means "punishable by death" or "of major importance." *Capitol* means "a building in which a legislature meets." It is capitalized when it refers to a building for a national legislature.

EXAMPLES
- Manila is the **capital** of the Philippines. [noun]
- Paris is the fashion **capital** of the world. [noun]
- The company has **capital** of $100,000. [noun]
- **Capital** punishment was the subject of the debate. [adjective]
- New York's **capitol** is in Albany.
- The United States Senate and House of Representatives meet in the **Capitol** in Washington, D.C.

case Case is the form of a noun or pronoun that shows how it is used. The three cases are the nominative, the objective, and the possessive. See pages 187–204.

NOMINATIVE	**Lorraine** said that **she** would bring salad.
OBJECTIVE	Will you give **Theo** and **me** a ride to the **mall?**
POSSESSIVE	**Mr. Chalmer's** car needs to have **its** muffler replaced.

censor, censure As a noun, *censor* means "an official with the authority to remove or prohibit material considered objectionable." As a verb, it means "to subject [a book, film, etc.] to removal or prohibition of material." As a noun, *censure* means "strong disapproval." As a verb, it means "to express strong disapproval."

EXAMPLES
- During World War II, military **censors** monitored the mail of armed-forces personnel to prevent military secrets from being revealed. [noun]

- The Senate committee heard testimony on the issue of whether rock music lyrics should be **censored.** [verb]
- Anxious to avoid his parents' **censure,** Dwight went home before his curfew. [noun]
- The teacher **censured** the student for plagiarizing a magazine article. [verb]

center about, center around   In formal situations, avoid using *center about* or *center around* for *center on,* meaning "to focus on."

INFORMAL   The controversy centered around the candidate's conflicting statements.

FORMAL   **Centering on** gun control, the discussion aroused strong emotions in both the panel members and the audience.

childish, childlike   Both *childish* and *childlike* are used to refer to persons of any age who have qualities considered typical of young children. *Childish* suggests unfavorable qualities such as immaturity or selfishness; *childlike* suggests favorable qualities such as innocence or trustfulness.

EXAMPLES
- Embarrassed by her prom date's **childish** behavior, Carol pretended that he wasn't with her.
- Even though he's over sixty, my grandfather retains a **childlike** enthusiasm for the circus.

choose, chose   *Choose* (chooz) is the present tense form; *chose* (chōz) is the past tense form.

EXAMPLES
- **Choose** one of the topics in the book or one of your own.
- Born Elaine Potter Richardson, Jamaica Kincaid **chose** her pen name as a young adult.

cite, sight, site   *Cite* is a verb meaning "to summon before a court of law," "to quote," "to refer to," or "to express approval of." As a noun, *sight* means "something seen" or "the ability to see." As a verb, it means "to see" or "to aim [a gun, binoculars, etc.]." *Site* is a noun meaning "location."

EXAMPLES
- The police officer **cited** the driver for speeding.

WRITER'S QUICK REFERENCE

- One way to support a persuasive argument is to **cite** facts and statistics from reliable sources.
- In his autobiography, Malcolm X **cites** his desire to write his ideas clearly as his motivation for copying the entire dictionary.
- Compiling her report, Lieutenant Sanchez **cited** two of the soldiers in her platoon for their outstanding work.
- The expression "a **sight** for sore eyes" means "something pleasant to see." [noun]
- Lost for days, the sailors rejoiced when they **sighted** land at last. [verb]
- Fitting an arrow on the bowstring, Odysseus **sights** the bow and sends the arrow flashing through all the socket rings without grazing a single ring. [verb]
- Kolomoki Mounds State Historic Park in southwest Georgia is the **site** of several mounds built by the Weeder Island, Kolomoki, and Lamar peoples.

classic, classical As a noun, *classic* in formal usage means "a literary or artistic work of the highest quality" or "a famous traditional event." In informal usage, it means "an item of apparel whose simple lines keep it from going out of style" or "an automobile manufactured between 1925 and 1942." As an adjective, *classic* is often used interchangeably with the adjective *classical*. In general, *classic* is preferred for describing something considered the finest of its kind. *Classical* is preferred for describing cultural periods of extraordinary achievement. *Classical* is also used to describe music that conforms to certain established standards of form and complexity, such as symphonies and concertos.

EXAMPLES
- *One Hundred Years of Solitude* by Gabriel García Márquez is a **classic** of magical realism. [noun]
- An automobile racing **classic,** the Indianapolis 500 is held annually on Memorial Day weekend. [noun]
- In updating your wardrobe, don't make the mistake of parting with **classics.** [noun]

- At the head of the parade was a completely restored 1928 Ford, a **classic** few of us had seen before. [noun]
- The Grimm brothers gathered their **classic** collection of German fairy tales during the nineteenth century. [adjective]
- The **classical** period in Indian literature lasted from the sixth century B.C. until about A.D. 1000. [adjective]
- Wynton Marsalis is a virtuoso of both **classical** and jazz music. [adjective]

clause A clause is a group of words that contains a subject and its predicate and is used as part of a sentence. See **independent clause, subordinate clause,** and **Chapter 7: Clauses.**

EXAMPLE
- **I washed the car,** and **mom waxed it.** [*I* is the subject of the first clause, and *washed the car* is the predicate. *Mom* is the subject of the second clause, and *waxed it* is the predicate.]

clothes, cloths *Clothes* means "wearing apparel." *Cloths* means "pieces of fabric."

EXAMPLES
- I'd like to buy some new school **clothes.**
- Use these **cloths** to clean the car.

coarse, course *Coarse* is an adjective meaning "rough; crude." *Course* is a noun meaning "a path of action," "one part of a meal," or "a series of studies." *Course* is also used after *of* to mean "naturally" or "certainly."

EXAMPLES
- The driveway was covered with **coarse** sand.
- His **coarse** language and manners prevented him from getting the job.
- What **course** do you think I should follow?
- My favorite main **course** is bolichi.
- The **course** in world history lasts a full year.
- Of **course,** you may go with us.

collective noun A collective noun names a group of persons or things. See pages 89 and 126–127.

EXAMPLE
- My **family** can't agree whether to call our **collection** of strange pets a **herd,** a **pack,** or a **pod.**

colonel, kernel A *colonel* is a military officer. A *kernel* is a grain or seed [of corn, wheat, etc.], or, by extension, the central, most important part of something.

EXAMPLES ■ Before she was promoted to brigadier general, Sherian Grace Cadoria was a **colonel** in the United States Army.
■ The tassel of an ear of corn is the plant's male flowers, and the **kernels** are the female flowers.
■ The **kernel** of the speaker's comments was a plea for unity.

comma splice A comma splice occurs when two complete thoughts are incorrectly joined by only a comma. See also **fused sentence, run-on sentence,** and pages 318–319.

COMMA SPLICE A new twelve-screen movie theater is under construction on the north side of town, our favorite pizza place is on the south side.
REVISED A new twelve-screen movie theater is under construction on the north side of town, **but** our favorite pizza place is on the south side.
REVISED A new twelve-screen movie theater is under construction on the north side of town; **however,** our favorite pizza place is on the south side.
REVISED A new twelve-screen movie theater is under construction on the north side of town. **Unfortunately,** our favorite pizza place is on the south side.

common noun A common noun is a general name for a person, place, thing, or idea; it is not usually capitalized. See page 88.

EXAMPLE ■ In Herman Melville's *Moby-Dick*, Captain Ahab sacrifices his **ship** and most of his **crew** during his obsessive **pursuit** of the white **whale.**

compare, contrast Used with *to, compare* means "to look for similarities between." Used with *with*, it means "to look for similarities and differences between." *Contrast* is always used to point out differences.

EXAMPLES ▪ Write a simile **comparing** a manufactured product **to** something in nature.
▪ How do the haiku of Taniguchi Buson **compare with** those of Matsuo Bashō?
▪ The tour guide **contrasted** the two castles' provisions for defense.

complement A complement is a word or group of words that completes the meaning of a verb. See **predicate adjective, predicate nominative, direct object, indirect object,** and pages 285–293.

complement, compliment As a noun, *complement* means "something that makes [something else] whole or complete." As a verb, it means "to make whole or complete." As a noun, *compliment* means "praise." In its plural form, it means "courteous greetings." As a verb, it means "to express praise."

EXAMPLES ▪ The diagram shows that angle *WXY* is the **complement** of angle *YXZ*. [noun]
▪ A good shortstop would **complement** the team. [verb]
▪ The performer was pleased and flattered by the critic's **compliment**. [noun]
▪ Please give my **compliments** to your parents. [plural noun]
▪ Did the critic **compliment** all of the other performers, too? [verb]

complex sentence A complex sentence has one independent clause and at least one subordinate clause. See pages 295–296.

EXAMPLE ▪ Whenever we go to a Chinese restaurant, Bob orders moo shu pork. [one subordinate clause and one independent clause]

compliment See **complement, compliment.**

compound-complex sentence A compound-complex sentence has two or more independent clauses and at least one subordinate clause. See page 296.

EXAMPLE
- Jay knew that something was wrong with the car, but he just didn't know what it was. [two independent clauses and two subordinate clauses]

compound sentence A compound sentence has two or more independent clauses but no subordinate clauses. See pages 294–295.

EXAMPLE
- That shirt needs to be ironed, and those slacks need to be hemmed. [two independent clauses]

compound subject A compound subject consists of two or more subjects that are joined by a conjunction and that have the same verb. See pages 124–125 and 282–283.

EXAMPLES
- **Rhonda** and **Max** are dancing the mambo.
- **Six** or **seven** in the morning is when I usually get up.

compound verb A compound verb consists of two or more verbs that are joined by a conjunction and that have the same subject. See pages 282–283.

EXAMPLE
- Many students **donated** a few dollars or **volunteered** some of their time to help us repaint the King Memorial Senior Citizens' Center.

concrete noun A concrete noun names an object that can be perceived by the senses. See pages 88–89.

EXAMPLE
- The **driver** swerved to miss the **dog** running across the **street.**

confidant, confident *Confidant* is a noun meaning "a close, trusted friend." *Confident* is an adjective meaning "certain" or "self-assured."

EXAMPLES
- Romeo and Juliet share the secret of their love with their **confidant,** Friar Laurence. [noun]
- The coach is **confident** that this year's team will make both the division and state finals. [adjective]
- Trying to appear **confident,** the applicant shook hands with the personnel director. [adjective]

conjugating   Conjugating means listing all the forms of a verb in all its tenses. See pages 157–158 and 172–173.

conjunction   A conjunction joins words or groups of words. See pages 109–113.

EXAMPLE   ▪ **Both** Gabriella **and** I will bring plates **and** napkins.

conjunctive adverb   A conjunctive adverb is an adverb used as a connecting word between independent clauses in a compound sentence. See pages 112–113.

EXAMPLE   ▪ We made sure to be at the Hendersons' by 6:30 P.M.; **however,** we arrived on the wrong day.

conscience, conscious   *Conscience* is a noun meaning "a knowledge or sense of right and wrong." *Conscious* is an adjective meaning "aware" or "in the normal waking state."

EXAMPLES   ▪ Tormented by his guilty **conscience,** Oedipus blinds himself.
▪ **Conscious** of the audience's hostility, the speaker told a joke to break the tension. [adjective]
▪ Falling asleep in the mountains, Rip Van Winkle doesn't become **conscious** again until twenty years later. [adjective]

consensus of opinion   *Consensus* means "an opinion held by all or most; general agreement." Therefore, the expression *consensus of opinion* is redundant. Use *consensus* alone.

EXAMPLES   ▪ After weeks of deliberation, House and Senate leaders finally reached a **consensus** [*not* consensus of opinion] on the budget.

consul, council, counsel   *Consul* is a noun meaning "a person appointed by a government to serve its citizens in a foreign country." *Council* is a noun meaning "a group called together to accomplish a job." As a noun, *counsel* means "advice." As a verb, it means "to advise."

EXAMPLES   ▪ The Israeli **consul** held a press conference to pledge his support for the peace talks.
▪ The student **council** meets this afternoon.

- Shandra sought **counsel** from Mr. Nakai. [noun]
- Mr. Nakai **counseled** her to apply for the scholarship. [verb]

continual, continuous   *Continual* means "repeated often." *Continuous* means "extending without interruption in either space or time."

EXAMPLES   ■ The child's **continual** questions amused and delighted her parents.
　　　　　■ Along the evacuation route flowed a **continuous** stream of cars, trucks, and motor homes.

continue on   Since *continue* means "to go on," the expression *continue on* is redundant. Use *continue* alone.

EXAMPLE   ■ After a brief stop in Atlanta, the flight **continued** [*not* continued on] to San Francisco.

continuous   See **continual, continuous.**

contraction   A contraction is a shortened form of a word, a figure, or a group of words, written with an apostrophe to indicate where letters or numerals have been omitted. See pages 424–425.

EXAMPLE   ■ **It's** four **o'clock,** and Brandon still **hasn't** called.

contrast   See **compare, contrast.**

coordinating conjunction   A coordinating conjunction joins parallel words, phrases, or clauses. See page 110.

EXAMPLE   ■ Vitamin A **and** niacin could be called beauty vitamins, **for** they help to keep the skin healthy.

core, corps   A *core* is the central or innermost part of something. A *corps* is a group of people under common direction; in its military sense, it means "a branch of the armed services having some specialized function."

EXAMPLES   ■ The **core** of the issue is whether adoptees have the right to meet their birth parents.
　　　　　■ Marina's ambition is to become a member of the diplomatic **corps.**
　　　　　■ When was the U.S. Marine **Corps** established?

correlative conjunctions Correlative conjunctions are used in pairs to join parallel words, phrases, or clauses. See page 110.

EXAMPLE   ■ **Either** Alison **or** JB will represent our school at the chess championships.

could of See **of.**

council See **consul, council, counsel.**

councilor, counselor A *councilor* is a member of a council. A *counselor* is one who gives advice.

EXAMPLES   ■ Although the council was in session for hours, the **councilors** did not reach an agreement.
           ■ Shandra's guidance **counselor** helped her complete the application.

counsel See **consul, council, counsel.**

counselor See **councilor, counselor.**

couple of In formal situations, avoid using *couple of* for *two of* or *several of.* Use a specific number instead.

INFORMAL   A couple of my friends and I volunteered to help with the Special Olympics this year.

  FORMAL   Two of my friends and I volunteered to help with the Special Olympics this year.

course See **coarse, course.**

credible, creditable, credulous *Credible* means "believable." *Creditable* means "deserving some praise." *Credulous* means "too ready to believe."

EXAMPLES   ■ Dylan thought hard to come up with a **credible** excuse for forgetting his homework.
           ■ The amateur theater group gave a **creditable** performance of *Richard III.*
           ■ The clerk's sales pitch convinced the **credulous** shopper that he couldn't live without the new kitchen appliance.

criteria, criterion *Criteria* is the plural form of *criterion.*

EXAMPLES   ■ Do you agree that loyalty is the single most important **criterion** of friendship?

- I can think of several **criteria** of success other than wealth.

D

dangling modifier A dangling modifier is a modifying word, phrase, or clause that does not clearly and sensibly modify a word or a group of words in a sentence. See pages 231–232.

DANGLING   Looking through the microscope, the paramecia seemed enormous.

REVISED   Looking through the microscope, I thought the paramecia seemed enormous.

data *Data* is the plural form of the word *datum*. In standard informal English, *data* is frequently used with singular pronouns and verbs. In formal usage, however, *data* takes plural pronouns and verbs.

INFORMAL   When the research data was published, it immediately became controversial.

FORMAL   When the research **data were** published, **they** immediately became controversial.

declarative sentence A declarative sentence makes a statement and is followed by a period. See pages 297 and 377.

EXAMPLE   - In 1991, South African writer Nadine Gordimer won the Nobel Prize for literature.

dependent clause See **subordinate clause.**

des'ert, desert', dessert *Desert* (des'ert) is a noun meaning "a dry region." *Desert* (desert') is a verb meaning "to leave or abandon." *Dessert* is a noun meaning "the final course of a meal."

EXAMPLES   - Irrigation has brought new life to the **desert.** [noun]
            - Good soldiers never **desert** their posts. [verb]
            - My favorite **dessert** is frozen yogurt with strawberries on top. [noun]

die, dye As a verb, *die* means "to stop living." As a noun, it means "a small, marked cube used in games of chance" (*dice* is the plural form of this sense) or "a tool or device for shaping or otherwise working metal or other substances." As a noun, *dye* means "color produced with a coloring agent" or "a substance that gives color [to fabric, hair, etc.]." As a verb, it means "to color with or as with a dye."

EXAMPLES
- Shakespeare **died** on April 23, 1616. [verb]
- One **die** from our backgammon set is missing. [noun]
- When we visited the U.S. Mint in Washington, D.C., we saw the **dies** used to stamp coins. [noun]
- The **dye** in this shirt ran the first time I washed it. [noun]
- Indigo is a blue **dye** native to India. [noun]
- In art class, we learned how to **dye** cloth using the batik method developed in Indonesia. [verb]

differ from, differ with *Differ from* means "to be unlike." *Differ with* means "to disagree."

EXAMPLES
- Earth **differs from** the other planets in our solar system in many ways.
- Jeremy **differs with** me about the value of space exploration.

different from, different than Use *different from* in most cases. When a subordinate clause follows, either *different from* or *different than* is acceptable. Never use *different to*.

EXAMPLES
- Alonso's reactions to the disclosures Prospero makes in the final act of *The Tempest* are quite **different from** Antonio's reactions.
- The outcome of the election was **different from** [*or* different than] what the polls had predicted.

direct object A direct object is a word or word group that receives the action of the verb or that shows the result of the action by telling *whom* or *what* after a transitive verb. See pages 287–288.

EXAMPLE
- Did you hear the **news**?

WRITER'S QUICK REFERENCE

direct quotation A direct quotation is a reproduction of a person's exact words, enclosed in quotation marks. See pages 412–416.

EXAMPLE
- Did Mr. Ramírez actually say, **"Don't study too hard"**?

discover, invent *Discover* means "to learn of the existence of [something]." *Invent* means "to bring something new into existence."

EXAMPLES
- Who **discovered** the remains of the ice-age hunter found in a glacier in the Alps?
- Linguists who study illiterate cultures must often **invent** alphabets that symbolize the sounds of spoken language.

discreet, discrete *Discreet* means "careful about what one says or does." *Discrete* means "separate and distinct."

EXAMPLES
- Please be **discreet** about what I'm about to tell you.
- The **discrete** sections of a pie chart graphically indicate relative quantities.

disinterested, uninterested *Disinterested* means "free from selfish motives; impartial." *Uninterested* simply means "not interested."

EXAMPLES
- A **disinterested** bystander confirmed every detail of the motorcyclist's version of the accident.
- **Uninterested** in the televised wrestling match, I went for a walk.

done *Done* is the past participle of *do.* Avoid using *done* for *did,* which is the past form of *do* and which does not require an auxiliary verb. When *done* is used as an adjective, it does not require an auxiliary verb.

NONSTANDARD	He done all of his homework over the weekend.
STANDARD	He **has done** all of his homework over the weekend.
STANDARD	He **did** all of his homework over the weekend.
STANDARD	My research paper is finally **done**.

don't, doesn't *Don't* is the contraction of *do not. Doesn't* is the contraction of *does not.* Use *doesn't,* not *don't,* with singular subjects except *I* and *you.*

EXAMPLES ■ She **doesn't** [*not* don't] like seafood.
■ The bookstore **doesn't** [*not* don't] have any copies of Faith Ringgold's *Tar Beach* in stock.

double comparison Double comparison is the use of two comparative forms (usually *more* and *–er*) or two superlative forms (usually *most* and *–est*) to express comparison. In standard usage, the single comparative form is sufficient. See pages 224–225.

NONSTANDARD   Letitia is a more better student than I am.
STANDARD   Letitia is a **better** student than I am.

double negative A double negative is a construction in which two negative words are used where one is enough. Although they were acceptable up to and during Shakespeare's time, double negatives are now considered nonstandard.

Common Negative Words		
barely	never	not (–n't)
but (meaning	no	nothing
"only")	nobody	nowhere
hardly	none	only

NONSTANDARD   She has not read none of Nadine Gordimer's books.
STANDARD   She has **not** read **any** of Nadine Gordimer's books.
STANDARD   She has read **none** of Nadine Gordimer's books.

NONSTANDARD   I do not know nothing about the Peloponnesian War.
STANDARD   I do **not** know **anything** about the Peloponnesian War.
STANDARD   I know **nothing** about the Peloponnesian War.

NONSTANDARD   Grandma said that she hadn't never seen another pumpkin as large as this one.

| STANDARD | Grandma said that she **hadn't ever** seen another pumpkin as large as this one. |
| STANDARD | Grandma said that she had **never** seen another pumpkin as large as this one. |

NOTE Avoid the common error of using –*n't*, the contraction of *not*, with another negative word, such as *barely*, *hardly*, or *scarcely*.

NONSTANDARD	I can't hardly take another step in these new boots.
STANDARD	I can **hardly** take another step in these new boots.
NONSTANDARD	The film is so long that we couldn't scarcely see it in one class period.
STANDARD	The film is so long that we could **scarcely** see it in one class period.

The words *but* and *only* are considered negative words when they are used as adverbs meaning "no more than." In such cases, the use of another negative word with *but* or *only* is considered informal.

| INFORMAL | I don't have only fifteen cents. |
| FORMAL | I have only fifteen cents. |

Winthrop reprinted by permission of NEA, Inc.

double subject   A double subject error is the use of an unnecessary pronoun after the subject of a sentence. See **he, she, it, they.**

due to   Avoid using *due to* for "because of" or "owing to."

EXAMPLE   ■ The game was postponed **because of** [*not due to*] rain.

WRITER'S QUICK REFERENCE

dye See **die, dye.**

E

each and every The expression *each and every* is redundant. Instead, use either *each* or *every* alone.

EXAMPLES
- **Each** [*not* Each and every] **runner who completes the race will receive a T-shirt.**
- **Every** [*not* Each and every] **student was invited to the party.**

eager See **anxious, eager.**

effect See **affect, effect.**

e.g., i.e. The abbreviation *e.g.* stands for the Latin phrase *exempli gratia,* meaning "for the sake of example; for example." The abbreviation *i.e.* stands for the Latin phrase *id est,* meaning "that is (to say)." It is used to cite a word or phrase equal in meaning to the one already used. In general, confine the use of *e.g.* and *i.e.* to parenthetical or technical matter. See also **Abbreviations,** pages 380–381.

EXAMPLES
- **Some hypertension medications (e.g., thiazide diuretics) may affect blood-fat levels adversely.**
- **The negative plates of the battery had sulfated, i.e., a deposit of lead sulfate had formed on them.**

either, neither *Either* usually means "one or the other of two." In referring to more than two, use *any one* or *any* instead. *Neither* usually means "not one or the other of two." In referring to more than two, use *none* instead.

EXAMPLES
- **Either of those two topics would be appropriate for a research paper.**
- **Consider writing about a recent scientific discovery, a medical breakthrough, or new uses for computers; any one of those topics would be interesting.**
- **Neither of the Perez twins is in school today.**

- Selma Lagerlöf forgot **none** of the Swedish legends and folk tales her grandmother had told her.

elicit, illicit *Elicit* is a verb meaning "to draw forth; evoke." *Illicit* is an adjective meaning "unlawful; unauthorized."

EXAMPLES
- Skillful interviewers **elicit** revealing responses from their subjects.
- Which newspaper uncovered the story about the group's **illicit** arms sales?

elliptical clause An elliptical clause is a clause from which words have been omitted. See pages 273–274.

EXAMPLE
- **If** [it is] **necessary,** we'll take the shuttle bus to the airport.

emerge, immerse *Emerge* means "to rise from" or "to come forth." *Immerse* means "to plunge, drop, or tip into." (*Immerge* is an archaic variant spelling of *immerse;* avoid using it.)

EXAMPLES
- The snow began just as the crowd **emerged** from the theater.
- Stories of many different cultures relate how the world was once **immersed** in flood waters.

emigrate, immigrate *Emigrate* means "to leave a country or a region to settle elsewhere." *Immigrate* means "to come into a country or a region to settle there."

EXAMPLES
- Thousands of people **emigrated** from Germany during the 1870s.
- Most of the German refugees **immigrated** to the United States.

eminent, imminent *Eminent* means "prominent" or "distinguished." *Imminent* means "likely to occur soon."

EXAMPLES
- Our **eminent** speaker today is the Honorable Rosemary Barkett, chief justice of the Florida Supreme Court.
- For his **eminent** achievements in photography, films, books, and music, Gordon Parks was awarded the National Medal of Arts.

WRITER'S QUICK REFERENCE

■ Warning that the hurricane was **imminent,** forecasters urged people in the area to evacuate.

end result, result   Since *result* suggests an end brought about by a cause, the expression *end result* is usually redundant. Use *end result* only to refer to the outcome of a series of causes and results.

EXAMPLES   ■ One **result** [*not* end result] of Gilgamesh's rejection of Ishtar is the death of Enkidu.
■ The **end result** of the series of collisions on the icy road was a massive traffic jam.

ensure, insure   *Ensure* means "to make sure or certain." *Insure* means "to arrange for monetary payment in case of loss, accident, or death."

EXAMPLES   ■ Elie Wiesel's writings **ensure** that the horrors of the Holocaust will not be forgotten.
■ What company **insures** your car?

essential clause, essential phrase   Also called **restrictive,** an essential clause or phrase is one that is necessary to the meaning of a sentence. It is not set off by commas. See pages 386–388.

EXAMPLE   ■ All students **who have not yet received their spring schedules** should report to Ms. Gretsky's office by Friday.

et al.   *Et al.* is the abbreviation for the Latin phrase *et alii,* meaning "and others." Its use is usually confined to citations of reference works with more than three authors. See **Abbreviations,** pages 380–381.

etc.   See **and etc.**

every   See **each and every.**

every day, everyday   The expression *every day* means "each day." *Everyday* is an adjective meaning "daily" or "usual."

EXAMPLES   ■ **Every day** presents it own challenges.
■ Lane watches his younger brother **every day** after school.
■ Walking the dog is one of my **everyday** chores.

- The party will be casual; wear **everyday** clothes.

every one, everyone   In the expression *every one, every* is an adjective modifying the pronoun *one.* Used together, the two words specify every person or thing of those named. *Everyone* is a pronoun meaning "every person; everybody." Often, pronunciation provides a clue to the meaning you intend.

EXAMPLES ■ **Every one** of the soloists received a standing ovation. [stress on *one*]
■ Did **everyone** have a chance to try out for the play? [stress on *every*]

everywheres   See **anyways, anywheres.**

except   See **accept, except.**

excess   See **access, excess.**

exclamatory sentence   An exclamatory sentence expresses strong feeling and is followed by an exclamation point. See pages 297–298 and 379–380.

EXAMPLE ■ What a fantastic concert that was!

explicit, implicit   *Explicit* means "clearly stated; openly expressed." *Implicit* means "suggested although not openly expressed."

EXAMPLES ■ Mom left us **explicit** instructions to clean the house.
■ **Implicit** in her instructions was the message that we'd be grounded if we didn't.

F

fair, fare   As an adjective, *fair* means "attractive," "clear and sunny," "just and honest," "according to the rules," or "average." As a noun, it means "a festival or carnival; bazaar." As an adverb, it means "in a fair manner." As a noun, *fare* means "money paid for transportation" or "food." As a verb, it means "to go through an experience."

WRITER'S QUICK REFERENCE

EXAMPLES ■ Speaking metaphorically, Romeo calls on Juliet, as "the **fair** sun," to destroy "the envious moon." [adjective]

■ Forecasters are predicting **fair** skies for the weekend. [adjective]

■ Even the defendant's lawyer found the judge's sentence **fair**. [adjective]

■ The third-base umpire ruled the disputed line drive **fair**. [adjective]

■ The party was **fair,** not great. [adjective]

■ Reminding the team to play **fair,** Coach Bluehouse waved the players onto the field. [adverb]

■ Have you seen the huge stuffed tiger Lennie won at the State **Fair?** [noun]

■ Once again the city council has raised bus **fares.** [noun]

■ During Kwanzaa, we prepare dishes representing the **fare** of Africa, the Caribbean, and South America. [noun]

■ China's writers **fared** poorly under Mao Tse-tung's Cultural Revolution. [verb]

famous, infamous, noted, notorious *Famous* means "widely known." *Infamous* means "having a bad reputation." *Noted* means "distinguished for a particular quality or achievement." *Notorious* means "widely but unfavorably known."

EXAMPLES ■ The Alamo is a **famous** historic building in Texas.

■ Charles Dickens's novels reveal the misery of nineteenth-century London's **infamous** sweatshops.

■ Appointed president of the University of Arizona in 1991, **noted** educator Manuel Pacheco hopes to make the school a model for minority students across the nation.

■ Al Capone was a **notorious** gangster in the 1920s.

farther, further *Farther* is the comparative degree of the adjective or adverb *far*. As an adjective or adverb, use *farther* to express physical distance. Use *further* as an adjective or adverb to express abstract relationships of degree or quantity.

EXAMPLES
- Your house is **farther** from school than mine is. [adjective]
- We swam **farther** today than we usually do. [adverb]
- The United Nations members had just decided that **further** debate was unnecessary when the ambassador from Haiti brought up a valid point. [adjective]
- After discussing the matter **further,** the nations reached an agreement. [adverb]

See also **all the farther, all the faster** and page 222.

faze, phase *Faze* is a verb meaning "to disturb." An informal usage, it is most commonly used in negative constructions. As a verb, *phase* means "to carry out in stages." As a noun, it means "stage" or "aspect."

EXAMPLES
- Matt didn't let the awkward situation **faze** him.
- The new federal job-training program will be **phased** in over the next three years. [verb]
- Among other things, *The Old Farmer's Almanac* includes detailed information on the **phases** of the moon. [noun]
- Held in Rio de Janeiro, Brazil, in June 1992, the United Nations' Earth Summit explored many **phases** of the environment. [noun]

fewer, less Use *fewer,* which tells "how many," to modify a plural noun. Use *less,* which tells "how much," to modify a singular noun.

EXAMPLES
- **Fewer** students are going out for football this year.
- I find that I have a lot more fun now that I spend **less** time watching TV.

figuratively, literally *Figuratively* means "in a metaphorical sense; not actually." *Literally* means "word for word; not imaginatively."

WRITER'S QUICK REFERENCE

EXAMPLES ■ Writing **figuratively,** the editor attached this headline to the lead story: "Superintendent of Schools Flunks Out."
■ Those who read the headline **literally** did not realize that the article referred to the superintendent's failed reelection bid.

first, firstly; second, secondly Using *firstly, secondly, thirdly,* and so on, to mean "in the first (second, third, etc.) place" is not incorrect, but these words tend to sound pretentious. The use of *first, second, third,* and so on, is generally preferred.

EXAMPLE ■ **First** [*not* Firstly], read your draft for content.

flammable, inflammable Both of these adjectives mean "capable of burning easily and quickly." Only *inflammable,* however, is used to describe a person who is hot-tempered or easily angered. Furthermore, *flammable* is preferred in technical writing to prevent readers from confusing the prefix *in–,* here meaning "into," with an identical prefix meaning "not."

EXAMPLES ■ Odysseus made an enemy of the **inflammable** god Poseidon by blinding Poseidon's son Polyphemus, the Cyclops.
■ Many common household cleansers are highly **flammable.**

flaunt, flout The verb *flaunt* means "to display defiantly or in a flashy way." The verb *flout* means "to mock; to show contempt for."

EXAMPLES ■ Even though Sarah is gifted, she never **flaunts** her knowledge.
■ In his novel *Don Quixote,* Miguel de Cervantes **flouts** the idealism of medieval courtly romances.

flounder, founder As a verb, *flounder* means "to move, speak, or act awkwardly or in a confused manner." *Founder* as a verb means "to stumble, fall, or collapse" or "to fill with water and sink."

EXAMPLES ■ **Floundering** through knee-deep snowdrifts, we wondered why the schools had opened after such a blizzard.

- As it approached the final hurdle, the horse suddenly **foundered.**
- Thousands of Africans captured for the slave trade drowned when their ships **foundered** on the long voyage.

flout See **flaunt, flout.**

formally, formerly *Formally* means "in a proper or dignified manner, according to strict rules." *Formerly* means "previously; in the past."

EXAMPLES
- Mayor Pérez will **formally** open the new recreation center on Wednesday.
- Mrs. Ling was **formerly** the head of the math department at Leland High School.

forth, fourth *Forth* is an adverb meaning "forward." As an adjective, *fourth* means "preceded by three others in a series" or "designating any of the four equal parts of something." As a noun, it means "the one following the third" or "any of the four equal parts of something."

EXAMPLES
- Step **forth** and take a bow; you deserve it!
- The **fourth** question on the test was the one that stumped me. [adjective]
- On **fourth** down, the center fumbled the ball. [adjective]
- Ben was the **fourth** to finish the marathon. [noun]
- The recipe calls for a **fourth** of a cup of chopped green pepper. [noun]

founder See **flounder, founder.**

fourth See **forth, fourth.**

fragment See **sentence fragment.**

further See **farther, further.**

fused sentence A fused sentence occurs when two or more complete thoughts have no punctuation between them. See also **comma splice, run-on sentence,** and pages 318–319.

FUSED   I'm afraid I offended Stan I certainly didn't mean to.

WRITER'S QUICK REFERENCE

REVISED   I'm afraid I offended Stan. I certainly didn't mean to.

REVISED   I'm afraid I offended Stan, although I certainly didn't mean to.

G

general reference A general reference error occurs when a pronoun refers to a general idea rather than to a specific word or group of words. See page 206.

GENERAL   My biology class is going on a field trip to the coast this week, which should be fun. [no specific antecedent for *which*]

CLEAR   My biology class is going on a field trip to the coast this week. The trip should be fun.

CLEAR   Going on a field trip to the coast with my biology class this week should be fun.

gerund A gerund is a verb form ending in *–ing* that is used as a noun. See pages 250–251.

EXAMPLE   ■ **Eavesdropping** is very rude behavior.

gerund phrase A gerund phrase consists of a gerund and its modifiers and complements. See page 251.

EXAMPLE   ■ Charles sought to impress Belinda by **serenading her on his tuba.**

go, say Avoid using *go* to mean *say.* Do not use *say* after a past-tense verb. *Said* is the past-tense form.

NONSTANDARD   Then she glares at me and goes, "Where have you been?"

NONSTANDARD   Then she glared at me and says, "Where have you been?"

STANDARD   Then she glared at me and **said,** "Where have you been?"

good, well *Good* is an adjective. *Well* may be used as an adjective or as an adverb. Avoid using *good* to modify an action verb. Instead, use *well* as an adverb meaning "capably" or "satisfactorily."

NONSTANDARD	The school orchestra played good.
STANDARD	The school orchestra played **well**.
NONSTANDARD	Although she was nervous, Aretha performed quite good.
STANDARD	Although she was nervous, Aretha performed quite **well**.

As an adjective, *well* means "in good health" or "satisfactory in appearance or condition."

EXAMPLES   ■ He says that he feels quite **well**.
            ■ It's midnight, and all is **well**.

Fox Trot, copyright 1989 Universal Press Syndicate. Reprinted with permission. All rights reserved.

graduate Use the expression *graduate from,* not *to be graduated from* or *graduate*.

EXAMPLE   ■ After she **graduated from** [*not* graduated] Barnard College, Zora Neale Hurston studied the oral tradition among African Americans in Florida.

H

had of See **of**.

had ought, hadn't ought Do not use *had* or *hadn't* with *ought*.

| NONSTANDARD | His test scores had ought to be back by now. |
| STANDARD | His test scores **ought** to be back by now. |

NONSTANDARD   She hadn't ought to have turned here.
STANDARD   She **ought not** to have turned here.

half Avoid using the article *a* both before and after *half.*

EXAMPLES ▪ We've already waited **half a day** [*not* a half a day] for the box office to open.
▪ Next, add **a half cup** [*not* a half a cup] of sliced black olives.

hardly See **double negative.**

he, she, it, they Avoid using a pronoun along with its antecedent as the subject of a verb. Such an error is called the *double subject.*

NONSTANDARD   The computer system it is down today.
STANDARD   The **computer system is** down today.

NONSTANDARD   Fay Stanley and Diane Stanley they collaborated on a biography of the Hawaiian princess Ka'iulani.
STANDARD   **Fay Stanley and Diane Stanley collaborated** on a biography of the Hawaiian princess Ka'iulani.

heard, herd *Heard,* meaning "listened," is the past participle of the verb *hear.* As a noun, *herd* means "a group of cattle, sheep, or other large animals." As a verb, it means "to tend or drive as a herd."

EXAMPLES ▪ Have you **heard** Willy Chirino's latest album?
▪ Vast **herds** of buffalo once provided Native Americans with hides for clothing and dwellings as well as with food. [noun]
▪ Among the Masai people of East Africa, one of the chief duties of boys is to **herd** the community's cattle and sheep. [verb]

hisself, theirselves In formal situations, do not use these words for *himself* and *themselves.*

EXAMPLE ▪ Is Arnold feeling very proud of **himself** [*not* hisself]?

hole, holey; holy; whole, wholly *Hole* is a noun meaning "opening." *Holey* is an adjective meaning "having a hole or holes." An adjective, *holy* means "sacred." As a noun, *whole* means "the entire amount, quantity, extent, or sum" or "a thing complete in itself." As an adjective, it means "intact; not broken or divided up." *Wholly* is an adverb meaning "entirely."

EXAMPLES
- According to legend, Pyramus and Thisbe, a young Babylonian couple, fell in love while talking to each other through a **hole** in the wall between their houses.
- Don't throw out that **holey** dish towel; it will make a good dust rag.
- Mecca, Saudi Arabia, where Mohammed was born, is one of the **holy** cities of Islam.
- The **whole** of Denali National Park in Alaska consists of 4,716,726 acres. [noun]
- The **whole** cast did a great job in last night's performance. [adjective]
- We were **wholly** surprised when the audience gave us a standing ovation. [adverb]

Honorable See **Reverend, Honorable.**

hopefully *Hopefully* is an adverb meaning "in a hopeful manner." In formal situations, avoid using it for *I hope* or *it is hoped.*

INFORMAL   Hopefully, the rain will let up before the parade starts.

FORMAL   **I hope** the rain will let up before the parade starts.

FORMAL   I looked **hopefully** for signs of sun behind the clouds.

however When *however* is used as an adverb within a clause, it is set off by commas. When it is used as a conjunctive adverb between independent clauses, it is preceded by a semicolon and followed by a comma.

EXAMPLES
- The shuttle was to have lifted off this morning; heavy rains at the launch site, **however,** postponed the flight.
- The shuttle was to have lifted off this morning; **however,** heavy rains at the launch site postponed the flight.

human, humane   As a noun, *human* means "a person." As an adjective, it means "of, belonging to, or typical of people" or "consisting of or produced by people." *Humane* is an adjective meaning "having qualities considered admirable in people, such as kindness, gentleness, and mercy."

EXAMPLES
- The Quiché Mayan myth "The Wooden People" explains the origins of **humans.** [noun]
- Myths of every world culture attempt to explain the **human** condition. [adjective]
- Appalled by conditions among the poor, Jane Addams founded Hull House in Chicago to provide **humane** services.

hypercritical, hypocritical   *Hypercritical* means "overly critical." *Hypocritical* means "pretending to possess worthy qualities but not actually possessing them."

EXAMPLES
- When you take part in peer review, try not to be **hypercritical.**
- How **hypocritical** it was of him to make friends with us before the election and then drop us once he was elected!

I

---

i.e.   See **e.g., i.e.**

if, whether   Use *if* to introduce clauses of condition; use *whether* (with *or*) to introduce alternatives. Also use *whether* (with or without *or*) in indirect questions and in expressions of doubt.

EXAMPLES
- **If** you haven't read Jung Chang's book *Wild Swans: Three Daughters of China,* I have a copy that you can borrow.
- We still must decide **whether** to drive **or** walk.
- Martina asked us **whether** we had seen Bruce.

- Jacy wondered **whether** they were showing off **or** trying to be helpful.

illicit See **elicit, illicit.**

illusion See **allusion, illusion.**

immerse See **emerge, immerse.**

immigrate See **emigrate, immigrate.**

imperative mood The imperative mood is the form of a verb used to express a direct command or request. See page 176.

EXAMPLE - **Be** ready to leave at 7:00 A.M.

imperative sentence An imperative sentence gives a command or makes a request. It is followed by either a period or an exclamation point. See pages 297 and 378.

EXAMPLES - Come out with your hands up**!**
- Please pass the salt and pepper**.**

implicit See **explicit, implicit.**

imply, infer *Imply* means "to suggest indirectly." *Infer* means "to interpret" or "to draw a conclusion."

EXAMPLES - The governor **implied** in her speech that she would support a statewide testing program.
- I **inferred** from the governor's speech that she would support a statewide testing program.

important, importantly The phrase *more (most) important* is an elliptical construction for "what is more (most) important." Consequently, do not add *–ly* to *important.*

EXAMPLE - More **important** [*not* importantly], leave the campsite as clean as you'd want it to be the next time you visit.

in, in to, into *In* generally shows location. In the construction *in to, in* is an adverb followed by the preposition *to*. *Into* generally shows direction.

EXAMPLES - Totem Bight Park, which preserves the totem heritage of the Tlingits, is **in** Ketchikan, Alaska.

- When she found a wallet on the bus, Rachel turned it **in to** the driver.
- We heard the phone ringing as we stepped **into** the house.

indefinite reference An indefinite reference error occurs when the pronoun *you, it,* or *they* refers to no particular person or thing. See pages 208–209.

INDEFINITE   In the new school regulations it states that student cars parked in the faculty lot will be towed.

REVISED   The new school regulations state that student cars parked in the faculty lot will be towed.

independent clause Also called a **main clause,** an independent clause expresses a complete thought and can stand by itself as a sentence. See pages 263–264.

EXAMPLES   ■ **Where's my umbrella?**
■ Before you leave, **make sure you've turned out all the lights.**

indicative mood The indicative mood is the form of a verb used to express a fact, an opinion, or a question. See pages 175–176.

EXAMPLE   ■ I **think** Michael Jordan **is** the best basketball player of all time.

indirect object An indirect object is a word or word group that comes between a transitive verb and its direct object and tells *to whom* or *to what* or *for whom* or *for what* the action of a verb is done. See pages 287–289.

EXAMPLES   ■ Lonnie, did you give the **baby** his bath?
■ We need to get our **dog** and **cat** rabies vaccinations.

indirect quotation An indirect quotation is a rewording, or paraphrasing, of something another person has said. See page 412.

EXAMPLE   ■ Did Mr. Ramírez actually say **that we shouldn't study too hard**?

See also **direct quotation.**

infamous See **famous, infamous, noted, notorious.**

infinitive An infinitive is a verb form, usually preceded by *to,* used as a noun, an adjective, or an adverb. See pages 252–254.

EXAMPLE ▪ Our goal is **to win** the state championship.

infinitive phrase An infinitive phrase consists of an infinitive and its modifiers and complements. See pages 253–254.

EXAMPLE ▪ Darlene is the person **to see for help in physics.**

inflammable See **flammable, inflammable.**

ingenious, ingenuous *Ingenious* means "clever; inventive." *Ingenuous* means "straightforward."

EXAMPLES ▪ An **ingenious** new radio allows listeners to automatically scan the airwaves for stations with a particular format, such as the blues, country, or rock.
▪ The **ingenuous** toddler told his parents' guests, "You go home now."

in regards to, with regards to Use instead *regarding, in regard to, with regard to,* or *as regards.*

EXAMPLE ▪ **Regarding** [*or* **In regard to** *or* **With regard to** *or* **As regards**] your proposal, my answer is still no.

insure See **ensure, insure.**

interjection An interjection expresses emotion and has no grammatical relation to the rest of the sentence. See page 114.

EXAMPLE ▪ **Wow!** What a great looking car that 1937 Packard convertible is!

interrogative sentence An interrogative sentence asks a question and is followed by a question mark. See pages 297 and 377–378.

EXAMPLE ▪ Have you read Erich Maria Remarque's classic novel *All Quiet on the Western Front*?

into See **in, in to, into.**

intransitive verb An intransitive verb is an action verb that does not take an object. See page 101.

EXAMPLE   ■ The soloist **bowed** humbly as the audience **rose** to their feet and **cheered.**

invent See **discover, invent.**

irregardless, regardless *Irregardless* is nonstandard. Use *regardless* instead.

EXAMPLE   ■ **Regardless** [*not* Irregardless] of the children's pleas, their father bought a plain cereal instead of a sugar-coated one.

irregular verb An irregular verb forms its past and past participle in some other way than by adding *–d* or *–ed* to the base form. See pages 147–153.

EXAMPLE   ■ I shouldn't have **eaten** just before I **swam** ten laps.

it See **he, she, it, they.**

its, it's *Its* is the possessive form of *it. It's* is the contraction of *it is* or *it has.*

EXAMPLES   ■ The community is proud of **its** school system.
■ **It's** [It is] a symbol of peace.
■ **It's** [It has] been a long time since your last visit.

J

join, join together Since *join* means "put or bring together," *join together* is redundant. Use *join* alone.

EXAMPLE   ■ Members of the community **joined** [*not* joined together] to aid the victims of the flood.

judicial, judicious *Judicial* means "of judges, law courts, or their functions." *Judicious* means "having, applying, or showing sound judgment."

EXAMPLES ■ The governor has appointed a special committee to investigate the need for **judicial**
reform.
■ The landlord's **judicious** handling of the dis-
pute satisfied both tenants.

K

kernel See **colonel, kernel.**

kind of, sort of   In formal situations, avoid using these
terms for the adverb *somewhat* or *rather.*

INFORMAL   You look kind of worried.
FORMAL   You look **rather** [*or* somewhat] worried.

kind of a, sort of a   In formal situations, omit the *a.*

INFORMAL   What kind of a car do you drive?
FORMAL   What **kind of** car do you drive?

kind(s), sort(s), type(s)   With the singular form of each of
these nouns, use *this* or *that.* With the plural form, use *these*
or *those.*

EXAMPLES ■ **This kind** of gas is dangerous, but **those kinds**
are harmless.
■ **These types** of reading assignments are always challenging.

L

later, latter   Both *later* and *latter* are comparative forms of
late meaning "more late." *Later* refers to time; it may be either an adjective or an adverb. *Latter,* an adjective, refers to
the second of two, as opposed to *former,* which refers to the
first of two things.

EXAMPLES ■ We will send the package at a **later** time.
[adjective]
■ I will help you **later.** [adverb]

■ When given the choice of coleslaw or a tossed salad, I chose the **latter** side dish.

lay, lie See **lie, lay.**

lead, led, lead *Lead,* pronounced "leed," is a verb meaning "to go first" or "to guide." *Led* is the past tense of *lead. Lead,* pronounced "led," is a noun meaning "a heavy metal" or "graphite in a pencil."

EXAMPLES ■ Who will **lead** the discussion group?
■ Elaine **led** the band onto the field.
■ The mechanic used small weights made of **lead** to balance the wheel.
■ My pencil **lead** broke during the test.

learn, teach *Learn* means "to gain knowledge." *Teach* means "to provide with knowledge."

EXAMPLE ■ The more you **teach** someone else, the more you **learn** yourself.

leave, let *Leave* means "to go away." *Let* means "to permit or to allow." Avoid using *leave* for *let.*

EXAMPLES ■ **Let** [*not* Leave] them stay where they are.
■ They **let** [*not* left] Jaime out early for a dentist appointment.

led See **lead, led, lead.**

lend See **borrow, lend, loan.**

less See **fewer, less.**

let See **leave, let.**

liable See **apt, likely, liable.**

lie, lay The verb *lie* means "to rest" or "to stay, to recline, or to remain in a certain state or position." *Lie* never takes an object. The verb *lay* means "to put [something] in a place." *Lay* usually takes an object. See pages 153–154.

EXAMPLES ■ The pasture **lies** in the valley. [no object]
■ Eduardo **lay** the strips of grilled meat on the tortilla. [*Strips* is the object of *lay.*]

like, as Informally, *like* is often used as a conjunction introducing a subordinate clause. In formal situations, however, do not use *like* for the conjunction *as* to introduce a subordinate clause.

INFORMAL   Placido Domingo sings like Caruso once did.

FORMAL   Placido Domingo sings **as** Caruso once did.

like, as if In formal situations, avoid using the preposition *like* for the conjunction *as if* or *as though* to introduce a subordinate clause.

INFORMAL   The singers sounded like they had not rehearsed.

FORMAL   The singers sounded **as if** [*or* as though] they had not rehearsed.

likely See **apt, liable, likely.**

likewise *Likewise* is an adverb meaning "in the same manner." Avoid using it as a conjunction to mean "and" or "together with."

NONSTANDARD   James Weldon Johnson wrote *God's Trombones,* likewise "Lift Every Voice and Sing."

STANDARD   James Weldon Johnson wrote *God's Trombones* **and** "Lift Every Voice and Sing."

STANDARD   Johnson collaborated with his brother, John, on a comic opera; **likewise,** the brothers worked as a team on more than two hundred songs.

linking verb A linking verb connects the subject of a sentence with a word that identifies or describes the subject. See pages 101–103.

EXAMPLE   ▪ The day **turned** dark and chilly.

literally See **figuratively, literally.**

loan See **borrow, lend.**

loose, lose, loss As an adjective, *loose,* pronounced "loos," means "free, unbound," "not tight," or "not firmly fastened." As an adverb, it means "in a loose manner." As a verb, it means "to let go." *Lose* is a verb, pronounced "looz," meaning "to misplace," "to suffer a loss," or "to fail to win or gain." *Loss* is a noun meaning "an instance of misplacing or of failing to win or gain" or "the person, thing, or amount lost."

EXAMPLES
- **Loose** dogs are not allowed in the city park. [adjective]
- Clothes with a **loose** fit are good to wear for tai chi practice. [adjective]
- The front wheel of your bike is **loose**. [adjective]
- At one time, huge herds of mustangs ran **loose** on this land. [adverb]
- Aileen **loosed** her frustration by playing a vigorous game of tennis. [verb]
- Where did you **lose** your contact lens?
- The trees will **lose** their leaves soon.
- I predict that the Oilers will **lose** the game.
- A **loss** now would drop our team to second place in the league.
- Fortunately, insurance covered the **loss** when the car was stolen.

lot See **a lot.**

may See **can, may.**

me and Avoid using the expression *me and* as part of a compound subject. Instead, use the nominative form *I,* and place the other person's name first.

NONSTANDARD   Me and Teresa created a new computer game.

STANDARD   **Teresa and I** created a new computer game.

might of, must of See **of.**

miner, minor *Miner* is a noun meaning "a worker in a mine." As a noun, *minor* means "a person under legal age." As an adjective, it means "less important."

EXAMPLES
- American **miners** lead the world in the production of coal.

- Normally a **minor** is not permitted to sign a legal paper. [noun]
- Let's not list any of the **minor** objections to the plan. [adjective]

misplaced modifier A misplaced modifier is a word, a phrase, or a clause that makes a sentence awkward because it seems to modify the wrong word or group of words. See pages 229–231.

MISPLACED   We learned that Mary Ann Evans wrote under the pseudonym George Eliot in our English class.

CORRECTED   In our English class we learned that Mary Ann Evans wrote under the pseudonym George Eliot.

modifier A modifier is a word, a phrase, or a clause that limits the meaning of a word. See **Chapter 5: Using Modifiers.**

EXAMPLE   - The **sweet** song **of a nightingale** filled the garden **with music.**

mood Mood is the form a verb takes to indicate the attitude of the person using the verb. There are three moods in English: **indicative, imperative,** and **subjunctive.** See pages 175–178.

moral, morale As an adjective, *moral* means "good; virtuous." As a noun, it means "a lesson of conduct." *Morale* is a noun meaning "spirit; mental condition."

EXAMPLES   - Proper conduct is often based on **moral** principles. [adjective]
- The **moral** of this old folk tale is "Be true to yourself." [noun]
- Teamwork is impossible without good **morale.**

most See **almost, most.**

myself, ourselves In formal situations, do not use pronouns ending in *–self* or *–selves* to replace personal pronouns as subjects or objects.

EXAMPLES   - Brenda and I [*not* myself] plan to attend Swarthmore.
- As for **us** [*not* ourselves], we'd like the fettucine Alfredo.

See pages 92–93 and 200–201 for more about pronouns that end in *–self* or *–selves*.

nauseated, nauseous   *Nauseated* means "sick." *Nauseous* means "disgusting" or "sickening."

EXAMPLES   ■ Bouncing on the trampoline right after lunch, Ron became **nauseated**.

　　　　　　 ■ Whatever is in this jar is certainly giving off a **nauseous** odor.

DRABBLE reprinted by permission of UFS, Inc.

neither   See **either, neither.**

no, none, no one, nobody, not, nothing, nowhere   See **double negative.**

nohow, noway   Avoid using these nonstandard expressions. However, *no way* written as two words is standard.

NONSTANDARD   Noway can the characters Geoffrey Chaucer created in *The Canterbury Tales* be considered dull.

STANDARD   In **no way** can the characters Geoffrey Chaucer created in *The Canterbury Tales* be considered dull.

STANDARD   There is **no way** in which the characters Geoffrey Chaucer created in *The Canterbury Tales* can be considered dull.

nominative case Nominative case is the form a noun or pronoun takes when it is the subject or predicate nominative of a sentence. See pages 187–191.

EXAMPLE
- The **headlines** declared that the **winner** was **he.**

nonessential clause, nonessential phrase Also called "nonrestrictive," a nonessential clause or phrase is one that adds information not necessary to the main idea in the sentence. It is set off by commas. See pages 386–388.

EXAMPLES
- This vase, **which is more than five hundred years old,** is quite valuable.
- My dad, **a true do-it-yourselfer,** is converting our attic into a playroom for the twins.

nonsexist language Nonsexist language is language that applies to people in general, both male and female. See pages 135–136.

EXAMPLE
- The **chairperson** asked each of us to give a report.

nor See **or, nor.**

noted See **famous, infamous, noted, notorious.**

nothing like, nowhere near These expressions are both used informally to mean "not nearly." In formal situations, use *nothing like* to mean "not at all like." Use *nowhere near* to mean "not anywhere near."

INFORMAL My new job is **nothing like** as much fun as my old one.
FORMAL My new job is **not nearly** as much fun as my old one.
FORMAL My new job is **nothing like** my old one.
INFORMAL Machine-tooled belts are **nowhere near** as elegant as hand-tooled ones.
FORMAL Machine-tooled belts are **not nearly** as elegant as hand-tooled ones.
FORMAL Machine-tooled belts are made **nowhere near** where I live.

notorious See **famous, infamous, noted, notorious.**

noun   A noun names a person, place, thing, or idea. See pages 87–90.

EXAMPLE   ■ After the **field trip, Mr. Reyes** asked the **students** to share some of their **impressions** of the **National Gallery of Art.**

noun clause   A noun clause is a subordinate clause used as a noun. See pages 268–269.

EXAMPLE   ■ **What I want to know** is **how much a car like that costs.**

noun of direct address   A noun of direct address identifies the person spoken to or addressed in a sentence. See pages 390–391.

EXAMPLE   ■ Who do you think will win the election, **Kim?**

nowhere near   See **nothing like, nowhere near.**

nowheres   See **anyways, anywheres.**

number   Number is the form of a word that indicates whether the word is singular or plural. See **Chapter 2: Agreement.**

SINGULAR   **John** really **likes his** new **mountain bike.**
PLURAL   **Indonesians use peanuts** in many of **their** traditional **dishes.**

number   See **amount, number.**

number of   Use a singular verb after the expression *the number of.* Use a plural verb after the expression *a number of.*

EXAMPLES   ■ **The number of** candidates **was** surprising.
■ **A number of** candidates **were** nominated.

O

object   An object is a complement that does not modify or identify the subject of the sentence. See pages 287–289.

EXAMPLE   ■ Riding our **bikes** to the **lake** would give **us** some **exercise.**

objective case Objective case is the form a noun or a pronoun takes when used as a direct object, an indirect object, or an object of a preposition. See pages 191–194.

EXAMPLE   ■ Alex asked **me** to go with **him** when he goes to get his **driver's license.**

objective complement An objective complement is a word or word group that helps complete the meaning of a transitive verb by identifying or modifying the direct object. See pages 289–290.

EXAMPLES   ■ My aunt called that hill a **butte.** [*Butte* identifies the direct object *hill.*]
■ Jennifer and her father painted the barn **red.** [*Red* modifies the direct object *barn.*]

object of a preposition An object of a preposition is the noun or pronoun that follows the preposition in a prepositional phrase. See pages 107–109.

EXAMPLE   ■ Somewhere in that **stack** of **photos** is a decent picture of **me.**

of *Of* is a preposition. Do not use *of* in place of *have* after verbs such as *could, should, would, might, must,* and *ought* [*to*]. Also, do not use *had of* for *had.*

NONSTANDARD   He could of had a summer job if he had applied earlier.
STANDARD   He **could have** [*or* **could've**] had a summer job if he had applied earlier.

NONSTANDARD   You ought to of studied Spanish.
STANDARD   You **ought to have** studied Spanish.

NONSTANDARD   If I had of known the word *raze,* I would of made a perfect score.
STANDARD   If I **had** known the word *raze,* I **would have** made a perfect score.

Avoid using *of* after other prepositions such as *inside, off,* and *outside.*

EXAMPLE   ■ Chian-Chu dived **off** [*not* off of] the side of the pool into the water.

off, off of Do not use *off* or *off of* for *from.*

NONSTANDARD You can get a program off of the usher.
STANDARD You can get a program **from** the usher.

on to, onto In the expression *on to, on* is an adverb and *to* is a preposition. *Onto,* written as one word, is a preposition.

EXAMPLES ▪ The lecturer moved **on to** her next main idea.
▪ Just learning to walk, the child still holds **on to** the furniture.
▪ The cat leapt gracefully **onto** the windowsill.

or, nor Use *or* with *either;* use *nor* with *neither.*

EXAMPLES ▪ On Tuesdays the school cafeteria offers a choice of **either** a taco salad **or** a pizza.
▪ I wonder why **neither** Ralph Ellison **nor** Robert Frost was given the Nobel Prize for literature.

oriented, orientated *Oriented* is the past tense of the verb *orient,* which means "to arrange with reference to the east," "to set [a map or chart] in agreement with the points of the compass," or "to adapt to a particular situation." Avoid using the nonstandard form *orientated.*

EXAMPLES ▪ The architects **oriented** the new courthouse to the east.
▪ Before setting out, the campers **oriented** their map of the terrain.
▪ Kimiko quickly **oriented** [*not* orientated] herself to the new school.

ought See **had ought, hadn't ought.**

ought to of See **of.**

outside, outside of *Outside* may be used as a noun, an adjective, an adverb, or a preposition. *Of* may follow *outside* only when *outside* is used as a noun.

EXAMPLES ▪ The devastated community welcomed **outside** help. [adjective]
▪ Has the cat gone **outside** lately? [adverb]
▪ Hiding some of their best soldiers inside, the Greeks left the Trojan horse **outside** [*not* outside of] the gates of Troy. [preposition]

- Originally, great blocks of polished limestone formed the **outside of** the Great Pyramid of Khufu. [noun]

P

pair, pare, pear   *Pair* is a noun meaning "two people or things." *Pare* is a verb meaning "to peel" or "to reduce [size, cost, etc.]." *Pear* is a noun meaning "a fruit tree of the rose family" or "the fruit of such a tree."

EXAMPLES
- London and Paris are the **pair** of cities in which Charles Dickens's novel *A Tale of Two Cities* is set.
- First, **pare** the yams and cut them into half-inch chunks.
- In Homer's *Odyssey,* **pears** are one of the fruits grown in the gardens of King Alcinous.

parallel structure   Parallel structure is the repetition of grammatical forms. See pages 311–313.

EXAMPLE
- Jim's hobbies include **hiking, swimming,** and **reading.**

pare   See **pair, pare, pear.**

parenthetical expression   A parenthetical expression is a remark that adds incidental information. See pages 391–392.

EXAMPLE
- **As a matter of fact,** I do plan to go.

participial phrase   A participial phrase consists of a participle and its complements and modifiers. See pages 247–249.

EXAMPLE
- On hot days, you can find our dog Roy **sleeping under the porch.**

participle   A participle is one of the principal parts of a verb or a verb form that can be used as an adjective. See pages 145–156 and 246–249.

EXAMPLE
- Ernest bounced the **laughing** baby on his knee.

WRITER'S QUICK REFERENCE

passed, past *Passed,* the past tense of the verb *pass,* means "went beyond." As a noun, *past* means "time gone by." As an adjective, it means "of a former time." As a preposition, it means "beyond."

EXAMPLES   ■ The runner from Central High **passed** me at the turn. [verb]

■ To understand the problems in the Middle East, you need to study that region's **past.** [noun]

■ Talented historians can make **past** events much more meaningful and interesting to the average person. [adjective]

■ Drive **past** the gas station, and turn right at the next light. [preposition]

passive voice A verb is in the passive voice when it expresses an action done *to* its subject. See pages 170–175.

EXAMPLE   ■ The ball **was thrown** too far to the left.

peace, piece *Peace* means "calmness; the absence of war or strife." *Piece* means "a part of something."

EXAMPLES   ■ Disarmament is an important step toward **peace.**

■ Four **pieces** of the puzzle are missing.

pear See **pair, pare, pear.**

perfect See **unique, perfect.**

persecute, prosecute *Persecute* means "to attack or annoy someone constantly." *Prosecute* means "to bring legal action against someone for unlawful behavior."

EXAMPLES   ■ Joseph Stalin **persecuted** the people who opposed him.

■ The district attorney's job is to **prosecute** persons accused of criminal acts.

personal, personnel *Personal* is an adjective meaning "individual; private." *Personnel* is a noun meaning "a group of people employed in the same work or service."

EXAMPLES   ■ My **personal** opinion has nothing to do with the case.

- Most large companies prefer to recruit their executive **personnel** from among college graduates.

phase See **faze, phase.**

phenomena *Phenomena* is the plural form of the word *phenomenon.* Do not use *phenomena* as a singular noun.

PLURAL   To re-create **those phenomena** in a laboratory setting proved impossible.

SINGULAR   We studied the northern lights, a **phenomenon** of nature that **is** quite spectacular.

phrase A phrase is a group of related words that does not contain both a verb and its subject and that is used as a single part of speech. See **Chapter 6: Phrases.**

EXAMPLE   - Josh and I **are planning** a surprise party **for Francine's birthday.**

piece See **peace, piece.**

plain, plane As an adjective, *plain* means "not fancy" or "clear." As a noun, it means "an area of flat land." *Plane* is a noun meaning "a flat surface" or "a tool" or "an airplane."

EXAMPLES   - Although the new uniforms are **plain,** they are quite attractive. [adjective]
- Does my explanation make things **plain** to you? [adjective]
- Many western movies are set on the Great **Plains.** [noun]
- Some problems in physics deal with the mechanical advantage of an inclined **plane.** [noun]
- Use this **plane** to smooth the board. [noun]
- We watched the **plane** circle for its landing. [noun]

plus In formal situations, avoid using *plus* as a substitute for *and* between main clauses or as a conjunctive adverb between main clauses or sentences.

INFORMAL   Maria jogs three miles a day, plus she lifts weights.

INFORMAL	Maria jogs three miles a day; plus, she lifts weights.
FORMAL	Maria jogs three miles a day, **and** she lifts weights.
FORMAL	Maria jogs three miles a day; **moreover,** she lifts weights.

P.M. See **A.M., P.M.**

possessive case Possessive case is the form a noun or pronoun takes when used to show ownership or relationship. See pages 195–196.

EXAMPLE ▪ **David's** and **my** report is almost finished.

precede, proceed *Precede* means "to be, come, or go before in time, place, order, rank, or importance." *Proceed* means "to advance or go on, especially after stopping."

EXAMPLES ▪ In the frame story for *The Thousand and One Nights,* each of the women who **precede** Scheherazade as the sultan's wife is killed after one night.
▪ To postpone her own execution, Scheherazade **proceeds** to tell the sultan a series of tales, leaving each one unfinished until the following night.

predicate The predicate is the part of a sentence that says something about the subject. See pages 280–283.

EXAMPLE ▪ We **have been studying all weekend for the chemistry mid-term.**

predicate adjective A predicate adjective is an adjective that follows a linking verb and that modifies the subject of the verb. See page 292.

EXAMPLE ▪ Of all the puppies, this one appears **healthiest** and most **friendly.**

predicate nominative A predicate nominative is a noun or a pronoun that follows a linking verb and that refers to the same person or thing as the subject of the verb. See pages 291–292.

EXAMPLE ▪ The top finishers in the marathon were **Reggie, Arturo,** and **she.**

preposition A preposition shows the relationship of a noun or a pronoun to some other word. See pages 107–109.

EXAMPLE ■ Elizabeth Barrett Browning wrote *Sonnets from the Portuguese* **for** her husband.

prepositional phrase A prepositional phrase is a group of words consisiting of a preposition, a noun or a pronoun called the object of the preposition, and any modifiers of that object. See pages 240–244.

EXAMPLE ■ Playing hide-and-seek **in Grandpa's old barn** is a treat **for my young cousins.**

principal, principle As a noun, *principal* means "the head of a school." As an adjective, it means "main or most important." *Principle* is a noun meaning "a rule of conduct" or "a fact or general truth."

EXAMPLES ■ The **principal** will address the student body tomorrow. [noun]
■ Florida and California are our **principal** citrus-growing states. [adjective]
■ The **principle** of the golden rule is found in many religions.
■ The design of this plane is based on the latest **principles** of aerodynamics.

proceed See **precede, proceed.**

pronoun A pronoun is used in place of a noun, more than one noun, or another pronoun. See pages 90–95.

EXAMPLE ■ Mr. Stevens says that **he** might be willing to postpone the quiz.

proper adjective A proper adjective is an adjective formed from a proper noun. See pages 354–356.

EXAMPLES ■ Spanish ■ Texan
■ Buddhist ■ Martian

proper noun A proper noun names a particular person, place, thing, or idea and is always capitalized. See pages 354–355.

EXAMPLES ■ Queen Elizabeth ■ Iowa
■ Christianity ■ Brooklyn Bridge

WRITER'S QUICK REFERENCE

Q
---

quiet, quit, quite   *Quiet* is an adjective meaning "still; silent." *Quit* is a verb meaning "to stop." *Quite* is an adverb meaning "completely; rather; very."

EXAMPLES
- The library is usually a **quiet** place to study.
- Why did you **quit** your job?
- Are you **quite** finished?
- We are **quite** proud of Angel's achievements.

R
---

rain, reign, rein   As a noun, *rain* means "water falling to earth in drops." As a verb, *rain* often takes an impersonal construction (*it rained*) and means "to fall as rain." As a noun, *reign* means "power, authority, or rule." As a verb, it means "to rule as a sovereign" or "to prevail." As a noun (usually plural) *rein* means "a strap fastened to a bit and used to control an animal." As a verb, *rein* is usually followed by *in* or *up* and means "to stop or slow a horse, etc., as with reins."

EXAMPLES
- When the **rain** stopped, we went for a walk. [noun]
- In December, it **rained** for two weeks straight. [verb, impersonal construction]
- The art of haiku was perfected in the seventeenth century, during the **reign** of the Tokugawa family. [noun]
- From the capital in Edo (now Tokyo), the Tokugawa shogun **reigned** over all of Japan. [verb]
- Instead of using the **reins** to guide Rocinante, Don Quixote lets the horse take whatever path it chooses. [noun]
- Harold wasn't able to **rein** in his horse until they had galloped almost to the edge of the ravine. [verb]

raise See **rise, raise.**

rarely ever See **double negative.**

real, really *Real* is an adjective. *Really* is an adverb meaning "actually" or "truly." Although *real* is commonly used as an adverb meaning "very" in everyday situations, avoid its use in formal speaking and writing.

INFORMAL   Our new neighbor is real nice.
FORMAL   Our new neighbor is **really** nice.

INFORMAL   Janine did real well on the SAT.
FORMAL   Janine did **really** well on the SAT.

reason . . . because See **because.**

refer back Since the prefix *re–* in *refer* means "back," the expression *refer back* is redundant. Use *refer* alone.

EXAMPLE   ▪ The word *fifties* in Alice Walker's poem "For My Sister Molly Who in the Fifties" **refers** [*not* refers back] to the 1950s.

regardless See **irregardless, regardless.**

regular verb A regular verb forms its past and past participle by adding *–d* or *–ed* to the base form.

EXAMPLE   ▪ When we **had reached** the pier, we **stopped** walking and **tossed** crumbs to the sea gulls.

reign See **rain, reign, rein.**

rein See **rain, reign, rein.**

result See **end result, result.**

Reverend, Honorable In formal writing, do not use these titles before a person's last name alone. Do use the word *the* before the title.

NONSTANDARD   Reverend Hill, the Reverend Hill, Honorable Jordan
STANDARD   **the Reverend** Robert Hill, **the Reverend** R. H. Hill, **the Reverend** Dr. Hill, **the Honorable** Barbara Jordan

right, rite, write As a noun, *right* means "what is just, lawful, morally good, etc."; "something that belongs to a person by law, nature, or tradition"; or "the side opposite the left." As a verb, it means "to restore [something] to its proper position," "to correct," or "to make amends for." *Rite* is a noun meaning "a ceremony" or "a customary practice." *Write* is a verb meaning "to form or inscribe [words, letters, symbols, etc.] on a surface."

EXAMPLES
- In the *Analects,* translated by Arthur Waley, Confucius is quoted as stating that at seventy what he desired "no longer overstepped the boundaries of **right**." [noun]
- Thomas Paine's ***Rights** of Man* is a ringing defense of the French Revolution. [noun]
- Our house is the third one on the **right**. [noun]
- In Robert Frost's "Birches," the speaker describes trees so weighted down by ice that they are unable to **right** themselves. [verb]
- Sojourner Truth argued that women working together could **right** the wrongs of the world. [verb]
- For her efforts to convince the government to **right** the injustices done to the people of Burma (now the Union of Myanmar), Daw Aung San Suu Kyi won the 1991 Nobel Prize for peace. [verb]
- Egyptian works of both the Old Kingdom and the New Kingdom contain magical spells for burial **rites**.
- What topic have you decided to **write** about?

rise, raise The verb *rise* means "to go up" or "to get up." *Rise* rarely takes an object. The verb *raise* means "to cause [something] to rise" or "to lift up." *Raise* usually takes an object. See pages 155–156.

EXAMPLES
- The speaker **rose** from her chair and walked to the podium. [no object]
- The movers **raised** the boxes onto their shoulders. [*Boxes* is the object of *raised.*]

rite See **right, rite, write.**

rout, route As a noun, *rout* means "a disorderly flight." As a verb, it means "to put to flight" or "to defeat overwhelmingly." *Route* is a noun meaning "a road" or "a way to go."

EXAMPLES
- What began as an orderly retreat ended as a **rout**. [noun]
- The coach predicts that his Bears will **rout** the Wildcats in the playoffs. [verb]
- This highway is the shortest **route** to the mountains.

run-on sentence A run-on sentence occurs when two complete sentences run together as if they were one sentence. See also **comma splice, fused sentence,** and pages 318–319.

RUN-ON
Ms. Jefferson asked each of us to choose a metaphysical poem and to write an essay about it I chose Donne's "The Bait" Renée chose Herbert's "The Pulley."

REVISED
Ms. Jefferson asked us to choose a metaphysical poem and write an essay about it. I chose Donne's "The Bait"; Renée chose Herbert's "The Pulley."

REVISED
When Ms. Jefferson asked us to choose a metaphysical poem and write an essay about it, I chose Donne's "The Bait," and Renée chose Herbert's "The Pulley."

S

same, said, such These words are sometimes used to act as pronouns in business or legal writing. Avoid using them in general writing.

LEGAL
I received your letter and have forwarded a copy of same to my associate.

GENERAL
I received your letter and have forwarded a copy of **it** to my associate.

LEGAL
Said letter sheds new light on our case.

GENERAL
This letter sheds new light on our case.

LEGAL
Your suggestion that we withhold this evidence appalls me; I cannot condone such.

GENERAL
Your suggestion that we withhold this evidence appalls me; I cannot condone **such behavior.**

say See **go, say.**

scarcely See **double negative.**

second, secondly See **first, firstly; second, secondly.**

seldom ever Since *seldom* means "not often," the expression *seldom ever* is redundant. Use *seldom* alone.

EXAMPLE   ■ We **seldom** [*not* seldom ever] see our former neighbors since they moved to Cincinnati.

sentence A sentence is a group of words that contains a subject and a verb and that expresses a complete thought. See page 279.

sentence fragment A sentence fragment is a group of words that looks like a sentence but that does not make sense by itself. See pages 279 and 313–317.

set See **sit, set.**

sexist language See **nonsexist language.**

she See **he, she, it, they.**

shone, shown *Shone* is the past tense of the verb *shine*, which means "to emit or reflect light" or "to exhibit [itself] clearly." *Shown* is the past participle of the verb *show*, which means "to exhibit."

EXAMPLES   ■ The old car **shone** once it was waxed.
            ■ Pride **shone** from Manolo's parents' faces.
            ■ Since its opening in 1991, the Museum of African-American Art in Tampa has **shown** the works of distinguished black artists to thousands of visitors.

Another meaning of *shine* is "to polish" or "to direct the light of," but the preferred past tense form for this meaning is *shined*, not *shone*.

EXAMPLES   ■ Preparing for a job interview, Dan **shined** [*not* shone] his old black shoes.
            ■ Nancy **shined** [*not* shone] the flashlight along the path.

should of See **of.**

shown See **shone, shown.**

sight See **cite, sight, site.**

simple sentence A simple sentence has one independent clause and no subordinate clauses. See page 294.

EXAMPLE ▪ Driving on that little-used country road just outside of town, we saw three deer.

sit, set The verb *sit* means "to rest in an upright, seated position." *Sit* seldom takes an object. The verb *set* means "to put [something] in a place." *Set* usually takes an object. See pages 154–155.

EXAMPLES ▪ Where do you want to **sit**? [no object]
▪ Please **set** the groceries on the table. [*Groceries* is the object of *set.*]

site See **cite, sight, site.**

slow, slowly *Slow* is an adjective. *Slowly* is an adverb. Although *slow* is also labeled as an adverb in many dictionaries, this usage applies only to informal situations and colloquial expressions, such as *drive slow* and *go slow.*

INFORMAL Do sloths always move that slow?
FORMAL Do sloths always move that **slowly**?

so, so that As an adverb, *so* means "to such an extent." It is often used in a correlative construction with *that.* Informally, it is used (and often overused) as a substitute for *very.* As a subordinating conjunction, it means "in order that." In formal situations, use *so that* instead.

INFORMAL That flight was so bumpy.
FORMAL That flight was **so** bumpy **that** we wished we had taken the train.

INFORMAL I rehearsed my speech so I'd be prepared.
FORMAL I rehearsed my speech **so that** I'd be prepared.

some day, someday In the colloquial expression *some day, some* is an adjective meaning "remarkable." *Someday* is an adverb meaning "on an unspecified future day."

EXAMPLES ▪ This has been **some day.** [stress equally on *some* and *day*]
▪ **Someday** we'll laugh about the experience. [stress on *some*]

some, somewhat In formal situations, avoid using *some* to mean "to some extent." Use *somewhat.*

INFORMAL   My grades have improved some during the past month.

FORMAL   My grades have improved **somewhat** during the past month.

some time, sometime, sometimes In the expression *some time, some* is an adjective modifying the noun *time. Sometime* is an adverb meaning "at an unspecified time." *Sometimes* is an adverb meaning "occasionally."

EXAMPLES ▪ I need **some time** to myself.
▪ Would you like to go to a movie with me **sometime**?
▪ The Realto Theater **sometimes** shows Mexican films.

somewheres See **anyways, anywheres.**

sort(s) See **kind(s), sort(s), type(s)** and **kind of a, sort of a.**

sort of See **kind of, sort of.**

stationary, stationery *Stationary* is an adjective meaning "in a fixed position." *Stationery* is a noun meaning "writing paper."

EXAMPLES ▪ The new power plant contains large **stationary** engines.
▪ I always save my best **stationery** for important letters.

straight, strait As an adjective, *straight* means "not crooked or curved" or "direct." As an adverb, *straight* means "directly." *Strait* is a noun meaning "a channel connecting two large bodies of water." Used in its plural form, *strait* means "difficulty" or "distress."

EXAMPLES ▪ Draw a **straight** line that connects points A and B.
▪ If you head **straight** north, you'll reach the lake in about five minutes.
▪ The **Strait** of Gibraltar links the Atlantic Ocean and the Mediterranean Sea.
▪ His family always helped him when he was in bad **straits.**

subject   The subject is the part of a sentence that tells whom or what the sentence is about. See pages 280–285.

EXAMPLE   ■ Thornton Wilder's **Our Town** is one of the most popular American plays ever written.

subject complement   A subject complement is a word or word group that completes the meaning of a linking verb and that identifies or modifies the subject. See pages 291–292

EXAMPLE   ■ Nadine's brother is a **computer programmer.**

subjunctive mood   The subjunctive mood is used to express a suggestion, a necessity, a condition contrary to fact, or a wish. See pages 176–178.

EXAMPLE   ■ I wish I **were** a better skier.

subordinate clause   Also called a **dependent clause,** a subordinate clause does not express a complete thought and cannot stand alone as a sentence. See pages 264–274.

EXAMPLE   ■ **Before you read The Great Gatsby,** let's talk a little about the Jazz Age.

subordinating conjunction   A subordinating conjunction begins a subordinate clause and links it to an independent clause. See pages 110–112.

EXAMPLE   ■ **When** Chilean poet Gabriela Mistral won the Nobel Prize for literature in 1945, she became the first woman ever to receive that honor.

subsequently   *Subsequently* means "coming after; following in time." Don't confuse it with *consequently,* which means "as a result."

EXAMPLE   ■ Leslie Marmon Silko grew up on the Laguna Pueblo Reservation in New Mexico; **subsequently** [*not* consequently], she attended the University of New Mexico.

such   See **same, said, such.**

sure, surely   Avoid using the adjective *sure,* meaning "certain," as an adverb. Instead, use *surely* or *certainly.*

WRITER'S QUICK REFERENCE

EXAMPLES ■ The ending of Naguib Mahfouz's story "Half a Day" **certainly** [*not* sure] came as a surprise to me. [adverb]
■ Until the story's last line, I was **sure** the narrator was simply lost. [adjective]

T

---

take See **bring, take.**

teach See **learn, teach.**

tense The tense of a verb indicates the time of the action or state of being the verb expresses. See pages 156–163.

EXAMPLE ■ I **thought** [past] that you **had** already **left** [past perfect].

than, then *Than* is a conjunction used in comparisons. *Then* is an adverb meaning "at that time" or "next."

EXAMPLES ■ Tyrone is more studious **than** I am.
■ Take your diploma in your left hand and shake hands with the principal; **then** leave the stage and return to your seat.
■ First, mix the wet ingredients; **then** slowly add the flour.

that See **who, which, that.** See also **general reference** and pages 265–267.

their, there, they're *Their* is a possessive form of *they*. As an adverb, *there* means "at that place." As an expletive, it is used to begin a sentence (see page 126). *They're* is the contraction of *they are*.

EXAMPLES ■ The performers are studying **their** lines.
■ I will be **there** after rehearsal. [adverb]
■ **There** will be four performances of the play. [expletive]
■ **They're** performing a play by Luis Valdez.

theirs, there's *Theirs* is a possessive form of the pronoun *they*. *There's* is the contraction for *there is*.

EXAMPLES ■ These posters are ours; **theirs** are the ones on the opposite wall.

■ **There's** a new biography of W.E.B. DuBois in the library.

theirselves See **hisself, theirselves.**

them Do not use *them* as an adjective. Use *those.*

EXAMPLE ■ Have you seen **those** [*not* them] murals by Judith Baca at the art museum?

then See **than, then.**

there See **their, there, they're.**

there's See **theirs, there's.**

therefore When *therefore* is used as an adverb within a clause, it is set off by commas. When it is used as a conjunctive adverb between independent clauses, it is preceded by a semicolon and followed by a comma.

EXAMPLES ■ I have to work Saturday; I won't, **therefore,** be able to go camping with you.

■ I have to work Saturday; **therefore,** I won't be able to go camping with you.

they See **he, she, it, they.**

they're See **their, there, they're.**

this here, that there Avoid using *here* or *there* after *this* or *that.*

EXAMPLE ■ **This** [*not* This here] magazine has an article about Japanese koto player Kazue Sawai.

this, that, these, those See **kind(s), sort(s), type(s).**

thusly Avoid using *thusly*. Instead, use *thus.*

EXAMPLE ■ The concert was sold out; **thus,** [*not* thusly] we were unable to attend.

till, until Although both *till* and *until* are standard usage, *until* is the preferred form for the first word of a sentence. Avoid using the spellings *til* and *'til.*

EXAMPLES ▪ **Until** [*not* Till] we studied August Wilson's *The Piano Lesson,* I didn't realize that Romare Bearden's painting of the same title inspired the play.

to, too, two *To* is used as a preposition or as the sign of the infinitive form of a verb. *Too* is an adverb meaning "also" or "overly." As an adjective *two* means "totaling one plus one." As a noun, it means "the number between one and three."

EXAMPLES ▪ Let's go **to** the movies. [preposition]
▪ After the rain, the birds began **to** sing. [sign of the infinitive]
▪ You, **too,** are invited to the sports banquet.
▪ Is it **too** far to walk?
▪ They only serve **two** flavors. [adjective]
▪ **Two** of my favorite writers are Nadine Gordimer and Ntozake Shange. [noun]

toward, towards Use *toward* rather than *towards,* which is the British usage.

EXAMPLE ▪ Rounding third, Flo headed **toward** [*not* towards] home plate.

Overboard copyright 1991 Universal Press Syndicate.
Reprinted with permission. All rights reserved.

transitional expressions Transitional expressions are words and phrases that indicate relationships between ideas in a paragraph or a composition. See pages 294–295.

transitive verb A transitive verb is an action verb that takes an object. See page 101.

EXAMPLE ▪ Joey **smacked** the baseball as hard as he could and **made** his first home run.

try and, try to   Use **try to,** not **try and.**

EXAMPLE   ▪ I will **try to** [*not* try and] be there by noon.

type, type of   Avoid using the noun *type* as an adjective. Add *of* after *type.*

NONSTANDARD   I prefer this type shirt.
STANDARD   I prefer this **type of** shirt.

type(s)   See **kind(s), sort(s), type(s).**

U

understood subject   The understood subject is the unstated *you* in a request or a command. See page 283.

EXAMPLE   ▪ [You] Please hand me those pliers.

uninterested   See **disinterested, uninterested.**

unique, perfect   *Unique,* meaning "the only one of its kind," and *perfect,* meaning "flawless" or "complete," are **absolute adjectives**—ones without degrees of comparison. Avoid using them in the comparative or superlative degree. See pages 227–228.

NONSTANDARD   Jenny's uncle brought her the most
            unique bracelet from Peru.
STANDARD   Jenny's uncle brought her a **unique**
            bracelet from Peru.

NONSTANDARD   Do you think human beings will ever cre-
            ate a more perfect society?
STANDARD   Do you think human beings will ever cre-
            ate a **perfect** society?

V

vain, vein   *Vain* is an adjective meaning "unsuccessful" or "conceited." Used with *in,* it forms the idiom *in vain,* meaning "fruitlessly" or "profanely." *Vein* is a noun meaning "a blood vessel that carries blood from some part of the body back to the heart," or "a natural substance deposited in rock."

EXAMPLES
- The candidate made several **vain** attempts to set the record straight.
- Marshall has never been **vain** about his looks.
- All my efforts to call her were in **vain.**
- The biblical commandment "Thou shalt not take the name of the Lord thy God in **vain**" appears in Exodus 20:7.
- Capillaries are the tiny blood vessels that connect the arteries with the **veins.**
- Often, gold is found in **veins** of quartz.

verb   A verb expresses an action or a state of being. See pages 100–103.

EXAMPLE
- Edmonia Lewis **became** a highly respected sculptor.

verb phrase   A verb phrase consists of a main verb preceded by at least one helping verb. See page 103.

EXAMPLE
- **Have** you ever **seen** a Florida panther?

verbal   A verbal is a form of a verb used as a noun, an adjective, or an adverb. See pages 246–255.

EXAMPLE
- **Whooping** and **whistling,** the fans celebrated the team's victory.

verbal phrase   A verbal phrase consists of a verbal and its modifiers and complements. See pages 246–255.

EXAMPLE
- **Trained in classical dance,** Mikhail Baryshnikov later began **to dance contemporary works** and eventually formed a creative partnership with choreographer Twyla Tharp.

voice   Voice is the form a transitive verb takes to indicate whether the subject of the verb performs or receives the action. See pages 170–175.

ACTIVE VOICE   Leon **caught** the pass and **made** the touchdown.
PASSIVE VOICE   The pass **was caught,** and the touchdown **was made** by Leon.

W

waist, waste   *Waist* is a noun meaning "the midsection of the body." As a noun, *waste* means "unused or useless material." As a verb, it means "to squander."

EXAMPLES ■ These slacks are too tight at the **waist**.
■ Our community is trying to find ways to recycle **waste** from the paper mill.
■ Don't **waste** your money on movies like that.

ways   Use *way*, not *ways*, when referring to distance.

INFORMAL   My home in Wichita is a long ways from Tokyo, where my pen pal lives.
FORMAL   My home in Wichita is a long **way** from Tokyo, where my pen pal lives.

weak reference   A weak reference occurs when a pronoun refers to an antecedent that has not been expressed. See pages 207–208

WEAK   Natalie is a multitalented performer. One of these is dancing.
CLEAR   Natalie is a multitalented performer. One of her talents is dancing.

well   See **good, well.**

what   Use *that,* not *what,* to introduce an adjective clause.

EXAMPLE ■ The part of Japanese author Sei Shōnagon's *Pillow Book* **that** [*not* what] intrigued me the most was "Embarrassing Things."

when, where   Avoid the use of *when* or *where* to begin a definition.

NONSTANDARD   A spoonerism is when you switch the beginning sounds of two words.
STANDARD   A spoonerism is **a slip of the tongue in which the beginning sounds of two words are switched.**

NONSTANDARD   A predicament is where you get into an embarrassing situation.
STANDARD   A predicament is **an embarrassing situation.**

WRITER'S QUICK REFERENCE

where, when Do not use *where* or *when* for *that.*

EXAMPLE   ■ I read **that** [*not* where] Demosthenes learned
              to speak clearly by practicing with pebbles in
              his mouth.

           ■ Do you remember the time **that** [*not* when]
              we spent all our money at the arcade and
              had to walk home in the rain?

where . . . at See **at.**

whether See **if, whether.**

which   Use *which,* not *that,* to introduce a nonessential
clause. In many cases, such clauses can be reduced to appositive phrases.

EXAMPLES   ■ Jamaica Kincaid grew up in St. John's,
              which [*not* that] is the largest city on the
              Caribbean island of Antigua. [nonessential
              clause]

           ■ Jamaica Kincaid grew up in St. John's, the
              largest city on the Caribbean island of
              Antigua. [appositive phrase]

See also **who, which, that; wordiness;** and pages 265–267.

while See **a while.**

who, which, that   *Who* refers to persons only. *Which* refers
to things only. *That* may refer to either persons or things.

EXAMPLES   ■ Wasn't Beethoven the composer **who** [*or*
              that] continued to write music after he lost
              his hearing?

           ■ First editions of Poe's first book, **which** is ti-
              tled *Tamerlane and Other Poems,* are worth
              thousands of dollars.

           ■ Is this the only essay **that** James Baldwin
              wrote?

See also **which.**

who, whom See pages 201–204.

whole, wholly See **hole, holey; holy; whole, wholly.**

who's, whose   *Who's* is the contraction of *who is* or *who has.*
Whose is the possessive form of *who.*

EXAMPLES ■ **Who's** going to portray the Navajo detective in the play?
■ **Who's** been using my typewriter?
■ **Whose** artwork is this?

–wise Avoid adding the adverb-forming suffix *–wise* to a word to mean "with regard to" or "in connection with."

NONSTANDARD Weatherwise, the fiesta was perfect.
BETTER The weather for the fiesta was perfect.

NONSTANDARD Moneywise, I can't help you.
BETTER I can't help you with money.

with regards to See **in regards to, with regards to.**

wordiness Wordiness is the use of unnecessary words. See pages 325–327.

WORDY It is at this point in time that we seniors should all begin to try to assess the courses of action that await us.
BETTER We seniors should now begin planning for our futures.

would of See **of.**

write See **right, rite, write.**

Y

your, you're *Your* is a possessive form of *you. You're* is the contraction of *you are.*

EXAMPLES ■ Is this **your** book?
■ I hope **you're** able to come to my graduation.

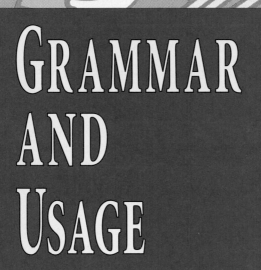

GRAMMAR
AND
USAGE

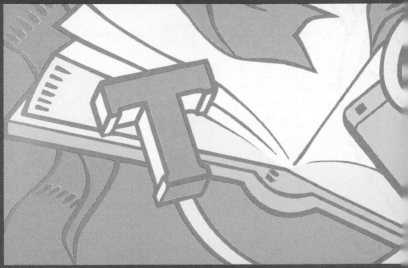

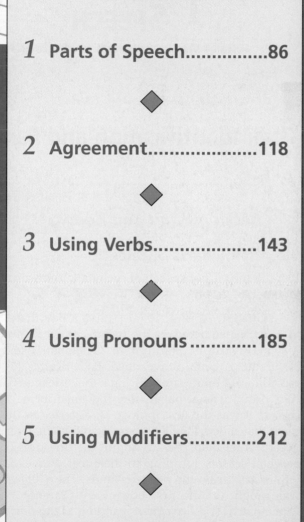

1 PARTS OF SPEECH

Their Identification and Function

 Checking What You Know

Identifying Parts of Speech

Identify the part of speech of each italicized word in the following paragraph.

Thursday, April 4, 1974, [1] *was* a day that will [2] *always* be remembered in the history of [3] *baseball.* At 2:40 P.M. in Riverfront Stadium in Cincinnati, Henry Aaron [4] *of* the Atlanta Braves tied Babe Ruth's [5] *unbroken* record of 714 home runs during a major league baseball career. Aaron was at bat for the first time in the [6] *baseball* season. It was the first inning. [7] *Nevertheless,* he hit a 3-1 pitch that sailed 400 feet, zooming [8] *neatly* over the fence in left center field and driving in the first runs of the 1974 baseball season. Jumping to their feet, Braves fans yelled [9] *"Bravo!"* from the packed stands. The [10] *horsehide* ball was caught on the first bounce by Clarence Williams, a Cincinnati [11] *police officer,* standing [12] *behind* the fence. "I couldn't see what was going on," said Williams, [13] *one* of Aaron's fans, [14] *"but* I knew he was up when I saw 44 on the scoreboard under the 'at bat' sign." While being interviewed by the press after the game, Aaron smiled in his usual gracious [15] *way* [16] *and* said he was [17] *positively* delighted to have tied the Babe's [18] *longstanding* record. Later that month, on April 8, Aaron [19] *broke* Babe Ruth's record, a feat that [20] *many* had thought they would never see.

✓

The Eight Parts of Speech		
noun	verb	conjunction
pronoun	adverb	interjection
adjective	preposition	

The Noun

1a. A *noun* is a word used to name a person, a place, a thing, or an idea.

PERSONS	PLACES	THINGS	IDEAS
architect	restaurant	computers	education
travelers	islands	sailboats	beliefs
family	wilderness	insects	ambition
Kira Alvarez	Utah	Mount Ida	democracy
B. B. King	Brooklyn	the Capitol	Utopianism

Dates and days of the week are also nouns.

EXAMPLES   November 22, 1963   321 B.C.   Saturday

NOTE Two kinds of verbals, the gerund and the infinitive, function as nouns. Compare the following sentences.

NOUN   Jeff likes winter **sports.**
GERUND   Jeff likes **skiing.**
INFINITIVE Jeff likes **to ski.**

 REFERENCE NOTE: For more about gerunds and infinitives, see pages 180–181, 250, and 252.

Common and Proper Nouns

A *common noun* is a general name for a person, place, thing, or idea. A *proper noun* names a particular person, place, thing, or idea. Common nouns are not capitalized unless they begin a sentence or are used in a title. Proper nouns are almost always capitalized.

COMMON NOUNS	PROPER NOUNS
woman	Sylvia Bryan, Eda Seasongood, Queen of England, Cleopatra, Indira Gandhi, Charlayne Hunter-Gault
nation	Switzerland, Canada, Mexico, South Africa, United Arab Emirates
event	World Series, Mardi Gras, Fall of Rome, Boston Marathon, State Fair of Texas
holiday	Memorial Day, Thanksgiving Day, Fourth of July, Kwanzaa, Rosh Hashanah
language	English, Spanish, Japanese, Arabic, Quechua, Hindustani, Bantu, Hebrew

 REFERENCE NOTE: For more on capitalizing proper nouns, see pages 354–365.

Concrete and Abstract Nouns

A *concrete noun* names an object that can be perceived by the senses. An *abstract noun* names a quality, a characteristic, or an idea.

CONCRETE NOUNS	fire, band, garlic, trumpet, cotton, telephone pole, horses, Liberty Bell, President Clinton
ABSTRACT NOUNS	confidence, optimism, strength, charm, divine right of kings, ability, Zen, jingoism, kinship, Pan-Americanism, sisterhood

Some nouns can be either concrete or abstract, depending on how they are used.

CONCRETE	Mrs. Reynolds contributed to her favorite **charity.** [*Charity* refers to a helpful organization or a good cause.]
ABSTRACT	**Charity** begins at home. [*Charity* refers to feelings of generosity or helpfulness.]
CONCRETE	The lemon's **sourness** made me wince. [*Sourness* refers to a taste.]
ABSTRACT	The **sourness** of my cat's expression told me not to bother him. [*Sourness* refers to a cross attitude.]
CONCRETE	An expert on the **writings** of James Baldwin spoke to our class. [*Writings* refers to such things as essays, short stories, and novels.]
ABSTRACT	**Writing** well requires much practice. [*Writing* refers to the art of composing written language.]

Collective Nouns

A *collective noun* names a group.

COLLECTIVE NOUNS	swarm, team, herd, crew, committee, fleet, family, class, group

Compound Nouns

A *compound noun* consists of two or more words used together as a single noun. Some compound nouns are written as one word, some as separate words, and others as hyphenated words.

ONE WORD	sidewalk, tablecloth, Greenland, backpack, Broadway, Tallchief
SEPARATE WORDS	attorney general, telephone pole, Empire State Building, mover and shaker, Wall Street, Amy Tan
HYPHENATED WORDS	daughter-in-law, great-grandfather, jack-o'-lantern, Day-Lewis

NOTE When you are not sure about the form of a compound noun, look it up in a dictionary.

STYLE NOTE   To make your writing clearer and more precise, replace general nouns with specific ones whenever you can.

GENERAL   The dog sat on the rug.
SPECIFIC   The **poodle** sat on the **Persian carpet.**

Notice how the specific nouns help you "see" the scene more clearly.

 QUICK CHECK 1   **Classifying Nouns**

Classify each of the following nouns as either *concrete* or *abstract*.

1. tradition
2. great-aunt
3. courage

4. cafeteria
5. dancers

The Pronoun

1b.   A *pronoun* is a word used in place of one or more nouns.

EXAMPLE   Angelo borrowed a hammer and some nails. **He** will return **them** tomorrow. [The pronoun *he* takes the place of the noun *Angelo.* The pronoun *them* takes the place of the nouns *hammer* and *nails.*]

The word that a pronoun stands for is called the *antecedent* of the pronoun. In the preceding example, *Angelo* is the antecedent of *he,* and *hammer* and *nails* are the antecedents of *them.*

 REFERENCE NOTE: See pages 133–139 for more information on the agreement of pronouns and their antecedents. For more about using pronouns, see **Chapter 4: Using Pronouns.**

A pronoun may also take the place of another pronoun or a verbal.

GRAMMAR/USAGE

EXAMPLES   **Several** of the students have entered the essay contest because **they** are extremely interested in the topic. [The pronoun *they* takes the place of the pronoun *several.*]

We treated **ourselves** to a night out. [The pronoun *ourselves* takes the place of the pronoun *we.*]

Mrs. Reynolds teaches candlemaking and flower arranging, but **these** are only two of the many crafts she knows. [The pronoun *they* takes the place of the gerunds *candlemaking* and *flower arranging.*]

Gina is learning **to surf,** and she has discovered that **it** is more difficult than she had thought. [The pronoun *it* takes the place of the infinitive *to surf.*]

☞ REFERENCE NOTE: For more about gerunds and infinitives, see pages 180–181, 250, and 252.

A pronoun may also take the place of a phrase or a clause.

EXAMPLES   Painting the garage took most of the day. **It** was a hot, dirty job. [The pronoun *It* takes the place of the gerund phrase *Painting the garage.*]

Whoever decides to become a marathon runner must be able to discipline **himself** or **herself** to eat right and train hard. [The pronouns *himself* and *herself* take the place of the noun clause *Whoever decides to become a marathon runner.*]

☞ REFERENCE NOTE: For more information about phrases, see **Chapter 6: Phrases.** For more about clauses, see **Chapter 7: Clauses.**

Personal Pronouns

A *personal pronoun* refers to the one speaking (first person), the one spoken to (second person), or the one spoken about (third person).

	SINGULAR	PLURAL
FIRST PERSON	I, me, my, mine	we, us, our, ours
SECOND PERSON	you, your, yours	you, your, yours
THIRD PERSON	he, him, his, she, her, hers, it, its	they, them, their, theirs

EXAMPLES   Can **you** help **me** with **my** homework?
            He said that **they** would meet **us** outside the theater.

NOTE   The pronoun *it* also has impersonal uses.

EXAMPLES   **It** is my job to cook supper. [*It* is used as an *expletive*—a word that fills out the structure of a sentence but does not add to its meaning. *It* may be omitted without changing the meaning of the sentence: *My job is to cook supper.*]
            It is raining. [*It* has no antecedent—we cannot replace It with a noun. Like the expressions *It's hot today* and *It is too late*, *It is raining* is an *idiom*, a word or phrase that means something different from its literal meaning.]

In this book the words *my, your, his, her, its, our,* and *their* are called possessive pronouns. Since these words precede nouns and tell which one or whose, some authorities prefer to call them possessive adjectives.

EXAMPLES   **my** job, **your** essay, **their** plans

Follow your teacher's instructions in labeling these words.

Reflexive and Intensive Pronouns

A *reflexive pronoun* refers to the subject of a sentence and directs the action of the verb back to the subject. A reflexive pronoun functions as an object of a verb, verbal, or preposition. An *intensive pronoun* emphasizes a noun or another pronoun. An intensive pronoun may be omitted froma sentence without changing the basic meaning of the sentence.

	SINGULAR	PLURAL
FIRST PERSON	myself	ourselves
SECOND PERSON	yourself	yourselves
THIRD PERSON	himself, herself itself	themselves

EXAMPLES   Kimiko wrote **herself** a note. [reflexive—*herself* is the indirect object of the verb *wrote*.]
All by **itself** the bloodhound tracked the escaped convict. [reflexive—*itself* is the object of the preposition *by*.]
Leonora **herself** organized the school's recycling program. [intensive]
Did you two plant the garden **yourselves?** [intensive]

 REFERENCE NOTE: For more about pronouns as objects of verbs, verbals, and prepositions, see pages 191–194.

Demonstrative Pronouns

A *demonstrative pronoun* points out a person, a place, a thing, or an idea.

this	that	these	those

EXAMPLES   **This** is our favorite song by Ella Fitzgerald.
The apples I picked today taste better than **those** from the store.

Interrogative Pronouns

An *interrogative pronoun* introduces a question.

who	whom	which	what	whose

GRAMMAR/USAGE

EXAMPLES   **What** is the answer to the last algebra
                     problem?
                 Whose car is parked outside?

Relative Pronouns

A *relative pronoun* introduces a subordinate clause.

that	which	who	whom	whose

EXAMPLES   The house **that** you saw is a historical land-
                 mark. [The relative pronoun introduces the
                 adjective clause *that you saw*.]
                 She is the woman **who** is running for mayor.
                 [The relative pronoun introduces the adjec-
                 tive clause *who is running for mayor*.]
                 Believe **what** he says. [The relative pronoun
                 introduces the noun clause *what he says*.]

 REFERENCE NOTE: For more information about relative
pronouns and subordinate clauses, see pages 264–267.

Indefinite Pronouns

An *indefinite pronoun* refers to a person, place, or thing
that is not specifically named.

all	each other	most	one another
another	either	much	other
any	everybody	neither	several
anybody	everyone	nobody	some
anyone	everything	none	somebody
anything	few	no one	someone
both	many	nothing	something
each	more	one	such

EXAMPLES   I have packed **everything** we will need for
                 the trip.
                 Has **anyone** seen my binoculars?
                 The delegates greeted **each other** warmly.

Some indefinite pronouns can be used as adjectives.

EXAMPLES   **Many** of the items at the garage sale were in good condition. [pronoun]
Many items at the garage sale were in good condition. [adjective]

 REFERENCE NOTE: For more about indefinite pronouns and subject-verb agreement, see pages 122–124. For more about pronoun-antecedent agreement and indefinite pronouns , see pages 134–136.

 QUICK CHECK 2   **Identifying Pronouns**

Identify the pronouns in the following sentences.

1. Deven himself knew everyone who either had a ticket or could get one for him at a low price.
2. Everybody has bought at least one of the records on sale at the discount store.
3. A friend of mine said you won several of the events at the 4-H competition.
4. Those are photographs of some of the many contemporary politicians who are women.
5. What is the large body of water that borders Ethiopia called?

The Adjective

1c. An *adjective* is a word used to modify a noun or a pronoun.

To *modify* a word means to describe or to make more definite the meaning of a word. Adjectives modify nouns or pronouns by telling *what kind, which one,* or *how many (how much).*

WHAT KIND?	WHICH ONE?	HOW MANY?	HOW MUCH?
brown shoes	**those** cars	**ten** boxes	**some** water
large animal	**this** street	**several** books	**less** time
narrow road	**first** step	**fewer** mistakes	**more** space
nice person	**last** one	**many** students	**enough** money

NOTE An adjective may also modify a gerund—a verbal used as a noun.

EXAMPLE Darryl's **loud** coughing echoed in the auditorium. [The adjective *loud* modifies the gerund *coughing* by telling *what kind*.]

Adjectives usually precede the words they modify.

EXAMPLE The **wild** and **graceful** deer ran through the forest.

For emphasis, however, adjectives are sometimes placed after the words they modify.

EXAMPLE The deer, **wild** and **graceful,** ran through the forest.

Adjectives may also be separated from the words they modify.

EXAMPLES The casserole was **delicious.**
Luis appeared **ill.**

The adjectives in these two examples are called *predicate adjectives.*

☞ REFERENCE NOTE: For more information about predicate adjectives, see page 292.

Calvin & Hobbes copyright 1989 Watterson.
Reprinted with permission of Universal
Press Syndicate. All rights reserved.

Compound Adjectives

A *compound adjective* consists of two or more words used together as one adjective. Some compound adjectives are written as a single word, some as separate words, and others as hyphenated words.

ONE WORD	childlike smile, noteworthy achievement, paperback book, campfire songs
SEPARATE WORDS	middle school principal, Native American peoples, soft drink dispenser
HYPHENATED WORDS	able-bodied volunteers, short-term loan, air-conditioned office

NOTE In the examples above, the compound nouns *middle school* and *soft drink* function as adjectives.

☞ REFERENCE NOTE: For more about nouns used as adjectives, see pages 98–99.

Articles

The most frequently used adjectives are *a, an,* and *the.* These words are called *articles.*

A and *an* are *indefinite articles,* which refer to any one of a group. *A* is used before a word beginning with a consonant sound. *An* is used before a word beginning with a vowel sound.

EXAMPLES Jorge drew pictures of **a** pelican and **an** albatross.
For **an** hour I rode through the park in **a** horse-drawn carriage.
Lakeview Drive is **a** one-way street.

Notice in the second example above that *an* is used before a noun beginning with the consonant *h,* because the *h* in *hour* is not pronounced. *Hour* is pronounced as if it began with a vowel (like *our*). In the third example, *a* is used before *one-way* because *one-way* is pronounced as though it begins with a consonant. The first *sound* of the word, not the first letter, determines which indefinite article to use.

The is the *definite article.* It indicates someone or something in particular. *The* can precede any word, regardless of the initial sound.

EXAMPLES **The** lion is often called **the** "king of **the** beasts."

Adjective or Pronoun?

A word may be used as one part of speech in one context and as a different part of speech in another context. For example, the following words may be used as *adjectives* or *pronouns*.

all	each	more	one	that	what
another	either	most	other	these	which
any	few	much	several	this	whose
both	many	neither	some	those	

Remember that an adjective *modifies* a noun and that a pronoun *takes the place* of a noun.

ADJECTIVE   **Which** museum did you visit? [*Which* modifies the noun *museum*.]

PRONOUN   **Which** did you visit? [*Which* takes the place of the noun *museum*.]

ADJECTIVE   Leslie Marmon Silko wrote **these** stories. [*These* modifies *stories*.]

PRONOUN   Leslie Marmon Silko wrote **these**. [*These* takes the place of the noun *stories*.]

 REFERENCE NOTE: Possessive pronouns may also be classified as adjectives. See page 195.

Nouns Used as Adjectives

Sometimes nouns are used as adjectives.

NOUNS	NOUNS USED AS ADJECTIVES
business	business letter
saxophone	saxophone player
tuna fish	tuna fish salad
United States	United States government

Some pairs or groups of nouns are considered compound nouns.

EXAMPLES   road map, blood bank, soap opera, country club, United States of America

GRAMMAR/USAGE

By checking an up-to-date dictionary, you can avoid confusing a noun that is used as an adjective with a noun that is part of a compound noun.

 REFERENCE NOTE: For more information about compound nouns, see page 89.

Verbals Used as Adjectives

Two types of verbals—participles and infinitives—may be used as adjectives.

EXAMPLES   A **chirping** cricket kept us awake all night.
[The present participle *chirping* modifies the noun *cricket* by telling *what kind*.]
Tuned and **polished,** the piano was ready for the evening's performance. [The past participles *tuned* and *polished* modify the noun *piano* by telling *what kind*.]
She is the one **to watch.** [The infinitive *to watch* modifies the pronoun *one* by telling *which one*.]

 REFERENCE NOTE: For more information about participles and infinitives, see pages 179–181, 246–247, and 252–253.

Adverbs Used as Adjectives

Some adverbs may be used as adjectives.

EXAMPLES   Tomorrow is my day **off.** [*Off* modifies the noun *day* by telling *what kind*.]
Aunt Margaret lives in a **nearby** town.
[*Nearby* modifies *town* by telling *what kind*.]

 REFERENCE NOTE: For more information about adverbs, see pages 104–106.

STYLE NOTE

To create vivid images in writing, use adjectives that appeal to the senses of sight, hearing, taste, touch, and smell. Words such as *silky, tangy, laughing, crisp, burnished, thunderous,* and *crimson* help readers to imagine the experience that a writer describes. Compare the following sentences.

> The dog wandered into town.
> **Hungry** and **lost,** the **three-legged** dog wandered into the **sleeping** town.

Notice how the adjectives dramatically change the second sentence. The added adjectives help you clearly "see" and "feel" the action of the scene.

 QUICK CHECK 3   **Identifying Adjectives and the Words They Modify**

Identify the adjectives and the words they modify in each of the following sentences. [Note: Do not include the articles *a, an,* and *the.*]

1. You need four cups of flour for this recipe.
2. Your new apartment, so spacious and sunny, certainly seems ideal for you.
3. The image of the eagle is quite powerful in many Native American cultures.
4. Neither film was enjoyable.
5. Speaking of the space program, which astronaut do you admire more—Lt. Colonel Bluford or Dr. Jemison?

The Verb

1d. A *verb* is a word used to express action or a state of being.

Action Verbs

An *action verb* expresses physical or mental activity.

PHYSICAL	write describe	sit receive	arise
MENTAL	remember consider	think understand	believe

(1) A **transitive verb** is an action verb that takes an **object**—a word that tells who or what receives the action.

EXAMPLES   Everyone in the school **cheered** the football **team**. [*Team* receives the action of *cheered*.]
Nikki Giovanni **writes** poetry. [*Poetry* receives the action of *writes*.]
Would you please **give** me a ride to school? [*Me* and *ride* receive the action of *would give*.]

(2) An **intransitive verb** is an action verb that does not take an object.

EXAMPLES   The gorilla **smiled** at the zoologist.
Suddenly, the child next to the door **screamed**.

A verb can be transitive in one sentence and intransitive in another.

EXAMPLES   We **ate** our lunch quickly. [transitive]
We **ate** quickly. [intransitive]
Ms. Marino **measured** the boards carefully. [transitive]
Ms. Marino **measured** carefully. [intransitive]

NOTE   Dictionaries usually group the definitions of verbs according to whether the verbs are used transitively (*v.t.*) or intransitively (*v.i.*).

    REFERENCE NOTE: For more on objects of verbs, see pages 287–290.

Linking Verbs

A **linking verb** is an intransitive verb that connects the subject with a word that identifies or describes it. The word that is linked to the subject is called the **subject complement**.

EXAMPLES   Patience **is** the best remedy for many troubles. [*Remedy* identifies the subject *patience*.]
The dessert **looks** delicious. [*Delicious* describes the subject *dessert*.]

Edmonia Lewis **became** a highly respected sculptor in America. [*Sculptor* identifies the subject *Edmonia Lewis*.]

 REFERENCE NOTE: For more about subject complements, see pages 291–293.

COMMONLY USED LINKING VERBS			
FORMS OF *BE*			
am	be	will be	had been
is	can be	could be	shall have been
are	may be	should be	will have been
was	might be	would be	could have been
were	must be	has been	should have been
being	shall be	have been	would have been
OTHERS			
appear	grow	seem	stay
become	look	smell	taste
feel	remain	sound	turn

Some linking verbs may be used as action verbs.

LINKING   The soup **tasted** spicy.
ACTION   We **tasted** the soup.

LINKING   She **felt** confident about her presentation.
ACTION   The explorers **felt** rain on their faces.

 To determine whether a verb in a sentence is a linking verb, substitute a form of the verb *be*. If the sentence makes sense, the verb is probably a linking verb.

LINKING   The milk **smelled** sour. [The verb *was* can replace *smelled: The milk was sour.*]
ACTION   I **smelled** the milk to see whether it was fresh. [The verb *was* cannot sensibly replace *smelled.*]

The verb *be* does not always link the subject with a noun, pronoun, or adjective in the predicate. *Be* can express a state of being without having a complement. In the sentences below, forms of the verb *be* are followed by an adverb and an adverb phrase telling *where*.

EXAMPLE My relatives from Ohio **will be here** tomorrow.
The cat **is in the cupboard!**

The Verb Phrase

A *verb phrase* consists of a main verb and at least one *helping verb* (also called an *auxiliary verb*). Notice in these examples that as many as three helping verbs may precede the main verb.

EXAMPLES Both Laurence Olivier and Kenneth Branagh
have played the role of Henry V. [*Have* is a
helping verb; *played* is the main verb.]
Should the VCR **have been set** to start
recording at 9:00 P.M.? [*Should, have,* and
been are helping verbs; *set* is the main
verb.]

COMMONLY USED HELPING VERBS				
Forms of *Be*	am	is	are	was
	were	be	being	been
Forms of *Have*	has	have	having	had
Forms of *Do*	do	does	doing	did
Others	may	can	could	
	might	shall	should	
	must	will	would	

The helping verb may be separated from the main verb by another word.

EXAMPLES **Should** we **leave** immediately?
I **have** not **read** Alice Walker's latest novel.

 REFERENCE NOTE: The word *not* and its contraction,
–n't, are never part of a verb phrase. Instead, they are
adverbs telling *to what extent*. For more information
about adverbs, see pages 104–106.

GRAMMAR/USAGE

 QUICK CHECK 4   **Identifying and Classifying Verbs and Verb Phrases**

Identify the verbs and verb phrases in the following sentences. Then classify each verb or verb phrase as *transitive, intransitive,* or *linking.* Be prepared to give the object(s) of each transitive verb and the complement(s) of each linking verb.

1. She was the judge who would have tried the case.
2. Teddy was here earlier, but he left at least an hour ago.
3. Do not ride that motorcycle until it is safe again.
4. Oatmeal tastes good on cold winter mornings, but I prefer cold cereal in summer.
5. The captain of the ship sounded the alarm, and the crew scrambled on deck.

The Adverb

1e. An *adverb* is a word used to modify a verb, an adjective, or another adverb.

Adverbs modify other words by telling *how, when, where,* or *to what extent* (*how much* or *how often*).

Adverbs Modifying Verbs

Most commonly, adverbs are used to modify verbs, verb phrases, and verbals.

EXAMPLES   Marian Anderson sang **magnificently.** [The adverb *magnificently* modifies the verb *sang,* telling *how.*]

We should have planted the tomatoes **earlier.** [The adverb *earlier* modifies the verb phrase *should have planted,* telling *when.*]

Looking **high** and **low,** the rescue team searched for the lost child. [The adverbs *high* and *low* modify a verbal (the participle *looking*), telling *where.*]

To overwhelm the opposition **completely** is their goal. [The adverb *completely* modifies a verbal (the infinitive *to overwhelm*), telling *to what extent.*]

Adverbs Modifying Adjectives

Adverbs may modify adjectives.

EXAMPLES   The players are **exceptionally** skillful. [The adverb *exceptionally* modifies the adjective *skillful*, telling *to what extent.*]

The documentary about global warming was **quite** interesting. [The adverb *quite* modifies the adjective *interesting*, telling *to what extent.*]

Adverbs Modifying Other Adverbs

Adverbs may also modify other adverbs.

EXAMPLES   Cheetahs can run **extremely** fast. [The adverb *extremely* modifies the adverb *fast*, telling *to what extent.*]

André reacted to the news **rather** calmly. [The adverb *rather* modifies the adverb *calmly*, telling *to what extent.*]

 NOTE Certain adverbs are used to express agreement, disagreement, or probability. Such adverbs include *indeed, OK, yes, all right, never, no, not, maybe,* and *perhaps.*

Nouns Used as Adverbs

Some nouns may be used as adverbs.

EXAMPLES   They were happy to return **home.** [The noun *home* is used as an adverb, telling *where.*]

Tanya will be arriving **tonight.** [The noun *tonight* is used as an adverb, telling *when.*]

The teacher reviewed what had been covered **yesterday.** [The noun *yesterday* is used as an adverb, telling *when.*]

In identifying parts of speech, label nouns used in this way as adverbs.

GRAMMAR/USAGE

STYLE NOTE

To keep your writing fresh, try to avoid using worn-out adverbs such as *very, really,* and *so*. When you can, replace these words with more exact and descriptive words.

EXAMPLES   The lions were **ravenous** [*not* very hungry] after their unsuccessful hunt.
In the land of the Lilliputians, Gulliver appears **gigantic** [*not* really tall].
Hundreds of [*not* So many] people were waiting in line for tickets.

 REFERENCE NOTE: For guidelines on using adverbs, see **Chapter 5: Using Modifiers.**

"I've just read your latest book and found it fast moving, full of suspense, and very well written. You're probably just the person who could clear up something that's been puzzling me for years. What's an adverb?"

© 1993 by Sidney Harris.

 QUICK CHECK 5 **Identifying Adverbs and the Words They Modify**

Identify the adverbs and the words they modify in the following sentences. Be prepared to state whether the adverb tells *how, when, where,* or *to what extent.*

1. I understand now what he was saying.
2. We thought that the decorations would be too costly.
3. Maurice and Gregory Hines tap-danced professionally when they were very young children.
4. The messenger apologized for being so late.
5. Visitors to China often bring back small figures that are delicately carved from solid blocks of jade.

The Preposition

1f. A *preposition* is a word that relates a noun or pronoun to another word.

Notice how the prepositions in the following sentences show different relationships between the words *ran* and *me*.

EXAMPLES   The playful puppy ran **beside** me.
The playful puppy ran **toward** me.
The playful puppy ran **around** me.
The playful puppy ran **past** me.
The playful puppy ran **after** me.
The playful puppy ran **behind** me.
The playful puppy ran **in front of** me.
The playful puppy ran **up to** me.

A preposition always introduces a phrase. The noun or pronoun that ends a prepositional phrase is called the **object of the preposition.** In each of the preceding examples, the object of the preposition is *me*.

 REFERENCE NOTE: For more information about prepositional phrases, see pages 240–244.

Commonly Used Prepositions			
about	beneath	in	through
above	beside	inside	throughout
across	besides	into	till
after	between	like	to
against	beyond	near	toward
along	but (meaning	of	under
amid	"except")	off	underneath
among	by	on	until
around	concerning	out	unto
as	down	outside	up
at	during	over	upon
before	except	past	with
behind	for	regarding	within
below	from	since	without

GRAMMAR/USAGE

You may want to store the lists of prepositions given on pages 107 and 109 in a computer file that you can access when you write. Use the lists each time to help you choose the preposition that most clearly expresses the relationship you intend.

Some words in this list may be used as other parts of speech.

NOUN To understand the present, we must study the **past**. [*Past* is a noun functioning as a direct object.]

PREPOSITION Go **past** the convenience store and turn right. [*Past* introduces a prepositional phrase ending with the object *convenience store*.]

VERB Is your older dog **regarding** the new puppy as a nuisance or as a playmate? [*Regarding* is the main verb in the complete verb phrase *is regarding*.]

PREPOSITION The principal will address the senior class **regarding** this year's commencement exercises. [*Regarding* introduces a prepositional phrase ending with the object *exercises*.]

ADVERB We drove **around** for a while. [*Around* modifies *drove*.]

PREPOSITION We drove **around** the parking lot. [*Parking lot* is the object of *around*.]

Do not confuse the prepositions *upon* and *into* with the adverbs *up* and *in* and the prepositions *on* and *to* used together.

EXAMPLES Peace be **upon** you.
Don't let Scruffy **up on** the sofa.

Jesse mixed the raisins **into** the bread dough.
We handed our tests **in to** the teacher.

A preposition that consists of more than one word is called a ***compound preposition.***

Commonly Used Compound Prepositions		
according to	by way of	in spite of
along with	due to	instead of
aside from	except for	next to
as for	in addition to	out of
as of	in front of	up to
because of	in place of	with regard to

EXAMPLES   The young sculptor made a scale model of
Mount Rushmore **out of** clay.
She placed a photograph of Mount Rushmore
next to her clay model.

STYLE NOTE   In formal writing and speaking situations,
it is generally best to avoid ending a
sentence with a preposition.

INFORMAL   Who should I give this package to?
FORMAL   **To** whom should I give this package?

Sometimes, however, a formal sentence may sound
particularly awkward or pompous.

EXAMPLE   This is the sort of English up with which I will
not put.

The sentence above is said to have been written by Sir
Winston Churchill, who wanted to poke fun at people who
do not use common sense when applying the rules of
grammar. Such a sentence should be revised to make it
sound more natural.

INFORMAL   This is the sort of English I will not put up with.
FORMAL   This is the sort of English I will not tolerate.

The Conjunction

1g.   A *conjunction* is a word used to join words or
groups of words.

Coordinating Conjunctions

A *coordinating conjunction* connects words or groups of words used in the same way.

Coordinating Conjunctions						
and	but	for	nor	or	so	yet

EXAMPLES   We couldn't find the bat **or** the glove. [connects two words]
Our hike took us up steep hills **and** along cool streams. [connects two phrases]
Will Rogers said, "My folks didn't come over on the *Mayflower,* **but** they were there to meet the boat." [connects two clauses]

Correlative Conjunctions

Correlative conjunctions are pairs of conjunctions that connect words or groups of words used in the same way.

Correlative Conjunctions	
both . . . and	not only . . . but (also)
either . . . or	whether . . . or
neither . . . nor	

EXAMPLES   **Both** athletes **and** singers must train for long hours. [connects two words]
Either your fuel line is clogged, **or** your carburetor needs adjusting. [connects two clauses]
Gnats are getting inside **not only** through open doors **but** through the screens. [connects two phrases]
I'm going to Galveston **whether** it rains **or** it shines. [connects two clauses]

Subordinating Conjunctions

A *subordinating conjunction* begins a subordinate clause and connects it to an independent clause.

Commonly Used Subordinating Conjunctions

after	because	since	when
although	before	so that	whenever
as	even though	than	where
as if	how	that	wherever
as much as	if	though	whether
as though	in order that	unless	while
as well as	provided	until	why

EXAMPLES We arrived late **because** our train was delayed.

Sherlock Holmes listened quietly **while** Dr. Watson explained his theory.

I'm glad **that** you were able to get here.

A subordinating conjunction does not always come between the groups of words it joins. It may come at the beginning of a sentence.

EXAMPLE **While** Dr. Watson explained his theory, Sherlock Holmes listened quietly.

 REFERENCE NOTE: Subordinating conjunctions are generally used to show relationships of time, manner, cause, place, comparison, condition, or purpose. For more information about subordinating conjunctions, see pages 271–272. For more information about subordinate clauses, see pages 264–274. For more about punctuating subordinate clauses, see pages 386–388.

Subordinating Conjunction or Preposition?

Some words may be used as either subordinating conjunctions or as prepositions. Remember that a preposition introduces a prepositional phrase and that a subordinating conjunction joins a subordinate clause to an independent clause.

CONJUNCTION Beethoven had lost his hearing **before** he completed his Ninth Symphony. [*Before joins the subordinate clause before he*

GRAMMAR/USAGE

completed his Ninth Symphony to an independent clause.]

PREPOSITION   The bridesmaids enter **before** the bride.
[*Before* introduces the prepositional phrase *before the bride*.]

CONJUNCTION   How long will it be **until** the United States is able to build a permanent space station?
[*Until* joins the subordinate clause *until the United States is able to build a permanent space station* to an independent clause.]

PREPOSITION   I can hardly wait **until** prom night! [*Until* introduces the prepositional phrase *until prom night*.]

Conjunctive Adverbs

A *conjunctive adverb* is an adverb that is used to connect independent clauses.

Common Conjunctive Adverbs		
accordingly	however	next
also	indeed	nonetheless
anyway	instead	otherwise
besides	likewise	still
consequently	meanwhile	then
finally	moreover	therefore
furthermore	nevertheless	thus

EXAMPLES   The wolverine is a fierce predator; **indeed,** animals such as reindeer and caribou, which are much larger than it, are the wolverine's prey.
We should do all we can to conserve the earth's natural resources; **otherwise,** future generations may not have sufficient raw materials.

Like other adverbs, the conjunctive adverb does not have a fixed position in a sentence.

EXAMPLES   Jerome is fascinated by African art; **accord-ingly,** he plans to attend the exhibit of Benin bronzes.

Jerome is fascinated by African art; he plans, **accordingly,** to attend the exhibit of Benin bronzes.

 REFERENCE NOTE: For more about punctuating sentences that contain conjunctive adverbs, see pages 398–399.

Correlative Adverbs

Correlative adverbs are pairs of adverbs that join words or groups of words used in the same way.

Common Correlative Adverbs	
as . . . as	the . . . the
so . . . as	then . . . when
so . . . that	there . . . where

EXAMPLES   The engine ran **so** hot **that** it overheated.
            The bigger they are, **the** harder they fall.
            Gilda is **as** skilled in karate **as** Matt is.

NOTE Sometimes the second half of a comparison like the one in the last example is not explicitly stated.

EXAMPLE   Manuel's computer program looks just **as** complicated **as** the instructor's [computer program looks].

In the example above, the omitted ideas may be inferred from the context of the sentence. The omissions are part of an *elliptical clause.*

 REFERENCE NOTE: For more information on elliptical clauses, see pages 273–274.

 QUICK CHECK 6   **Identifying Prepositions and Conjunctions; Classifying Conjunctions**

For each of the following sentences, identify every word or word group that is the part of speech indicated in parenthe-

GRAMMAR/USAGE

ses. Classify each conjunction as *coordinating, correlative,* or *subordinating.*

1. Seeds were removed from cotton bolls by hand until Eli Whitney invented the cotton gin. (*conjunction*)
2. Eli Whitney invented not only the cotton gin but also the interchangeable part. (*conjunction*)
3. Nowadays we take the idea of interchangeable parts for granted, but it was a revolutionary concept at that time. (*conjunction*)
4. For example, when a rifle is constructed with inter-changeable parts, a defective part can be replaced quickly and easily with an identical piece. (*preposition*)
5. Before Eli Whitney introduced the idea of interchange-able parts, manufacturers had to employ many skilled workers. (*preposition*)

The Interjection

1h. An *interjection* is a word used to express emotion. It has no grammatical relation to other words in the sentence.

EXAMPLES
ah	oh	whew	yahoo
gee	ouch	whoa	yikes
hey	well	wow	yippee

An interjection is set off from the rest of the sentence by an exclamation point or a comma. An exclamation point in-dicates strong emotion. A comma indicates mild emotion.

EXAMPLES
Ouch! That hurts!
Ugh! I don't think that fish is fresh.
Well, I think you should apologize to her.
He's been known to, **ah,** procrastinate from time to time.
Yeah! Our double-dutch jump-rope team is going to the national finals!

 REFERENCE NOTE: For more about punctuating interjec-tions, see page 379.

GRAMMAR/USAGE

Determining Parts of Speech

1i. The part of speech of a word is determined by the way the word is used in a sentence.

EXAMPLES   The coach decided that the team needed more **practice.** [noun]
The girls **practice** every Saturday afternoon. [verb]
They will have a **practice** session after school on Wednesday. [adjective]

Winston-Salem, North Carolina, is the **home** of the talented writer Maya Angelou. [noun]
The last **home** game will be played tomorrow night. [adjective]
We walked **home** after the movie. [adverb]

Celine has won the citizenship award **before.** [adverb]
The two candidates debated each other **before** the election. [preposition]
Read the directions **before** you begin answering the questions. [conjunction]

 QUICK CHECK 7   **Identifying the Parts of Speech**

Identify the part of speech of each italicized word in the following sentences.

1. Two workers were trapped in the mine when the tunnel caved *in.*
2. Carol's mother, a busy parent herself, was forever telling her, "*Busy* yourself with some work."
3. Red Cross workers help in any emergency where their *help* is needed.
4. The girl with the *black* hair was dressed entirely in black.
5. That delivery truck had driven *past* our house three times in the past hour.

✓ Chapter Review 1

Identifying Parts of Speech

For each sentence in the following paragraph, write each underlined item and identify its part of speech.

EXAMPLE   [1] In the past <u>few</u> years, African American film directors have <u>suddenly</u> begun to flourish.
            1. few—*adjective;* suddenly—*adverb*

[1] <u>Hey, nobody</u> who goes to the movies <u>fairly</u> often can fail to notice <u>this</u> exciting trend! [2] In 1991 alone, nineteen <u>feature</u> films directed <u>by</u> African Americans <u>were released</u>. [3] <u>Whether</u> you know it <u>or</u> not, that's more <u>than</u> there were in the <u>whole</u> previous decade. [4] <u>Furthermore</u>, the success of Spike Lee's films, <u>which</u> include the blockbuster *Do the Right Thing,* has inspired other young black directors to create <u>their</u> own movies <u>about</u> the black experience. [5] The absorbing stories and real-life settings of these films <u>attract</u> many <u>thousands</u> of moviegoers, not just African Americans. [6] <u>Who</u> are some of <u>the</u> black directors building their careers in Hollywood <u>nowadays</u>? [7] Rising <u>stars</u> <u>include</u> Charles Lane, Mario Van Peebles, John Singleton, Bill Duke, and <u>Matty Rich</u>. [8] Their success helps create <u>job</u> opportunities for <u>all</u> types of black film workers, including hairdressers, actors, stuntpersons, <u>cinematographers</u>, and sound technicians. [9] For example, the crew <u>that</u> worked <u>along with</u> John Singleton on his 1991 hit film *Boyz N the Hood* was 90 percent <u>black</u>! [10] <u>After</u> you've read these facts, maybe you'll <u>watch</u> the movie listings in your <u>local</u> newspaper for <u>some</u> upcoming films from young black directors.

✓ Chapter Review 2

Writing Sentences with Words Used as Specific Parts of Speech

Write sentences according to the following guidelines.
    1. Use *hammer* as a noun.

2. Use *sink* as a transitive verb.
3. Use *whose* as an adjective.
4. Use *fast* as an adverb.
5. Use *inside* as a preposition.
6. Use *well* as an interjection.
7. Use *that* as a demonstrative pronoun.
8. Use *which* as an interrogative pronoun.
9. Use *both . . . and* as a correlative conjunction.
10. Use *before* as a subordinating conjunction.

SUMMARY OF PARTS OF SPEECH

Rule	Part of Speech	Use	Examples
1a	noun	names	**Shane** is playing **soccer** in the **park**.
1b	pronoun	takes the place of a noun	**She herself** said **that all** of **us** have been invited.
1c	adjective	modifies a noun or a pronoun	**This rare Roman** coin is **valuable**.
1d	verb	shows action or a state of being	Shelby **is** the candidate who **will win**.
1e	adverb	modifies a verb, an adjective, or another adverb	I jogged **nearly** five miles **today,** but I think I ran **too fast**.
1f	preposition	relates a noun or a pronoun to another word	Some of the streets were closed **on** Friday **because of** flooding.
1g	conjunction	joins words or groups of words	**Either** Brandon **or** I will meet you **and** Darla at the airport **so that** you won't have to take a taxi.
1h	interjection	shows emotion	**Hooray!** We're home! **Well,** we'll see.

2 AGREEMENT

Subject and Verb, Pronoun and Antecedent

 Checking What You Know

A. Choosing Correct Forms for Subject-Verb and Pronoun-Antecedent Agreement

For each of the following sentences, choose the word in parentheses that completes the sentence correctly.

EXAMPLE 1. Both Arapaho and Cheyenne (*is, are*) part of the Algonquian language group of Native Americans.
1. *are*

1. When I begin cutting out this skirt pattern, I know I'll discover that my scissors (*need, needs*) sharpening.
2. British sailors are frequently called "limeys" because years ago their diet (*was, were*) supplemented with limes to prevent scurvy during long sea voyages.
3. Either Dad or my brother (*go, goes*) down to the store to buy a newspaper each morning.

4. In San Ildefonso Village, two days (*is, are*) not considered a long time to spend polishing one piece of black pottery.
5. A small number of adults (*is, are*) coming along on our trip to Washington, D.C.
6. When Suzanne and Anita arrive, would you please help (*her, them*) find some good seats?
7. (*Here's, Here are*) those extra two tickets for tonight's rap concert at the arena.
8. Exactly one third of the students in my American history class (*is, are*) African American.
9. To read her poems aloud (*embarrass, embarrasses*) Amelia.
10. *The Borrowers*, a fantasy story about some tiny people, (*was, were*) my favorite book when I was ten years old.

B. Choosing Correct Forms for Subject-Verb and Pronoun-Antecedent Agreement

For each sentence in the following paragraph, choose the word in parentheses that will complete the sentence correctly.

EXAMPLE   Kenny Walker is the only player in the NFL who [1] (*has, have*) a hearing impairment.
           1. *has*

The Denver Broncos, my favorite team, [11] (*was, were*) smart to choose Walker in the 1990 football draft. Walker certainly [12] (*don't, doesn't*) let his deafness keep him from being a great linebacker. Passed over by many a coach because [13] (*he, they*) thought a player who was deaf would be a problem, Walker was finally picked two hundred twenty-eighth by Denver. Even today, not everyone [14] (*know, knows*) that spinal meningitis cost Kenny Walker his hearing when he was two years old. Sign language and lip reading [15] (*was, were*) taught to him at a special school, beginning when he was four. Because of Walker's hearing impairment, most of the neighborhood boys [16] (*was, were*) unwilling to choose him to be on a team. But after they saw him play, everyone wanted him on [17] (*their, his*) team! Now that Walker is a professional football player, neither he nor his coaches **[18]** (*has, have*) much difficulty with his deafness. One of the accommodations the Broncos made **[19]** (*was, were*) to hire a full-time interpreter to sign plays to Walker. Although he can't hear a sound, Walker feels the vibrations in his shoulder pads when the crowd **[20]** (*cheers, cheer*) him. ✓

Number

Number is the form of a word that indicates whether the word is singular or plural.

a. A word that refers to one person or thing is *singular* in number. A word that refers to more than one is *plural* in number.

SINGULAR	computer woman	brush this	story it
PLURAL	computers women	brushes these	stories they

In general, nouns that end in *s* are plural, and verbs that end in *s* are singular.

Agreement of Subject and Verb

b. A verb should agree with its subject in number.

(1) Singular subjects take singular verbs.

EXAMPLES   My **grandfather trains** dogs.
The **senator is** in favor of the bill.
She owns and **operates** a video store.

NOTE The pronouns *I* and *you* take plural verbs. The only exceptions to this rule are *I am* and *I was*.

(2) Plural subjects take plural verbs.

GRAMMAR/USAGE

EXAMPLES   My **grandparents train** dogs.
Many **senators are** in favor of the bill.
They own and **operate** a video store.

Like the one-word verb in each of the preceding examples, a verb phrase must also agree in number with its subject. The number of a verb phrase is indicated by the form of its first auxiliary (helping) verb.

EXAMPLES   This **song was performed** by Bonnie Raitt.
[singular subject and verb phrase]
These **songs were performed** by Bonnie Raitt.
[plural subject and verb phrase]

The **dancer has been rehearsing** since noon.
[singular subject and verb phrase]
The dancers **have been rehearsing** since noon. [plural subject and verb phrase]

 REFERENCE NOTE: For more information about verb phrases, see page 103.

Intervening Phrases and Clauses

2c. The number of the subject is not changed by a phrase or a clause following the subject.

EXAMPLES   The **characters represent** abstract ideas.
The **characters** in an allegory **represent** abstract ideas. [The prepositional phrase *in an allegory* does not affect the number of the subject *characters*.]

Today's newspaper reports that **The Ramírez Group has won** the contract for the new office complex downtown.
Today's newspaper reports that **The Ramírez Group,** one of Delta City's foremost architectural firms, **has won** the contract for the new office complex downtown. [The appositive phrase *one of Delta City's foremost architectural firms* does not affect the number of the subject *The Ramírez Group.*]

GRAMMAR/USAGE

Langston Hughes was a major influence in the Harlem Renaissance.

Langston Hughes, who wrote *The Weary Blues* and other books of poems, **was** a major figure in the Harlem Renaissance.
[The adjective clause *who wrote* The Weary Blues *and other books of poems* does not affect the number of the subject *Langston Hughes.*]

The subject's number is also not affected when the subject is followed by a phrase beginning with an expression such as *along with, as well as, in addition to,* and *together with.*

EXAMPLES   The history **teacher,** as well as her students, **was fascinated** by the exhibit of artifacts at the Du Sable Museum of African-American History. [singular subject and verb]
The history **students,** as well as their teacher, **were fascinated** by the exhibit of artifacts at the Du Sable Museum of African-American History. [plural subject and verb]

STYLE NOTE   In formal writing and speaking, be sure to use a singular verb after a singular subject. In informal situations, you may use a plural verb if the meaning is clearly plural.

FORMAL   Jeremy, along with Denise and Raúl, has applied to Stanford.
INFORMAL   Jeremy, along with Denise and Raúl, have applied to Stanford.

Indefinite Pronouns

2d.   Indefinite pronouns may be singular, plural, or either.

(1) The following indefinite pronouns are singular: *anybody, anyone, anything, each, either, everybody,*

everyone, everything, neither, nobody, no one, nothing, one, somebody, someone, and *something.*

EXAMPLES   **Neither** of the books **contains** any charts or illustrations.

Is everyone in the pep club **wearing** the school colors?

Nothing I have heard so far **has changed** my mind.

One of the most beautiful places in North Carolina **is** the Joyce Kilmer Memorial Forest.

(2) The following indefinite pronouns are plural: *both, few, many,* and *several.*

EXAMPLES   **Both** of the poems **were written** by Claude McKay.

Many of our words **are derived** from Latin.

Several of the juniors **have volunteered.**

(3) The following indefinite pronouns may be singular or plural: *all, any, most, none,* and *some.*

These pronouns are singular when they refer to singular words and are plural when they refer to plural words.

EXAMPLES   The police officer told us that **none** of the equipment **was damaged.** [*None* refers to the singular noun *equipment.*]

The police officer told us that **none** of the machines **were damaged.** [*None* refers to the plural noun *machines.*]

Has most of the food been **eaten?** [*Most* refers to the singular noun *food.*]

Have most of the sandwiches **been eaten?** [*Most* refers to the plural noun *sandwiches.*]

Some of her artwork **is** beautiful, and all of it is expensive. [*Some* and *all* refer to the singular noun *artwork.*]

Some of her paintings **are** beautiful, and all of them are expensive. [*Some* and *all* refer to the plural noun *paintings.*]

GRAMMAR/USAGE

When the word *none* refers to a plural noun, it is singular when it means "not one" and plural when it means "not any."

EXAMPLES   **None** of the hats **fits.** [*Not one* fits.]
            None of the hats **fit.** [*Not any* fit.]

If you use a computer when you write, you may want to create a "help" file containing lists of indefinite pronouns and their rules for agreement. Fill this file with information that will help you determine whether an indefinite pronoun is used correctly. Then, as you proofread your work, you can access the file whenever you have a question about the agreement between an indefinite pronoun and a verb or another pronoun.

 QUICK CHECK 1   **Identifying Subjects and Verbs That Agree in Number**

For each of the following sentences, identify the subject of the verb in parentheses. Then choose the verb form that agrees in number with the subject.

1. I know that all the workers (*is, are*) proud to help restore the Statue of Liberty.
2. Most of the English classes in my school (*stresses, stress*) composition skills.
3. (*Do, Does*) each of you know what you're supposed to bring tomorrow?
4. Both of the paintings (*shows, show*) the influence of the work of Joan Miró.
5. Our class in photographic techniques (*begins, begin*) next Tuesday; all of us (*is, are*) excited about it.

Compound Subjects

A *compound subject* is two or more subjects that have the same verb.

GRAMMAR/USAGE

2e. Subjects joined by *and* usually take a plural verb.

EXAMPLES   **Basil** and **thyme are** plants of the mint family.
Following Julius Caesar's death, **Antony, Octavian,** and **Lepidus became** the rulers of Rome.
Are blueberries, gooseberries, and **strawberries** all used in making pies?

A compound subject may name a single person or thing. Such a compound subject takes a singular verb.

EXAMPLES   The **secretary** and **treasurer is** Gretchen. [one person]
Grilled chicken and **rice is** the restaurant's specialty. [one dish]

2f. Singular subjects joined by *or* or *nor* take a singular verb.

EXAMPLES   **Neither Juan** nor **Jeff wants** to see the movie.
Either Felicia or **Terry plans** to report on Chinese philosopher Lao-tzu.
Has your **mother** or your **father met** your teacher?

2g. When a singular subject and a plural subject are joined by *or* or *nor,* the verb agrees with the subject nearer the verb.

EXAMPLES   Neither the **performers** nor the **director was** eager to rehearse the scene again. [The singular subject *director* is nearer to the verb.]
Neither the **director** nor the **performers were** eager to rehearse the scene again. [The plural subject *performers* is nearer to the verb.]

NOTE   Whenever possible, revise the sentence to avoid this awkward construction.

EXAMPLE   The **director was** not eager to rehearse the scene again, and neither **were** the **performers.**

Special Problems in Subject-Verb Agreement

2h.   The verb agrees with its subject, even when the verb precedes the subject.

The verb usually comes before its subject in sentences beginning with *Here* or *There* and in questions.

EXAMPLES   Here **is** a **copy** of my report.
Here **are** two **copies** of my report.

There **was** a **message** on her answering machine.
There **were** no **messages** on her answering machine.

Where **is Arsenio?**
Where **are Arsenio** and **his brother?**

Why **is the referee clearing** all the players off the field?
Why **are the players leaving** the field?

In what part of the program **does the figure skater do** her triple axel?
In what part of the program **do the fans begin clapping** to the music?

 REFERENCE NOTE: For more information about finding the subject in a question or in a sentence beginning with *Here* or *There,* see pages 283–285.

 NOTE   *Here is, there is,* and *where is* can form the contractions *here's, there's,* and *where's.* Use these contractions only with subjects that are singular in meaning.

NONSTANDARD   Here's your keys.
STANDARD   Here **are** your **keys.**
STANDARD   Here**'s** your **set** of keys.

NONSTANDARD   Where's the islands located?
STANDARD   Where **are** the **islands** located?
STANDARD   Where**'s** the **island** located?

2i.   Collective nouns may be either singular or plural.

A *collective noun* is singular in form but names a group of persons or things.

GRAMMAR/USAGE

Common Collective Nouns			
army	committee	fleet	pack
assembly	congregation	flock	posse
audience	couple	group	public
band	crew	herd	squadron
cast	crowd	jury	staff
class	dozen	majority	swarm
clique	ensemble	mob	team
club	family	number	troop

A collective noun takes a singular verb when the noun refers to the group as a unit and takes a plural verb when the noun refers to the parts or members of the group.

SINGULAR　The **cast** of the play **is made** up entirely of students. [The cast as a unit is made up of students.]

PLURAL　After the play, the **cast are joining** their families and friends for a celebration. [The members of the cast are joining their families and friends.]

SINGULAR　The tour **group is** on the bus. [The group as a unit is on the bus.]

PLURAL　The tour **group are talking** about what they expect to see. [The members of the group are talking to one another.]

SINGULAR　A **flock** of geese **is flying** over. [The flock is flying as a unit.]

PLURAL　The **flock** of geese **are joining** together in a V-shaped formation. [The members of the flock are joining together.]

NOTE　In the expression *number of,* the word *number* is singular when preceded by *the* and plural when preceded by *a.*

EXAMPLES　**The number of** students taking computer courses **has increased.**

A number of students taking computer courses **belong** to a computer club and **subscribe** to computer magazines.

GRAMMAR/USAGE

PEANUTS reprinted by permission of UFS, Inc.

2j. An expression of an amount (a measurement, a statistic, or a fraction, for example) may be singular or plural.

An expression of an amount is
■ singular when the amount is thought of as a unit
■ plural when the amount is thought of as many parts

EXAMPLES **Five thousand tiles is** a heavy load for this truck. [The tiles are thought of as a unit.]
Five thousand tiles, each carefully placed, **were used** to create the building's floor. [The tiles are thought of separately.]

Three days is the amount of time we will spend visiting college campuses. [one unit]
Three days of this month **are** school holidays. [separate days]

A fraction or a percentage is singular when it refers to a singular word and plural when it refers to a plural word.

EXAMPLES   **One fourth** of the student body **works** part time after school. [The fraction refers to the singular noun *student body*.]
One fourth of the students **work** part time after school. [The fraction refers to the plural noun *students*.]

Seventy-five percent of the junior class **is** sixteen years old. [The percentage refers to the singular noun *class*.]
Seventy-five percent of the juniors **are** sixteen years old. [The percentage refers to the plural noun *juniors*.]

 REFERENCE NOTE: For more information on using hyphens in expressions stating amounts, see page 428.

Expressions of measurement (length, weight, capacity, area) are usually singular.

EXAMPLES   **Four and seven-tenths inches is** the diameter of a CD.
Eight fluid ounces of water **equals** one cup.
Two hundred kilometers was the distance we flew in the hot-air balloon.

 REFERENCE NOTE: For information on when to spell out numbers and when to use numerals, see pages 596–598.

 QUICK CHECK 2   **Selecting Verbs That Agree with Their Subjects**

For each of the following sentences, identify the subject of each verb in parentheses. Then choose the verb form that agrees in number with the subject.

1. The stage crew (*is, are*) working together to make a rapid scene change for Rita Moreno's entrance.
2. Where (*is, are*) the other flight of stairs that goes up to the roof?
3. Of the world's petroleum, approximately one third (*was, were*) produced by the United States at that time.
4. Red beans and rice (*is, are*) often served as a side dish at Cajun meals.

5. Either brisk walks or jogging (*serves, serve*) as a healthful way to get daily exercise.

2k. The title of a creative work (such as a book, song, film, or painting), the name of an organization, or the name of a country or city (even if it is plural in form) takes a singular verb.

EXAMPLES   ***Those Who Ride the Night Winds* was written** by the poet Nikki Giovanni.
"Tales from the Vienna Woods" is only one of Johann Strauss's most popular waltzes.
The **United Nations was formed** in 1945.
Avalon Textiles is located on King Street.
The **United States calls** its flag "Old Glory."
The **Philippines comprises** more than seven thousand islands.
Des Moines is the capital of Iowa.

NOTE The names of some organizations may take singular or plural verbs. When the name refers to the organization as a unit, it takes a singular verb. When the name refers to the members of the organization, it takes a plural verb.

EXAMPLES   The **New York Yankees has won** the World Series twenty-two times. [The New York Yankees has won as a unit.]
The **New York Yankees are signing** autographs. [The players are signing autographs.]

2l. Some nouns that are plural in form are singular in meaning.

(1) The following nouns always take singular verbs.

civics	genetics	measles	news
economics	gymnastics	molasses	physics
electronics	mathematics	mumps	summons

EXAMPLES   **Measles is** a contagious disease.
The **news was** disappointing.

GRAMMAR/USAGE

(2) The following nouns always take plural verbs.

binoculars	pants	shears
eyeglasses	pliers	shorts
Olympics	slacks	scissors

EXAMPLES
The **scissors are** in the sewing basket.
The first modern **Olympics were held** in Athens.

NOTE Many nouns ending in *-ics,* such as *acoustics, athletics, ethics, politics, statistics,* and *tactics,* may be singular or plural. In general, such a noun is considered singular when it names a science, a system, or a skill. It is considered plural when it names qualities, operations, activities, or individual items.

EXAMPLES
Statistics is the collection of mathematical data. [*Statistics* refers to a system of analyzing data.]
The **statistics are** misleading. [*Statistics* refers to a set of numerical data.]

If you do not know whether a noun that is plural in form is singular or plural in meaning, look in a dictionary.

2m. A subject that is a phrase or a clause takes a singular verb.

EXAMPLES
Living in the woods appeals to Alan, whose hero is Henry David Thoreau. [The gerund phrase *Living in the woods* is the subject of *appeals.*]
Is before lunch a good time for us to meet? [The prepositional phrase *before lunch* is the subject of *Is.*]
Whoever plans to vote in the primary needs to register soon. [The noun clause *Whoever plans to vote in the primary* is the subject of *needs.*]
Has what's in the attic been inventoried? [The noun clause *what's in the attic* is the subject of *Has been inventoried.*]

A verb agrees with its subject, not with its predicate nominative.

EXAMPLES   Sore **muscles are** one symptom of flu.
One **symptom** of flu **is** sore muscles.

Perhaps the greatest **contribution** of ancient African scholars **was** a number of concepts used in higher mathematics.
A number of the concepts used in higher mathematics **were** perhaps the greatest contribution of ancient African scholars.

2o. Subjects preceded by *every* or *many a* take singular verbs.

EXAMPLES   **Every sophomore** and **junior is participating.**
Many a person supports the cause.

p *Doesn't,* not *don't,* is used with singular subjects except *I* and *you.*

Remember that *doesn't* is the contraction for *does not,* and that *don't* is the contraction for *do not.*

NONSTANDARD He don't [do not] know what the word means.
STANDARD **He doesn't [does not]** know what the word means.

NONSTANDARD It don't [do not] belong to me.
STANDARD **It doesn't [does not]** belong to me.

NONSTANDARD Don't [do not] that boy understand the rules?
STANDARD **Doesn't [does not]** that boy understand the rules?

2q. When a relative pronoun (*that, which,* or *who*) is the subject of an adjective clause, the verb in the clause agrees with the word to which the relative pronoun refers.

EXAMPLES   Ganymede, **which is** one of Jupiter's satellites, is the largest satellite in our solar system.

GRAMMAR/USAGE

[*Which* refers to the singular noun
Ganymede.]
I have neighbors **who raise** tropical fish.
[*Who* refers to the plural noun *neighbors.*]

NOTE When preceded by *one of* [*plural word*], the relative
pronoun takes a plural verb. When preceded by *the
only one of* [*plural word*], the relative pronoun takes
a singular verb.

EXAMPLES   The dodo is **one of the birds that are**
extinct.
Pluto is **the only one of the planets that
crosses** the orbit of another planet.

 QUICK CHECK 3 **Selecting Verbs That Agree
with Their Subjects**

For each of the following sentences, choose the correct verb
form in parentheses.

1. Two teaspoonfuls of cornstarch combined with a small
amount of cold water (*makes, make*) an ideal thickener for
many sauces.
2. "Seventeen Syllables" (*recounts, recount*) the story of a
Japanese American family.
3. This (*doesn't, don't*) make sense to me.
4. When she is doing needlepoint, Aunt Ching's scissors always (*hang, hangs*) around her neck on a red ribbon.
5. Healthy teeth (*is, are*) one of the rewards of regular
brushing.

Agreement of Pronoun and Antecedent

A pronoun usually refers to a noun or another pronoun.
The word to which a pronoun refers is called its *antecedent.*

 REFERENCE NOTE: For more on antecedents, see pages
90–91 and 204–209.

2r. A pronoun agrees with its antecedent in number,
gender, and person.

(1) Singular pronouns refer to singular antecedents. Plural pronouns refer to plural antecedents.

EXAMPLES   **Sammy Davis, Jr.,** made **his** movie debut in 1931. [singular]
The **joggers** took **their** canteens with **them.** [plural]

(2) A few singular pronouns indicate gender.

FEMININE	she	her	hers	herself
MASCULINE	he	him	his	himself
NEUTER	it	it	its	itself

EXAMPLES   **Shay** has more credits than **he** needs. [masculine]
Maria has misplaced **her** class ring. [feminine]
A **snake** swallows **its** prey whole. [neuter]

(3) *Person* indicates whether a pronoun refers to the one speaking (first person), the one spoken to (second person), or the one spoken about (third person).

FIRST PERSON   **I** have almost finished **my** report.
SECOND PERSON   Have **you** finished **yours?**
THIRD PERSON   **They** finished **theirs** yesterday.

NOTE   Indefinite pronouns such as *someone, everyone, few,* and *several* are in the third person. Use third-person pronouns to refer to these words.

EXAMPLES   **Everyone** should bring **his** or **her** [*not* your] canned-food donations on Friday.
Several in the class have volunteered to deliver **their** [*not* your] donations to the shelter in person.

2s.   As antecedents, indefinite pronouns may be singular, plural, or either.

(1) Singular pronouns are used to refer to the following indefinite pronouns: *anybody, anyone, anything, each, either, everybody, everyone, everything, neither,*

nobody, no one, nothing, one, somebody, someone, and *something.*

These words do not indicate gender. To determine their gender, look at the phrases following them.

EXAMPLES **Each** of the **girls** has memorized her **part.**
One of the **boys** left **his** helmet on the bus.

If the antecedent may be either masculine or feminine, use both the masculine and feminine pronouns to refer to it.

EXAMPLES **Anyone** who is going on the field trip needs to bring **his** or **her** lunch.
Any qualified **person** may submit **his** or **her** résumé and application.

You can often avoid the awkward *his or her* construction by substituting an article (*a, an,* or *the*) for the possessive pronouns or by rephrasing the sentence, using the plural forms of both the pronoun and its antecedent.

EXAMPLES Any interested **person** may submit **a** résumé and application.
All interested **persons** may submit **their** résumés and applications.

STYLE NOTE   In conversation, plural pronouns are often used to refer to singular antecedents that can be either masculine or feminine.

EXAMPLES **Everybody** wanted Ms. Hirakawa to sign **their** yearbooks.
Each of the employees will receive **their** new ID cards tomorrow.

This usage of a plural pronoun to refer to a singular antecedent is becoming more popular in writing. In fact, using a singular pronoun to refer to a singular antecedent that is clearly plural in meaning may be misleading.

MISLEADING **Nobody** left the prom early, because **he** or **she** was enjoying **himself** or **herself.** [Since *nobody* is clearly plural in meaning, the singular pronouns *he* or *she* and *himself* or *herself,* though grammatically correct, are confusing.]

IMPROVED   **Nobody** left the prom early, because **they** were enjoying **themselves.**

MISLEADING   **Everyone** in the audience had enjoyed the performance so much that **he** or **she** called for an encore.

IMPROVED   **Everyone** in the audience had enjoyed the performance so much that **they** called for an encore.

---

(2) Plural pronouns are used to refer to the following indefinite pronouns: *both, few, many,* and *several.*

EXAMPLES   **Both** of the finalists played **their** best.
Many of the spectators leapt from **their** seats and cheered.

(3) Singular or plural pronouns may be used to refer to the following indefinite pronouns: *all, any, most, none,* and *some.*

These indefinite pronouns are singular when they refer to singular words. They are plural when they refer to plural words.

EXAMPLES   **All** of our **planning** served **its** purpose.
All of your **suggestions** had **their** good points.

None of the renovated **structure** matches **its** original beauty.
None of the **caribou** have left on **their** annual migration.

2t.   A plural pronoun is used to refer to two or more singular antecedents joined by *and.*

EXAMPLES   If **Jerry and Francesca** call, tell **them** that I will not be home until this evening.
Pilar, Kimberly, and Laura have donated **their** time to the hospital.

2u. A singular pronoun is used to refer to two or more singular antecedents joined by *or* or *nor.*

EXAMPLES **Either Rinaldo or Philip** always finishes **his** geometry homework in class.
Neither Cindy nor Carla thinks **she** is ready to write the final draft.

2v. When a singular and a plural antecedent are joined by *or* or *nor,* the pronoun usually agrees with the nearer antecedent.

EXAMPLES Neither the **twins** nor Jerry likes **his** new books.
Neither Jerry nor the **twins** like **their** new books.

Whenever possible, revise the sentence to avoid such an awkward construction.

EXAMPLE The **twins** don't like **their** new books, and **Jerry** doesn't like **his** new books either.

STYLE NOTE — Sometimes, following the rules results in an awkward or misleading sentence. In such cases, revise the sentence so that the pronoun reference is clear.

AWKWARD **Either Leo or Rose will give his or her report.** [The pronouns agree in gender with their antecedents, but the sentence is awkward to read.]

MISLEADING **Either Leo or Rose will give her report.** [The pronoun agrees with the nearer of the two antecedents; however, the antecedents are of different genders.]

REVISED **Either Leo will give his report, or Rose will give hers.**

2w. Collective nouns may act as singular or plural antecedents.

GRAMMAR/USAGE

REFERENCE NOTE: For a list of common collective nouns, see page 127.

A collective noun takes a singular pronoun when the noun refers to the group as a unit. A collective noun takes a plural pronoun when the noun refers to the parts or members of the group.

SINGULAR   Last Wednesday, the **debate club** elected **its** new officers. [The club held its election as a unit.]

PLURAL   The **debate club** practice **their** speeches in a weekly workshop. [The members of the club practice individually.]

SINGULAR   After listening to two weeks of testimony, the **jury** reached **its** decision in only one hour. [The jury decided as a unit.]

PLURAL   The **jury** disagree on how much importance **they** should give to one of the defendant's statements. [The members of the jury disagree.]

x.   The title of a creative work (such as a book, song, film, or painting), the name of an organization, or the name of a country or city (even if it is plural in form) takes a singular pronoun.

EXAMPLES   Because **it** has been used in many television and movie scores, Vivaldi's ***The Four Seasons*** is one piece of classical music that is familiar to many people.

Anderson Outfitters advertises **itself** as "the first step in getting away from it all."

The **United Arab Emirates** generates most of **its** revenue from the sale of oil.

Los Alamos, New Mexico, gets **its** name from the Spanish word for a poplar tree.

y.   Some words that are plural in form are singular in meaning.

(1) The following nouns always take singular pronouns.

GRAMMAR/USAGE

civics	genetics	measles	news
economics	gymnastics	molasses	physics
electronics	mathematics	mumps	summons

EXAMPLES   **Measles** is an uncomfortable disease, but **it** usually isn't fatal.

Quite unexpectedly, Mr. Quinn was handed a **summons** and told to bring **it** and himself to court the next day.

(2) The following nouns always take plural pronouns.

binoculars	pants	shears
eyeglasses	pliers	shorts
Olympics	slacks	scissors

EXAMPLES   Please find the **pliers** and bring **them** to me.

These **pants** are too long. I'll have to hem **them**.

NOTE Many nouns ending in *-ics,* such as *acoustics, athletics, ethics, politics, statistics,* and *tactics,* may be singular or plural in meaning. Generally, such a noun takes a singular pronoun when it names a science, a system, or a skill. It takes a plural pronoun when it names qualities, operations, activities, or individual items.

EXAMPLES   At this university, **athletics** is generously supported because **it** generates money for the school through ticket sales and broadcast fees. [*Athletics* refers to the athletic program.]

Sign up for intramural **athletics; they** include soccer, field hockey, baseball, and lacrosse. [*Athletics* refers to different athletic activities.]

2z. Nouns preceded by *every* or *many a* take singular pronouns.

EXAMPLES   **Every hammer, screwdriver,** and **power tool** was in **its** place, and the garage practically sparkled.

Many a boy soprano in New York City dreams of singing **his** way into the famous Boys Choir of Harlem.

 NOTE The phrase *the number of* is singular; the phrase *a number of* is plural.

EXAMPLES   **The number of** summer jobs offered by the city is increasing; this year **it** reached an all-time high of twelve hundred.

Janelle bought **a number of** those colorful batik shirts because **they** were on sale.

 QUICK CHECK 4   **Supplying Pronouns That Agree with Their Antecedents**

Complete each of the following sentences by supplying at least one pronoun that agrees with its antecedent. Use standard formal English.

1. Each student prepares _____ own outline.
2. Both Jane and Ruth wrote _____ essays about ecology.
3. If anyone else wants to drive, _____ should tell Mrs. Cruz.
4. Neither Angela nor Carrie has given _____ dues to me.
5. This month, Beacon Associates will be testing _____ new product.

 Chapter Review
_____

A. Proofreading Sentences for Subject-Verb and Pronoun-Antecedent Agreement

Most of the following sentences contain errors in agreement. If the sentence is correct, write C. If it contains an error in agreement, identify the incorrect verb or pronoun, and supply the correct form.

EXAMPLE   **1.** Each of the members of the school board are hoping to be reelected this fall.
       1. *are hoping—is hoping*

1. Half the members of my history class this year is in the National Honor Society.
2. Over one thousand miles of tunnels travels through El Teniente, the largest copper mine in the world.
3. If she already has needle-nose pliers, she can exchange them for something else at the hardware store.
4. The etchings of Mary Cassatt, a leading impressionist painter, reflects the influence of Japanese prints.
5. Before the banquet, servers had placed every utensil, plate, and goblet in their proper place.
6. If you see either Veronica or Sabrena in the cafeteria, will you please tell them that I won't be able to go with them after school today?
7. Neither Adrianne nor Lillian expect to make the varsity softball team this year; nevertheless, both girls are trying out for it.
8. To learn more about our municipal government, our civics class is planning to invite a number of guest speakers to school.
9. Unfortunately, neither Mayor Ella Hanson nor Mrs. Mary Ann Powell, the assistant mayor, have responded to our invitations yet.
10. *Blue Highways* by William Least Heat-Moon tell about the fascinating people he met on a trip through small-town America.

B. Proofreading a Paragraph for Subject-Verb and Pronoun-Antecedent Agreement

Most of the sentences in the following paragraph contain errors in agreement. If a sentence contains an error in agreement, identify the incorrect verb or pronoun, and supply the correct form. If a sentence is correct, write *C*.

EXAMPLE   [1]My friends and I have stopped buying records in favor of its more modern competitor, the compact disc.
             1. *its—their*

[11] Do you know what the differences between records and compact discs is? [12] One of the differences are that

the music is encoded onto a compact disc by a computer, not pressed into the disc mechanically. [13] Another difference is that a CD recording is played back with a laser beam instead of a needle. [14] There's several built-in advantages to this technology; for example, because a needle never touches the disc's surface, a CD never wears out. [15] And although a CD is usually more expensive than a record album or cassette tape, they can hold over seventy minutes of music on each side. [16] You may ask, "Doesn't a record and a compact disc yield the same high-fidelity sound?" [17] Yes, both kinds of technology does play the same music, but the compact disc also offers total freedom from unwanted noise and distortion. [18] My aunt recently told me that a CD of mine has a brighter treble and a truer bass than their record of the same album. [19] This great sound quality is obvious even when you play a compact disc on one of the tiny, inexpensive portable players. [20] Because virtually all CD players offers the same excellent performance, you should choose the lowest-priced player that has the features you want.

3 Using Verbs

Principal Parts; Tense, Voice, Mood

 Checking What You Know

A. Choosing the Correct Verb Forms

For each of the following sentences, choose the correct form of the verb in parentheses.

EXAMPLE   **1.** (*Sit, Set*) this pitcher of juice on the table, please.
           1. *Set*

1. A beautiful oak banister (*rises, raises*) along the staircase.
2. If you (*would have, had*) visited Mexico City, you would have seen the great pyramids at Tenochtitlán.
3. Tammie says that yesterday she should have (*went, gone*) to the beach.
4. Edward said that he wanted (*to go, to have gone*) to the Diez y Seis party, where his friends were celebrating Mexico's independence from Spain.
5. One of the statues has (*fell, fallen*) off its base.
6. How long did it (*lie, lay*) on the floor?

7. Since last September, I (*missed, have missed*) only one day of school.

8. The U.S. Census Bureau has predicted that by the year 2000 the Hispanic population in the United States (*will grow, will have grown*) to more than 25 million.

9. Fortunately, I have never been (*stinged, stung*) by a bee.

10. The unusual pattern in this wool material was (*weaved, woven*) by Seamus MacMhuiris, an artist who uses bold geometric designs.

11. The house became very quiet once everyone (*left, had left*).

12. I (*began, begun*) this homework assignment an hour ago.

13. My parents' old car has (*broke, broken*) down again.

14. Everyone who (*saw, seen*) Greg Louganis dive in the 1988 Olympics recognized his superior talent.

15. Uncle Bart likes to (*sit, set*) on the porch in his rocking chair.

B. Revising Verb Voice or Mood

Revise the following sentences by correcting verbs that use an awkward passive voice and verbs that are not in the appropriate mood.

16. If I was you, I would not skate on that lake; the ice is too thin.

17. The ball that was thrown by me was caught by the dog.

18. He now wishes that he was on the field trip to the Diego Rivera exhibit.

19. The quilt that was made by me won second prize at the county fair.

20. The half-time show was enjoyed by the crowd. ✓

 REFERENCE NOTE: Depending on their function, verbs may be classified as *action verbs* or *linking verbs*, as *transitive verbs* or *intransitive verbs*, and as *main verbs* or *helping verbs*. For a discussion of these different kinds of verbs, see pages 100–103. The information presented in this chapter applies to all of these types of verbs.

The Principal Parts of Verbs

3a. Every verb has four basic forms called the *principal parts:* the *base form*, the *present participle*, the *past*, and the *past participle*. All other forms of a verb are derived from these principal parts.

The following examples include *is* and *have* in parentheses to indicate that helping verbs (forms of *be* and *have*) are used with the present participle and past participle forms of verbs.

BASE FORM	PRESENT PARTICIPLE	PAST	PAST PARTICIPLE
cling	(is) clinging	clung	(have) clung
forsake	(is) forsaking	forsook	(have) forsaken
grin	(is) grinning	grinned	(have) grinned
hurt	(is) hurting	hurt	(have) hurt
join	(is) joining	joined	(have) joined
receive	(is) receiving	received	(have) received

All verbs form the present participle in the same way: by adding *-ing* to the base form. All verbs, however, do not form the past and past participle in the same way. A verb is classified as *regular* or *irregular* depending on the way it forms its past and past participle.

Regular Verbs

3b. A *regular verb* is a verb that forms its past and past participle by adding *-d* or *-ed* to the base form.

 REFERENCE NOTE: Adding endings to some verbs can pose a spelling problem. For information on adding suffixes to verbs, see page 448.

BASE FORM	PRESENT PARTICIPLE	PAST	PAST PARTICIPLE
happen	(is) happening	happened	(have) happened
outline	(is) outlining	outlined	(have) outlined
pin	(is) pinning	pinned	(have) pinned
try	(is) trying	tried	(have) tried
use	(is) using	used	(have) used
watch	(is) watching	watched	(have) watched

A few regular verbs have alternative past and past participle forms ending in -t.

BASE FORM	PRESENT PARTICIPLE	PAST	PAST PARTICIPLE
burn	(is) burning	burned *or* burnt	(have) burned *or* burnt
dream	(is) dreaming	dreamed *or* dreamt	(have) dreamed *or* dreamt
leap	(is) leaping	leaped *or* leapt	(have) leaped *or* leapt

NOTE The regular verbs *deal* and *mean* always form the past and past participle by adding *-t: dealt, (have) dealt; meant, (have) meant.*

Faulty pronunciation can lead to spelling errors. One common mistake is to leave off the *-d* or *-ed* ending of verbs such as *ask, prejudice, risk, suppose,* and *use.*

NONSTANDARD We use to live in Bakersfield.
STANDARD We **used** to live in Bakersfield.

NONSTANDARD I was suppose to be home by now.
STANDARD I was **supposed** to be home by now.

Another common error is to add unnecessary letters to the past and past participle of verbs such as *attack* and *drown.*

NONSTANDARD Is it true that your dog attackted a burglar?
STANDARD Is it true that your dog **attacked** a burglar?

NONSTANDARD   If the lifeguard hadn't been paying attention, Jeremy might have drownded.
STANDARD   If the lifeguard hadn't been paying attention, Jeremy might have **drowned.**

Sally Forth reprinted with
special permission of King
Features Syndicate, Inc.

Irregular Verbs

3c. An *irregular verb* forms the past and the past
participle in some other way than by adding *-d* or
-ed to the base form.

The best way to learn the principal parts of irregular verbs
is to memorize them. No single usage rule applies to the
different ways that these verbs form their past and past
participle forms. However, there are some general guidelines that you can use. Irregular verbs form the past and
past participle by

■ changing vowels *or* consonants
■ changing vowels *and* consonants
■ making no change

	BASE FORM	PRESENT PARTICIPLE	PAST	PAST PARTICIPLE
Vowel Change	swim	(is) swimming	swam	(have) swum
Consonant Change	bend	(is) bending	bent	(have) bent
Vowel and Consonant Change	teach	(is) teaching	taught	(have) taught
No Change	burst	(is) bursting	burst	(have) burst

When forming the past and the past participle of irregular verbs, avoid these common errors:

(1) using the past form with a helping verb

NONSTANDARD I have never swam in this lake before.
    STANDARD I **have** never **swum** in this lake before.

(2) using the past participle form without a helping verb

NONSTANDARD She swum to shore to get help.
    STANDARD She **swam** to shore to get help.

(3) adding -d, -ed, or -t to the base form

NONSTANDARD We bursted into laughter as soon as we
             saw the comedian.
    STANDARD We **burst** into laughter as soon as we saw
             the comedian.

NOTE If you are not sure about the principal parts of a verb, look in a dictionary. Entries for irregular verbs give the principal parts. If no principal parts are listed, the verb is a regular verb.

The alphabetical lists on pages 148–153 contain the principal parts of many common irregular verbs. You may use these lists as a reference; however, keep in mind that the lists do not include every irregular verb.

COMMON IRREGULAR VERBS			
GROUP I: Each of these irregular verbs has the same form for its past and past participle.			
BASE FORM	**PRESENT PARTICIPLE**	**PAST**	**PAST PARTICIPLE**
bend	(is) bending	bent	(have) bent
bind	(is) binding	bound	(have) bound
bleed	(is) bleeding	bled	(have) bled
bring	(is) bringing	brought	(have) brought
build	(is) building	built	(have) built
buy	(is) buying	bought	(have) bought
catch	(is) catching	caught	(have) caught
dig	(is) digging	dug	(have) dug
feel	(is) feeling	felt	(have) felt
fight	(is) fighting	fought	(have) fought

(continued)

COMMON IRREGULAR VERBS (*continued*)			
GROUP I			
BASE FORM	PRESENT PARTICIPLE	PAST	PAST PARTICIPLE
find	(is) finding	found	(have) found
fling	(is) flinging	flung	(have) flung
grind	(is) grinding	ground	(have) ground
have	(is) having	had	(have) had
hold	(is) holding	held	(have) held
keep	(is) keeping	kept	(have) kept
kneel	(is) kneeling	knelt	(have) knelt
lay	(is) laying	laid	(have) laid
lead	(is) leading	led	(have) led
leave	(is) leaving	left	(have) left
lend	(is) lending	lent	(have) lent
lose	(is) losing	lost	(have) lost
make	(is) making	made	(have) made
meet	(is) meeting	met	(have) met
pay	(is) paying	paid	(have) paid
say	(is) saying	said	(have) said
seek	(is) seeking	sought	(have) sought
sell	(is) selling	sold	(have) sold
send	(is) sending	sent	(have) sent
shine	(is) shining	shone *or* shined	(have) shone *or* shined
shoot	(is) shooting	shot	(have) shot
sit	(is) sitting	sat	(have) sat
spend	(is) spending	spent	(have) spent
spin	(is) spinning	spun	(have) spun
stand	(is) standing	stood	(have) stood
stick	(is) sticking	stuck	(have) stuck
sting	(is) stinging	stung	(have) stung
swing	(is) swinging	swung	(have) swung
teach	(is) teaching	taught	(have) taught
tell	(is) telling	told	(have) told
think	(is) thinking	thought	(have) thought
weep	(is) weeping	wept	(have) wept
win	(is) winning	won	(have) won
wind	(is) winding	wound	(have) wound

QUICK CHECK 1   **Using the Past and Past Participle Forms of Verbs**

For each of the following sentences, give the correct form (past or past participle) of the verb in parentheses.

1. Bob and Terri have (*lead*) our class in math scores for two years.
2. Have you (*teach*) your little brother Bobby how to throw a curveball yet?
3. Mrs. Torres (*tell*) us yesterday that Mexican ballads are called *corridos*.
4. Ever since we met last year, Kitty and I have (*sit*) together in assembly.
5. The tiger-striped cat (*creep*) down the hallway and into the dark room.

COMMON IRREGULAR VERBS			
GROUP II: Each of these irregular verbs has a different form for its past and past participle.			
BASE FORM	**PRESENT PARTICIPLE**	**PAST**	**PAST PARTICIPLE**
be	(is) being	was, were	(have) been
bear	(is) bearing	bore	(have) borne
beat	(is) beating	beat	(have) beaten *or* beat
become	(is) becoming	became	(have) become
begin	(is) beginning	began	(have) begun
bite	(is) biting	bit	(have) bitten
blow	(is) blowing	blew	(have) blown
break	(is) breaking	broke	(have) broken
choose	(is) choosing	chose	(have) chosen
come	(is) coming	came	(have) come
dive	(is) diving	dove *or* dived	(have) dived
do	(is) doing	did	(have) done
draw	(is) drawing	drew	(have) drawn
drink	(is) drinking	drank	(have) drunk
drive	(is) driving	drove	(have) driven
eat	(is) eating	ate	(have) eaten
fall	(is) falling	fell	(have) fallen
fly	(is) flying	flew	(have) flown

(continued)

COMMON IRREGULAR VERBS (*continued*)			
GROUP II			
BASE FORM	**PRESENT PARTICIPLE**	**PAST**	**PAST PARTICIPLE**
forbid	(is) forbidding	forbade *or* forbad	(have) forbidden
forget	(is) forgetting	forgot	(have) forgotten *or* forgot
forgive	(is) forgiving	forgave	(have) forgiven
freeze	(is) freezing	froze	(have) frozen
get	(is) getting	got	(have) gotten *or* got
give	(is) giving	gave	(have) given
go	(is) going	went	(have) gone
grow	(is) growing	grew	(have) grown
hide	(is) hiding	hid	(have) hidden
know	(is) knowing	knew	(have) known
lie	(is) lying	lay	(have) lain
ride	(is) riding	rode	(have) ridden
ring	(is) ringing	rang	(have) rung
rise	(is) rising	rose	(have) risen
run	(is) running	ran	(have) run
see	(is) seeing	saw	(have) seen
shake	(is) shaking	shook	(have) shaken
show	(is) showing	showed *or* shown	(have) showed *or* shown
shrink	(is) shrinking	shrank *or* shrunk	(have) shrunk
sing	(is) singing	sang	(have) sung
sink	(is) sinking	sank	(have) sunk
speak	(is) speaking	spoke	(have) spoken
spring	(is) springing	sprang *or* sprung	(have) sprung
steal	(is) stealing	stole	(have) stolen
stink	(is) stinking	stank *or* stunk	(have) stunk
strike	(is) striking	struck *or* stricken	(have) struck
swear	(is) swearing	swore	(have) sworn
swim	(is) swimming	swam	(have) swum

(*continued*)

COMMON IRREGULAR VERBS (*continued*)			
GROUP II			
BASE FORM	**PRESENT PARTICIPLE**	**PAST**	**PAST PARTICIPLE**
take	(is) taking	took	(have) taken
tear	(is) tearing	tore	(have) torn
throw	(is) throwing	threw	(have) thrown
wake	(is) waking	wakened *or* woke	(have) wakened, waked, *or* woken
wear	(is) wearing	wore	(have) worn
write	(is) writing	wrote	(have) written

 QUICK CHECK 2 **Using the Past and Past Participle Forms of Verbs**

For each of the following sentences, give the correct form (past or past participle) of the verb in parentheses.

1. Your friends have (*come*) to see you.
2. He (*do*) his best on the PSAT last Saturday.
3. Elizabeth has finally (*begin*) her research report.
4. The poem I submitted was (*choose*) to receive a prize.
5. Strong winds (*drive*) the Dutch galleon off its course.

COMMON IRREGULAR VERBS			
GROUP III: Each of these irregular verbs has the same form for its infinitive, past, and past participle.			
BASE FORM	**PRESENT PARTICIPLE**	**PAST**	**PAST PARTICIPLE**
burst	(is) bursting	burst	(have) burst
cast	(is) casting	cast	(have) cast
cost	(is) costing	cost	(have) cost
cut	(is) cutting	cut	(have) cut
hit	(is) hitting	hit	(have) hit
hurt	(is) hurting	hurt	(have) hurt
let	(is) letting	let	(have) let
put	(is) putting	put	(have) put
read	(is) reading	read	(have) read

(continued)

COMMON IRREGULAR VERBS *(continued)*			
GROUP III			
BASE FORM	**PRESENT PARTICIPLE**	**PAST**	**PAST PARTICIPLE**
set	(is) setting	set	(have) set
spit	(is) spitting	spit *or* spat	(have) spit *or* spat
spread	(is) spreading	spread	(have) spread

GRAMMAR/USAGE

QUICK CHECK 3

Using the Past and Past Participle Forms of Verbs

Most of the following sentences contain an incorrect verb form. If a verb form is incorrect, give the correct form. If a sentence is correct, write *C*.

1. The roots of the plant had bursted the flowerpot.
2. After we've cut the grass, we'll weed the garden.
3. The angry hornet stung me right on the end of my nose, and it hurted all afternoon.
4. Sam spreaded his pita bread with hummus.
5. Both Felina and Fernanda hitted home runs in last week's softball game.

Six Troublesome Verbs

Each verb in the irregular verb pairs *lie/lay, sit/set,* and *rise/raise* has numerous definitions. The information on the next few pages shows you how to use these verbs correctly in some common situations. Keep in mind that these examples reflect only some, not all, uses of these verbs.

Lie and *Lay*

The verb *lie* means "to rest" or "to stay, to recline, or to remain in a certain state or position." *Lie* never takes an object. The verb *lay* means "to put [something] in a place." *Lay* usually takes an object.

BASE FORM	PRESENT PARTICIPLE	PAST	PAST PARTICIPLE
lie (to rest)	(is) lying	lay	(have) lain
lay (to put)	(is) laying	laid	(have) laid

EXAMPLES

The printout **is lying** there next to the computer. [no object]
The secretary **is laying** a copy of the report on everyone's desk. [*Copy* is the object of *is laying*.]

The explorers saw that a vast wilderness **lay** before them. [no object]
She carefully **laid** the holiday decorations in the box. [*Decorations* is the object of *laid*.]

My basset hound **has lain** in front of the fireplace since early this morning. [no object]
Tranh **has** already **laid** the fishing gear in the boat. [*Gear* is the object of *has laid*.]

Sit and *Set*

The verb *sit* means "to rest in an upright seated position." *Sit* seldom takes an object. The verb *set* means "to put [something] in a place." *Set* usually takes an object.

BASE FORM	PRESENT PARTICIPLE	PAST	PAST PARTICIPLE
sit (to rest)	(is) sitting	sat	(have) sat
set (to put)	(is) setting	set	(have) set

EXAMPLES

May I sit here? [no object]
May I set the chair here? [*Chair* is the object of *May set*.]

The Arc de Triomphe **sits** at the center of Place Charles de Gaulle in Paris. [no object]
This machine **sets** the body of the car onto its chassis. [*Body* is the object of *sets*.]

Is Ricardo **sitting** here? [no object]
Are you **setting** those leftovers aside for the cat? [*Leftovers* is the object of *Are setting.*]

We **sat** in the theater for an hour, waiting for the play to begin. [no object]
Kishi **set** the candles on the piano. [*Candles* is the object of *set.*]

We **have sat** on this bus for an hour. [no object]
Sue and I **have set** that large houseplant near the bay window. [*Houseplant* is the object of *have set.*]

Rise and *Raise*

The verb *rise* means "to go up" or "to get up." *Rise* never takes an object. The verb *raise* means "to cause [something] to rise" or "to lift up." *Raise* usually takes an object.

BASE FORM	PRESENT PARTICIPLE	PAST	PAST PARTICIPLE
rise (to go up)	(is) rising	rose	(have) risen
raise (to lift up)	(is) raising	raised	(have) raised

EXAMPLES   Every morning, Grandpa **rises** early and does an hour of yoga. [no object]
A heavy rain usually **raises** the water level in the lake by several inches. [*Level* is the object of *raises.*]

The temperature **is rising** fast today. [no object]
Workers **are raising** the foundation of that old house. [*Foundation* is the object of *are raising.*]

She **rose** from the wheelchair and walked toward the door. [no object]
Willis **raised** the window blinds to brighten the room. [*Window blinds* is the object of *raised.*]

The prices of fresh fruits and vegetables **have risen** considerably because of the drought. [no object]
Salim **has** already **raised** the flag. [*Flag* is the object of *has raised*.]

 QUICK CHECK 4

Choosing the Forms of *Lie* and *Lay*, *Sit* and *Set*, and *Rise* and *Raise*

For each of the following sentences, choose the correct verb form in parentheses. Be prepared to explain your choices.

1. I think I will (*lay*, *lie*) here and rest awhile.
2. They (*sit*, *set*) the yearbooks in Mr. Cohen's office.
3. Let's (*set*, *sit*) down and talk about the problem.
4. The price of citrus fruit (*rises*, *raises*) after a freeze.
5. Hours of driving (*lay*, *laid*) ahead of us.

Tense

3d. The *tense* of a verb indicates the time of the action or the state of being expressed by the verb.

Every verb has six tenses: *present, past, future, present perfect, past perfect,* and *future perfect.* These tenses are formed from the four principal parts of a verb.

This time line shows how the six tenses are related to one another.

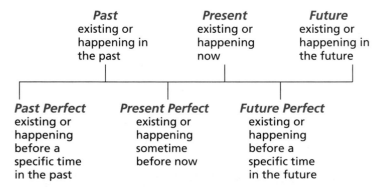

Past existing or happening in the past

Present existing or happening now

Future existing or happening in the future

Past Perfect existing or happening before a specific time in the past

Present Perfect existing or happening sometime before now

Future Perfect existing or happening before a specific time in the future

Listing all of the forms of a verb according to tense is called *conjugating* a verb.

CONJUGATION OF THE VERB *SEE*			
PRINCIPAL PARTS			
BASE FORM	**PRESENT PARTICIPLE**	**PAST**	**PAST PARTICIPLE**
see	seeing	saw	seen

PRESENT TENSE

SINGULAR	PLURAL
I see	we see
you see	you see
he, she, it sees	they see

PAST TENSE

SINGULAR	PLURAL
I saw	we saw
you saw	you saw
he, she, it saw	they saw

FUTURE TENSE
(*will* or *shall* + base form)

SINGULAR	PLURAL
I will (shall) see	we will (shall) see
you will see	you will see
he, she, it will see	they will see

PRESENT PERFECT TENSE
(*have* or *has* + past participle)

SINGULAR	PLURAL
I have seen	we have seen
you have seen	you have seen
he, she, it has seen	they have seen

(continued)

CONJUGATION OF THE VERB *SEE (continued)*	
PAST PERFECT TENSE (had + past participle)	
SINGULAR	*PLURAL*
I had seen	we had seen
you had seen	you had seen
he, she, it had seen	they had seen
FUTURE PERFECT TENSE (will have or shall have + past participle)	
SINGULAR	*PLURAL*
I will (shall) have seen	we will (shall) have seen
you will have seen	you will have seen
he, she, it will have seen	they will have seen

For Better or For Worse copyright 1993 Lynn Johnston Prod. Reprinted with permission of Universal Press Syndicate. All rights reserved.

The Uses of the Tenses

3e. Each of the six tenses has its own special uses.

(1) The *present tense* is used mainly to express an action or a state of being that is occurring now.

EXAMPLES   Martina **races** down the court and **shoots** the
               ball.
               The fans **cheer** wildly.

The present tense is also used

- to show a customary or habitual action or state of being
- to convey a general truth—something that is always true

- to make a historical event seem current (such use is called the *historical present*)
- to summarize the plot or subject matter of a literary work, or to refer to an author's relationship to his or her work (such use is called the *literary present*)
- to express future time

EXAMPLES   For breakfast I usually **eat** some cereal and **drink** orange juice. [customary action]
The earth **revolves** around the sun, which **is** at the center of our solar system. [general truth]
In a surprise move, the Greeks **construct** a huge wooden horse and **leave** it outside the walls of Troy. [historical present]
Camara Laye's *The Dark Child* **tells** the story of a boy growing up in an African village. [literary present]
The workshop that **begins** tomorrow **continues** for two weeks. [future time]

(2) The ***past tense*** is used to express an action or a state of being that occurred in the past but did not continue into the present.

EXAMPLES   In the last lap the runner **fell** and **injured** his knee.
The injury **prevented** him from competing in the relay race.

NOTE   A past action or state of being may also be shown in another way.

EXAMPLE   I **used to hate** spicy food.

(3) The ***future tense*** is used to express an action or a state of being that will occur. The future tense is formed with *will* or *shall* and the base form.

EXAMPLES   The president of the company **will** not **return** to headquarters today.
We **will** (or **shall**) **hold** a press conference at noon.

REFERENCE NOTE: *Shall* and *will* are both acceptable in forming the first-person future tense. For more information on the uses of *shall* and *will*, see page 167.

A future action or state of being may also be expressed by using

- the present tense of *be* followed by *going to* and the base form of a verb
- the present tense of *be* followed by *about to* and the base form of a verb
- the present tense of a verb with a word or phrase that expresses future time

EXAMPLES   My cousins **are going to visit** Japan in July.

Mrs. Scheirer **is about to announce** the winners.

The chess player **defends** her title at Bass Hall **next Friday night.**

(4) The ***present perfect tense*** is used mainly to express an action or a state of being that occurred at some indefinite time in the past. The present perfect tense always includes the helping verb *have* or *has.*

EXAMPLES   **Has** Miguel already **entered** the information into the computer?

The squirrels **have eaten** all of the bread-crumbs and birdseed.

 Avoid the use of the present perfect tense to express a *specific* time in the past. Instead, use the past tense.

NONSTANDARD   They have bought a computer last week. [*Last week* indicates a specific time in the past.]

STANDARD   They **bought** a computer last week. [past tense]

The present perfect tense is also used to express an action or a state of being that began in the past and continues into the present.

EXAMPLES   Mr. Steele **has taught** school for twenty-one years.

He **has coached** soccer since 1986.

(5) The ***past perfect tense*** is used to express an action or a state of being that was completed in the past before some other past occurrence. The past perfect tense always includes the helping verb *had.*

EXAMPLES   Paul **had traveled** several miles before he realized his mistake. [The traveling occurred before the realizing.]

He discovered that he **had misread** the road
map. [The misreading occurred before the
discovering.]

NOTE Use the past perfect tense in "if" clauses that express
the earlier of two past actions.

EXAMPLES   If he **had taken** [not *would have taken* or
took] more time, he would have won.

I would not have been late if I **had had**
[not *would have had* or *had*] a watch.

If you **had stopped** [not *would have*
stopped or *stopped*] by, you could
have met my cousin.

(6) The *future perfect tense* is used to express an action
or a state of being that will be completed in the future
before some other future occurrence. The future perfect
tense always includes the helping verbs *will have* or
shall have.

EXAMPLES   By the time school begins in August, we **will**
(or **shall**) **have saved** enough money to
buy the car.

By May, you **will have worked** here a year.

The Sequence of Tenses

3f. Use tense forms carefully to show the correct
relationship between verbs in a sentence.

(1) Use verbs in the same tense in the following
situations:
- in a compound predicate
- in compound and complex sentences, to describe
  events that occur at the same time or at nearly the
  same time

NONSTANDARD   The sprinter springs off the block and
raced to the finish line.

STANDARD   The sprinter **sprang** off the block and **raced** to the finish line. [compound predicate]

STANDARD   The sprinter **springs** off the block and **races** to the finish line.

NONSTANDARD   The coach blew the whistle, and the swimmers dive into the pool.

STANDARD   The coach **blew** the whistle, and the swimmers **dived** into the pool. [The events in this compound sentence are occurring at nearly the same time.]

STANDARD   The coach **blows** the whistle, and the swimmers **dive** into the pool.

NONSTANDARD   While the crowd had roared, Michael Jordan made the three-point shot.

STANDARD   While the crowd **roared,** Michael Jordan **made** the three-point shot. [In this complex sentence, the events occur at the same time.]

STANDARD   While the crowd **roars,** Michael Jordon **makes** the three-point shot.

NOTE   In some cases, a tense shift in a compound predicate is acceptable.

EXAMPLE   I **was, am,** and always **will be** a fan of Beatrix Potter.

(2) When describing events that occur at different times, use verbs in different tenses to show the order of events.

EXAMPLES   She now **works** for *The New York Times,* but she **worked** for *The Wall Street Journal* earlier this year. [Because her work for *The New York Times* is occurring now, the present tense form *works* is the correct form. Her work for *The Wall Street Journal* occurred at a specific time in the past and preceded her work at the *Times;* therefore, the past tense form **worked** is the correct form.]

Since the new band director **took** over, our band **has won** all of its contests. [Because the new director took over at a specific time in the past, the use of the past tense is correct. The winning has taken place over a period of time and continues into the present; therefore, the present perfect tense is used.]

The tense you use depends on the meaning that you want to express.

EXAMPLES   **I think I have** a B average in math. [Both verbs are in the present tense to indicate that both actions are occurring now.]
I think I had a B average in math. [The change to the past tense in the second verb implies that I once had, but no longer have, a B average in math.]

Lia **said** that she **lived** near the park. [Both verbs are in the past tense to indicate that at the time Lia spoke, she was living near the park.]
Lia **said** that she **had lived** near the park. [The change from past to past perfect indicates that at the time Lia spoke, she no longer lived near the park.]
Lia said that Yom Kippur **falls** on a different date every year. [The subordinate clause shifts to the present tense because it indicates a permanent fact.]

 QUICK CHECK 5   **Using Tenses Correctly**

Each of the following sentences contains an error in the use of tense. Identify the error, and then give the correct form of the verb.

1. By the time we get to the picnic area, the rain will stop.
2. I would have agreed if you would have asked me sooner.
3. Val claims that cats made the best pets.
4. As a witness to the accident, Pam told what happened.
5. Ever since he came to this country, he studied diligently.

GRAMMAR/USAGE

Progressive Forms, Emphatic Forms, and Modal Forms

The Progressive Form

3g. Each verb tense has an additional form called the *progressive form,* which expresses a continuing action or state of being. In each tense, the progressive form consists of the appropriate tense of *be* plus the present participle of the main verb. Some forms also include helping verbs.

(1) The *present progressive* form is used to express a continuing action or state of being that is happening in the present.

EXAMPLES   **Is** the baby **being** cranky?
Josh and I **are giving** the dog a bath.

NOTE   When used with a word or phrase that indicates future time, the present progressive can express future action.

EXAMPLE   We **are going** spelunking next weekend.

(2) The *past progressive* form is used to express a continuing action or state of being that happened in the past.

EXAMPLES   During the fourteenth century, Italy **was experiencing** a cultural rebirth that became known as the Renaissance.
Josh and I **were giving** the dog a bath when you called.

(3) The *future progressive* form is used to express a continuing action that will happen in the future.

EXAMPLES   In April, all of us **will be planning** how we'll spend our summer vacations.
Josh and I **will be giving** the dog a bath tomorrow.

(4) The ***present perfect progressive*** form is used to express a continuing action that began in the past and is still happening in the present.

EXAMPLES Andrew Lloyd Webber's new musical **has been receiving** rave reviews.
     Josh and I **have been giving** the dog a bath every week.

(5) The ***past perfect progressive*** form is used to express a continuing action that happened before another action in the past.

EXAMPLES The engine **had** not **been running** properly for a month before Dana finally figured out what was wrong with it.
     Until the weather turned warmer, Josh and I **had been giving** the dog a bath only once a month.

(6) The ***future perfect progressive*** form is used to express a continuing action that will have happened by a particular time in the future.

EXAMPLES By the time we reach the summit, we **will have been climbing** for two hours.
     By October, Josh and I **will have been giving** the dog weekly baths for six months.

The Emphatic Form

3h. The ***emphatic form*** of a verb is used to show emphasis.

This form consists of the present or the past tense of *do* with the base form of the main verb. Only present tense and past tense verbs have emphatic forms.

PRESENT EMPHATIC Although the grass is green, the lawn **does need** watering.
       Your little brother and sister certainly **do make** a lot of noise.
PAST EMPHATIC The patient suffered many setbacks, yet he **did** finally **make** a full recovery.

The emphatic form is also used in questions and in negative statements. These uses do not place any special emphasis on the verb.

QUESTIONS   **Does** this latex paint really **cover** in one coat?
            Why **do** fire ants **have** to be so hard to kill?

NEGATIVE   Because of the water shortage, I didn't
STATEMENTS   [**did** not] **wash** my car as often as I would
            have liked to.
            If your new CD player doesn't [**does** not]
            work, take it back to the store.

The Modal Forms

3i.   *Modals* are helping verbs that are joined with main verbs to express attitudes such as necessity or possibility toward the action or the state of being of the main verb. The helping verbs *can, could, may, might, must, ought, shall, should, will,* and *would* are modals.

(1) *Can* and *could* are used to express ability to perform the action of the main verb.

EXAMPLES   **Can** you **carry** that easy chair by yourself?
           A raccoon **could have knocked** the garbage can over.

(2) *May* is used to express permission or possibility.

EXAMPLES   You **may leave** when you finish the test. [permission]
           The mechanic said that the car's starter **may need** to be replaced. [possibility]

(3) *Might,* like *may,* is used to express a possibility. Often, the possibility expressed by *might* is less likely than the one expressed by *may.*

EXAMPLE   Kevin Costner **might be** at the press conference, but I doubt it.

(4) *Must* is most often used to express a requirement. Sometimes, *must* is used to express an explanation.

EXAMPLES   At our school, all students **must take** four
years of English. [requirement]
You **must have been** tired after making such
a long drive. [explanation]

(5) *Ought* is used to express obligation or likelihood.

EXAMPLES   Does Mrs. Lewis think that we **ought to have
auditioned** for the play? [obligation]
The thunderstorm **ought to be** over soon.
[likelihood]

(6) *Shall* and *will* are used to express future time.

EXAMPLES   Where **will** (or **shall**) we **go** for dinner?
The pharmacist **will fill** your prescription next.

NOTE In the past, careful writers and speakers of English
made a distinction between the modals *shall* and *will*.
They used *shall* only with first-person subjects (*I* and
we) and *will* with all other subjects. Nowadays, however, *will* tends to be used in all cases. *Shall* is rarely
used, except in certain questions.

EXAMPLE   **Shall** we go?

(7) *Should* is used to express a recommendation, an
obligation, or a possibility.

EXAMPLES   I told Lionel he **should see** a dentist about
that toothache. [recommendation]
Gina really **should have called** Lauren and
Todd before she ordered tickets for them.
[obligation]
Should you **have** any questions about your
account, please don't hesitate to ask.
[possibility]

(8) *Would* is used to express the ***conditional form*** of a
verb. A conditional verb form usually appears in an
independent clause that is joined with an "if" clause.
The "if" clause explains under what *condition(s)* the
action or state of being of the conditional verb takes
place. It may also be used to express future time in a
subordinate clause when the main verb is in the past
tense. Finally, *would* can be used to express a polite

request, an invitation, or an action that was repeated in the past.

EXAMPLES   If they had read the chapter, they **would have been prepared** for the pop quiz. [conditional]

He told me that he **would be** here by eight o'clock. [subordinate clause]

Would you please **tell** me how to get to Sycamore Street? [request]

Would you **like** to dance, Danielle? [invitation]

Every winter we **would build** a snowman and decorate it for Christmas. [repeated past action]

Frank & Ernest reprinted by permission of NEA, Inc.

The Verb *Be*

The verb *be* is the most frequently used verb in the English language. The conjugation of the verb *be* differs from that of other verbs. Only the present and past tenses of *be* have the progressive form, and none of the tenses has the emphatic form.

CONJUGATION OF THE VERB *BE*			
PRINCIPAL PARTS			
BASE FORM	PRESENT PARTICIPLE	PAST	PAST PARTICIPLE
be	being	was, were	been

(continued)

GRAMMAR/USAGE

CONJUGATION OF THE VERB *BE (continued)*	
PRESENT TENSE	
SINGULAR	*PLURAL*
I am	we are
you are	you are
he, she, it is	they are
Present Progressive: am, are, is being	
PAST TENSE	
SINGULAR	*PLURAL*
I was	we were
you were	you were
he, she, it was	they were
Past Progressive: was, were being	
FUTURE TENSE (*will* or *shall* + base form)	
SINGULAR	*PLURAL*
I will (shall) be	we will (shall) be
you will be	you will be
he, she, it will be	they will be
PRESENT PERFECT TENSE (*have* or *has* + past participle)	
SINGULAR	*PLURAL*
I have been	we have been
you have been	you have been
he, she, it has been	they have been
PAST PERFECT TENSE (*had* + past participle)	
SINGULAR	*PLURAL*
I had been	we had been
you had been	you had been
he, she, it had been	they had been

(continued)

GRAMMAR/USAGE

CONJUGATION OF THE VERB *BE (continued)*	
FUTURE PERFECT TENSE (***will have*** or ***shall have*** + past participle)	
SINGULAR	*PLURAL*
I will (shall) have been	we will (shall) have been
you will have been	you will have been
he, she, it will have been	they will have been

Active Voice and Passive Voice

3j. *Voice* is the form a transitive verb takes to indicate whether the subject of the verb performs or receives the action.

 REFERENCE NOTE: For more discussion of transitive verbs, see page 101.

When the subject of a verb performs the action, the verb is in the *active voice.* When the subject receives the action, the verb is in the *passive voice.*

As the following examples show, verbs in the active voice have objects, and verbs in the passive voice do not.

ACTIVE VOICE Gloria Naylor **wrote** *The Women of Brewster Place.* [*The Women of Brewster Place* is the direct object.]

PASSIVE VOICE *The Women of Brewster Place* **was written** by Gloria Naylor.

ACTIVE VOICE The optometrist **adjusted** the eyeglasses. [*Eyeglasses* is the direct object.]

PASSIVE VOICE The eyeglasses **were adjusted** by the optometrist.

PASSIVE VOICE The eyeglasses **were adjusted.**

ACTIVE VOICE Carol **has adopted** the two puppies. [*Puppies* is the direct object.]

PASSIVE VOICE The two puppies **have been adopted** by Carol.

PASSIVE VOICE **The two puppies have been adopted.**

From these examples, you can see how an active construction can become a passive construction.

- The verb from the active sentence becomes a past participle preceded by a form of *be.*
- The object of the verb becomes the subject of the verb in a passive construction.
- The subject in an active construction becomes the object of the preposition *by* in a passive construction. (As the last example shows, this prepositional phrase is not always necessary.)

 REFERENCE NOTE: For more information on direct objects and indirect objects, see pages 287–289.

The Retained Object

A transitive verb in the active voice often has an indirect object as well as a direct object. Either object can become the subject or can remain a complement in the passive construction. A complement in a passive construction is called a *retained object,* not a direct object or an indirect object.

     S V   IO   DO
ACTIVE **Ms. Ribas gave each student a thesaurus.**

     S   V   RO
PASSIVE **Each student was given a thesaurus (by Ms. Ribas).** [The indirect object *student* becomes the subject, and the direct object *thesaurus* becomes the retained object.]

     S   V   RO
PASSIVE **A thesaurus was given to each student (by Ms. Ribas).** [The direct object *thesaurus* becomes the subject, and the indirect object *student* becomes the retained object.]

The verb in a passive construction always includes a form of *be* and the past participle of a transitive verb. Notice in the following conjugation of the verb *see* in the passive voice that the form of *be* determines the tense of the passive verb.

CONJUGATION OF THE VERB *SEE* IN THE PASSIVE VOICE

PRESENT TENSE

SINGULAR	PLURAL
I am seen	we are seen
you are seen	you are seen
he, she, it is seen	they are seen

Present Progressive: am, are, is being seen

PAST TENSE

SINGULAR	PLURAL
I was	we were
you were	you were
he, she, it was	they were

Past Progressive: was, were being

FUTURE TENSE

SINGULAR	PLURAL
I will (shall) be seen	we will (shall) be seen
you will be seen	you will be seen
he, she, it will be seen	they will be seen

Future Progressive: will (shall) be being seen

PRESENT PERFECT TENSE

SINGULAR	PLURAL
I have been seen	we have been seen
you have been seen	you have been seen
he, she, it has been seen	they have been seen

PAST PERFECT TENSE

SINGULAR	PLURAL
I had been seen	we had been seen
you had been seen	you had been seen
he, she, it had been seen	they had been seen

(continued)

CONJUGATION OF THE VERB *SEE (continued)*	
FUTURE PERFECT TENSE	
SINGULAR	*PLURAL*
I will (shall) have been seen	we will (shall) have been seen
you will have been seen	you will have been seen
he, she, it will have been seen	they will have been seen

 REFERENCE NOTE: The conjugation of *see* in the active voice is on pages 157–158.

The Uses of the Passive Voice

3k. Use the passive voice sparingly.

Choosing between the active voice and the passive voice is a matter of style, not correctness. In general, however, the passive voice is less direct, less forceful, and less concise than the active voice. In some cases, the passive voice may simply sound awkward.

AWKWARD PASSIVE	Last night, the floor was scrubbed by my father, and the faucet was fixed by my mother.
ACTIVE	Last night, my father **scrubbed** the floor, and my mother **fixed** the faucet.

AWKWARD PASSIVE	The first wristwatch was created by a court jeweler when a watch set in a bracelet was requested by Empress Josephine.
ACTIVE	When Empress Josephine **requested** a watch set in a bracelet, a court jeweler **created** the first wristwatch.

Notice that the use of the passive voice in a long passage is particularly awkward.

AWKWARD PASSIVE	When my mother was asked by the local camera club to give a lecture on modern photography, she was amazed by the request. Mom had never been chosen to do anything

GRAMMAR/USAGE

like this before. Since I am considered by my mother to be the most imaginative member of our family, I was given by her the task of choosing the topics that would be presented by her. Dad was asked by her to select the slides that would be shown to the amateur photographers. Within a few days, the lecture had been prepared by Mom. On the night of the presentation, everyone in the audience was impressed by Mom's knowledge of modern photography.

ACTIVE When the local camera club **asked** my mother to give a lecture on modern photography, the request **amazed** her. No one **had** ever **chosen** Mom to do anything like this before. Since my mother **considers** me the most imaginative member of our family, she **gave** me the task of choosing the topics that she **would present.** She **asked** Dad to select the slides that she **would show** to the amateur photographers. Within a few days, Mom **had prepared** the lecture. On the night of the presentation, Mom's knowledge of modern photography **impressed** everyone in the audience.

Passive voice constructions are not always awkward. In fact, the passive voice is appropriate and useful in the following situations:

(1) when you do not know the performer of the action

EXAMPLES Asbestos **was used** for making fireproof materials.

An anonymous letter **had been sent** to the police chief.

(2) when you do not want to reveal the performer of the action

EXAMPLES Many careless errors **were made** in some of these essays.

The missing paintings **have been returned** to the museum.

(3) when you want to emphasize the receiver of the action

EXAMPLES   Penicillin **was discovered** accidentally.
             This book **has been translated** into more than
                 one hundred languages.

If you use a computer when you write,
you may want to find out more about the
different kinds of style-checking software
that are available. One such program checks for overuse of
passive voice verbs. Remember, though, the computer can
only highlight the passive voice verbs it finds. It can't determine whether they are used intentionally for a particular
stylistic effect.

 QUICK CHECK 6   **Revising Sentences in the
                                          Passive Voice**

Revise the following sentences by changing the passive
voice to the active voice wherever the change is desirable. If
the passive voice is preferable, write *C*.

1. For his bravery, he was awarded a Silver Star Medal.
2. The proposal had been heard by every member of the
   committee.
3. The dishes should have been washed by your brother.
4. Before Friday, a replacement will have been named by
   the coach.
5. This beautiful example of Spanish lace was made by
   hand.

Mood

Mood is the form a verb takes to indicate the attitude of the
person using the verb. Verbs may be in one of three moods:
the *indicative,* the *imperative,* or the *subjunctive.*

31.   The *indicative mood* is used to express a fact, an
           opinion, or a question.

GRAMMAR/USAGE

EXAMPLES   Andrei Sakharov **was** the nuclear physicist who **won** the Nobel Prize for peace in 1975.

All of us **think** that our baseball team **is** the best one in the state.

Can you **explain** the difference between a meteor and a meteorite?

 REFERENCE NOTE: For examples of all of the tense forms in the indicative mood, see the conjugations on pages 157–158 and 172–173.

3m. The *imperative mood* is used to express a direct command or request.

The imperative mood of a verb has only one form. It is the same as the infinitive form of a verb.

EXAMPLES   **Explain** the difference between a meteor and a meteorite.

Please **fasten** your seat belt.

3n. The *subjunctive mood* is used to express a suggestion, a necessity, a condition contrary to fact, or a wish.

EXAMPLES   The guidance counselor recommended that Tina **apply** to a small liberal arts college. [suggestion]

It is imperative that we **be** on time for the appointment. [necessity]

If Ron **were** any taller, he'd have a hard time getting through regular doorways. [condition contrary to fact]

I wish that you **were** coming with us. [wish]

Only the present tense has a distinctive subjunctive form. The other tense forms in the subjunctive mood are the same as those in the indicative mood. The exception to this rule is the verb *be,* which does have a distinctive past subjunctive form.

The following partial conjugation of *be* shows how the present and past tense forms in the subjunctive mood differ from those in the indicative mood. [Note: The use of *that*

GRAMMAR/USAGE

and *if,* which are shown in parentheses, is explained on this page and the next page.]

PRESENT INDICATIVE		PRESENT SUBJUNCTIVE	
SINGULAR	*PLURAL*	*SINGULAR*	*PLURAL*
I am	we are	(that) I be	(that) we be
you are	you are	(that) you be	(that) you be
he, she, it is	they are	(that) he, she, it be	(that) they be
PAST INDICATIVE		**PAST SUBJUNCTIVE**	
I was	we were	(if) I were	(if) we were
you were	you were	(if) you were	(if) you were
he, she, it was	they were	(if) he, she, it were	(if) they were

The present subjunctive form of a verb is the same as the base form. For all verbs except *be,* the past subjunctive form is the same as the past indicative form.

(1) The *present subjunctive* is used to express a suggestion or a necessity.

Generally, the verb in a subordinate clause beginning with *that* is in the subjunctive mood when the independent clause contains a word indicating a suggestion (such as *ask, move, prefer, propose, urge, request, suggest,* or *recommend*) or a word indicating a necessity (such as *demand, insist, order, require, necessary,* or *essential*).

EXAMPLES   Ms. Gutiérrez suggested that he **apply** for the job.

The moderator at the convention requested that the state delegates **be seated.**

It is necessary that she **attend** the convention.

It is required that you **be** here on time.

(2) The *past subjunctive* is used to express a condition contrary to fact or to express a wish.

In general, a clause beginning with *if, as if,* or *as though* expresses a condition contrary to fact—something that is not

GRAMMAR/USAGE

true. In such a clause, use the past subjunctive. Remember that *were* is the only past subjunctive form of *be*.

EXAMPLES   If I **were** you, I'd have those tires checked.
              If he **were** to proofread his writing, he would
                  make fewer errors.
              Because of the bad telephone connection,
                  Gregory sounded as though [as if] he **were**
                  ten thousand miles away.

Similarly, use the past subjunctive to express a wish—a condition that is desirable.

EXAMPLES   I wish I **were** more patient than I am.
              Reiko wishes that her best friend **were**n't
                  moving away.
              I wish you **could go** with me.

Frank & Ernest reprinted by
permission of NEA, Inc.

   QUICK CHECK 7   **Identifying the Mood of Verbs**

For each of the following sentences, identify the mood of the italicized verb as *indicative, imperative,* or *subjunctive.*

1. Theo, *stand* back a safe distance while I try again to start this lawnmower.
2. Did you know that Tamisha's mother *is* the new manager at the supermarket?
3. Bradley says that if he *were* president, he'd take steps to reduce the federal deficit.
4. I suggest that these young maple trees *be* planted quickly, before they wilt.

5. This Lenni-Lenape moccasin *was* found near Matawan, New Jersey.

Verbals

A *verbal* is a verb form used as a noun, an adjective, or an adverb. Even though verbals are used as other parts of speech, they retain many of the qualities of verbs, including tense and voice. The three kinds of verbals are the *participle,* the *gerund,* and the *infinitive.* All three are formed from the principal parts of verbs.

 REFERENCE NOTE: For more information about verbals and how they are used, see pages 246–255.

The Participle

Participles, which function as adjectives, are formed from two principal parts of a verb—the present participle and the past participle.

PRESENT PARTICIPLE	Pour the **boiling** water into a bowl, and stir in the gelatin.
PAST PARTICIPLE	**Deceived** by appearances, Othello unjustly accuses Desdemona of infidelity.
PRESENT PERFECT PARTICIPLE	Janet and Leon, **having finished** their exams, decided to celebrate. [active voice] **Having been discovered** by reporters, the movie star looked for a more remote hideaway. [passive voice]

3o. The *present participle* or the *past participle* is used to express an action or a state of being that occurs at the same time as that of the main verb.

EXAMPLES **Gazing** through the telescope, I saw the rings around Saturn. [The action expressed by *Gazing* occurs at the same time as the action expressed by *saw.*]
Driven by curiosity, I found the encyclopedia entry on our solar system's moons. [The ac-

GRAMMAR/USAGE

tion expressed by *Driven* occurs at the same
time as the action expressed by *found*.]

3p. The *present perfect participle* is used to express
an action or a state of being that happens before
that of the main verb.

EXAMPLES **Having completed** her outline, Kate wrote
the first draft of her research paper. [The action expressed by *Having completed* precedes
the action expressed by *wrote*.]
Having been proofread, Kate's research paper
was ready for publication. [The action expressed by *Having been proofread* precedes
the action expressed by *was*.]

 REFERENCE NOTE: For more information about participles and how they are used, see pages 246–249.

The Gerund

A gerund, which functions as a noun, is formed from the present participle of a verb. Gerunds have the following forms:

PRESENT **Competing** in an Olympic diving competition
has been Arnold's dream ever since he first
watched Greg Louganis dive. [active voice]
The high point of Tina's junior year was **being
chosen** for the pep squad. [passive voice]

PRESENT The authorities suspected him of **having
PERFECT stolen** that painting. [active voice]
My **having been accepted** at Princeton was
cause for celebration. [passive voice]

 REFERENCE NOTE: For more information about gerunds
and how they are used, see pages 250–251.

The Infinitive

The infinitive is formed by the base form of the verb, preceded by *to*. It can function as either a modifier or a noun.
Infinitives have the following forms:

PRESENT **Wasn't it great to see** Jeremy again? [active
INFINITIVE voice]

GRAMMAR/USAGE

To be given an important test early on a Monday morning seems like cruel and unusual punishment to me. [passive voice]

PRESENT
PERFECT
INFINITIVE

I was pleased **to have seen** so many cranes in the nature preserve. [active voice]
Richelle said that just **to have been nominated** was a wonderful honor. [passive voice]

3q. The *present infinitive* is used to express an action or a state of being that follows that of the main verb.

EXAMPLES   Latrice hopes **to attend** the Super Bowl. [The action expressed by *to attend* follows the action expressed by *hopes*.]
Latrice asked **to be allowed** some time off. [The action expressed by *to be allowed* follows the action expressed by *asked*.]

3r. The *present perfect infinitive* is used to express an action or a state of being that precedes that of the main verb.

EXAMPLES   The divers claim **to have located** an ancient sailing vessel. [The action expressed by *to have located* precedes the action expressed by *claim*.]
They claimed **to have been exploring** the reef when they found the ship. [The action expressed by *to have been exploring* precedes the action expressed by *claimed*.]

STYLE
NOTE

Because the tenses of infinitives and main verbs help to show the relationships between these words, it's important to use tense forms precisely.

EXAMPLES   Amanda **would like to see** the performing Lipizzaner horses. [Amanda wants to see the horses at some time in the future.]

Amanda **would have liked to see** the performing Lipizzaner horses. [Amanda wanted to see the horses at some time in the past, but she didn't see them.]
Amanda **would like to have seen** the performing Lipizzaner horses. [Amanda now wishes that she had seen the horses at some time in the past.]

 REFERENCE NOTE: For more information about infinitives and how they are used, see pages 252–255.

 QUICK CHECK 8 **Using Verbal Tenses Correctly**

Each of the following sentences contains an error in the tense of a verbal. Identify the error, and then give the correct form of the verbal.

1. When you charge the battery in the car, be sure to have protected your eyes and hands from the sulfuric acid in the battery.
2. Deciding to attend the concert at Boyer Hall, we bought four tickets for Saturday night.
3. I would have liked to have gone swimming yesterday.
4. After singing the aria, Jessye Norman received a standing ovation.
5. Anthropologists believe these ancient cave dwellers to live somewhere north of the Red Sea.

 Chapter Review

A. Proofreading Sentences for Correct Verb Usage

Most of the following sentences contain errors in the use of verbs. If a sentence has a verb error, revise the sentence, using the correct verb form. If a sentence is correct, write *C*.

EXAMPLE
1. If I would have seen the accident, I would have reported it.
1. *If I had seen the accident, I would have reported it.*

1. If modern society was an agricultural one, more of us would know about farming and about the difficulties faced by farmers.
2. At the time the census tally was taken, more than thirty-nine thousand Native Americans have been living in Wisconsin.
3. How many of us possess the skills to have survived on our own without the assistance of store-bought items?
4. If you would have taken the nutrition class, you would have learned how to shop wisely for food.
5. Wacky, my pet hamster, was acting as if she was trying to tell me something.
6. Yesterday, Dad's pickup truck was washed and waxed by my brother.
7. According to this news article, the concert last Saturday night is "a resounding success."
8. Janet Jackson's concerts have broke all attendance records at the City Arena.
9. Because of the excessive amount of rain this spring, the water behind the dam has raised to a dangerous level.
10. Spending the entire morning working in the garden, Jim is now lying down for a rest.

B. Proofreading Sentences for Correct Verb Usage

Most of the following sentences contain errors in the use of verbs. If a sentence has a verb error, revise the sentence, using the correct verb form. If a sentence is correct, write *C*.

EXAMPLE   1. From our studies we had concluded that women had played many critical roles in the history of our nation.

      1. *From our studies we have concluded that women have played many critical roles in the history of our nation.*

11. In Daytona Beach, Florida, Mary McLeod Bethune founded a tiny school, which eventually become Bethune-Cookman College.
12. Jane Addams founded Hull House in Chicago to educate the poor and to acquaint immigrants with

American ways; for her efforts she had received the Nobel Prize for peace in 1931.

13. In 1932, after a flight lasting almost fifteen hours, Amelia Earhart became the first woman to have flown solo across the Atlantic Ocean.

14. Pearl Buck, a recipient of the Nobel Prize for literature in 1938, strived to bring understanding and peace to people all over the world.

15. When the Republican National Convention met in San Francisco in 1964, Margaret Chase Smith, senator from Maine, received twenty-seven delegate votes for the presidential nomination.

16. Lorraine Hansberry wrote the successful play *A Raisin in the Sun,* which had been translated into thirty languages.

17. Have you ever heard of Belva Lockwood, a woman whose accomplishments paved the way for women in politics?

18. By the end of her career, Lockwood claimed the distinction of being the first woman lawyer to argue a case before the United States Supreme Court.

19. Although Lockwood is not well known nowadays, she did receive more than four thousand votes for the presidency in 1884.

20. By the time you leave high school, you will learn many interesting facts about history.

4 USING PRONOUNS

Case Forms of Pronouns; Special Problems; Clear Reference

 Checking What You Know

A. Selecting Correct Forms of Pronouns

For each of the following sentences, choose the correct form of the pronoun in parentheses.

EXAMPLE   **1.** Since (*he, him*) and I now have our licenses, Aunt Arabella allowed us to drive her car to the lake.
      1. *he*

1. This afternoon the talent committee will audition Tina and (*myself, me*).

2. As I waited for the elevator, I heard the receptionist say, "(*Who, Whom*) shall I say is calling?"

3. The best tennis players in school, Adele and (*he, him*), are going to the regional finals.

4. I helped Two Bear and (*she, her*) take down the tepee and load it onto the travois.

5. (*Who, Whom*) did you talk to at the information desk?

6. Because Alberto and (*they, them*) have taken dancing lessons, they were chosen to be in the chorus line.

7. My math teacher objects to (*me, my*) yelling out answers before I have been called on.

8. I learned about life in post-World War II Cuba from my great-grandmother and (*he, him*).

9. Between you and (*I, me*), I'm glad it's almost lunchtime.

10. When we were small, Ellie always got into more trouble than (*I, me*).

B. Revising Sentences by Correcting Unclear References

Most of the following sentences contain pronouns without clear antecedents. Revise each sentence to correct any unclear pronoun references. [Note: Although sentences can be corrected in more than one way, you need to give only one revision.] If a sentence is correct, write *C*.

EXAMPLE   **1.** Chip studied the Chinese poet T'ao Ch'ien in his world literature class last semester.

          1. *In his world literature class last semester, Chip studied the Chinese poet T'ao Ch'ien.*

11. T'ao Ch'ien loved to work in his garden, which is evident in his poetry.

12. T'ao Ch'ien's topics came from his own simple life. One of these was worrying about his five sons.

13. In our literature book it states that the Chinese consider Tu Fu to be their greatest poet.

14. Many people admire poetry, but most people don't think they can be used for medicinal purposes.

15. In this book, you will find a story about Tu Fu's suggesting that his poetry could cure malarial fever.

16. That more than a thousand of Tu Fu's poems survive is amazing.

17. The poet Li Po liked to travel and to enjoy nature. This gave him many poetry subjects but no family life.

18. Ms. Johnson explained to Alicia the meaning of the Li Po poem she had just read.

19. John Jay liked Po Chü-i's poetry, and he wanted to copy one of the poems.

20. Darnell took almost the whole class period to describe the tragic love story related in Po Chü-i's narrative poem *The Song of Everlasting Regret*. It went by very quickly. ✓

Case

Case is the form of a noun or a pronoun that shows how it is used. In English, there are three cases: *nominative, objective, and possessive.*

The form of a noun is the same for both the nominative case and the objective case. For example, a noun used as a subject (nominative case) will have the same form if used as an object (objective case).

NOMINATIVE CASE The **general** explained the strategy. [*General* is the subject.]

OBJECTIVE CASE The strategy was explained by the **general**. [*General* is the object of the preposition.]

A noun changes its form for the possessive case, usually by adding an apostrophe and an *s* to most singular nouns and only the apostrophe to most plural nouns.

POSSESSIVE CASE The **general's** explanation was clear and concise. [singular modifier]
The **generals'** explanations were clear and concise. [plural modifier]

☞ REFERENCE NOTE: For more information about possessive forms, see pages 421– 424.

Unlike nouns, most personal pronouns have three forms—one for each case. The form a pronoun takes depends on its function in a sentence.

NOMINATIVE CASE **We** listened closely to the teacher's directions. [subject]

OBJECTIVE CASE The teacher gave **us** a vocabulary quiz. [indirect object]

POSSESSIVE CASE The teacher collected **our** papers. [modifier]

Within each case, the forms of the personal pronouns indicate *number, person,* and *gender.*

- **Number** is the form of a pronoun that indicates whether it is *singular* or *plural.*
- **Person** is the form of a pronoun that indicates the one(s) speaking (*first person*), the one(s) spoken to (*second person*), or the one(s) spoken of (*third person*).
- **Gender** is the form of a pronoun that establishes it as *masculine, feminine,* or *neuter* (neither masculine nor feminine).

PERSONAL PRONOUNS		
SINGULAR		
	NOMINATIVE CASE	**OBJECTIVE CASE**	**POSSESSIVE CASE**
FIRST PERSON	I	me	my, mine
SECOND PERSON	you	you	your, yours
THIRD PERSON	he, she, it	him, her, it	his, her, hers, its
PLURAL		
	NOMINATIVE CASE	**OBJECTIVE CASE**	**POSSESSIVE CASE**
FIRST PERSON	we	us	our, ours
SECOND PERSON	you	you	your, yours
THIRD PERSON	they	them	their, theirs

Notice in the chart that *you* and *it* have the same forms for the nominative and the objective cases. All other personal pronouns have different forms for each case. Notice also that only third-person singular pronouns indicate gender.

Mother Goose & Grimm reprinted by permission:
Tribune Media Services.

STYLE
NOTE

Use the neuter pronoun *it* when referring to an animal unless the gender of the animal is made clear by another word in the sentence.

EXAMPLES   A stablehand led the horse to **its** stall.
That rooster is known for **his** bad temper.
[The word *rooster* indicates that the animal is male.]
The grizzly bear is very protective of **her** cubs.
[The words *protective* and *cubs* indicate that the animal is female.]

The Nominative Case

Personal pronouns in the nominative case—*I, you, he, she, it, we,* and *they*—are used as subjects of verbs and as predicate nominatives.

 REFERENCE NOTE: Personal pronouns in the nominative case may also be used as appositives. See pages 256–257.

4a. A subject of a verb is in the nominative case.

EXAMPLES   **We** ordered the concert tickets. [*We* is the subject of the verb *ordered*.]
Why does **she** think that **they** are too expensive? [*She* is the subject of the verb *does think. They* is the subject of the verb *are*.]
Could **Lionel** or **she** fix the lawnmower? [*Lionel* and *she* are the subjects of the verb *could fix*.]

 REFERENCE NOTE: For more information about subjects of verbs, see pages 280–285.

As you can see in the last example above, a subject may be compound, with a pronoun appearing in combination with a noun or another pronoun. To help you choose the correct pronoun form in a compound subject, try each form as the simple subject of the verb.

CHOICES: After everyone had voted, Onawa and (*he, him*) counted the votes. [*He counted* or *him counted*?]

ANSWER:	After everyone had voted, Onawa and **he** counted the votes.
CHOICES:	*(She, Her)* and *(I, me)* will make the piñata for my nephew's birthday party. [*She will make* or *Her will make? I will make* or *me will make*?]
ANSWER:	**She** and **I** will make the piñata for my nephew's birthday party.

4b. A predicate nominative is in the nominative case.

A *predicate nominative* follows a linking verb and explains or identifies the subject of the verb.

A pronoun used as a predicate nominative always follows some form of the verb *be: am, is, are, was, were, be,* or *been.*

EXAMPLES	The chairperson of the prom committee is **she.** [*She* follows *is* and identifies the subject *chairperson.*]
	The one who made the comment was **I.** [*I* follows *was* and identifies the subject *one.*]
	The lucky winners may have been **they.** [*They* follows *may have been* and identifies the subject *winners.*]

 REFERENCE NOTE: For more information on predicate nominatives, see pages 291–292.

As you can see in the examples above, the predicate nominative and the subject of the verb both indicate the same individual(s). To identify the correct pronoun form to use as a predicate nominative, try each form as the subject of the verb.

CHOICES:	The only applicant for the job was *(he, him).* [*He was* or *him was*?]
ANSWER:	The only applicant for the job was **he.**

Like a subject, a predicate nominative may be compound.

EXAMPLES	The only students who auditioned for the part of King Arthur were **he** and **Carlos.** [*He* and *Carlos* identify the subject *students.*]

The two debaters are **she** and **I**. [*She* and *I* identify the subject *debaters*.]

NOTE Expressions such as *It's me, This is her*, and *It was them* are examples of informal usage. Though acceptable in everyday situations, such expressions should be avoided in formal speaking and writing. (The formal versions of the expressions above are *It is I, This is she*, and *It was they*.)

 QUICK CHECK 1 | **Using Pronouns in the Nominative Case**

For each of the following sentences, choose the correct form of the pronoun in parentheses. Then identify its use in the sentence either as a *subject* or a *predicate nominative*.

1. In the morning, Dana and (*they, them*) will begin the long trip back.
2. You and (*me, I*) have really contributed to the success of the fund drive.
3. Neither Sally nor (*he, him*) can attend the conference.
4. If you hear a knock at the door, it will probably be (*she, her*).
5. The most successful contestants were (*us, we*).

The Objective Case

Personal pronouns in the objective case—*me, you, him, her, it, us,* and *them*—are used as objects of verbs and as objects of prepositions.

 REFERENCE NOTE: Personal pronouns in the objective case may also be used as appositives. See pages 197–198.

4c. An object of a verb is in the objective case.

The object of a verb may be a *direct object* or an *indirect object*. A **direct object** follows an action verb and tells *whom* or *what*.

EXAMPLES My pen pal from Manila visited **me** last summer. [*Me* tells *whom* my pen pal visited.]
The car stalled, and we couldn't restart **it**. [*It* tells *what* we couldn't restart.]

GRAMMAR/USAGE

Did our Mardi Gras masks frighten **Joey** and **her**? [*Joey* and *her* tell *whom* the masks frightened.]

An *indirect object* comes between a transitive verb and a direct object and tells *to whom, to what, for whom,* or *for what.*

EXAMPLES   The coach awarded **her** a varsity letter. [*Her* tells *to whom* the coach awarded a varsity letter.]

We gathered the chickens and gave **them** some feed. [*Them* tells *to what* we gave some feed.]

My little sister calmed down when Grandpa told **her** and **me** stories about growing up on a farm. [*Her* and *me* tell *to whom* Grandpa told stories.]

My mother studies Japanese, so I got **her** a bonsai for her birthday. [*Her* tells *for whom.*]

An object of a verb may be compound. To help you choose the correct pronoun form in a compound object, try each form as the object of the verb.

CHOICES: The new student asked Kelly and (*I, me*) for directions. [*The new student asked I* or *asked me*?]

ANSWER: The new student asked Kelly and **me** for directions.

CHOICES: The editor-in-chief gave (*he, him*) and (*she, her*) an interesting assignment. [*The editor-in-chief gave he* or *gave him*? *The editor-in-chief gave she* or *gave her*?]

ANSWER: The editor-in-chief gave **him** and **her** an interesting assignment.

CHOICES: Did the fog delay Karl and (*she, her*)? [First, restate the question as a declarative sentence: The fog did delay Karl and (*she, her*). *The fog delayed she* or *delayed her*?]

ANSWER: Did the fog delay Karl and **her**?

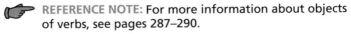 REFERENCE NOTE: For more information about objects of verbs, see pages 287–290.

4d.   An *object of a preposition* is in the objective case.

An *object of a preposition* comes at the end of a phrase that begins with a preposition.

EXAMPLES   for **me**   after **her**   next to **them**
           with **us**   beside **him**   between **you** and me

 REFERENCE NOTE: For lists of common prepositions, see pages 107 and 109. For more discussion of prepositional phrases, see pages 240–244.

An object of a preposition may be compound, as in the phrase *between you and me*. To help you determine which pronoun form to use, read each form separately with the preposition.

CHOICES: Esteban wants to go camping with you and (*I*, *me*). [*With I* or *with me*?]

ANSWER: Esteban wants to go camping with you and **me**.

CHOICES: Please return these videotapes to Ms. Chang and (*he*, *him*). [*To he* or *to him*?]

ANSWER: Please return these videotapes to Ms. Chang and **him**.

CHOICES: Did you show your new CD player to (*he*, *him*) and (*she*, *her*)? [*To he* or *to him*? *To she* or *to her*?]

ANSWER: Did you show your new CD player to **him** and **her**?

STYLE NOTE   As a matter of courtesy, first-person pronouns are placed at the end of compound constructions.

EXAMPLES   Joel and **I** went to the movies. [compound subject]

Are the finalists in the chess contest Sarah and Gerald or Shi-ho and **I**? [compound predicate nominative]

Please call Annette and **me** when you get home. [compound direct object]

Whenever she's away on business, Mom sends Dad and **me** postcards every day. [compound indirect object]

Do you want to go with them or **us**? [compound object of a preposition]

4e. The objects of verbals are in the objective case.

EXAMPLES   Before the big swim meet, Mark shaved his head, making **him** more streamlined in the water. [*Him* is the direct object of the participle *making*.]

Protecting **them** is not enough; we must preserve the habitat of these unusual creatures. [*Them* is the direct object of the gerund *protecting*.]

I don't know whether Leonora wants me to bring **her** a memento. [*Her* is the indirect object of the infinitive *to bring*.]

 As you can see in the last example above, infinitives may have subjects. [*Me* is the subject of the infinitive *to bring*.] The subject and the predicate nominative of an infinitive are in the objective case. This usage is an exception to the rules given earlier in this chapter.

EXAMPLES   Did Mr. Withers ask **them** to work next weekend? [*Them* is the subject of the infinitive *to work*.]

No one expected the winner to be **her**. [*Her* is the predicate nominative of the infinitive *to be*.]

 REFERENCE NOTE: For more information about verbals and verbal phrases, see pages 246–255.

 QUICK CHECK 2   **Using Pronouns in the Objective Case**

Complete the following sentences by using personal pronouns in the objective case.

1. Would you please lend _____ and _____ the manual for the fax machine?

GRAMMAR/USAGE

2. Marcia drove _____ to the civic center.
3. Teammates like Dave and _____ can almost read each other's minds on the basketball court.
4. Please tell _____ the plans for the prom.
5. The small puppy stayed close behind the girls, following _____ all the way home.

The Possessive Case

The personal pronouns in the possessive case—*my, mine, your, yours, his, her, hers, its, our, ours, their, theirs*—are used to show ownership or relationship.

NOTE   In this book the words *my, your, his, her, its, our,* and *their* are called possessive pronouns. Some authorities prefer to call these words possessive adjectives because they are used to limit the meaning of nouns.

EXAMPLES   **My** watch is broken.
           His first public performance as a concert pianist was in 1968.
           Do you know **their** address?

Follow your teacher's instructions in labeling these words.

4f.   The possessive pronouns *mine, yours, his, hers, its, ours,* and *theirs* are used in the same ways that the pronouns in the nominative and the objective cases are used.

SUBJECT	Both your car and **mine** badly need tune ups.
PREDICATE NOMINATIVE	This yearbook is **hers.**
DIRECT OBJECT	We ordered **ours** yesterday.
INDIRECT OBJECT	Ms. Kwan gave **theirs** a quick look.
OBJECT OF PREPOSITION	My Siamese cat looks puny next to **yours.**

4g.   A noun or a pronoun preceding a gerund is in the possessive case.

A *gerund* is a verb form that ends in -*ing* and functions as a noun.

GRAMMAR/USAGE

EXAMPLES   We were all thrilled by **Joetta's** scoring in the top 5 percent. [*Joetta's* modifies the gerund *scoring*. Whose scoring? Joetta's scoring.]
Todd's parents objected to **his** working late on school nights. [*His* modifies the gerund *working*. Whose working? His working.]

NOTE   Do not confuse a gerund with a present participle, which is also a verb form that ends in *-ing*.

EXAMPLES   She nearly stepped on the **puppy** frolicking around her. [*Puppy* is modified by the participial phrase *frolicking around her.*]
We found **him** sitting on a bench in the park. [*Him* is modified by the participial phrase *sitting on a bench in the park.*]

STYLE NOTE   The form of a noun or pronoun before an *-ing* word often depends on the meaning you want to express. If you want to emphasize the *-ing* word, use the possessive form. If you want to emphasize the noun or pronoun preceding the *-ing* word, avoid the possessive form. Notice the difference in meaning between the two sentences in each of the following pairs.

EXAMPLES   Can you imagine **my** driving in the desert? [emphasis on *driving*]
Can you imagine **me** driving in the desert? [emphasis on *me*]

The **Glee Club's** singing of "Hail, Columbia!" got the most applause. [emphasis on *singing*]
The **Glee Club** singing "Hail, Columbia!" got the most applause. [emphasis on *Glee Club*]

   QUICK CHECK 3   **Using Pronouns with Gerunds and Present Participles**

For each of the following sentences, identify the *-ing* word as either a *gerund* or a *present participle,* and then choose the correct noun or pronoun in parentheses. Be prepared to explain your choices. [Note: A sentence may be correctly completed in more than one way.]

1. Hao didn't see the huge green wave until she felt (*it, its*) crashing over her shoulders.
2. I like my stepfather, but I just can't get used to (*him, his*) cooking.
3. The baby reached out to touch the shiny (*ribbons, ribbon's*) decorating the gift.
4. (*Him, His*) being sarcastic has ruined our chance to win the debate.
5. Did you mind (*me, my*) telling Denzel that you entered the essay contest?

Special Pronoun Problems

Appositives

An *appositive* is a noun or a pronoun placed next to another noun or pronoun to explain or identify it.

 REFERENCE NOTE: For more information about appositives, see pages 256–258.

4h. An *appositive* is in the same case as the noun or pronoun to which it refers.

EXAMPLES   My best friends, **Raúl** and **she**, have been nominated for class treasurer. [*Raúl* and *she* are in apposition with the subject *friends*. Since a subject is always in the nominative case, an appositive to a subject is in the nominative case.]

My grandfather paid the two boys, **Mario** and **him**, for raking leaves. [*Mario* and *him* are in apposition with the direct object *boys*. Since a direct object is always in the objective case, an appositive to a direct object is in the objective case.]

The deciding factor in this campaign has been the grassroots supporters, **we** who went door-to-door. [*We* is in apposition with the predicate nominative *supporters*. Since a predicate nominative is always in the nominative case, an appositive to the predicate nominative is also in the nominative case.]

To identify which pronoun form to use as an appositive, try each form in the position of the word it refers to.

CHOICES: Two juniors, Erin and (*she, her*), conducted the survey. [The appositive refers to *juniors,* the subject of the verb *conducted. She conducted* or *her conducted*?]

ANSWER: Two juniors, Erin and **she,** conducted the survey.

CHOICES: The survey was conducted by two juniors, Erin and (*she, her*). [The appositive refers to *juniors*, the object of the preposition *by. Conducted by she* or *by her*?]

ANSWER: The survey was conducted by two juniors, Erin and **her.**

NOTE Sometimes the pronoun *we* or *us* is followed by a noun appositive. To determine which pronoun form to use, try each form without the noun appositive.

CHOICES: On our field trip to the planetarium, (*we, us*) students learned many interesting facts about our solar system. [*We learned* or *us learned*?]

ANSWER: On our field trip to the planetarium, **we** students learned many interesting facts about our solar system.

CHOICES: The guidance counselor talked to (*we, us*) students about the requirements for graduation. [*The guidance counselor talked to we* or *to us*?]

ANSWER: The guidance counselor talked to **us** students about the requirements for graduation.

Elliptical Constructions

An *elliptical construction* is a clause from which words have been omitted. An elliptical construction often begins with the word *than* or *as.*

REFERENCE NOTE: For more information about elliptical clauses, see pages 273–274.

4i. A pronoun following *than* or *as* in an elliptical construction is in the same case as it would be if the construction were completed.

GRAMMAR/USAGE

ELLIPTICAL Keiko was more frustrated by the assignment **than he.**

COMPLETED Keiko was more frustrated by the assignment **than he was frustrated.** [*He* is the subject of the elliptical clause.]

ELLIPTICAL The assignment frustrated me as much **as him.**

COMPLETED The assignment frustrated me as much **as it frustrated him.** [*Him* is the direct object in the elliptical clause.]

Notice how the meaning of each of the following sentences depends on the pronoun form in the elliptical construction.

EXAMPLES I have known Leigh longer **than she.** [I have known Leigh longer *than she has known Leigh.*]
I have known Leigh longer **than her.** [I have known Leigh longer *than I have known her.*]

Did Mr. Chandra pay you as much **as I?** [Did Mr. Chandra pay you as much *as I paid you?*]
Did Mr. Chandra pay you as much **as me?** [Did Mr. Chandra pay you as much *as he paid me?*]

 QUICK CHECK 4   **Selecting Pronouns for Incomplete Constructions**

For each of the following sentences, add words to complete the elliptical clause. Include in the clause the appropriate pronoun form. Then tell whether the pronoun is a *subject* or an *object*. [Note: Some of the elliptical clauses may be completed in more than one way; you need to give only one option.]

1. No one else in my class is as shy as (*I, me*).

2. Can you whistle as loudly as (*he, him*)?
3. If you want to sell more raffle tickets than Bradley, you should call on more people than (*he, him*).
4. I am more interested in Spike Lee's films than (*she, her*).
5. Did Ms. Finn give them as much work as (*us, we*)?

Reflexive and Intensive Pronouns

Reflexive and intensive pronouns (sometimes called *compound personal pronouns*) have the same forms.

REFLEXIVE AND INTENSIVE PRONOUNS		
	SINGULAR	**PLURAL**
FIRST PERSON	myself	ourselves
SECOND PERSON	yourself	yourselves
THIRD PERSON	himself, herself, itself	themselves

A *reflexive pronoun* refers to another word that indicates the same individual(s) or thing(s).

EXAMPLES   I hurt **myself.** [*Myself* refers to *I.*]
These computers can repair **themselves.**
[*Themselves* refers to *computers.*]

An *intensive pronoun* emphasizes another word that indicates the same individual(s) or thing(s).

EXAMPLES   My grandfather and I restored the car **ourselves.** [*Ourselves* emphasizes *grandfather* and *I.*]
The weather **itself** seemed to be our enemy. [*Itself* emphasizes *weather.*]

NOTE   A reflexive pronoun is necessary to the meaning of a sentence. An intensive pronoun may be omitted from a sentence without a significant change in meaning. To determine whether a pronoun is reflexive or intensive, try removing it from the sentence.

EXAMPLES   The children decorated the gym **themselves.** [Since *The children decorated the*

gym makes sense, the pronoun is intensive.]

Let's treat **ourselves** to frozen yogurt.
[Since *Let's treat to frozen yogurt*
doesn't make sense, the pronoun is
reflexive.]

 REFERENCE NOTE: The words *hisself* and *theirselves* are
nonstandard usage. See page 46.

4j. A pronoun ending in *-self* or *-selves* should not be
used in place of a simple personal pronoun.

NONSTANDARD   Lupe and myself went to the ballet.
STANDARD   Lupe and **I** went to the ballet.

NONSTANDARD   Did Rosa make lunch for herself and yourself?
STANDARD   Did Rosa make lunch for herself and **you**?

Who and *Whom*

Like most personal pronouns, the pronoun *who* (*whoever*)
has three case forms.

NOMINATIVE CASE	who	whoever
OBJECTIVE CASE	whom	whomever
POSSESSIVE CASE	whose	whosever

These pronouns may be used in two ways: to form
questions and to introduce subordinate clauses. When they
are used to form questions, they are called ***interrogative
pronouns.*** When they are used to introduce subordinate
clauses, they are called ***relative pronouns.***

4k. The form an interrogative pronoun takes depends
on its use in the question.

Who is used as a subject or as a predicate nominative.
Whom is used as an object of a verb or as an object of a
preposition.

NOMINATIVE   **Who** played this role on Broadway? [*Who*
is the subject of the verb *played*.]

Who could it have been? [*Who* is the predicate nominative identifying the subject *it*.]

OBJECTIVE **Whom** did the president recommend? [*Whom* is the direct object of the verb *did recommend*.]

With **whom** did Moss Hart write the play? [*Whom* is the object of the preposition *with*.]

STYLE NOTE

In informal English, the use of *whom* is gradually disappearing. In formal speech and writing, though, it's still important to distinguish between *who* and *whom*.

4l. The form a relative pronoun takes depends on its use in the subordinate clause.

When choosing between *who* and *whom* in a subordinate clause, follow these steps:

STEP 1: Find the subordinate clause.

STEP 2: Decide how the relative pronoun is used in the clause—subject, predicate nominative, direct object, indirect object, or object of a preposition.

STEP 3: Determine the case for this use of the relative pronoun.

STEP 4: Select the correct case form of the relative pronoun.

EXAMPLE: Ms. Gonzalez, (*who, whom*) I greatly admire, operates a shelter for homeless people in our community.

STEP 1: The subordinate clause is (*who, whom*) *I greatly admire.*

STEP 2: The relative pronoun serves as the direct object of the verb *admire.*

STEP 3: A direct object is in the objective case.

STEP 4: The objective form of the relative pronoun is *whom.*

ANSWER: Ms. Gonzalez, **whom** I greatly admire, operates a shelter for homeless people in our community.

The case of the relative pronoun in a subordinate clause is not affected by any word outside the subordinate clause.

EXAMPLE: The prize goes to (*whoever, whomever*) is the first to solve the riddles.

STEP 1: The subordinate clause is (*whoever, whomever*) *is the first to solve the riddles.*

STEP 2: The relative pronoun serves as the subject of the verb *is*, not the object of the preposition *to.* (The entire clause is the object of the preposition *to.*)

STEP 3: A subject of a verb is in the nominative case.

STEP 4: The nominative form of the relative pronoun is *whoever.*

ANSWER: The prize goes to **whoever** is the first to solve the riddles.

EXAMPLE: We'll support (*whoever, whomever*) they nominate.

STEP 1: The subordinate clause is (*whoever, whomever*) *they nominate.*

STEP 2: The relative pronoun serves as the direct object of the verb *nominate.* The entire subordinate clause is the direct object of the verb *support.*

STEP 3: A direct object is in the objective case.

STEP 4: The objective form of the relative pronoun is *whomever.*

ANSWER: We'll support **whomever** they nominate.

 REFERENCE NOTE: For more information about subordinate clauses, see pages 264–267.

 NOTE When choosing between *who* and *whom* to begin a question or a subordinate clause, do not be misled by a parenthetical expression consisting of a subject and a verb, such as *I think, do you suppose, he feels,* or *they believe.* Select the pronoun form you would use if the expression were not in the clause.

EXAMPLES **Who** do you think will win the Super Bowl? [The clause *do you think* is paren-

thetical. *Who* is the subject of the verb
will win.]

**She is the one whom we believe they will
name Teacher of the Year.** [The clause *we
believe* is parenthetical. *Who* is the subject of the verb *will name.*]

 REFERENCE NOTE: For more information about parenthetical expressions, see pages 391–392.

 QUICK CHECK 5 **Using *Who* and *Whom*
Correctly**

For each of the following sentences, choose the correct form
of the pronoun in parentheses. Then identify its use in the
sentence—as a *subject*, a *predicate nominative*, a *direct object*,
an *indirect object*, or an *object of the preposition*.

1. (*Who, Whom*) was that on the phone just now?
2. Give the door prize to (*whoever, whomever*) buys the one-
hundredth ticket.
3. He is one person (*who, whom*) we could not do without.
4. (*Who, Whom*) did they choose for the role of Puck?
5. (*Who, Whom*) do you suppose won first place?

Shoe, by Jeff MacNelly, reprinted by permission:
Tribune Media Services.

Clear Pronoun Reference

A pronoun has no definite meaning in itself. Its meaning is
clear only when the reader knows what word it stands for.
This word is called the ***antecedent*** of the pronoun.

GRAMMAR/USAGE

4m. A pronoun should always refer clearly to its antecedent.

In the following examples, arrows point from the pronouns to their antecedents.

 REFERENCE NOTE: For more information about pronouns and antecedents, see pages 90–91 and 133–139.

EXAMPLES   The Pope asked **Leonardo** to do the sculpture, but **he** refused.

The math teacher gave **us** a problem that **we** couldn't solve.

After trying on the long blue **dress,** Mary said, **"This** fits perfectly."

Ambiguous Reference

4n. Avoid an *ambiguous reference,* which occurs when a pronoun refers to either of two antecedents.

AMBIGUOUS   Colleen called Alicia while she was doing her homework. [The antecedent of *she* and *her* is unclear. Who was doing her homework, Colleen or Alicia?]

CLEAR   While Colleen was doing her homework, she called Alicia.

CLEAR   While Alicia was doing her homework, Colleen called her.

AMBIGUOUS   The ship's officer explained to the passenger the meaning of the regulation he had just read. [The antecedent of *he* is unclear. Who had just read the regulation?]

CLEAR   After the ship's officer read the regulation, he explained its meaning to the passenger.

CLEAR   After reading the regulation, the ship's officer explained its meaning to the passenger.

CLEAR   After the passenger read the regulation, the ship's officer explained its meaning to him.

General Reference

4o. Avoid a *general reference*, which occurs when a pronoun refers to a general idea rather than to a specific noun.

The pronouns commonly used in making general references are *it, this, that, which,* and *such.* You can correct a general reference error by (1) replacing the pronoun with an appropriate noun or (2) rephrasing the sentence.

GENERAL   The wind rose, and dark clouds rolled in from the distant hills. This prompted the campers to seek shelter. [*This* has no specific antecedent.]

CLEAR   The wind rose, and dark clouds began rolling in from the distant hills. These ominous conditions prompted the campers to seek shelter.

CLEAR   As the wind rose and dark clouds began rolling in from the distant hills, the campers sought shelter.

GENERAL   More than 20 percent of students who enter college never graduate, which is a shame. [*Which* has no specific antecedent.]

CLEAR   That more than 20 percent of students who enter college never graduate is a shame.

 *QUICK CHECK 6* **Revising Sentences by Correcting Ambiguous and General References**

Revise each of the following sentences, correcting the ambiguous or general pronoun reference. [Note: Although these sentences can be corrected in more than one way, you need to give only one revision.]

GRAMMAR/USAGE

1. England invaded France in 1337. It began a series of wars known as the Hundred Years' War.
2. On California's San Miguel Island we had a guided tour by a ranger, which made the visit especially interesting.
3. My parents bought a new carpet and new curtains, and they hired someone to paint the walls and ceiling. That certainly improved the appearance of the room.
4. The loyal forces fought the guerrillas until they were almost entirely destroyed.
5. The police officer told the sergeant that she had lost a button from her uniform.

Weak Reference

4p. Avoid a *weak reference*, which occurs when a pronoun refers to an antecedent that has not been expressed.

You can correct a weak reference error by (1) replacing the pronoun with an appropriate noun or (2) giving the pronoun a clear antecedent.

WEAK	Every time a circus came to town, my sister Erin wanted to become one of them. [The antecedent of *them* is not expressed.]
CLEAR	Every time a circus came to town, my sister Erin wanted to become one of the troupe.
WEAK	Our dog Grover is jealous of my new baby sister. To help him get over it, I try to give him extra attention. [The antecedent of *it* is not expressed.]
CLEAR	Our dog Grover is jealous of my new baby sister. To help him get over his jealousy, I try to give him extra attention.
CLEAR	To help our dog Grover get over his jealousy of my new baby sister, I try to give him extra attention.
WEAK	He was a very superstitious person. One of these was that walking under a ladder would bring bad luck. [The antecedent of *these* is not expressed.]

CLEAR   He was a very superstitious person. One of his superstitions was that walking under a ladder would bring bad luck.

CLEAR   He believed in many superstitions. One of these was that walking under a ladder would bring bad luck.

CLEAR   He believed in many superstitions, one of which was that walking under a ladder would bring bad luck.

Indefinite Reference

4q. In formal writing, avoid the indefinite use of the pronouns *it, they*, and *you*.

An *indefinite reference* occurs when a pronoun refers to no particular person or thing. Such a pronoun is unnecessary to the meaning of the sentence. You can correct an indefinite reference error by rephrasing the sentence to eliminate the personal pronoun.

INDEFINITE   In the newspaper it reported that a volcano had erupted in the Indian Ocean. [*It* is not necessary to the meaning of the sentence.]

CLEAR   The newspaper reported that a volcano had erupted in the Indian Ocean.

INDEFINITE   In this history book, they refer to the American Civil War as the War Between the States. [*They* does not refer to any specific persons.]

CLEAR   This history book refers to the American Civil War as the War Between the States.

INDEFINITE   In some nineteenth-century novels, you will find the vocabulary quite difficult. [*You* has no clear antecedent in the sentence.]

CLEAR   In some nineteenth-century novels, the vocabulary is quite difficult.

NOTE   The indefinite use of *it* in familiar expressions such as *it is snowing, it is early,* and *it seems* is acceptable.

Use the word processor's search-and-replace function to locate all occurrences of the pronoun *it* in your writing. Every time the pronoun appears, check its reference carefully. Is the reference clear, or is it general or indefinite? If necessary, use the replace function to substitute a better word for the pronoun, or rewrite the sentence so that the pronoun has a clear reference. Use the same procedure to check your use of the pronouns *this, that, which, such, they,* and *you.*

GRAMMAR/USAGE

  QUICK CHECK 7

Revising Sentences by Correcting Weak or Indefinite Pronoun References

Revise each of the following sentences, correcting the weak or indefinite pronoun references. [Note: Although these sentences can be corrected in more than one way, you need to give only one revision.]

1. In Japan they have the world's tallest roller coaster.
2. In *The Diary of Anne Frank* it shows a young Jewish girl's courage during two years of hiding from the Nazis.
3. The pet-sitting service takes care of them when you can't.
4. When Grandpa was a child, you were supposed to be absolutely silent at the table.
5. They had whirled so fast it made them dizzy.

 *Chapter Review*

A. Proofreading a Paragraph for Correct Pronoun Forms

Identify each incorrect pronoun form in the following sentences, and then give the correct form. [Note: There may be more than one error in a sentence.] If a sentence is correct, write *C*.

GRAMMAR/USAGE

EXAMPLE   [1] Meriwether Lewis hired me when him and
                 William Clark set out to explore the
                 Louisiana Purchase.
            1. *him—he*

[1] My cousin John and me were proud to be included
in the group that went along with Lewis and Clark. [2] Us
cousins were jacks-of-all-trades; both of us did everything
from loading pack animals to building campfires. [3] For
John and I, one of the best things about the trip was getting
to know the other members of the group. [4] Someone who
we became good friends with was York, a strong, friendly
African American.   [5] Everyone, including myself, found
York to be one of the most valuable members of the expedition.   [6] Many people know that Sacagawea, a Shoshone
woman, was an interpreter on the expedition, but York was
just as valuable an interpreter as her. [7] In fact, communicating with Native Americans would have been practically impossible without both Sacagawea and himself.
[8] Whenever the expedition met with Native Americans,
Sacagawea would tell her French husband Charbonneau
what was said between her and them.   [9] Charbonneau
would then repeat the message in French to York, who
would translate the French into English for Lewis, Clark,
and the rest of we expedition members.   [10] When we
needed food and horses, York himself did much of the trading with Native Americans because him and them got
along very well.

B. Revising Sentences by Correcting Faulty
Pronoun References

Most of the following sentences contain ambiguous, general, weak, or indefinite references. Revise each faulty sentence. If a sentence is correct, write *C*. [Note: Although
sentences can be corrected in more than one way, you need
to give only one revision.]

EXAMPLE   **1.** Carl Sagan praised Stephen W. Hawking
                 after he wrote *A Brief History of Time*.
            1. *Carl Sagan praised Stephen W. Hawking*
                 after Hawking wrote A Brief History of
                 Time.

11. In the review of the book, it calls Hawking one of the greatest physicists of the twentieth century.
12. Hawking's 1988 book about physics and the universe became a bestseller, which was surprising.
13. Jamie told Rick that he should have read Hawking's chapter about black holes in space before writing his report.
14. Whenever Francine reads a good book about science, she wants to become one of them.
15. According to Hawking, Galileo was a talented science writer. One of these was the work *Two New Sciences*, the basis of modern physics.
16. In Hawking's book, you will find concepts about quantum mechanics, which can be difficult for nonscientists to understand.
17. In this magazine article on Hawking, they tell about his personal battle with motor neuron disease.
18. Because the disease affects his speech and movement, Hawking wrote his book by using a voice synthesizer and a personal computer on his wheelchair.
19. Even though Hawking carefully explains his theories on the thermodynamic and cosmological arrows of time, it still confuses some readers.
20. That Hawking apparently understands the applications of Einstein's theories to time and the universe does not seem astonishing.

5 USING MODIFIERS

Forms and Uses of Adjectives and Adverbs; Comparison; Placement of Modifiers

 Checking What You Know

A. Selecting Modifiers to Complete Sentences

Select the correct modifier in parentheses for each of the following sentences.

EXAMPLE   **1.** When you feel (*nervous, nervously*), take a deep breath and concentrate on relaxing images.
              1. *nervous*

   1. When Rosa and I had the flu, Rosa was (*sicker, more sicker*).

   2. As a student, Edmonia Lewis watched (*careful, carefully*) when her teacher demonstrated sculpting techniques.

   3. As you approach the next intersection, drive (*cautious, cautiously*).

   4. Our new car is roomier than (*any, any other*) car we ever had.

5. The leaders of the Underground Railroad acted (*quick, quickly*) to help runaway slaves.
6. If you look at the two kittens carefully, you will see that the smaller one is (*healthier, healthiest*).
7. It was obvious from his response at the press conference that the candidate had a very (*unusual, unique*) perspective on the budget deficit.
8. This movie is awful; it must be the (*baddest, worst*) movie ever made.
9. You will drive more (*steady, steadily*) if you keep your eyes on the road.
10. Don't you think Gerard's behavior seemed (*oddly, odd*) last night?

B. Revising Sentences by Correcting Faulty Modifiers

Most of the following sentences contain errors in the use of modifiers. Revise each faulty sentence so that its meaning is clear. If a sentence is correct, write *C*.

EXAMPLE   1. Carrie Green dreamed of touring Virginia's Historic Triangle while reading travel brochures.
          1. *While reading travel brochures, Carrie Green dreamed of touring Virginia's Historic Triangle.*

11. The Greens and the Alvarezes decided to visit the historic town of Williamsburg, Virginia, which has been painstakingly restored on the spur of the moment.
12. Decorated in colonial style, the two families registered at a quaint inn.
13. After resting for an hour or so, the Governor's Palace, the College of William and Mary, the Capitol, and many other sites were visited.
14. Joel Green quickly snapped a great shot of a candlemaker focusing his camera.
15. A tour guide at DeWitt Wallace Decorative Arts Gallery explained how eighteenth-century costumes were sewn.

16. The tour guide said when the families asked she would be happy to go into greater detail.
17. Dressed in colonial garb, a woman at the Raleigh Tavern asked the families to imagine how eighteenth-century residents may have spread news.
18. Having seen enough for the day, a quiet dinner at the inn was enjoyed by all of them.
19. Kevin dipped his spoon into a bowl of peanut-butter soup filled with great apprehension.
20. With fond memories and many photographs, the trip to Williamsburg will not soon be forgotten. ✓

What Is a Modifier?

A *modifier* is a word or group of words that limits the meaning of another word or group of words. The two kinds of modifiers are *adjectives* and *adverbs*.

 REFERENCE NOTE: For information on phrases and clauses used as modifiers, see **Chapter 6: Phrases** and **Chapter 7: Clauses.** For information on the placement of phrases and clauses used as modifiers, see pages 229–231.

One-Word Modifiers

Adjectives

5a. Use an *adjective* to limit the meaning of a noun or a pronoun.

EXAMPLES   Ross got a **perfect** score on the test. [*Perfect* limits the meaning of the noun *score.*]
Did you buy the **last** one? [*Last* limits the meaning of the pronoun *one.*]

An adjective may also limit the meaning of a gerund—a verbal used as a noun.

EXAMPLE   **Professional cake** decorating is one service that that bakery offers. [*Professional* and *cake* limit the meaning of the gerund *decorating.*]

 REFERENCE NOTE: For more information about gerunds, see pages 250–251.

As you can see from the examples above, adjectives are usually placed before the words they modify. For emphasis, however, adjectives may follow the word or words they modify.

EXAMPLE   The night, **clear** and **crisp**, was ideal for stargazing. [*Clear* and *crisp* modify the noun *night.*]

More than one adjective may modify the same word or words.

EXAMPLE   All I need is a **small, dependable, fuel-efficient** car. [*Small, dependable,* and *fuel-efficient* modify the noun *car.*]

 REFERENCE NOTE: See pages 95–100 for more about adjectives. For information about punctuating adjectives in a series, see pages 384–385.

A linking verb is often followed by a *predicate adjective*—a word that modifies the subject. The most common linking verbs are the forms of *be: am, is, are, was, were, be, been,* and *being.*

EXAMPLES   Our new computer system is **efficient.**
           The governor's comments on the controversial issue were **candid.**

 REFERENCE NOTE: For more about predicate adjectives, see pages 96 and 292–293.

 Some word-processing software packages include a thesaurus. Like a printed thesaurus, thesaurus software can help make your writing more precise by suggesting just the adjective you need. To make sure that an adjective offered by the thesaurus has exactly the meaning you intend, however, you should check the word in a dictionary.

Cathy copyright 1992 Cathy Guisewite. Reprinted with permission of Universal Press Syndicate. All rights reserved.

Adverbs

5b. Use an *adverb* to limit the meaning of a verb, an adjective, or another adverb.

EXAMPLES   Every morning my grandmother walks **briskly** for thirty minutes. [*Briskly* limits the meaning of the action verb *walks*.]

That dog does **not** look friendly. [*Not* limits the meaning of the linking verb *does look*.]

The jury believed that the defendant was **completely** innocent. [*Completely* limits the meaning of the adjective *innocent*.]

After working **remarkably** hard for several hours, Clarence figured out what was wrong with his computer program. [*Remarkably* limits the meaning of the adverb *hard*.]

As you can see from the examples above, adverbs can be placed either before or after the words they modify.

An adverb may also limit the meaning of a *verbal*—a verb form used as another part of speech.

EXAMPLES   Stopping **often** to ask for directions, we arrived at our destination more than an hour late. [*Often* limits the meaning of the participle *Stopping*.]

After **carefully** rolling out the dough, Katrina began cutting out different shapes with the cookie cutter. [*Carefully* limits the meaning of the gerund *rolling*.]

If Denzel wants Rhonda to forgive him, he needs to apologize **sincerely**. [*Sincerely* limits the meaning of the infinitive *to apologize*.]

 REFERENCE NOTE: For a discussion of verbals, see pages 246–255.

More than one adverb may modify the same word or words.

EXAMPLE   **Slowly** and **timidly,** my goldfish Fred approached the large snail that I had put in his bowl. [*Slowly* and *timidly* modify the verb *approached*.]

Most modifiers with an *-ly* ending are adverbs. Many adverbs, in fact, are formed by adding *-ly* to an adjective.

ADJECTIVES	perfect	clear	quiet	abrupt
ADVERBS	perfectly	clearly	quietly	abruptly

However, not all adverbs end in *-ly*.

EXAMPLES   often   too   quite   not
            very   so   again   seldom

 NOTE Some adverbs have two forms, one that is identical to the adjective form and one that adds *-ly* to the adjective form. As a rule, the longer form is preferred in formal writing. Occasionally, though, these forms have very different meanings.

EXAMPLES   Come here **quick**! [informal]
            I set the table **quickly** because dinner was almost ready. [formal]

            How **high** can he jump? [meaning "to a high level"]
            This novel has been **highly** praised. [meaning "very much"]

            The concert started **late**. [meaning "after it was supposed to"]
            Have you been to any concerts **lately**? [meaning "recently"]

REFERENCE NOTE: For more information about adverbs, see pages 104–106.

Some modifiers ending in *-ly* are used as adjectives.

EXAMPLES   **monthly** budget   **early** indication
            likely outcome

A few modifiers have the same form whether they are used as adjectives or as adverbs.

ADJECTIVES	ADVERBS
hard job	work **hard**
long wait	wait **long**
early arrival	arriving **early**

Adjective or Adverb?

5c. Linking verbs, especially the verbs of sense (*taste, touch, smell, feel, sound,* etc.) are often followed by adjectives. Action verbs are often followed by adverbs.

To help you determine whether a verb is a linking verb or an action verb, replace the verb with a form of *seem*. If the substitution sounds reasonable, the original verb is a linking verb and should be followed by an adjective. If the substitution sounds absurd, the original verb is an action verb and should be followed by an adverb.

EXAMPLES   Carmen looked frantic. [Since *Carmen seemed frantic* sounds reasonable, *looked* is a linking verb.]
            Carmen looked frantically for her class ring. [Since *Carmen seemed frantically for her class ring* sounds absurd, *looked* is an action verb.]

 REFERENCE NOTE: The following pairs of modifiers are frequently confused: *bad, badly; good, well; real, really;* and *slow, slowly.* For discussions of the correct uses of these modifiers, look up each pair in the **Writer's Quick Reference.** For more information about linking verbs and action verbs, see pages 100–103.

"This is Dr. Grumbacher, professor emeritus of comparative philology. Perhaps he could tell you the difference between an adverb and an adjective."

 QUICK CHECK 1 **Selecting Modifiers to Complete Sentences**

Select the correct modifier in parentheses for each of the following sentences. Then identify the word or words it modifies.

1. Stunned, the audience looked (*quick, quickly*) at the judge.
2. (*Slow, Slowly*), the damaged ship sailed to safe harbor.
3. These instructions do not seem (*clear, clearly*).
4. I heard the sound of footsteps (*soft, softly*) falling on the carpet.
5. (*Skillful, Skillfully*) fly-fishing requires great concentration.

Comparison of One-Word Modifiers

5d. *Comparison* refers to the change in the form of an adjective or an adverb to show increasing or decreasing degrees in the quality the modifier expresses.

The three degrees of comparison are *positive, comparative,* and *superlative.*

	POSITIVE	COMPARATIVE	SUPERLATIVE
ADJECTIVES	neat	neater	neatest
	careful	more careful	most careful
	optimistic	less optimistic	least optimistic
	good	better	best
ADVERBS	soon	sooner	soonest
	calmly	more calmly	most calmly
	commonly	less commonly	least commonly
	well	better	best

Regular Comparison

(1) Most one-syllable modifiers form the comparative and superlative degrees by adding *-er* and *-est.*

POSITIVE	COMPARATIVE	SUPERLATIVE
soft	softer	softest
big	bigger	biggest
clean	cleaner	cleanest
dry	drier	driest
long	longer	longest

NOTE There are some exceptions to the rule for one-syllable modifiers. Words such as *just, like, real*, and *wrong*

would be awkward or misleading to pronounce with the endings -*er* or -*est*.

EXAMPLE   In this story, the female characters seem **more real** [*not* realer] than the male characters.

 REFERENCE NOTE: For guidelines on spelling words with suffixes such as -*er* and -*est*, see pages 451–452. For information on determining the syllables in a word, see page 439.

(2) Some two-syllable modifiers form the comparative and superlative degrees by adding -*er* and -*est*. Other two-syllable modifiers form the comparative and superlative degrees by using *more* and *most*.

POSITIVE	COMPARATIVE	SUPERLATIVE
simple	simpler	simplest
likely	likelier	likeliest
cautious	more cautious	most cautious
freely	more freely	most freely

If you are not sure how a two-syllable modifier is compared, use a dictionary.

(3) Modifiers of more than two syllables form the comparative and superlative degrees by using *more* and *most*.

POSITIVE	COMPARATIVE	SUPERLATIVE
efficient	more efficient	most efficient
punctual	more punctual	most punctual
frequently	more frequently	most frequently
skillfully	more skillfully	most skillfully

(4) To show a decrease in the qualities they express, all modifiers form the comparative and superlative degrees by using *less* and *least*.

GRAMMAR/USAGE

POSITIVE	COMPARATIVE	SUPERLATIVE
proud	less proud	least proud
honest	less honest	least honest
patiently	less patiently	least patiently
reasonably	less reasonably	least reasonably

Irregular Comparison

Some modifiers do not follow the regular methods of forming the comparative and superlative degrees.

POSITIVE	COMPARATIVE	SUPERLATIVE
bad	worse	worst
far	farther *or* further	farthest *or* furthest
good	better	best
ill	worse	worst
little	less	least
many	more	most
much	more	most
well	better	best

STYLE NOTE   In formal English, the words *farther* and *farthest* are used to compare physical distance. *Further* and *furthest* are used to compare amounts, degrees, and abstract concepts.

EXAMPLES   How much **farther** is it to Asheville? [physical distance]
The effects of the new incinerator on the surrounding neighborhoods require **further** study. [amount]

NOTE   Like other modifiers, compound adjectives have comparative and superlative degrees.

POSITIVE	COMPARATIVE	SUPERLATIVE
foolhardy	foolhardier	foolhardiest
well-known	better-known	best-known

As you can see, one way that compound adjectives show comparison is by using the comparative and superlative degrees of one part of the compound. When such constructions prove difficult to pronounce or awkward to use, form the comparative and superlative by adding *more* and *most*.

POSITIVE	COMPARATIVE	SUPERLATIVE
footloose	more footloose	most footloose
worldly-wise	more worldly-wise	most worldly-wise

 REFERENCE NOTE: For more information about compound adjectives, see pages 96–97.

Uses of Comparative and Superlative Forms

5e. Use the comparative degree when comparing two things. Use the superlative degree when comparing more than two.

COMPARATIVE Although both puppies look cute, the **more active** one seems **healthier.** [comparison of two puppies]
After reading *King Lear* and *A Winter's Tale*, I can understand why *King Lear* is **more widely** praised. [comparison of two plays]

SUPERLATIVE Of the four plays that we saw, I think *Death of a Salesman* was the **most moving.** [comparison of four plays]

I sat in the front row because it provided the **best** view of the chemistry experiment. [comparison of many views]

NOTE In informal situations the superlative degree is sometimes used to emphasize the comparison of only two things. Avoid such use of the superlative degree in formal speaking and writing.

INFORMAL   Which was hardest to learn, French or Spanish?

FORMAL   Which was **harder** to learn, French or Spanish?

The superlative degree is also used to compare two things in some idiomatic expressions.

EXAMPLES   Put your **best** foot forward.
May the **best** person win.

Frank & Ernest reprinted by permission of NEA, Inc.

Problems with Comparative and Superlative Forms

Double Comparisons

A *double comparison* is the use of two comparative forms (usually *-er* and *more*) or two superlative forms (usually *-est* and *most*) to modify the same word.

5f.   Avoid double comparisons.

NONSTANDARD   This week's program is more funnier than last week's.

STANDARD   This week's program is **funnier** than last week's.

NONSTANDARD	In our school, the most farthest you can go in math is Calculus II.
STANDARD	In our school, the **farthest** you can go in math is Calculus II.
NONSTANDARD	This word-processing software is more better suited to our needs.
STANDARD	This word-processing software is **better** suited to our needs.

Illogical Comparisons

5g. Include the word *other* or *else* when comparing one member of a group with the rest of the group.

ILLOGICAL	Anita has hit more home runs this season than any member of the team. [Anita is a member of the team. Logically, Anita could not have hit more home runs than herself.]
LOGICAL	Anita has hit more home runs this season than any **other** member of the team.
ILLOGICAL	I think that Jean-Pierre Rampal plays the flute better than anyone. [The pronoun *anyone* includes Rampal. Logically, Jean-Pierre Rampal cannot play better than himself.]
LOGICAL	I think Jean-Pierre Rampal plays the flute better than anyone **else.**

5h. Avoid comparing items that cannot logically be compared.

ILLOGICAL	Ben has a new car that is as sleek and shiny as Eric. [Is Eric sleek and shiny? The sentence makes an illogical comparison between a car and a person.]
LOGICAL	Ben has a new car that is as sleek and shiny as Eric's **(car).** [The sentence compares Ben's car and Eric's car.]
ILLOGICAL	Our team's winning streak is longer than the John Tyler Lions. [The sentence makes an il-

logical comparison between a winning streak and a team.]

LOGICAL Our team's winning streak is longer than the John Tyler Lions' (winning streak). [The sentence compares our winning streak and the John Tyler Lions' winning streak.]

Incomplete Comparisons

5i. State both parts of a comparison completely if there is any possibility of misreading.

UNCLEAR I tutor Ryan more often than Isabel. [Out of context, the sentence is unclear because the elliptical clause *than Isabel* may be completed in more than one way.]

CLEAR I tutor Ryan more often **than Isabel does.**

CLEAR I tutor Ryan more often **than I tutor Isabel.**

UNCLEAR Do you see movies more often than your friend?

CLEAR Do you see movies **more often than your friend does?**

CLEAR Do you see movies **more often than you see your friend?**

👉 **REFERENCE NOTE:** For information about elliptical clauses, see pages 273–274. For a discussion of pronouns used in elliptical clauses, see pages 198–199.

5j. Include all the words necessary to complete a compound comparison.

A *compound comparison* uses both the positive and comparative degrees of a modifier. One common error people make with compound comparisons is to omit the second *as* in the positive degree.

NONSTANDARD The soloist from our school performed as well, if not better than, the one from Central High.

STANDARD The soloist from our school performed **as well as, if not better than,** the one from Central High.

To make sure a sentence contains all the words necessary for a compound comparison, try making a sentence using each part of the compound separately.

EXAMPLES   The soloist from our school performed **as well as** the one from Central High.

The soloist from our school performed **better than** the one from Central High.

 REFERENCE NOTE: For information about punctuating compound comparisons, see page 391.

Absolute Adjectives

A few adjectives express a quality that either exists completely or doesn't exist at all. As a result, these adjectives have no comparative or superlative forms; they do not vary in degree. Such adjectives are called *absolutes.*

Common Absolute Adjectives		
complete	equal	perfect
correct	eternal	round
dead	full	square
empty	impossible	true
endless	infinite	unique

NONSTANDARD   Of all my friends, Jill is the most unique.
STANDARD   Of all my friends, Jill is the **most unusual.**
STANDARD   Jill is **unique** among all my friends.

NONSTANDARD   I can't imagine a day more perfect than today.
STANDARD   I can't imagine a day being **any better** than today has been.
STANDARD   Today has been **perfect;** I can't imagine a day being better.

Absolute adjectives may be used in comparisons if the absolute is accompanied by *more nearly* or *most nearly.*

EXAMPLES   The frame Kim made is **more nearly square** than the one I made.

Of the three answers, Kim's was **most nearly correct.**

STYLE NOTE Throughout the years, the rules regarding absolute adjectives have changed, becoming alternately more and less strict. The trend nowadays is increasingly to allow comparisons of absolutes. One historical precedent for this usage occurs in no less than the preamble of the Constitution of the United States of America:

> We the People of the United States, in order to form a **more perfect** Union, establish Justice, insure domestic Tranquility, provide for the common defense, promote the general Welfare, and secure the Blessings of Liberty to ourselves and our Posterity, do ordain and establish this Constitution for the United States of America.

Follow your teacher's instructions regarding the use of absolute adjectives.

QUICK CHECK 2

Using the Comparative and Superlative Forms of Modifiers

The following sentences contain errors in the use of modifiers. Revise each sentence to eliminate the error.

1. Which is the most famous Russian ballet company, the Kirov or the Bolshoi?
2. When Barbara-Rose Collins served as a state representative in Michigan, my aunt thought that she fought harder than any representative for key legislation to help minorities.
3. Lucia has the most uncommonest hobby I've ever heard of—collecting insects.
4. The night before last, the worse snowstorm ever to hit the metropolitan area swept in from the frigid seas of the Arctic.
5. Of the three tennis teams, our partnership is the more nearly equal.

Placement of Modifiers

The placement of some modifiers affects the meaning of a sentence.

 Place one-word modifiers such as *even, hardly, just, merely, nearly, only,* and *scarcely* immediately before the words they modify.

EXAMPLES   The movie star **just** smiled at Miriam as he signed her autograph book. [He just smiled; he didn't speak.]
The movie star smiled **just** at Miriam as he signed her autograph book. [He smiled just at Miriam and at no one else.]
The movie star smiled at Miriam **just** as he signed her autograph book. [He smiled just as he was writing, not before or after.]

Only you should bring a number 2 pencil. [Only you—no one else—should bring a pencil.]
You should **only** bring a number 2 pencil. [You should only bring a pencil, not use it.]
You should bring **only** a number 2 pencil. [Bring a pencil and nothing else.]

Misplaced Modifiers

A modifying word, phrase, or clause that sounds awkward because it modifies the wrong word or group of words is called a *misplaced modifier.*

 Avoid using misplaced modifiers.

To correct a misplaced modifier, place the word, phrase, or clause as close as possible to the word or words you intend it to modify.

 REFERENCE NOTE: For more on phrases and clauses, see **Chapter 6: Phrases** and **Chapter 7: Clauses.**

MISPLACED   Even horses can sense when bad weather is coming. [The sentence is grammatically correct as written. However, the writer intended to imply that horses have many abilities, one of which is that they can sense approaching storms.]

CLEAR   Horses can **even** sense when bad weather is coming.

MISPLACED   They were delighted to see a field of daffodils climbing up the hill. [The participial phrase *climbing up the hill* is misplaced. They, not the daffodils, were walking up the hill.]

CLEAR   **Climbing up the hill,** they were delighted to see a field of daffodils.

MISPLACED   The anxious hunter watched the raging lion come charging at him while he readied a bow and arrow. [The adverb clause *while he readied a bow and arrow* is misplaced. The hunter, not the lion, readied the bow and arrow.]

CLEAR   **While he readied a bow and arrow,** the anxious hunter watched the raging lion come charging at him.

MISPLACED   Uncle Bill saw a dog chasing a cat while walking to the park. [The elliptical clause *while walking to the park* is misplaced. Uncle Bill, not the dog, was walking to the park.]

CLEAR   **While walking to the park,** Uncle Bill saw a dog chasing a cat.

Two-Way Modifiers

Avoid placing a phrase or clause so that it seems to modify either of two words. Such a misplaced modifier is often called a *two-way, or squinting, modifier.*

MISPLACED   The prime minister said in the press interview her opponent spoke honestly. [Did the prime minister speak in the press interview, or did her opponent?]

CLEAR   **In the press interview,** the prime minister said her opponent spoke honestly.

CLEAR   The prime minister said her opponent spoke honestly **in the press interview.**

MISPLACED   Aurora's mayor said when the city council met she would discuss the proposed budget.

CLEAR   **When the city council met,** Aurora's mayor said she would discuss the proposed budget.

CLEAR   Aurora's mayor said she would discuss the proposed budget **when the city council met.**

MISPLACED   The manager told the two rookies after the game to report to the dugout.

CLEAR   **After the game,** the manager told the two rookies to report to the dugout.

CLEAR   The manager told the two rookies to report to the dugout **after the game.**

 REFERENCE NOTE: For information about using commas with modifying phrases and clauses, see pages 386–390.

Dangling Modifiers

A modifying word, phrase, or clause that does not sensibly modify any word or words in a sentence is called a *dangling modifier.*

5m.   Avoid using dangling modifiers.

You may correct a dangling modifier by

■ adding a word or words that the dangling word, phrase, or clause can sensibly refer to
■ adding a word or words to the dangling word, phrase, or clause
■ rewording the sentence

DANGLING   Alone, the mountain is virtually impossible to climb. [*Alone* does not sensibly modify any other word in the sentence. Who or what is alone?]

CLEAR   **For a person alone,** the mountain is virtually impossible to climb.

CLEAR   The mountain is virtually impossible for a person to climb **alone.**

GRAMMAR/USAGE

DANGLING	Having selected a college, a trip to the campus was promptly planned. [The participial phrase *Having selected a college* does not sensibly modify any word in the sentence. Who selected a college?]
CLEAR	**Having selected a college,** my friend and I promptly planned a trip to the campus.
CLEAR	**After we selected a college,** my friend and I promptly planned a trip to the campus.
DANGLING	After winning the Pulitzer Prize for poetry, the novel *Maud Martha* was written. [The participial phrase *After winning the Pulitzer Prize for poetry* does not sensibly modify any word in the sentence. Who won the Pulitzer Prize?]
CLEAR	**After winning the Pulitzer Prize for poetry,** Gwendolyn Brooks wrote the novel *Maud Martha.*
CLEAR	**After Gwendolyn Brooks won the Pulitzer Prize for poetry,** she wrote the novel *Maud Martha.*
DANGLING	While correcting papers, the message came from the principal. [The elliptical clause *While correcting papers* does not sensibly modify any word in the sentence. Who was correcting papers?]
CLEAR	**While correcting papers,** the teacher received the message from the principal.
CLEAR	**While the teacher was correcting papers,** the message came from the principal.

NOTE   A few dangling modifiers have become standard in idiomatic expressions.

| EXAMPLES | **Generally speaking,** Americans today have a longer life expectancy than ever before. |
| | **To be honest,** the surprise party was rather boring. |

☞ REFERENCE NOTE: For information about using a comma after an introductory word, phrase, or clause, see pages 388–390.

QUICK CHECK 3 | **Revising Sentences by Using Modifiers Correctly**

The following sentences contain errors in the use of modifiers. Revise each faulty sentence so that its meaning is clear and correct.

1. Waiting at the bus stop, my older brother drove by in his new car.
2. I found a good book about Virginia Woolf written by her husband at a garage sale.
3. Mr. Martinez promised in the morning he would tell a Native American trickster tale.
4. To interpret this poem, a knowledge of mythology is helpful.
5. Louise projected the photographs on a large screen that she had taken at the zoo.

 Chapter Review

A. Using Modifiers Correctly

Most of the following sentences contain errors in the use of modifiers. If the sentence is incorrect, revise it to eliminate the error. If it is correct, write *C*.

EXAMPLE   **1.** Janine, who is the most brightest student in both physics and trigonometry classes, is also a whiz in chemistry.

     1. *Janine, who is the brightest student in both physics and trigonometry classes, is also a whiz in chemistry.*

1. After listening to "The Battle of the Bands," we thought that the jazz band performed even more better than the rock group.
2. When the treasurer presented the annual report, most of the statistics showed that the company had done badder this year than last.
3. The most impossible job I ever undertook was to find something in my brother's closet.
4. The more even you distribute the workload among the

group members, the more satisfied and productive
everyone will be.

5. In 1949, Jackie Robinson was voted the Most Valuable
Player in the National League.

6. Last night the weather forecaster announced that this
spring was going to be even more rainy than last
spring.

7. This is the most tasty piece of sourdough bread I have
ever eaten.

8. The ticket to New Haven is more expensive than
Hartford.

9. Because of a recent volcanic eruption, the sunsets have
looked wonderfully all month.

10. When she danced at the Paris Opera, American ballet
star Maria Tallchief was received enthusiastic by
French audiences.

B. Placing Modifiers Correctly

Most of the following sentences contain errors in the use of
modifiers. Revise each faulty sentence so that its meaning is
clear and correct. If a sentence is correct, write *C*.

EXAMPLE   1. Did you know that before they had computers, all newspaper layout work was
done by hand?

1. *Did you know that before they had computers, newspaper editors did all layout
work by hand?*

11. Computer whiz Kim Montgomery said in the computer resource center anyone can learn to master basic
desktop publishing.

12. To prove her point, the editor of the school newspaper
was asked to give desktop publishing a try.

13. Kim led Terri, a novice computer user, to an unoccu-
pied terminal with an encouraging smile.

14. In a short tutorial session, Kim emphasized the need to
practice adding, deleting, and moving paragraphs.

15. While looking over her shoulder, Terri hit various keys
to call up menus on the computer screen.

16. Terri sometimes stared blankly at the computer screen, not knowing what to do next.
17. In need of more information, the tutor was asked many questions by the pupil.
18. "To prepare professional-quality illustrations, a graphics package is what you need," Kim said.
19. Kim said when the computer sounded an error warning she would be happy to offer assistance.
20. Kim was pleased to see Terri confidently keyboarding information as she went to help another student.

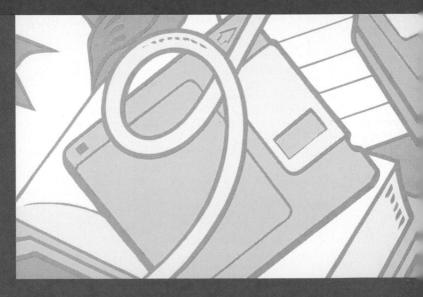

PART THREE

PHRASES, CLAUSES, SENTENCES

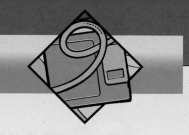

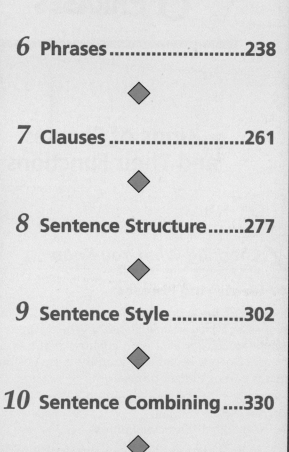

237

6 PHRASES

Kinds of Phrases
and Their Functions

✓ *Checking What You Know*

A. Identifying Phrases

In each of the following sentences, identify the italicized phrase as a *prepositional phrase*, a *gerund phrase*, a *participial phrase*, an *absolute phrase*, an *infinitive phrase*, or an *appositive phrase*. Do not separately identify a prepositional phrase that is part of a larger phrase.

EXAMPLE   **1.** *Smiling warmly,* they greeted us on our arrival.
            1. *participial phrase*

1. In Israel, farmers use innovative agricultural methods to meet the difficulties of *growing food in a desert country*.
2. *Her anti-slavery sentiments aroused,* Harriet Beecher Stowe wrote her now-famous novel to raise the country's consciousness.
3. Woodrow Wilson, *the U.S. President during World War I,* tried with his Fourteen Points to prevent another world war.

4. *In the Roaring Twenties,* the Teapot Dome scandal contributed to America's dissatisfaction with the presidency of Warren Harding.

5. During our vacation in Hawaii, we saw Mauna Loa, a volcano *rising six miles from the floor of the ocean.*

6. Thomas Nast, *a nineteenth-century illustrator and political cartoonist,* is famous for his numerous drawings of Santa Claus.

7. Withdrawing from the race, the candidate cited the following reasons for returning to private life: *her poor health and her desire to spend more time with her family.*

8. To conserve water, farmers water only the roots of plants, using a series *of underground irrigation pipes.*

9. *In a speech delivered to the graduating class,* the principal encouraged the graduates to improve the quality of life in our world.

10. *Using an opponent's strength against himself or herself* is the basis of the martial art jujitsu.

B. Identifying Phrases

Identify each italicized phrase in the following paragraph as a *prepositional phrase,* a *gerund phrase,* a *participial phrase,* an *infinitive phrase,* or an *appositive phrase.* Do not separately identify a prepositional phrase that is part of a larger phrase.

EXAMPLE   [1] Have you heard of Susan Butcher, *the four-time winner of the grueling Iditarod Sled Dog Race?*

         1. *appositive phrase*

[11] *A woman of rare determination,* Butcher raises her own dogs. [12] *Tucked away in the Alaskan wilderness not far from the Arctic Circle,* her kennel is a four-hour drive from the nearest grocery store. [13] Butcher believes that only when she is this isolated from society can she concentrate on *creating a tight bond with her 150 dogs.* [14] *For more than ten years,* she has raised huskies in her own unique way. [15] From the moment each puppy is born, she spends plenty of time with it *to get it used to her voice and her touch.* [16] She handles and talks *to the newborn puppy* fre-

quently and breathes on it so that it can also learn her scent. [17] *Growing closer and closer to Butcher,* the puppy is personally fed, trained, and even sung to and massaged by her. [18] When the puppy is four and one-half months old, Butcher begins *to train it in harness.* [19] By *showing the dogs her love for them,* Butcher gains the devotion needed to create championship teams. [20] The Iditarod, *1,130 miles of mountains, frozen seas, and snowy wilderness between Anchorage and Nome,* is the ultimate test of a dog team's devotion. ✓

What Is a Phrase?

6a. A *phrase* is a group of related words that is used as a single part of speech and that does not contain a verb and its subject.

VERB PHRASE	will commence [no subject]
APPOSITIVE PHRASE	the company picnic [no verb]
PREPOSITIONAL PHRASE	at two o'clock [no subject or verb]

The phrases above function as different parts of speech.

EXAMPLE **At two o'clock, the event of the year, the company picnic, will commence.** [*At two o'clock* functions as an adverb, *the company picnic* functions as a noun, and *will commence* is a verb.]

 REFERENCE NOTE: A group of words that has a subject and a verb is called a *clause.* For more about independent and subordinate clauses, see **Chapter 7: Clauses.** For more information on verb phrases, see **Chapter 3: Using Verbs.**

The Prepositional Phrase

6b. A *prepositional phrase* is a group of words consisting of a preposition, the *object of the preposition,* and any modifiers of that object.

The object of a preposition may be a noun, a pronoun, or a verbal.

EXAMPLES   The tall building **with the red roof** is our new library. [The noun *roof* is the object of the preposition *with.*]
Next to it is the old community hall, which is now being used for **entertaining.** [The pronoun *it* is the object of the compound preposition *Next to.* The gerund *entertaining* is the object of the preposition *for.*]

The object of a preposition may be a phrase or a clause.

EXAMPLES   The Johnsons didn't leave **until after eleven o'clock.** [The prepositional phrase *after eleven o'clock* is the object of the preposition *until.*]
Instead of rolling out the biscuit dough, Elaine dropped it by spoonfuls onto a baking sheet. [The gerund phrase *rolling out the biscuit dough* is the object of the compound preposition *Instead of.*]
The weather report advised people to take shelter **in whatever was available.** [The clause *whatever was available* is the object of the preposition *in.*]
The judges award the gold medal **to whoever accumulates the most points in all five events.** [The clause *whoever accumulates the most points in all five events* is the object of the preposition *to.*]

The object of a preposition may be compound.

EXAMPLE   *Brian's Song* is an inspiring story **about friendship and courage.** [Both *friendship* and *courage* are objects of the preposition *about.*]
The selection committee was impressed **by Lauren's volunteer work and her academic record.** [Both *work* and *record* are objects of the preposition *by.*]
After swimming all morning and sailing all afternoon, we decided to spend the evening

quietly playing cards. [Both *swimming all morning* and *sailing all afternoon* are objects of the preposition *After.*]

 REFERENCE NOTE: For lists of prepositions, see pages 107 and 109.

The Adjective Phrase

6c. An *adjective phrase* is a prepositional phrase that modifies a noun or a pronoun.

An adjective phrase tells *what kind* or *which one.*

EXAMPLES   Cassie Soldierwolf used a recipe very similar to that **of her ancestors** to make a batch **of fry bread.** [*Of her ancestors* modifies the pronoun *that,* telling *which one. Of fry bread* modifies the noun *batch,* telling *what kind.*]

An adjective phrase always follows the word it modifies. That word may be the object of another preposition.

EXAMPLE   Sarah Kemble Knight kept a journal **of her trip to New York.** [*Of her trip* modifies the direct object *journal. To New York* modifies *trip,* which is the object of the preposition *of.*]

More than one adjective phrase may modify the same word.

EXAMPLE   Sarah Knight's journey **on horseback from Boston to New York** was long and difficult. [The three phrases *on horseback, from Boston,* and *to New York* modify the noun *journey.*]

The Adverb Phrase

6d. An *adverb phrase* is a prepositional phrase that modifies a verb, an adjective, or an adverb.

An adverb phrase tells *how, when, where, why,* or *to what extent* (*how long* or *how far*).

An adverb phrase may modify a verb.

EXAMPLE   **During the Civil War,** Louisa May Alcott
worked **in a hospital as a nurse for six weeks.**
[Each phrase modifies the verb *worked.*
During the Civil War tells   *when, in a hospital*
tells *where, as a nurse* tells *how,* and *for six
weeks* tells *how long.*]

As you can see in this example, more than one adverb
phrase can modify the same word. The example also shows
that an adverb phrase, unlike an adjective phrase, can precede the word it modifies.

An adverb phrase may modify an adjective.

EXAMPLE   Louisa May Alcott wrote *Little Women,* a
novel rich **in New England traditions.** [*In New
England traditions* modifies the adjective *rich,*
telling *how* the novel is rich.]

An adverb phrase may modify an adverb.

EXAMPLE   Too late **for Alcott and other early suffragists,**
U.S. voting laws were changed to include
women in the process. [*For Alcott and other
early suffragists* modifies the adverb *late,*
telling *how late.*]

An adverb phrase may also be modified by an adverb.

EXAMPLE   Early **in June,** my family holds a big reunion
for all of our relatives. [The adverb *early*
modifies the adverb phrase *in June,* telling
when.]

NOTE   Be sure to place prepositional phrases carefully so
that they express the meaning you intend.

EXAMPLES   **On the bus,** I counted the children. [Both
the children and I were on the bus. The
adverb phrase *On the bus* modifies
counted and tells *where.*]
I counted the children **on the bus.** [I may
or may not have been on the bus, but
the children definitely were. The adjective phrase *on the bus* modifies *children*
and tells *which ones.*]

Prepositional Phrases Used as Nouns

Prepositional phrases are usually used as adjectives or adverbs. Occasionally, a prepositional phrase is used as a noun.

EXAMPLES   **Before rehearsal** is a good time to make the announcement. [*Before rehearsal* is used as a noun; it is the subject of the sentence.]

The kitten peeked out from **behind the sofa.** [*Behind the sofa* is used as a noun; it is the object of the preposition *from.*]

The best place to swim is **below the bridge.** [*Below the bridge* is used as a noun; it is a predicate nominative.]

STYLE NOTE   Prepositional phrases are handy for adding descriptive information to writing. Used excessively, however, these phrases can make writing wordy and stilted.

WORDY   With great haste, Marilyn grabbed her bag of books for school, pulled on her sweater made from Shetland wool, and moved with alacrity to the waiting school bus.

REVISED   Hastily, Marilyn grabbed her book bag, pulled on her Shetland wool sweater, and ran to the waiting school bus.

Whenever possible, try to replace prepositional phrases with more precise words.

COMPUTER NOTE   Do you use too many prepositional phrases in your writing? There's an easy way to find out, if you use a computer and have access to style-checking software. Use a program that will highlight prepositional phrases. Then, check each highlighted phrase in a piece of your writing to be sure that you have expressed yourself as concisely as possible.

SENTENCES

Overly thorough, lesser known Founding Father Clive Fishburne delivers his Preposition Proclamation.

 QUICK CHECK 1

Identifying Prepositional Phrases and the Words They Modify

Each of the following sentences contains a prepositional phrase. Identify each prepositional phrase as an *adjective*, an *adverb*, or a *noun*.

1. Duncan waited patiently, eating a bowl of oatmeal and raisins.
2. I got the twins ready for bed.
3. Heavy traffic on the highway delayed them.
4. Especially for the children, the mariachi band played "The Mexican Hat Dance."
5. Behind the sofa is the place to hide presents.

Verbals and Verbal Phrases

A *verbal* is a form of a verb used as a noun, an adjective, or an adverb. The three kinds of verbals are the *participle*, the *gerund*, and the *infinitive*.

A *verbal phrase* consists of a verbal and its modifiers and complements. The three kinds of verbal phrases are the *participial phrase*, the *gerund phrase*, and the *infinitive phrase*.

 REFERENCE NOTE: For more information on verbals, see pages 179–182.

The Participle

6e. A *participle* is a verb form that is used as an adjective.

There are two kinds of participles—the *present participle* and the *past participle*.

(1) Present participles end in *-ing.*

EXAMPLES   Esperanza has taken **singing** lessons for several years. [*Singing*, a form of the verb *sing*, modifies the noun *lessons.*]
Waving, the campers boarded the bus. [*Waving*, a form of the verb *wave*, modifies the noun *campers.*]
He felt himself **falling.** [*Falling*, a form of the verb *fall*, modifies the pronoun *himself.*]

(2) Most past participles end in *-d* or *-ed.* Others are irregularly formed.

EXAMPLES   The **baked** chicken with yellow rice tasted delicious. [*Baked*, a form of the verb *bake*, modifies the noun *chicken.*]
In your own words, define each term **given** in the first column. [*Given*, a form of the verb *give*, modifies the noun *term.*]
Confused and **frightened,** they fled into the jungle. [*Confused*, a form of the verb *confuse*, and *frightened*, a form of the verb *frighten*, modify the pronoun *they.*]

Because they are verbs, participles have different tenses and voices.

EXAMPLES   The **nominating** committee announced its choices. [present tense]

Nathan, **nominated** for treasurer, was pleased to accept. [past tense]

Having nominated only the best-qualified candidates, the committee members had done their job well. [present perfect tense, active voice]

Having been nominated, Nathan turned his attention to organizing his campaign. [present perfect tense, passive voice]

 REFERENCE NOTE: For more about the tense and voice of verbs, see pages 156–163 and 170–175.

Do not confuse a participle used as an adjective with a participle used as part of a verb phrase.

ADJECTIVE   Washington D.C.'s Vietnam Veterans Memorial, **designed** by Maya Ying Lin, was completed in 1982.

VERB PHRASE   Washington D.C.'s Vietnam Veterans Memorial, which **had been designed** by Maya Ying Lin, was completed in 1982.

 NOTE Some words that look like participles are actually adjectives.

EXAMPLES   cunning   willing   talented
rugged   unwashed   cold-blooded

If you are not sure whether a word is a participle or an adjective, look in a dictionary.

The Participial Phrase

6f.   A *participial phrase* consists of a participle and all of the words related to the participle.

Participles may be modified by adverbs and may also have complements.

EXAMPLES   **Speaking eloquently,** Barbara Jordan enthralled the audience. [The participial phrase modifies the noun *Barbara Jordan*. The adverb *eloquently* modifies the present participle *speaking*.]

Nodding his head, the defendant admitted his guilt. [The participial phrase modifies the noun *defendant*. The noun *head* is the direct object of the present participle *nodding*.]

We all laughed at the clown **juggling bananas.** [The participial phrase modifies the noun *clown*. The noun *bananas* is the direct object of the present participle *juggling*.]

Encouraged by his family, he submitted his book of poems for publication. [The participial phrase modifies the pronoun *he*. The adverb phrase *by his family* modifies the past participle *Encouraged*.]

Florence Griffith Joyner, **often called Flo Jo,** holds the U.S. national record for the women's 100-meter dash. [The participial phrase modifies the noun *Florence Griffith Joyner*. The adverb *often* modifies the past participle *called*. The noun *Flo Jo* is the direct object of *called*.]

Having caught the biggest fish, Pujari won the trophy. [The participial phrase modifies the noun *Pujari*. The noun *fish* is the direct object of the present perfect participle, *having caught*.]

When writing a sentence that contains a participial phrase, be sure to place the phrase as close as possible to the word it modifies.

MISPLACED   Singing in the trees, the explorers heard the birds walking along the path.

IMPROVED   **Walking along the path,** the explorers heard the birds **singing in the trees.**

 REFERENCE NOTE: For more information about misplaced or dangling participial phrases, see pages 229–232. For information about verbal phrases that are sentence fragments, see pages 314–315.

The Absolute Phrase

6g. An *absolute phrase* consists of a participle and the noun or pronoun it modifies. The entire phrase functions as an adverb and is used to modify an independent clause.

An absolute phrase has no direct grammatical connection with any word in the clause it modifies. Rather, the phrase modifies the independent clause by telling *why, when,* or *how.*

EXAMPLES   **Their ivory tusks being valuable,** elephants have been hunted almost to extinction.
[*Being valuable* modifies the noun *tusks.* The absolute phrase modifies the independent clause by telling *why* elephants have been hunted.]

The chores having been done, we can now go to a movie. [*Having been done* modifies the noun *chores.* The absolute phrase modifies the independent clause by telling *when* we can go.]

The tomcat next door kept us awake all night, **his yowls filling the night air.** [*Filling the night air* modifies the noun *yowls.* The absolute phrase modifies the independent clause by telling *how* the tomcat kept us awake.]

SENTENCES

 QUICK CHECK 2   **Identifying Participles and Participial Phrases and the Words They Modify**

Each of the following sentences contains at least one participial phrase. Identify each participial phrase and the word or words it modifies.

1. Known as Johnny Appleseed, John Chapman distributed apple seeds and saplings to families headed West.
2. Having been aided by good weather and clear skies, the sailors rejoiced as they sailed into port.

3. Searching through old clothes in a trunk, John found a map showing the location of a buried treasure.
4. Sparta and Athens, putting aside their own rivalry, joined forces to fight the Persians.
5. I would love to see it bursting into bloom in the spring; it must be quite a sight!

The Gerund

6h. A *gerund* is a verb form ending in *-ing* that is used as a noun.

SUBJECT	Mountain **climbing** is excellent exercise.
PREDICATE NOMINATIVE	Janetta's least favorite chore is **vacuuming.**
DIRECT OBJECT	She has always loved **dancing.**
INDIRECT OBJECT	He gave **studying** all his attention.
OBJECT OF PREPOSITION	In **cooking,** use salt sparingly.

NOTE Some words that look like gerunds are actually nouns.

EXAMPLES
clothing	wedding	understanding
roofing	ending	beginning

If you are not sure whether a word is a gerund or a noun, look in a dictionary.

Do not confuse a gerund with a present participle used as an adjective or as part of a verb phrase.

GERUND	I enjoy **reading** late at night. [direct object of the verb *enjoy*]
PRESENT PARTICIPLE	I sometimes fall asleep **reading** late at night.[adjective modifying the pronoun *I*]
PRESENT PARTICIPLE	Sometimes, I listen to classical music while I am **reading** late at night. [part of the verb phrase *am reading*]

NOTE A noun or a pronoun directly before a gerund is in the possessive case.

EXAMPLES **Rodrigo's** winning the contest surprised no one.
Mom was upset about **our** being late.

The Gerund Phrase

6i.   A *gerund phrase* consists of a gerund and all of the words related to the gerund.

Like participles, gerunds may have modifiers and complements.

EXAMPLES   **Exercising regularly** is important to your health. [The gerund phrase is the subject of the verb *is.* The adverb *regularly* modifies the gerund *Exercising.*]

My brother likes **working at the travel agency.** [The gerund phrase is the direct object of the verb *likes.* The adverb phrase *at the travel agency* modifies the gerund *working.*]

Walter Mitty daydreamed of **being a courageous pilot.** [The gerund phrase is the object of the preposition *of.* The noun *pilot* is a predicate nominative completing the meaning of the gerund *being.*]

An excellent way to build your vocabulary is **reading good literature.** [The gerund phrase is a predicate nominative explaining the subject *way.* The noun *literature* is the direct object of the gerund *reading.*]

 QUICK CHECK 3   **Identifying Participial Phrases and Gerund Phrases**

Identify the verbal phrase in each of the following sentences as a *participial phrase* or a *gerund phrase.*

1. Mary Shelley wrote *Frankenstein* after having had a nightmare about a scientist and his strange experiments.

2. Beginning with *Pippi Longstocking,* Astrid Lindgren has written a whole series of stories for children.

3. Marian Anderson was the first African American employed as a member of the Metropolitan Opera.

4. Fighting for women's suffrage was Carrie Chapman Catt's mission in life.

5. Mildred "Babe" Didrikson, entering the 1932 Olympics as a relative unknown, won gold and silver medals.

SENTENCES

Funky Winkerbean reprinted with special permission
of North America Syndicate, Inc.

The Infinitive

6j. An *infinitive* is a verb form that can be used as a
noun, an adjective, or an adverb. An infinitive
usually begins with *to.*

NOUNS **To fly** was an ambition of humans for many
centuries. [subject of *was*]
Some fish must swim constantly, or they start
to sink. [direct object of *start*]
Darius Freeman's dream is **to act.** [predicate
nominative identifying the subject *dream*]

ADJECTIVES Early attempts **to fly** were failures. [adjective
modifying the noun *attempts*]
The one **to ask** is your guidance counselor.
[adjective modifying the pronoun *one*]

ADVERBS With his dog Wolf, Rip Van Winkle went into
the woods **to hunt.** [adverb modifying the
verb *went*]
Everyone in the neighborhood was willing **to
help.** [adverb modifying the adjective *willing*]

 NOTE Do not confuse an infinitive with a prepositional
phrase that begins with *to.* An infinitive is a verb
form. A prepositional phrase begins with *to* and ends
with a noun or a pronoun.

INFINITIVES **To have** a friend, you need **to be** a
friend.
PREPOSITIONAL Please give one sample **to each** of
PHRASES the customers, and return the extras
to Rhonda.

Infinitives, like participles, have different tenses and voices. Helping verbs are added to the present infinitive to make these other forms.

EXAMPLES   **To see** film director Spike Lee is my cousin Jerome's greatest wish. [present tense, active voice]

Industry experts expect Lee's new film **to be seen** by millions. [present tense, passive voice]

By the time Jerome leaves New York, he hopes **to have seen** the director. [present perfect tense, active voice]

He was delighted **to have been seen** talking to his hero. [present perfect tense, passive voice]

 REFERENCE NOTE: For more about the tense and voice of verbs, see pages 156–163 and 170–175.

The word *to,* the sign of the infinitive, is sometimes omitted.

EXAMPLES   Let us [to] **sit** down.
Please make him [to] **stop** that noise.
We wouldn't dare [to] **disobey.**
Will you help me [to] **finish?**

The Infinitive Phrase

6k.   An *infinitive phrase* consists of an infinitive and all of the words related to the infinitive.

Like other verbals, infinitives may have modifiers and complements.

EXAMPLES   **To finish early** is our primary goal. [The infinitive phrase is the subject of the verb *is.* The adverb *early* modifies the infinitive *to finish.*]

Julia wants **to go to the beach with us on Saturday.** [The infinitive phrase is the direct object of the verb *wants.* The adverb phrases *to the beach, with us,* and *on Saturday* modify the infinitive *to go.*]

S E N T E N C E S

Napoleon's plan **to conquer the world** failed. [The infinitive phrase modifies the noun *plan.* The noun *world* is the direct object of the infinitive *to conquer.*]

Because of his sprained ankle, Chico was unable **to play in the football game.** [The infinitive phrase modifies the adjective *unable.* The adverb phrase *in the football game* modifies the infinitive *to play.*]

He did nothing but **waste time.** [The infinitive phrase is the object of the preposition *but.* The noun *time* is the direct object of the infinitive *(to) waste.*]

Hummingbirds' wings beat too rapidly **to be seen by the human eye.** [The infinitive phrase modifies the adverb *rapidly.* The adverb phrase *by the human eye* modifies the infinitive *to be seen.*]

The Infinitive Clause

6l. Unlike other verbals, an infinitive may have a subject. Such a construction is called an *infinitive clause.*

EXAMPLES The director of the theater has asked **Rebecca to star in the play.** [*Rebecca* is the subject of the infinitive *to star.* The entire infinitive clause is the direct object of the verb *has asked.*]

The sergeant commanded **them to march faster.** [*Them* is the subject of the infinitive *to march.* The entire infinitive clause is the direct object of the verb *commanded.*]

My friends and I want **the next president to be him.** [*President* is the subject of the infinitive *to be.* The entire infinitive clause is the direct object of the verb *want.*]

Notice in the last example that both the subject and the predicate nominative of an infinitive are in the objective case.

REFERENCE NOTE: For information about the objective case of pronouns, see pages 191–194. For more about clauses, see **Chapter 7: Clauses.**

STYLE NOTE — Words placed between the sign of the infinitive, *to,* and the verb create a *split infinitive.* Split infinitives are common in everyday speaking and writing but should be avoided in formal situations.

SPLIT	It's best to always tell the truth.
REVISED	It's best always **to tell** the truth.
REVISED	It's best **to tell** the truth always.
REVISED	It's always best **to tell** the truth.

Sometimes, however, it is necessary to split an infinitive to make the sentence clear.

UNCLEAR	To practice his signing regularly gives Ron confidence when he talks to people with hearing impairments. [Does *regularly* modify the verb *gives* or the infinitive phrase *To practice his signing*?]
CLEAR	**To regularly practice** his signing gives Ron confidence when he talks to people with hearing impairments.

SENTENCES

 QUICK CHECK 4 **Identifying Infinitives and Infinitive Phrases**

Identify the infinitive or infinitive phrase in each of the following sentences. Then tell whether it is used as a *noun,* an *adjective,* or an *adverb.* If the infinitive is used as a noun, decide whether it is a *subject,* a *direct object,* or a *predicate nominative.* If the infinitive is used as a modifier, give the word it modifies.

1. Swans and geese are fascinating to watch.
2. To land an American on the moon became the national goal of the United States during the 1960s.
3. Did you find that book difficult to understand?

4. Mom says I need to finish the dishes before I can go to the movies.
5. I did not have the time to watch the football game on television.

Appositives and Appositive Phrases

6m. An *appositive* is a noun or a pronoun placed beside another noun or pronoun to identify or explain it.

An appositive usually follows the word it identifies or explains.

EXAMPLES   We went to the Navajo Gallery in Taos, New Mexico, to see R. C. Gorman's painting ***Freeform Lady.*** [The noun *Freeform Lady* identifies the noun *painting.*]
Did Dan Namhinga complete *Red Desert,* **one** of his colorful acrylic paintings, in 1980? [The pronoun *one* refers to the noun *Red Desert.*]
Namhinga, a Hopi-Tewa **artist,** often paints abstract images of Hopi pueblos. [The noun *artist* explains the noun *Namhinga.*]
Can you believe that I **myself** plan to become a painter? [The intensive pronoun *myself* refers to the pronoun *I.*]

For emphasis, however, an appositive may come at the beginning of a sentence.

EXAMPLE   A younger **painter,** Jaune Quick-to-See Smith shows a deep awareness of her French, Cree, and Shoshone heritage. [The noun *painter* refers to the noun *Jaune Quick-to-See Smith.*]

Appositives are sometimes introduced by a colon or by the expressions *or, namely, such as, for example, for instance, i.e.,* or *e.g.*

SENTENCES

EXAMPLES
The homeless shelter is accepting donations of the following items: canned **foods, blankets,** and winter **coats.** [The nouns *foods, blankets,* and *coats* identify the noun *items.*]
Beneficial insects, such as **lady bugs** and **praying mantises,** can help control the population of harmful insects in a garden. [The nouns *lady bugs* and *praying mantises* explain the noun *insects.*]

NOTE An appositive can also be a verbal phrase or a noun clause.

EXAMPLES
I devote Saturday mornings to my favorite hobby, **cleaning my car.** [The gerund phrase explains the noun *hobby.*]
The winner, **whoever gets the highest score,** will receive a prize. [The noun clause identifies the noun *winner.*]

REFERENCE NOTE: For more information about noun clauses, see pages 268–269.

6n. An *appositive phrase* consists of an appositive and its modifiers.

EXAMPLES
We visited Boston Harbor, **the site of the Boston Tea Party.** [The adjective *the* and the adjective phrase *of the Boston Tea Party* modify the appositive *site.*]
The Kenai Peninsula is the home of the Alaska moose, **the largest deer in the world.** [The adjectives *the* and *largest* and the adjective phrase *in the world* modify the appositive *deer.*]
Our graduating class is planning to hold a reunion on Monday, January 1, 2001, **the first day of the twenty-first century.** [The adjectives *the* and *first* and the adjective phrase *of the twenty-first century* all modify the appositive *day.*]

An appositive phrase usually follows the word it explains or identifies but may precede it.

S E N T E N C E S

EXAMPLE   **A riot of colorful sights, intriguing aromas, and noise,** a Cairo bazaar is great fun for a tourist to visit.

 REFERENCE NOTE: For information on how to punctuate appositives, see page 390. For a discussion of the use of appositives, see pages 335–336.

 QUICK CHECK 5   **Identifying Appositives and Appositive Phrases**

Identify the appositive or appositive phrase and the word it explains or identifies.

1. Would you care to recite your poem "Block Party," Carlos?
2. These reptiles, natives of Africa, eventually found their way to North America.
3. A keen-eyed trouble-shooter, she quickly spotted the problem.
4. The task, designing a new filing system, should take about a month.
5. The botany club still needs specimens of the following leaves: persimmon tree, mango tree, and hawthorn.

 ## Chapter Review 1

A. Identifying Phrases

Identify the italicized phrase in each of the following sentences as a *prepositional phrase,* a *participial phrase,* a *gerund phrase,* an *absolute phrase,* an *infinitive phrase,* or an *appositive phrase.* Do not separately identify a prepositional phrase that is part of a larger phrase.

EXAMPLE   1. *Talking after the bell rings* is strictly forbidden.
                1. *gerund phrase*

1. *Working on the school newspaper* has taught me how to handle responsibility.
2. *Our flight delayed by the snowstorm,* we settled in for a long wait at the airport.

3. The Sunday newspaper's crossword puzzle is difficult *to complete correctly.*

4. If you want *to go to the concert tonight,* give me a call after school.

5. At the beginning of class today, we sang "La Marseillaise," *the French national anthem.*

6. Preserving rare and valuable books and documents is one of the challenges *facing the Library of Congress.*

7. *Startled by the knock at my door,* I lost my place in the book I was reading.

8. Franklin's history research report was on Booker T. Washington, founder *of Tuskegee Institute.*

9. Refreshed by the cool breeze, I didn't object to *going back to work.*

10. The United States has been greatly enriched *by many diverse cultures.*

B. Identifying Phrases

Identify each italicized phrase in the following paragraph as a *prepositional phrase,* a *participial phrase,* a *gerund phrase,* an *infinitive phrase,* or an *appositive phrase.* Do not separately identify a prepositional phrase that is part of a larger phrase.

By [11] *being elected to the Baseball Hall of Fame in 1953,* Charles Albert Bender became a symbol of pride for all Native Americans. Bender, [12] *born in 1883 in Crow Wing County, Minnesota,* was half Chippewa. "Chief," [13] *the nickname given to him by his teammates,* stuck with him throughout his career. [14] *Pitching for the Philadelphia Athletics* was his first job in baseball. Although he never played [15] *on a minor league team,* he pitched a four-hit victory in his first game. He won twenty-three games and lost only five during the 1910 season, [16] *the best season of his career.* [17] *During that same year,* he had an earned-run average of 1.58. If it was crucial [18] *to win a game,* Connie Mack, the Athletics' manager, would always send Bender to the mound. [19] *Finishing with a lifetime total of 212 wins and only 128 losses,* Bender led the American League three times in winning percentage. His last full active year as a pitcher was 1917, but he returned to the mound [20] *to pitch one inning for the White Sox in 1925.*

✓ Chapter Review 2

Writing Sentences with Phrases

Write ten sentences according to the following guidelines. In each of your sentences, underline the italicized phrase given, and tell what kind of phrase it is.

1. Use *whistling softly* as a participial phrase.
2. Use *to go* as an infinitive used as a modifier.
3. Use *with the green shirt* as an adjective phrase.
4. Use *with kindness* as an adverb phrase modifying an adjective.
5. Use *for me* as an adverb phrase modifying a verb.
6. Use *of fruits and vegetables* as an adjective phrase.
7. Use *the concert having been canceled* as an absolute phrase.
8. Use *diving into the pool* as a gerund phrase.
9. Use *to be happy* as an infinitive phrase used as a noun.
10. Use *a city in Mexico* as an appositive phrase.

7 CLAUSES

The Functions of Clauses

✓ Checking What You Know

A. Identifying Independent and Subordinate Clauses

Identify the italicized word group in each of the following sentences as an *independent clause* or a *subordinate clause.* Then classify each italicized subordinate clause as an *adjective clause,* an *adverb clause,* or a *noun clause.*

EXAMPLE
1. This novel, *which is the latest bestseller,* will be the perfect birthday gift for my mother.
1. *subordinate clause; adjective clause*

1. *If there is an increase in the amount of carbon dioxide present in the atmosphere,* plant growth also will increase.
2. *Many Americans believed in and supported the New Deal,* which was the political philosophy of Franklin D. Roosevelt.
3. *When you travel abroad,* you gain greater perspective on being American.

4. Amy thought *that "The Rockpile" was the best short story in our literature book,* and she asked the librarian to help her find other stories by James Baldwin.

5. *Since both of Len's parents are short,* Len doesn't expect to be tall.

6. The governor had to answer several questions about the budget *after he addressed the legislature.*

7. Please turn down that stereo *so that I can do my math homework.*

8. In 1981, Sandra Day O'Connor, *who had been an Arizona judge,* became the first female Supreme Court Justice.

9. Scientists are carefully monitoring *how much carbon dioxide is present in the atmosphere.*

10. *The Civil War, often referred to by southerners as the War Between the States, resulted in the deaths of more than 600,000 Americans;* it devastated the nation socially, politically, and economically.

B. Identifying Independent and Subordinate Clauses

In the following paragraph, identify each italicized clause as *independent* or *subordinate.* If the italicized clause is subordinate, tell whether it is used as an *adverb,* an *adjective,* or a *noun.*

EXAMPLE   [1] *When thinking of Native Americans,* many people immediately picture the Dakota Sioux.
            1. *subordinate—adverb*

Do you know [11] *why the Dakota spring to mind*? I think it is [12] *because they are known for their impressive eagle-feather headdresses.* Until recently, [13] *if an artist painted or drew Native Americans of any region,* the people were often shown wearing Dakota headdresses, fringed buckskin shirts, and elaborately beaded moccasins. Even paintings of the Pemaquid people meeting the Pilgrims [14] *as they landed on Cape Cod* show the Pemaquid dressed in the style of the Dakota, [15] *who lived far away in the northern plains region.* Artists apparently did not recognize [16] *that there are many different groups of Native Americans.* Each group has its own traditional clothing, and   [17] *the variety of Native American dress is truly amazing.* For example, [18] *the turbans and bear-claw necklaces of the Fox people are very different from the headbands and turquoise jewelry of the Navajo.*   [19] *While such images may not be familiar to you,* they are just as authentic as the image of the Dakota. To find out about other colorful and unique styles of dress, you might want to research the clothing worn by Native Americans [20] *that live in different regions of the United States.* ✓

7a.   A *clause* is a group of words that contains a verb and its subject and that is used as part of a sentence.

Every clause has a subject and a verb. Not every clause, however, expresses a complete thought.

SENTENCE	Lichens are small plants that are composed of both fungi and algae.
CLAUSE	Lichens are small plants. [complete thought]
CLAUSE	that are composed of both fungi and algae [incomplete thought]

There are two kinds of clauses: the *independent clause* and the *subordinate clause.* An independent clause that stands alone is a complete sentence. Like a word or a phrase, a subordinate clause functions as a single part of speech in a sentence.

 REFERENCE NOTE: The infinitive clause is discussed on page 254.

The Independent Clause

7b.   An *independent* (or *main*) *clause* expresses a complete thought and can stand by itself as a sentence.

EXAMPLES
$$\overset{\text{S}}{} \qquad \overset{\text{V}}{}$$
Ms. Martin explained the binary number system. [one independent clause]

SENTENCES

S
In the binary number system, each number
V
is expressed in powers of two, and **only the**
S   V
digits *0* and *1* are used. [two independent clauses joined by *and*]

S   V
The binary number system is important to
S   V
know because **it is used by computers.** [an independent clause combined with a subordinate clause]

NOTE An independent clause used by itself is called a sentence. The term *independent clause* is used only when such a clause is joined with at least one additional clause (either independent or subordinate) to make a sentence.

The Subordinate Clause

7c. A *subordinate* (or *dependent*) *clause* does not express a complete thought and cannot stand alone as a sentence.

EXAMPLES   that we collected last Saturday
what Hui Su named her pet beagle
when Rudy proofread his essay on Mark
Twain

The thought expressed by a subordinate clause becomes complete when the clause is combined with an independent clause.

EXAMPLES   Mr. Platero and I took the aluminum cans **that
we collected last Saturday** to the
recycling center.
Do you know **what Hui Su named her pet
beagle?**
**When Rudy proofread his essay on Mark
Twain,** he found several typographical errors.

 QUICK CHECK 1 **Identifying Independent and Subordinate Clauses**

Identify each word group as either an *independent clause* or a *subordinate clause*.

1. since I was angry about an article in the newspaper
2. I decided to write a letter to the editor
3. as I spelled out my objections and countered the article's reasoning
4. I began to see the other point of view
5. that moment was the beginning of my true thinking on the subject

The Adjective Clause

7d. An *adjective clause* is a subordinate clause that modifies a noun or a pronoun.

An adjective clause always follows the word or words that it modifies.

EXAMPLES In the 1930s, Dr. Charles Richter devised a scale **that is used to measure the magnitude of earthquakes.** [The adjective clause modifies the noun *scale*.]

Ferdinand Magellan, **who was the commander of the first expedition around the world**, was killed before the end of the journey. [The adjective clause modifies the noun *Ferdinand Magellan*.]

Didn't John Kieran once say, "I am a part of all **that I have read**"? [The adjective clause modifies the pronoun *all*.]

Relative Pronouns

Usually, an adjective clause begins with a *relative pronoun*—a word that relates an adjective clause to the word or words the clause modifies.

Relative Pronouns				
that	which	who	whom	whose

A relative pronoun
- refers to its antecedent—a preceding noun or pronoun
- connects the adjective clause with the rest of the sentence
- performs a function within its own clause by serving as a subject, an object of a verb, an object of a preposition, or a modifier in the adjective clause

EXAMPLES   Grandma Moses, **who began painting at the age of seventy-six,** became famous for her primitive style of art. [The relative pronoun *who* relates the adjective clause to the noun *Grandma Moses* and serves as the subject of the verb *began*.]

I have read nearly every novel **that Shirley Ann Grau has written.** [The relative pronoun *that* relates the adjective clause to the noun *novel* and serves as the direct object of the verb *has written*.]

The treasure **for which Dr. Diaz-Paraguas and her crew are searching** belonged to the Aztec emperor Montezuma II. [The relative pronoun *which* relates the adjective clause to the noun *treasure* and serves as the object of the preposition *for*.]

Those two movie critics, the ones with the television show, are the only ones **whose opinions he values.** [The relative pronoun *whose* relates the clause to its pronoun antecedent *ones* and modifies the noun *opinions* by showing possession.]

An adjective clause may begin with a relative adverb, such as *when* or *where*.

EXAMPLES   Uncle Chim told Lori and me about the time **when he backpacked across the island of Luzon.** [The adjective clause modifies the noun *time*.]
From 1914 to 1931, Isak Dinesen lived in Kenya, **where she operated a coffee plantation.** [The adjective clause modifies the noun *Kenya*.]

Sometimes the relative pronoun or relative adverb is not expressed, but its meaning is understood.

EXAMPLES   The book **[that] I am reading** is a biography of Harriet Tubman.

We will never forget the wonderful summer **[when] we stayed with our grandparents in Mayagüez, Puerto Rico.**

Depending on how it is used, an adjective clause is either essential or nonessential. An *essential clause* provides information that is necessary to the meaning of a sentence. A *nonessential clause* provides additional information that can be omitted without changing the meaning of a sentence. A nonessential clause is always set off by commas.

ESSENTIAL   Students **who are going to the track meet** can take the bus at 7:45 A.M. [Omitting the adjective clause would change the meaning of the sentence.]

NONESSENTIAL   Austin Stevens, **whose mother is a pediatrician,** plans to study medicine. [The adjective clause gives extra information. Omitting the clause would not affect the meaning of the sentence.]

 REFERENCE NOTE: For more about punctuating nonessential clauses, see pages 386–388.

 QUICK CHECK 2   **Identifying Adjective Clauses and the Words They Modify**

Identify the adjective clause in each of the following sentences, and give the noun or pronoun that it modifies. Then tell whether the relative pronoun is used as the *subject*, the *direct object*, an *object of a preposition,* or a *modifier* in the adjective clause.

1. Some of us have read *Native Son*, which was written by Richard Wright.
2. The fish that I caught yesterday weighed three pounds.
3. Please indicate the people to whom we should go for help.

4. The guide advised those who enjoy Native American art to visit the new exhibit of Hopi weaving and pottery.
5. The mare, whose colt grazed nearby, cantered over to greet us.

The Noun Clause

7e. A noun clause is a subordinate clause used as a noun.

A noun clause may be used as a subject, a predicate nominative, a direct object, an indirect object, an object of a preposition, or an object of a verbal.

SUBJECT **That Ntozake Shange is a talented writer** is an understatement.

PREDICATE NOMINATIVE A catchy slogan is **what we need for this campaign.**

DIRECT OBJECT The Greek astronomer Ptolemy believed **that the sun orbited the earth.**

INDIRECT OBJECT The choreographer will give **whoever can dance the best** the role of Snow Princess.

OBJECT OF A PREPOSITION Grandmother Gutiérrez has a kind word for **whomever she meets.**

OBJECT OF A VERBAL Learning **how early hunters made stone tools** was the best part of the demonstration.

NOTE Another type of noun clause is an appositive clause. Don't confuse an appositive clause with an adjective clause. An adjective clause modifies another word. An appositive clause identifies or explains the noun or pronoun beside it.

EXAMPLES Jason's dream **that he will someday win an Olympic medal** motivates him to train hard. [The appositive clause identifies *dream.*]
The dream **that Jason treasures most** is to win an Olympic medal. [The adjective clause modifies *dream* without identifying it.]

Common Introductory Words for Noun Clauses		
how	where	whoever
that	wherever	whom
what	whether	whomever
whatever	which	whose
when	whichever	why
whenever	who	

The word that introduces a noun clause may or may not have another function in the clause.

EXAMPLES   Do you know **who painted *Washington Crossing the Delaware*?** [The word *who* introduces the noun clause and serves as the subject of the verb *painted*.]

Ms. Picard, an environmentalist, will explain **what the greenhouse effect is.** [The word *what* introduces the noun clause and serves as the predicate nominative to complete the meaning of the verb *is*.]

She said **that she would be late.** [The word *that* introduces the noun clause but does not have any function within the noun clause.]

The word that introduces a noun clause is not always expressed. Sometimes, its meaning is understood.

EXAMPLES   I think [that] **we took a wrong turn**.

Do scientists know for sure [that or whether] **the universe is expanding?**

 QUICK CHECK 3   **Identifying Noun Clauses**

Identify the noun clause in each of the following sentences. Tell whether the noun clause is a *subject*, a *direct object*, an *indirect object*, a *predicate nominative,* or an *object of a preposition.*

1. I will listen carefully to whatever you say.
2. Give whoever wants one a free pass.

3. That Jill was worried seemed obvious to us all.
4. The teacher said that we could leave now.
5. A remote desert island was where the pirates buried their treasure.

The Adverb Clause

7f. An *adverb clause* is a subordinate clause that modifies a verb, an adjective, or an adverb.

Unlike an adjective clause, an adverb clause may come before or after the word or words it modifies. An adverb clause tells *how, when, where, why, to what extent,* or *under what condition.*

EXAMPLES The pitcher felt **as though all eyes were on her.** [The adverb clause modifies the verb *felt*, telling *how* the pitcher felt.]
Frédéric Chopin made his debut as a concert pianist **when he was eight years old.** [The adverb clause modifies the verb *made*, telling *when* Chopin made his debut.]
Ariel takes his new camera **wherever he goes.** [The adverb clause modifies the verb *takes*, telling *where* Ariel takes his new camera.]
At first, communicating with my deaf friend was hard **because I did not know how to sign.** [The adverb clause modifies the adjective *hard*, telling *why* communicating was hard.]
Zoë can explain the theory of relativity to you better **than I can.** [The adverb clause modifies the adverb *better*, telling *to what extent* Zoë can better explain the theory of relativity.]
If we leave now, we will avoid the rush-hour traffic. [The adverb clause modifies the verb *will avoid*, telling *under what condition* we will avoid the traffic.]

NOTE An adverb clause that begins a sentence is set off by a comma.

REFERENCE NOTE: For more about punctuating adverb clauses, see page 390.

An adverb clause can also modify a verbal.

EXAMPLES   Taken **after the Ennisville Eagles won the championship game,** the photo shows a group of tired, sweaty, and very happy young men. [The adverb clause modifies the participle *taken.*]

Blaming the bat or the pitch **when you hit a foul ball** doesn't make a great deal of sense. [The adverb clause modifies the gerund *blaming.*]

Rachel has promised to mow the lawn **as soon as she finishes practicing her layup shot.** [The adverb clause modifies the infinitive *to mow.*]

 REFERENCE NOTE: For more information about verbals and verbal phrases, see pages 246–255.

 Because an adverb clause does not have a fixed location in a sentence, the writer must choose where to put the clause. The "best" place for it is usually a matter of personal taste and style, but often the placement is determined by the context. If you use a computer, you can easily experiment with the placement of adverb clauses in sentences. Print out different versions of the sentence containing the adverb clause, along with the sentences that immediately precede and follow it. Read each version aloud to see how the placement of the clause affects the flow, rhythm, and overall meaning of the passage.

Subordinating Conjunctions

An adverb clause is introduced by a *subordinating conjunction*—a word or word group that relates the adverb clause to the word or words the clause modifies. Subordinating conjunctions show relationships of time, manner, cause, place, comparison, condition, or purpose.

COMMONLY USED SUBORDINATING CONJUNCTIONS	
TIME	after, as, as long as, as soon as, before, since, until, when, whenever, while
MANNER	as, as if, as though
CAUSE	because, since, that
PLACE	where, wherever
COMPARISON	as, as much as, than
CONDITION	although, as long as, even if, even though, if, provided that, though, unless, while
PURPOSE	in order that, so that

 REFERENCE NOTE: The words *after, as, before, since,* and *until* may also be used as prepositions. See page 107.

STYLE NOTE In casual conversation, native speakers of English regularly use inexact or nonstandard forms of subordinating conjunctions. Such usage is appropriate in conversation for two reasons: (1) the context of the conversation makes the inexact form clear, and (2) the participants likely agree on the meanings of any nonstandard forms. In most writing and in formal speaking situations, however, such usage should be avoided.

EXAMPLES   I can see **why** [*not* where] your feelings might be hurt by his remark.
Do it **because** [*not* 'cause] I said so.
She acted **as though** [*not* like] it was the end of the world.

 NOTE Some of the words that introduce adverb clauses may also introduce adjective clauses and noun clauses. To determine what type of clause the introductory word introduces, look at how the clause is used in the sentence.

ADJECTIVE CLAUSE	On the day when we first met, I knew we'd soon be good friends. [The clause modifies the noun *day*.]
NOUN CLAUSE	Do you remember when we first met? [The clause is the direct object of the verb *remember*.]
ADVERB CLAUSE	We were in seventh grade when we first met. [The clause modifies the verb *were*.]

The Elliptical Clause

7g. Part of a clause may be left out when the meaning can be understood from the context of the sentence. Such a clause is called an *elliptical clause.*

Most elliptical clauses are adverb clauses. In each of the adverb clauses in the following examples, the part given in brackets may be omitted because its meaning is clearly understood.

EXAMPLES   Roger knew the rules better **than Elgin** [did].
While [he was] **painting,** Rembrandt concentrated completely on his work.
If I can save enough money, I'll buy a car. **If** [I can] **not,** I'll buy a mountain bike.
Gerald may ride with us **if he wants to** [ride with us].
Whenever [it is] **necessary,** Beth takes the package to the express-delivery office herself.
The pot roast is tasty **though** [it is] **a bit dry.**
Kristine's costume is much more elaborate **than Michael's** [costume is].

Often the meaning of an elliptical clause depends on the form of the pronoun in it.

EXAMPLES   I play duets with Ramona **as often as he** [plays duets with Ramona].
I play duets with Ramona **as often as** [I play duets with] **him.**

REFERENCE NOTE: For more about the correct use of pronouns in elliptical clauses, see pages 198–199. For information about making logical comparisons, see pages 225–226.

Hagar the Horrible reprinted with special permission of King Features Syndicate, Inc.

 QUICK CHECK 4   **Identifying Adverb Clauses and the Words They Modify**

Identify the adverb clause in each of the following sentences, and give the word or words that the clause modifies. Then state whether the clause tells *how, when, where, why, to what extent,* or *under what condition.* [Note: If a clause is elliptical, be prepared to supply the omitted word or words.]

1. When we have a fire drill, we all must go outside.
2. Gazelles need to be able to run fast so that they can escape their enemies.
3. Return this revolutionary, new, sonic potato peeler for a full refund if not completely satisfied.
4. You understand the situation much better than I.
5. Reading while the doctor was busy, I did not mind the wait.

✓ *Chapter Review*

A. Identifying Independent and Subordinate Clauses

Identify the italicized clause in each of the following sentences as *independent* or *subordinate.* If the italicized clause is subordinate, tell whether it is used as an *adverb*, an *adjective*, or a *noun*.

EXAMPLE 1. Miguel and Bette, *who were visiting us over the weekend*, have returned to Rhode Island.
1. *subordinate; adjective*

1. *Whenever Jorge practices the clarinet,* his neighbor's beagle howls.
2. Advertisements encourage people to want products, and *many people cannot distinguish between their wants and their needs.*
3. In science class we learned *that chalk is made up mostly of calcium carbonate.*
4. Liliuokalani, *who was the last queen of Hawaii,* was an accomplished songwriter.
5. Does each of you know how you can protect yourself *if a tornado strikes*?
6. *If there is a tornado warning,* go quickly to the lowest level in your house or apartment, cover your head with your hands, and lie flat or crouch low until the danger is past.
7. The Native Americans *who inhabited the area of Connecticut around the Naugatuck River* were called the Pequots.
8. *When you enter the school,* you will find the principal's office on your right.
9. *That the girls' volleyball team was well coached* was clearly demonstrated last night when the team won the state championship.
10. *American music has been enriched by Ella Fitzgerald, Sarah Vaughan, and Lena Horne,* who are all famous African American vocalists.

B. Identifying and Classifying Subordinate Clauses

Identify the subordinate clause or clauses in each of the following sentences. Tell whether each one is used as an *adjective*, a *noun*, or an *adverb*.

SENTENCES

11. In general, national monuments cover a relatively small area, although Death Valley National Monument and Glacier Bay National Monument are exceptions.

12. Fort Laramie, which is called a national historic site, was first a fur-trading post and later an army post.

13. The White House is in a category of its own, since nothing else in the United States is really similar to it.

14. The Appalachian Trail is what is known as a national scenic trail.

15. When area alone is considered, the most awesome tract is the 6.5-million-acre (2,630,550-hectare) Noatak National Preserve in Alaska.

16. At the other extreme is the Benjamin Franklin statue that stands in the rotunda of Philadelphia's Franklin Institute.

17. That this statue is in a museum of science is a tribute to Franklin's wide-ranging scientific interests.

18. Everyone who goes to Philadelphia should also see Independence National Historical Park, "America's most historic square mile."

19. The bureau administers a number of parks in which famous Revolutionary and Civil War battles were fought.

20. Perhaps the most famous of all the battlefields is Gettysburg, which is located in Pennsylvania.

Subjects, Predicates, Complements; Types of Sentences

 Checking What You Know

A. Identifying Subjects, Verbs, and Complements

Identify the italicized word or word group in each of the following sentences as a *subject,* a *verb,* a *direct object,* an *indirect object,* a *predicate nominative,* or a *predicate adjective.*

EXAMPLE   1. Computers *have provided* work and play in today's world.
            1. *verb*

1. Frances Perkins, the first woman in the history of the United States to hold a Cabinet post, was *secretary of labor* during Franklin Roosevelt's administration.
2. Thanks to my "green thumb," these squash *plants* are spreading vines and fruits all over the garden!
3. Did Kimi write *you* a letter about her trip to Norway?

4. Since the ballots have not yet been counted, the names of next year's class representatives are not *available* yet.

5. At the end of World War I, the United States signed separate peace *treaties* with Germany, Austria, and Hungary.

6. Please bring *me* the hacksaw and two pipe wrenches from the garage.

7. Edward MacDowell's orchestral work based on Iroquois, Dakota, Chippewa, and Kiowa melodies *was performed* for the first time in 1896.

8. Martin Luther King, Jr., a nonviolent activist and civil rights leader, was a *recipient* of the Nobel Prize for peace.

9. Do *you* know that the difference between wasps and bees is that wasps have long bodies and slim waists?

10. How stirringly *Sidney Poitier* portrayed Justice Thurgood Marshall!

B. Classifying Sentences According to Purpose

Classify each sentence in Part A as *declarative, interrogative, imperative,* or *exclamatory.*

EXAMPLE   1. Computers have provided work and play in today's world.
            1. *declarative*

C. Classifying Sentences According to Structure

Classify each of the following sentences as *simple, compound, complex,* or *compound-complex.*

21. A familiar proverb states that the longest journey begins with a single step; another tells us that little strokes fell great oaks.

22. Many people have heard these wise sayings but haven't applied the sayings to their own lives.

23. For example, suppose you are required to read a 400-page novel before a test at the end of the school year.

24. If you don't start reading the book until the last possible weekend, you will probably not read it well; furthermore, you may not have time to finish the book, and you will almost certainly not enjoy it!

25. Instead, if you start early and read just ten pages a day, you'll be finished within six weeks. ✓

Sentence or Fragment?

8a. A *sentence* is a group of words that expresses a complete thought.

A thought is complete when it makes sense by itself.

EXAMPLES   The weary executive had left her briefcase on the commuter train.

For how many years was Winston Churchill the prime minister of England?

What extraordinary courage the early settlers must have had!

As you can see, a sentence begins with a capital letter and ends with a period, a question mark, or an exclamation point.

 REFERENCE NOTE: For information on the different types of sentences, see pages 294–296 and 297–298. See pages 377–380 for more on end marks.

Do not be misled by a group of words that looks like a sentence but that does not make sense by itself. Such a word group is called a *sentence fragment.*

FRAGMENT   Athletes representing 160 nations.
SENTENCE   Athletes representing 160 nations will compete in the Summer Olympics.

FRAGMENT   The offices designed for high efficiency.
SENTENCE   The offices have been designed for high efficiency.

FRAGMENT   Plans every month for future growth.
SENTENCE   The board of directors plans every month for future growth.

SENTENCES

REFERENCE NOTE: For information about how to correct sentence fragments, see pages 313–317.

 QUICK CHECK 1 **Identifying Sentences and Sentence Fragments**

Identify each of the following word groups as a *sentence* or a *fragment*.

1. In a dark silence, broken only by the low moan of an angry wind.
2. I awoke on a cold, hard, and unfamiliar cot.
3. Through painful yellow light, a man's voice booming.
4. It's roundup time.
5. Sent my thoughts racing to the long day ahead.

The Subject and the Predicate

8b. A sentence consists of two parts: a *subject* and a *predicate*. A **subject** tells *whom* or *what* the sentence is about. A **predicate** tells something about the subject.

Subject   Predicate
Lightning | struck.

Subject   Predicate
Everyone | enjoyed reading *The Piano Lesson*.

   Subject   Predicate
All of the seeds | sprouted.

    Predicate   Subject
Into the sky soared | the young eagle.

Predicate   Subject   Predicate
Where did | your family | go on vacation?

As you can see, a subject or a predicate may consist of one word or more than one word. In these examples, all the words labeled *subject* make up the *complete subject,* and all the words labeled *predicate* make up the *complete predicate.*

The Simple Subject

8c. A *simple subject* is the main word or group of words that tells *who* or *what* the sentence is about.

EXAMPLES Who was the **coach** of the hockey team in 1988? [The complete subject is *the coach of the hockey team.*]
Supported by grants, **scientists** constantly search for a cure for cancer. [The complete subject is *Supported by grants, scientists.*]
The **scenes** that you see in these tapestries show the beauty of Pennsylvania in the 1700s. [The complete subject is *The scenes that you see in these tapestries.*]
The **Corn Palace** in Mitchell, South Dakota, is quite a popular tourist attraction. [The complete subject is *The Corn Palace in Mitchell, South Dakota.*]

 REFERENCE NOTE: A compound noun, such as *Corn Palace,* is considered one noun and may therefore be used as a simple subject. For more about compound nouns, see page 89.

 In this book, the term *subject* refers to the simple subject unless otherwise indicated.

The Simple Predicate

8d. A *simple predicate* is a verb or verb phrase that tells something about the subject.

EXAMPLES Catalina **ran** swiftly and gracefully. [The complete predicate is *ran swiftly and gracefully.*]
The puppy **chased** its tail frantically. [The complete predicate is *chased its tail frantically.*]

SENTENCES

Another space probe **was** successfully
launched today. [The complete predicate is
was successfully launched today.]
Did Ethan ever **find** his history book? [The
complete predicate is *Did ever find his history
book.*]

In this book, the term *verb* refers to the simple predicate (a one-word verb or a verb phrase) unless otherwise indicated.

REFERENCE NOTE: For more information about verbs
and verb phrases, see pages 100–103.

The Compound Subject and the Compound Verb

8e. A *compound subject* consists of two or more
subjects that are joined by a conjunction and that
have the same verb.

Compound subjects are usually joined by the conjunction
and or *or.*

EXAMPLES   The **ship** and its **cargo** had been lost.
Marva or **Antonio** will drive us to the track
meet.
Athens, Delphi, and **Nauplia** are on the main-
land of Greece.

8f. A *compound verb* consists of two or more verbs
that are joined by a conjunction and that have
the same subject.

Compound verbs are usually joined by the conjunction *and,
but,* or *or.*

EXAMPLES   We chose a seat near the door and quietly **sat**
down.
Kendra **recognized** the song but **could** not **remember** its title.
For exercise I **swim** or **play** racquetball nearly
every day.
Truth **enlightens** the mind, **frees** the spirit,
and **strengthens** the soul.

NOTE   Do not mistake a sentence containing a compound subject or a compound predicate for a compound sentence. A compound sentence contains two independent clauses.

EXAMPLES   **Hamsters** and **guinea pigs are** small and quiet and **can be** good pets for people with allergies to cats and dogs. [compound subject and compound predicate]
Hamsters and **guinea pigs are** small and quiet, and **they can be** good pets for people with allergies to cats and dogs. [compound sentence]

 REFERENCE NOTE: For more information about compound sentences, see pages 294–295.

How to Find the Subject of a Sentence

8g.   To find the subject of a sentence, ask *Who?* or *What?* before the verb.

EXAMPLES   The **crew** of the whaling ship had worked hard. [Who worked? Crew worked.]
On the quarterdeck stood **Captain Ahab.** [Who stood? Captain Ahab stood.]
Stormy was the **sea.** [What was stormy? Sea was stormy.]

(1) The subject of a sentence expressing a command or a request is always understood to be *you,* although *you* may not appear in the sentence.

COMMAND   Turn left at the next intersection. [Who is being told to turn? *You* is understood.]
REQUEST   Please tell me the story again. [Who is being asked to tell? *You* is understood.]

The subject of a command or a request is *you* even when the sentence contains a *noun of direct address*—a word naming the one or ones spoken to.

EXAMPLE   Jordan, (you) close the window.

(2) The subject of a sentence is never within a prepositional phrase.

SENTENCES

EXAMPLES   **A group** of students gathered near the library. [Who gathered? Group gathered. *Students* is the object of the preposition *of*.]
One of the paintings by Vincent van Gogh sold for $82.5 million. [What sold? One sold. *Paintings* is the object of the preposition *of*. *Vincent van Gogh* is the object of the preposition *by*.]
Out of the stillness came the loud **sound** of laughter. [What came? Sound came. *Stillness* is the object of the preposition *out of*. *Laughter* is the object of the preposition *of*.]

NOTE   Occasionally a prepositional phrase itself is a subject.

EXAMPLE   **Before nine o'clock** is too early!

REFERENCE NOTE: For a discussion of prepositional phrases, see pages 121–122 and 240–244.

(3) The subject of a sentence expressing a question usually follows the verb or a part of the verb phrase.

EXAMPLES   Is the **dog** in the house? [What is in the house? Dog is.]
When was **Katherine Ortega** appointed the Treasurer of the United States? [Who was appointed? Katherine Ortega was appointed.]

Turning the question into a statement will often help you find the subject.

QUESTION   Have you read Ernesto Galarza's *Barrio Boy*?
STATEMENT   **You** have read Ernesto Galarza's *Barrio Boy*. [Who has read? You have read.]

QUESTION   Were Shakespeare's plays popular during his lifetime?
STATEMENT   Shakespeare's **plays** were popular during his lifetime. [What were popular? Plays were popular.]

(4) The word *there* or *here* is never the subject of a sentence.

EXAMPLES   There is the famous ***Mona Lisa***. [What is there? The *Mona Lisa* is there.]

Here are your gloves. [What are here? Gloves are here.]

In these two examples, the words *there* and *here* are used as adverbs telling *where*. The word *there* may also be used as an **expletive**—a word that fills out the structure of a sentence but that does not add to the meaning. In the following example, *there* does not tell *where* but serves only to make the structure of the sentence complete.

EXAMPLE   **There is a soccer game after school this Friday.** [What is? Game is. The subject is *game*.]

 QUICK CHECK 2   **Identifying Subjects and Verbs**

For each of the following sentences, identify the simple subject and the verb. Be sure to include all parts of a compound subject or a compound verb and all words in a verb phrase.

1. Under the stairs were a litter of kittens and their mother.
2. Martin, please stand up and tell us about the French Revolution.
3. All of the shipment was lost in transit.
4. Could Ms. Odoski have been wrong about her?
5. Here is the entrance to the cave.

Complements

8h. A *complement* is a word or a group of words that completes the meaning of a verb.

A sentence may contain only a subject and a verb. The subject may be expressed or understood.

EXAMPLES
       S   V
Everyone participated.

    V
Stop! [The subject *you* is understood.]

SENTENCES

Generally, however, a sentence also includes at least one complement. Without the complement or complements in the sentence, the subject and the verb may not express a complete thought.

INCOMPLETE   Jose Canseco caught
                       S   V

COMPLETE   Jose Canseco caught the **ball.**
                   S   V   C

INCOMPLETE   They sent
                     S V

COMPLETE   They sent us an **invitation.**
                 S V C   C

INCOMPLETE   The judges named
                     S   V

COMPLETE   The judges named **Consuelo** the **winner.**
                 S   V   C   C

INCOMPLETE   The ancient Picts dyed
                      S V

COMPLETE   The ancient Picts dyed their **skin blue.**
                         S V   C C

INCOMPLETE   Denzel Washington became
                      S   V

COMPLETE   Denzel Washington became a versatile **actor.**
                      S   V   C

INCOMPLETE   The players seem
                     S V

COMPLETE   The players seem **weary.**
                     S V   C

As you can see in the examples above, a complement may be a noun, a pronoun, or an adjective. Do not mistake an adverb for a complement.

ADVERB   Janna writes **well.** [The adverb *well* tells *how* Janna writes.]

COMPLEMENT   **Janna writes adventure stories.** [The noun *stories* completes the meaning of *writes.*]

Also, do not confuse a word in a prepositional phrase with a complement.

PREPOSITIONAL   **Janna also writes for the school literary**
PHRASE   **magazine.** [The noun *magazine* is the object of the preposition *for.*]

 REFERENCE NOTE: For more about prepositional phrases, see pages 240–244.

The Direct Object and the Indirect Object

Direct objects and *indirect objects* are two types of complements used with transitive verbs.

8i.   A ***direct object*** is a word or word group that receives the action of a verb or that shows the result of the action. A direct object tells *whom* or *what* after a transitive verb.

A direct object may be a noun, a pronoun, or a word group that functions as a noun.

EXAMPLES   **Drought destroyed the crops.** [Destroyed what? Crops.]
The journalist interviewed the astronauts before and after their flight. [Interviewed whom? Astronauts.]
Kerry called me at noon. [Called whom? Me.]
Regina likes to water-ski on Horseshoe Lake. [Likes what? To water-ski on Horseshoe Lake.]
Our puppy tried burrowing under the fence. [Tried what? Burrowing under the fence.]
Do you know where Anton lives? [Know what? Where Anton lives.]

A direct object may be compound.

EXAMPLES   **The dog chased Eli and me through the park.**
Beethoven composed sonatas, symphonies, and chorales.

SENTENCES

In addition, each part of a compound action verb can have its own direct object.

EXAMPLES   Mrs. Reynolds bent the **grapevines** and tied **them** together to make a wreath.

Savitha took a deep **breath** and began her **speech.**

 Verbals may take direct objects.

EXAMPLE   Terry practiced **roping calves.** [*Calves* is the object of the gerund *roping*.]

 REFERENCE NOTE: For more information on verbals and verbal phrases, see pages 246–256.

8j. An ***indirect object*** is a word or word group that comes between a transitive verb and a direct object and tells *to whom* or *to what* or *for whom* or *for what* the action of the verb is done.

An indirect object may be a noun, a pronoun, or a word group that functions as a noun.

EXAMPLES   Ms. Cruz showed our **class** a video about Moorish architecture. [Showed to whom? Class.]

The animal trainer fed the **bears** fish. [Fed to what? Bears.]

Their artistic skill won **them** many honors. [Won for whom? Them.]

Raymond gives **rehearsing for a play** his whole attention. [Gives his whole attention to what? Rehearsing for a play.]

 Some common verbs that may take indirect objects include *give, grant, ask, pay, lend, hand, send, offer, write, tell, teach,* and *get.*

Do not confuse an indirect object with an object of the preposition *to* or *for.*

INDIRECT OBJECT   The principal awarded **her** the academic scholarship.

OBJECT OF THE PREPOSITION   The principal awarded the academic scholarship to **her.** [*Her* is the object of the preposition *to*.]

An indirect object may be compound.

EXAMPLES The architect showed **Mom** and **Dad** the plans
for the new family room.
Years ago, Uncle Eugene built my **cousin** and
me a fort in the back yard.

Verbals may take indirect objects.

EXAMPLE **Handing Ms. Romero** my research paper,
I remembered I still needed a works cited
list. [*Ms. Romero* is the indirect object of
the participle *handing*.]

 REFERENCE NOTE: For more information on verbals and
verbal phrases, see pages 246–256.

The Objective Complement

8k. An *objective complement* is a word or word
group that helps complete the meaning of a
transitive verb by identifying or modifying the
direct object.

An objective complement may be a noun, a pronoun, an adjective, or a word group that functions as a noun or adjective.

EXAMPLES The members elected Carlotta **secretary.** [The
noun *secretary* identifies the direct object
Carlotta.]
He believed the Academy Award **his.** [The
possessive pronoun *his* modifies the direct object *Academy Award*.]
Everyone considered her **dependable.** [The
adjective *dependable* modifies the direct object *her*.]
The judge declared herself **satisfied with the
jury's verdict.** [The participial phrase *satisfied
with the jury's verdict* modifies the direct object *herself*.]

Word order usually indicates whether or not a word is
an objective complement. An objective complement
almost always follows the direct object it modifies. In
most cases, an adjective or pronoun that precedes a
direct object is not an objective complement.

SENTENCES

EXAMPLE   Speech class can make a **shy** speaker **more confident.** [*Shy* simply modifies *speaker.* But the objective complement *more confident* not only modifies *speaker* but also completes the meaning of *can make.*]

Only a few verbs take an objective complement: *consider, make,* and verbs that can be replaced by *consider* or *make,* such as *appoint, believe, call, choose, dye, elect, keep, name, cut, paint,* and *sweep.*

EXAMPLES   Many literary historians call Shakespeare **the greatest dramatist of all time.** [*or* consider Shakespeare the greatest dramatist of all time]
The flood had swept the valley **clean.** [*or* had made the valley clean]

 REFERENCE NOTE: For more information about participles and participial phrases, see pages 246–249.

An objective complement may be compound.

EXAMPLES   The Gibsons named their two cats **Bruno** and **Waldo.**
Charlena painted her old bicycle **black** and **silver.**

 NOTE Verbals may take objective complements.

EXAMPLE   Bisby is set on **calling** his dog **François.** [The objective complement *François* completes the meaning of the gerund *calling.*]

 ☑ *QUICK CHECK 3*   **Identifying Direct Objects, Indirect Objects, and Objective Complements**

Find the complements in the following sentences, and identify each as a *direct object,* an *indirect object,* or an *objective complement.*

1. In the northern part of the county, high winds swept into trailer parks and demolished many homes.
2. Do you consider her qualified for the job?

3. The committee appointed Sam chairperson then handed him the gavel.
4. Mother gave my cousin and me the old records but reserved the posters for my older sister.
5. What a beautiful voice you have!

The Subject Complement

A *subject complement* is a word or word group that completes the meaning of a linking verb and that identifies or modifies the subject.

 REFERENCE NOTE: For a list of linking verbs, see page 102.

There are two kinds of subject complements: the *predicate nominative* and the *predicate adjective*.

8l. A *predicate nominative* is the word or group of words that follows a linking verb and that refers to the same person or thing as the subject of the verb.

A predicate nominative may be a noun, a pronoun, or a word group that functions as a noun.

EXAMPLES   Adela Rogers St. Johns was a famous **journalist.** [The noun *journalist* refers to the subject *Adela Rogers St. Johns.*]
Of the three applicants, Carlos is the most competent **one.** [The pronoun *one* refers to the subject *Carlos.*]
On our photo safari, we had a terrific guide whose talent was **tracking big game.** [The gerund phrase *tracking big game* refers to the subject *talent.*]

 NOTE Gerunds and gerund phrases can act as predicate nominatives. However, do not confuse a gerund used as a predicate nominative with a present participle used as the main verb in a verb phrase.

VERB   This week Grandma **is planting** her vegetable garden.
PREDICATE NOMINATIVE   One of Grandma's great joys is **planting her vegetable garden.**

SENTENCES

REFERENCE NOTE: For more information about gerunds and gerund phrases, see pages 250–251.

A predicate nominative may be compound.

EXAMPLES   The two candidates for class treasurer are **Marco** and **I.**
South Dakota's chief crops are **corn, wheat,** and **oats.**

8m.   A *predicate adjective* is an adjective that follows a linking verb and modifies the subject of the verb.

EXAMPLES   The ocean is **calm.** [The adjective *calm* modifies the subject *ocean.*]
Does that orange taste **bitter?** [The adjective *bitter* modifies the subject *orange.*]
All of the astronauts look **confident.** [The adjective **confident** modifies the subject *All.*]

 A participle or a participial phrase can act as a predicate adjective. But don't confuse a predicate adjective with a participle used as a main verb in a verb phrase.

PREDICATE
ADJECTIVE   In Shakespeare's *Othello,* the character of Iago is sly and **scheming.**
Othello is a great man, but his character is **flawed.**

VERB   Throughout the play, Iago **is plotting** against Othello.
Finally, Othello **is thwarted** by Iago's scheming and by his own jealousy.

Don't automatically assume that an adjective that appears in a predicate is a predicate adjective.

EXAMPLES   Adrienne Rich is **talented.** [The predicate adjective *talented* modifies the subject *Adrienne Rich.*]
Adrienne Rich is a **talented** poet. [The adjective *talented* modifies the predicate nominative *poet.*]

A predicate adjective may be compound.

EXAMPLES   Illuminated manuscripts are **rare** and **valuable.**
Eben Flood felt **old, lonely,** and **sad.**

STYLE NOTE You don't always need to use the subject-verb-complement construction in your writing. For variety, you may occasionally want to place the subject complement before the subject and the verb.

PREDICATE ADJECTIVE	**Warm** and **winsome** is my true love's smile. [The adjectives *warm* and *winsome* modify the subject *smile*.]
PREDICATE NOMINATIVE	**What an outstanding basketball player Charles Barkley is!** [The noun *player* refers to the subject *Charles Barkley*.]

Placing the complement first changes the tone and the emphasis of your sentence. If you do experiment with word order in your sentence, be sure the result has the tone and emphasis you intend.

 NOTE Verbals may take subject complements.

EXAMPLE   Maureen was determined **to become** a world-class **gymnast**. [*Gymnast* is the predicate nominative of the infinitive *to become*.]
Nate hates **being late** for a movie. [*Late* is the predicate adjective of the gerund *being*.]

✓ *QUICK CHECK 4*   **Identifying Linking Verbs and Subject Complements**

Identify the linking verb and the subject complement in each of the following sentences. Indicate whether the complement is a *predicate nominative* or a *predicate adjective*.

1. Icy is the stare of the glacier.
2. Was Jane Austen the author of *Pride and Prejudice*?
3. Many people feel concerned about the spread of AIDS, not just in the United States but throughout the world.
4. Why does the spaghetti sauce taste too spicy?
5. A massive work of carved stone is the Great Sphinx.

Sentences Classified According to Structure

8n. According to their structure, sentences are classified as *simple, compound, complex,* and *compound-complex.*

(1) A *simple sentence* has one independent clause and no subordinate clauses.

EXAMPLES   Uncle Alan taught me how to play the mandolin.

The spotted owl of the northwestern United States is an endangered species.

Covered with mildew, dust and cobwebs, the old bicycle looked terrible but worked just fine.

(2) A *compound sentence* has two or more independent clauses but no subordinate clauses.

Independent clauses may be joined by a comma and a coordinating conjunction (*and, but, for, nor, or, so,* or *yet*), by a semicolon, or by a semicolon and a conjunctive adverb or a transitional expression.

EXAMPLES   Lorenzo's story about the pit bull terrier, the canoe, and the cabbage sounded incredible, but it was true. [two independent clauses joined by a comma and the coordinating conjunction *but*]

Agatha Christie was a prolific writer; she wrote more than eighty books in less than sixty years. [two independent clauses joined by a semicolon]

The defeat of Napoleon at the Battle of Waterloo was a victory for England; however, it brought to an end an era of French grandeur. [two independent clauses joined by a semicolon and the conjunctive adverb *however*]

Common Conjunctive Adverbs		
also	incidentally	next
anyway	indeed	nonetheless
besides	instead	otherwise
consequently	likewise	still
finally	meanwhile	then
furthermore	moreover	therefore
however	nevertheless	thus
Common Transitional Expressions		
after all	even so	in fact
as a result	for example	in other words
at any rate	for instance	on the contrary
by the way	in addition	on the other hand

NOTE Do not confuse a simple sentence that has a compound subject or a compound predicate with a compound sentence.

EXAMPLES The archaeological discovery was made in the fall and was widely acclaimed the following spring. [simple sentence with compound predicate]
The archaeological discovery was made in the fall, and it was widely acclaimed the following spring. [compound sentence]

(3) A *complex sentence* has one independent clause and at least one subordinate clause.

EXAMPLES Thurgood Marshall, who served on the United States Supreme Court for twenty-four years, retired in 1991. [The independent clause is *Thurgood Marshall retired in 1991.* The subordinate clause is *who served on the United States Supreme Court for twenty-four years.*]
While we were on our vacation in Washington, D.C., *we visited the Folger Shakespeare Library.* [The independent clause

SENTENCES

is *we visited the Folger Shakespeare Library.*
The subordinate clause is *While we were on
vacation in Washington, D.C.*]

 REFERENCE NOTE: For more about independent clauses
and subordinate clauses, see **Chapter 7: Clauses.**

(4) A ***compound-complex*** sentence has two or more
independent clauses and at least one subordinate
clause.

EXAMPLES   The two eyewitnesses told the police officer
what they saw, but their accounts of the accident were quite different. [The two independent clauses are *The two eyewitnesses told
the police officer* and *their accounts of the
accident were quite different.* The subordinate clause is *what they saw.*]
Chelsea is only seven years old, but she can already play the violin better than her tutor
can. [The two independent clauses are
Chelsea is only seven years old and *she can already play the violin better.* The subordinate
clause is *than her tutor can.*]

Computers can help you get a better sense
of your own sentence style. If you have
access to style-checking software, run a style
check on a paragraph or two (or more) of your writing. The
style checker will analyze your writing sample and will provide information such as the number of sentences per paragraph, the kinds of sentences, the average number of
words per sentence, and the lengths of the longest and
shortest sentences. If, for example, you discover that you
consistently use only one or two sentence structures and
that your sentences all tend to be of a similar length, you
can focus your attention on revising for greater variety.

 REFERENCE NOTE: For more information on improving
your sentence style, see **Chapter 9: Sentence Style.**

Sentences Classified According to Purpose

80. Sentences may be classified according to purpose.

(1) A *declarative sentence* makes a statement. It is followed by a period.

EXAMPLES   The lock on the front door is broken.
            Jorge Farragut led naval forces against the British in two wars.

(2) An *interrogative sentence* asks a question. It is followed by a question mark.

EXAMPLES   Have you seen a sculpture by Augusta Savage?
            Is Santa Fe the capital of New Mexico?

 NOTE A sentence of any type may be spoken in a way that makes it interrogative. In such cases, the sentence should end with a question mark.

EXAMPLES   Larry made dinner? [Declarative becomes interrogative.]
            Turn left here? [Imperative becomes interrogative.]
            How pleased I must be? [Exclamatory becomes interrogative.]

(3) An *imperative sentence* makes a request or gives a command. It is usually followed by a period. A very strong command, however, is followed by an exclamation point.

EXAMPLES   Please give me the dates for the class meetings. [request]
            Call this number in case of an emergency. [mild command]
            Help me! [strong command]

(4) An *exclamatory sentence* expresses strong feeling or shows excitement. It is followed by an exclamation point.

SENTENCES

EXAMPLES   What a noble leader he was**!**
             Ah, Dr. Emecheta, you have discovered the
                 secret at last**!**

NOTE   A sentence of any type may be spoken in a way that
             makes it exclamatory. In such cases, the sentence
             should end with an exclamation point.

EXAMPLES   I beg your pardon**!** [Declarative becomes
             exclamatory.]
             Listen carefully, class**!** [Imperative be-
             comes exclamatory.]
             What on earth makes you say something
             like that**!** [Interrogative becomes exclam-
             atory.]

  REFERENCE NOTE: For more information about end
marks, see pages 377–380.

Shoe, by Jeff MacNelly, reprinted by permission: Tribune Media Services.

 QUICK CHECK 5 **Identifying the Four Kinds of Sentences**

Identify each of the following sentences as *declarative, inter-rogative, imperative,* or *exclamatory.* Also supply the appro-priate end mark after the last word in the sentence.

1. Do you understand algebraic equations
2. Wow, that last eight hundred meter race just broke the high school track record
3. Please pass the pepper
4. Water is composed of oxygen and hydrogen
5. Call an ambulance right now

✓ **Chapter Review 1**

A. Identifying Subjects, Verbs, and Complements in the Sentences of a Paragraph

Identify the italicized word or word group in each sentence in the following paragraph as a *subject*, a *verb*, or a *complement*. If it is a complement, identify it as a *direct object*, an *indirect object*, a *predicate nominative*, a *predicate adjective*, or an *objective complement*.

EXAMPLE   [1]The National Science Foundation (NSF) is undergoing a great *surge* of growth.
               1. *complement (direct object)*

     [1] The NSF is relatively *small* compared with other government agencies like the National Institutes of Health and the National Aeronautics and Space Administration. [2] Recently, however, it *has accepted* more and more challenges. [3] In 1991, with funding of only $2.3 billion, the *foundation* participated heavily in several big government programs. [4] *One* of these important programs investigates global climate change. [5] There is another *program* for which the NSF is developing sophisticated computer technology. [6] In a third project, the foundation boosts science and mathematics *education* and *literacy*. [7] How important this project *must be* to the foundation's enthusiastic director, physicist Walter E. Massey! [8] Throughout his career, Dr. Massey has shown *hundreds* of students the excitement of physics, chemistry, biology, and the other sciences. [9] Dr. Massey is able to apply his own *experience* as an African American to the needs of minority students. [10] Perhaps through the programs of the National Science Foundation, many more students will now make themselves *candidates* for rewarding careers in science.

B. Classifying Sentences According to Purpose

Classify each of the following sentences as *declarative, interrogative, imperative,* or *exclamatory.* Then supply the appropriate end mark after the last word in the sentence.

SENTENCES

EXAMPLE   **1.** The school is five blocks from here
               1. *declarative—here.*

11. The umpire called a strike
12. The pear tree grew well in our back yard
13. His hard work earned him a promotion
14. Anita ran errands during most of the day
15. Why did Earl leave the party so early
16. Debbie Allen is a choreographer
17. What a wonderful day we had yesterday
18. Please hold my umbrella for a minute
19. Where did you park the car
20. Leave your classrooms quickly

C. Classifying Sentences According to Structure

Classify each of the following sentences as *simple, compound, complex,* or *compound-complex.*

21. The championship golfer Chi Chi Rodriguez knows about completing a large project in small sections.
22. When Rodriguez was a child in Puerto Rico, he learned this approach from his father, who wanted to plant corn in a field that was overgrown with bamboo.
23. Mr. Rodriguez could not afford to take several weeks off from his job to clear the whole field, so every evening after work, he would cut down a single bamboo plant.
24. Gradually, the field was cleared, and by the next spring, the Rodriguez family was eating corn for dinner.
25. Today, Chi Chi Rodriguez and his dedicated staff at the Chi Chi Rodriguez Youth Foundation help hundreds and hundreds of disadvantaged youngsters—one child at a time.

 Chapter Review 2

Writing Sentences

Write your own sentences according to the following guidelines. In your sentences, underline the words that indicate the italicized sentence parts. Also, use a variety of subjects, verbs, and complements in your sentences.

1. a declarative sentence with a *compound subject*
2. an interrogative sentence with a *compound verb*
3. an exclamatory sentence with a *direct object*
4. an imperative sentence with a *compound direct object*
5. a declarative sentence with an *indirect object*
6. a declarative sentence with a *predicate nominative*
7. an interrogative sentence with a *compound predicate adjective*
8. a declarative sentence with an *objective complement*
9. an imperative sentence with an *indirect object*
10. a declarative sentence with a *predicate adjective*

SUMMARY OF COMMON SENTENCE PATTERNS

Together the subject and the verb produce the most basic sentence pattern. All other sentence patterns are combinations of the subject, the verb, and various complements.

```
  S    V
Emilia sang.
```

```
  S    V    DO
Emilia sang a solo.
```

```
       S      V    IO              DO
The audience gave Emilia a standing ovation.
```

```
         S      V    DO             OC (N)
Some people called her an inspired performer.
```

```
    S        V           DO      OC (Adj)
Everyone considered her performance outstanding.
```

```
   S    V    PN
Emilia was the star of the show.
```

```
          S      V    PA
Her performance was flawless.
```

SENTENCES

9 SENTENCE STYLE

Clarity, Variety, Conciseness

✓ *Checking What You Know*

A. Revising Sentences by Correcting Weak Coordination and Faulty Parallelism

Most of the following sentences need revision because of either weak coordination or faulty parallelism. Make any necessary revisions. If a sentence does not need revision, write C.

EXAMPLE   1. Many museums offer special services to schools, and these include lectures and giving guided tours.
      1. *Many museums offer schools special services including lectures and guided tours.*

1. Isabella Stewart Gardner built a palace on a Boston dump, and she filled it with art treasures, and then in her will she said that each item must stay forever where she placed it.
2. Many immigrants came to America to seek their fortune or because they desired freedom of worship.
3. If you listen hard enough, you will be able to distinguish the singing of Leontyne Price from that of Marilyn Horne.

4. Willa Cather was a high school teacher, and it is believed that her short story "Paul's Case" was based on an experience in her school, and it is a very moving story.
5. Advertising executives place great emphasis on arousing needs for a product, making the product attractive, and that the product be fairly inexpensive.

B. Revising a Paragraph to Eliminate Sentence Fragments and Run-on Sentences

Rewrite the following paragraph by changing the punctuation and capitalization to eliminate sentence fragments and run-on sentences. You should be able to create five complete sentences if you use periods rather than colons or semicolons. (Your revised paragraph will contain fewer than five sentences if you use colons or semicolons.)

EXAMPLE   We liked to think of our childhood the scenes we recalled were part of another world. A world very unlike our present surroundings.

We liked to think of our childhood. The scenes we recalled were part of another world, a world very unlike our present surroundings.

or

We liked to think of our childhood: the scenes we recalled were part of another world, a world very unlike our present surroundings.

As we walked down the jungle trail, our thoughts turned to Vermont, we recalled the long summer days in the woods and meadows of the family farm our grandfather had taught us to move among the animals there quietly. Without alarming them. Our family always respected. Loved, in fact, animals. Who would have guessed that one day we would be hiking through a rain forest? Trying to feel at home with its creatures.

SENTENCES

C. Revising a Paragraph to Improve Sentence Variety and to Eliminate Wordiness and Unnecessary Shifts

Rewrite the following paragraph to vary sentence beginnings and sentence structure. Also, eliminate wordiness and unnecessary shifts. You may move or delete words or phrases, and you may combine sentences.

EXAMPLE   [1] Most of us know what a headache feels like, but many of us may not know what causes these uncomfortable-feeling headaches.

1. Although most of us know what a headache feels like, many of us do not know what causes headaches.

Headaches have a variety of different causes. [6] There are two common types of serious and severe headaches. [7] A tension headache is a headache that is caused by a tightening of scalp and neck muscles. [8] These headaches result from stress. [9] A migraine headache is caused by swelling of arteries in the brain. [10] The arteries become swollen, and nerve endings in the brain are pressed by the arteries.   ✓

Ways to Achieve Clarity

Often, the clarity of a sentence is a matter of focus, or emphasis: placing the weight of meaning exactly where you want it. You can sharpen the focus of your sentences by *coordinating* and *subordinating* ideas.

Coordinating Ideas

9a. Ideas of equal weight in a sentence are called *coordinate* ideas.

To balance two or more ideas, or to give them equal emphasis, link them with a connecting word, an appropriate mark of punctuation, or both.

EXAMPLES   The watch was ended at last**, and** we took supper and went to bed.

> Mark Twain, *Life on the Mississippi*

But that L-shaped rip on the left sleeve got bigger**;** bits of stuffing coughed out from its wound after a hard day of play.

> Gary Soto, "The Jacket"

As we hoisted the net on poles to the top of the tree, the clinging mesh snagged on every twig on the way up**; then,** as we squinted into the sun and gave helpful and confusing suggestions to each other on how to free the net to slide down as directed, we found that it could descend only by being profanely and scrupulously removed from twig to clutching twig.

> Hildegard Flanner, *Brief Cherishings: A Napa Valley Harvest*

Different connectives show different kinds of relationships between ideas. The following chart illustrates some possibilities.

ADDITION	CONTRAST	CHOICE	RESULT
also	but	either . . . or	as a result
and	however	neither . . . nor	accordingly
besides	instead	nor	consequently
both . . . and	nevertheless	or	hence
likewise	still	otherwise	therefore
futhermore	yet	whether . . . or	thus

You can use connecting words to join words, phrases, or clauses. The result is a compound element in your sentence.

EXAMPLES   Some **distant lamp or lighted window** gleamed below me. [compound subject]

> James Joyce, "Araby"

SENTENCES

I cleared my throat and coughed tentatively.
[compound predicate]

> Robert Cormier, "The Moustache"

We lived **with our grandmother and uncle** in the rear of the Store (it was always spoken of with a capital *s*), which she had owned some twenty-five years. [compound object of a preposition]

> Maya Angelou, *I Know Why the Caged Bird Sings*

For three days the fire had been burning and Evans, **red-armed in his shirt sleeves and sweating along the seams of his brow,** was prodding it with a garden fork. [coordinate verbal phrases]

> V. S. Pritchett, "The Wheelbarrow"

No man is an island entire of itself; every man is a piece of the continent, a part of the main. [compound sentence]

> John Donne, "Meditation 17"

 REFERENCE NOTE: For more about punctuating compound sentences, see pages 294, 385–386, and 397–399.

Subordinating Ideas

Sometimes, whether for meaning or for style, you do not want to give ideas equal emphasis within a sentence. Instead, you can express ideas so that one of them is grammatically *subordinate* to (or *dependent* on) another.

9b. One way to subordinate an idea is to use a subordinate clause.

A *subordinate clause* is a group of words that has a subject and verb but that depends on the sentence's main clause for its full meaning. You can use a subordinate clause to

- add details to an idea
- emphasize one idea over another
- specify the relationship between ideas

The kinds of subordinate clauses you will use most often are *adverb clauses* and *adjective clauses.*

EXAMPLES   Maria, **who likes Kevin Costner,** saw the movie *Dances with Wolves* three times. [adjective clause]

Dances with Wolves is a rare movie-going experience **because it uses Native American dialogue with English subtitles.** [adverb clause]

 REFERENCE NOTE: For more about the types of subordinate clauses, see pages 264–273.

Adverb Clauses

An *adverb clause* modifies a verb, an adjective, or an adverb in a sentence. Adverb clauses are introduced with subordinating conjunctions, such as *although, after, because, if, since, when, whenever, where,* and *while.* The conjunction shows how the adverb clause relates to the main clause. Usually, the relationship is *time, cause* or *reason, purpose* or *result,* or *condition.*

TIME   **Whenever the memory of those marigolds flashes across my mind,** a strange nostalgia comes with it and remains long after the picture has faded.

Eugenia Collier, "Marigolds"

CAUSE OR REASON   This confession he spoke harshly **because its unexpectedness shook him**.

Bernard Malamud, "The Magic Barrel"

PURPOSE OR RESULT   Rage made him weak, **so that he stumbled.**

Carson McCullers, *The Heart Is a Lonely Hunter*

CONDITION   **"If there'd been any farther west to go,** he'd have gone."

John Steinbeck, *The Red Pony*

This chart lists subordinating conjunctions you can use to express the different kinds of relationships.

SENTENCES

SUBORDINATING CONJUNCTIONS	
TIME	after, as, before, since, until, whenever, while
CAUSE	as, because, even though, since, that
PURPOSE	in order that, so that
CONDITION	although, if, provided that, though, unless, while

NOTE You can place an adverb clause at the beginning, the middle, or the end of a sentence. The position can affect the sentence's focus, so read it aloud with the clause in each position to see which sounds better. When you begin with an adverb clause, be sure to put a comma after the clause.

Adjective Clauses

An *adjective clause* modifies a noun or a pronoun in a sentence. It usually begins with *who, whom, whose, which, that,* or *where.*

EXAMPLES   Stashed somewhere in the larder there was always a jar of raisins and some vanilla pods **which appeared in the kitchen only on special occasions.**

Ernesto Galarza, *Barrio Boy*

Chicago seemed an unreal city **whose mythical houses were built of slabs of black coal wreathed in palls of gray smoke,** houses **whose foundations were sinking slowly into the dank prairie.**

Richard Wright, *American Hunger*

Before you use an adjective clause in a sentence, you need to decide which idea you want to emphasize. Suppose you want to combine these two ideas in one sentence:

Award-winning novelist Rolando Hinojosa-Smith writes in both Spanish and English. He was raised in a bilingual family.

If you want to emphasize that Hinojosa-Smith writes in Spanish and English, put that information in an independent clause and the other information in an adjective clause.

> Award-winning novelist Rolando Hinojosa-Smith, **who was raised in a bilingual family,** writes in both Spanish and English.

If you want to emphasize that Hinojosa-Smith was raised in a bilingual family, put that information in an independent clause and the other information in an adjective clause.

> Award-winning novelist Rolando Hinojosa-Smith, **who writes in both Spanish and English,** was raised in a bilingual family.

 REFERENCE NOTE: For more about combining sentences by subordinating ideas, see pages 339–342. For information on the use of commas with adjective clauses, see pages 386–388.

 QUICK CHECK 1 **Supplying Connectives**

For each of the following sentences, supply an appropriate coordinating conjunction, subordinating conjunction, correlative conjunction, relative pronoun, or relative adverb.

1. The clock, _____ has been in our family for generations, was originally made in Germany.
2. _____ you make a B average, you may be excused from the final exam.
3. Thunderclouds gathered overhead, _____ no rain fell on the hot streets.
4. Bad weather has delayed many flights to the North; _____ , we do not expect our guests to arrive today.
5. _____ the disk drive has failed, _____ someone has erased one of the system files on the computer.

Correcting Weak Coordination

In conversation, people tend to string together ideas with coordinating conjunctions: *I really want to go,* **and** *I'm trying* *to convince my parents,* **so** *I'll let you know later.* In formal situations, though, it's important to show the relative importance of ideas or their logical connections. The overuse of coordination can result in *weak focus*—poor definition of points or details. Another result of overusing coordination is *weak connection*—fuzzy bridges between ideas.

9c. Avoid using weak coordination.

Check each compound sentence to be sure that the ideas are equally significant and therefore best linked by the coordinating conjunctions *and, but,* or *so.* If not, subordinate an idea by placing it in a subordinate clause or phrase. You may need to rearrange some of the words in the sentence.

WEAK   Mrs. Willis was going to the mall, and so she offered us a ride there, and she is our neighbor.

BETTER   **Because our neighbor Mrs. Willis was going to the mall,** she offered us a ride there.

or

Mrs. Willis, **who was going to the mall,** offered us a ride there.

WEAK   My uncle is one of the performers in the musical, and he was able to get us tickets, and the tickets were for opening night.

BETTER   **Because my uncle is one of the performers in the musical,** he was able to get us tickets **for opening night.**

or

My uncle, **who is one of the performers in the musical,** was able to get us tickets **for opening night.**

Is weak coordination a problem in your writing? Use the "search" function on a computer to make a diagnosis. You can instruct the computer to look for every instance of **, and**; **, so**; and

, but in your paper (three separate searches), and then you can examine each instance. Decide whether the coordination is effective or whether subordination would sharpen the focus of the sentence.

 REFERENCE NOTE: For more about using phrases in sentences, see pages 332–336.

Using Parallel Structure

9d. Use the same grammatical form to express parallel ideas or ideas of equal weight.

Using the same grammatical form for equal ideas creates *parallel structure.*

(1) Use parallel structure when you *link coordinate ideas.*

NOT PARALLEL   In winter I usually like skiing and to skate. [gerund paired with infinitive]

PARALLEL   In winter I usually like **to ski** and **to skate**. [infinitive paired with infinitive]

NOT PARALLEL   The company guaranteed that salaries would be increased and shorter working days. [noun clause paired with a noun]

PARALLEL   The company guaranteed **that salaries would be increased** and **that working days would be shorter.** [noun clause paired with noun clause]

(2) Use parallel structure when you *compare* or *contrast* ideas.

NOT PARALLEL   To think logically is as important as calculating accurately. [infinitive compared with a gerund]

PARALLEL   **Thinking** logically is as important as **calculating** accurately. [gerund compared with a gerund]

NOT PARALLEL   Einstein liked mathematical research more than to supervise a large laboratory. [noun contrasted with an infinitive]

S E N T E N C E S

PARALLEL   Einstein liked mathematical **research** more than laboratory **supervision.** [noun contrasted with a noun]

(3) Use parallel structure when you *link ideas with correlative conjunctions* (*both . . . and, either . . . or, neither . . . nor,* or *not only . . . but also*).

NOT PARALLEL   With *Ship of Fools*, Katherine Anne Porter proved she was talented not only as a short-story writer but also in writing novels.

PARALLEL   With *Ship of Fools*, Katherine Anne Porter proved she was talented not only as a short-story writer but also as a novelist.

 NOTE   Be sure to place correlative conjunctions directly before the parallel terms. Otherwise, the relationship between the ideas won't be parallel.

UNCLEAR   A president of the United States must not only represent his own political party but also the entire American people.

CLEAR   A president of the United States must represent *not only* **his own political party** *but also* **the entire American people.**

When you revise for parallel structure, you may need to repeat an article, a preposition, or a pronoun before each of the parallel terms. Leaving key words out of the second half of a parallel construction can result in an elliptical construction that may be misread.

UNCLEAR   On our class trip to the bank, I met the president and head teller. [The sentence indicates that you met only one person.]

CLEAR   On our class trip to the bank, I met **the** president and **the** head teller.

UNCLEAR   Through Kate Chopin's stories, we can learn almost as much about the author as the social condition of women in her era.

CLEAR   Through Kate Chopin's stories, we can learn almost as much **about** the author as **about** the social condition of women in her era.

To make your meaning clear, you may need to add a few words to the second part of the parallel structure.

UNCLEAR   I admire the poems of Byron more than Wordsworth.

CLEAR   I admire the poems of Byron more than **those of** Wordsworth.

 REFERENCE NOTE: For more on elliptical constructions, see pages 198–199.

 QUICK CHECK 2   **Revising Sentences by Subordinating Ideas and by Using Parallel Structure**

Some of the following sentences have weak coordination or lack balance. Revise the sentences by subordinating ideas and by putting ideas in parallel structure. You may need to delete, add, or move some words.

1. Sports fans may disagree over whether going to baseball games or to watch football is more fun, and few people can ignore the importance of sports in America.
2. Many Americans are passionate about sports, so sports has always been a topic for friendly and not-so-friendly arguments.
3. Some sports fans argue endlessly and with anger about whether football or baseball is truly the American pastime.
4. Baseball backers may insist that baseball is the more important game, and it requires intelligence and dexterity.
5. On the other hand, football fans may praise a quarterback's speed, skill, and how agile he is.

Obstacles to Clarity

Sentence Fragments

A sentence should express a complete thought. If you punctuate a part of a sentence as if it were a complete sentence, you create a *sentence fragment.*

REFERENCE NOTE: For more on sentence fragments, see page 279.

9e.   In general, avoid using sentence fragments.

FRAGMENT	Has large horns shaped like corkscrews. [The subject is missing. What has large horns shaped like corkscrews?]
SENTENCE	**A male kudu** has large horns shaped like corkscrews.
FRAGMENT	The kudu, a type of antelope, in Africa. [The verb is missing.]
SENTENCE	The kudu, a type of antelope, **lives** in Africa.
FRAGMENT	The kudu, a type of antelope, found in Africa. [The helping verb is missing.]
SENTENCE	The kudu, a type of antelope, **is** found in Africa.
FRAGMENT	While the kudu stands five feet high at the shoulder. [This has a subject and a verb, but the subordinating conjunction *while* indicates that the clause needs to be combined with an independent clause to express a complete thought.]
SENTENCE	While the kudu stands five feet high at the shoulder, **its total height with its long horns can reach past eleven feet.**

Born Loser reprinted by permission of NEA, Inc.

Phrase Fragments

A *phrase* is a group of related words that doesn't contain both a subject and a verb. Because a phrase doesn't express a complete thought, it can't stand on its own as a sentence.

REFERENCE NOTE: The types of phrases include prepositional, appositive, and verbal phrases. For explanations
of these types of phrases, see **Chapter 6: Phrases.**

Often, you will be able to correct a phrase fragment in
your writing by attaching it to the sentence that comes before or after it.

FRAGMENT	During her long and productive life. Nina Otero excelled as an educator, writer, and public official. [prepositional phrase]
SENTENCE	**During her long and productive life,** Nina Otero excelled as an educator, writer, and public official.
FRAGMENT	Descended from a long line of political leaders. Otero became active in politics soon after she graduated from college. [verbal phrase— participial]
SENTENCE	**Descended from a long line of political leaders,** Otero became active in politics soon after she graduated from college.
FRAGMENT	She was one of the first Mexican American women. To hold important public posts in New Mexico. [verbal phrase—infinitive]
SENTENCE	She was one of the first Mexican American women **to hold important public posts in New Mexico.**
FRAGMENT	In 1917, she became superintendent of schools in Santa Fe County. An unusual position for a woman at that time. [appositive phrase]
SENTENCE	In 1917, she became superintendent of schools in Santa Fe County, **an unusual position for a woman at that time.**

Subordinate Clause Fragments

A *subordinate clause* contains a subject but doesn't express
a complete thought and can't stand alone as a sentence.

FRAGMENT	Michael Jackson made his film debut as the Scarecrow in *The Wiz*. Which was based on *The Wizard of Oz*. [adjective clause]

CORRECT   Michael Jackson made his film debut as the Scarecrow in *The Wiz*, **which was based on *The Wizard of Oz*.**

FRAGMENT   The former Jackson Five member topped his earlier popularity. When he performed in his first music video. [adverb clause]

CORRECT   The former Jackson Five member topped his earlier popularity **when he performed in his first music video**.

Compound-Structure Fragments

While checking over your work, you may find that two other constructions cause you trouble. They are items in a series and compound verbs.

FRAGMENT   I packed only casual clothes. A pair of jeans, two T-shirts, a sweater, and sneakers. [series of appositives]

CORRECT   I packed only casual clothes. I packed **a pair of jeans, two T-shirts, a sweater, and sneakers.**

or

I packed only casual clothes: **a pair of jeans, two T-shirts, and a sweater.**

FRAGMENT   Jay went strolling through the museum on his own. But caught up with the rest of the group later. [compound verb]

CORRECT   Jay went strolling through the museum on his own **but caught up with the rest of the group later.**

STYLE NOTE   Experienced writers sometimes deliberately use fragments for effect. For example, in the following excerpt, the author uses fragments to imitate the sounds of natural speech. Notice that the meaning of the fragments is made clear by the sentences that come before and after them.

SENTENCES

> "This was an unusual goose," my uncle said. "Called at the back door every morning for its food, answered to its name. An intelligent creature. Eddie's sisters tied a blue silk ribbon around its neck and made a pet of it. It displayed more personality and understanding than you'd believe possible in a bird. Came Christmas, of course, and they couldn't kill it."
>
> Leslie Norris, "A Flight of Geese"

Fragments can be effective when they are used as a stylistic technique. You may want to experiment with using them in expressive and creative writing such as journals, poems, and short stories. You can also use fragments when an informal, shorthand style is appropriate. However, don't use fragments in a research paper or a book report. In these kinds of writing, your readers expect formal, straightforward language.

 QUICK CHECK 3   **Revising to Eliminate Fragments**

Some of the following items are sets of complete sentences, while others contain fragments. If an item has only complete sentences, write C. If it contains a fragment, revise it to include the fragment in a complete sentence.

1. One colorful figure of the Old West. Andrew García, tells of his exploits in his autobiography *Tough Trip Through Paradise.*
2. García describes some of the tough characters he met when he traveled with an outlaw band. One of the most notorious characters was the horse thief George Reynolds, better known as "Big Nose George."
3. Like many of the outlaws García knew. Reynolds died a violent death.
4. Although tempted to become an outlaw himself. García eventually settled down. And began writing his exciting account of his life.

5. García didn't live to see his memoirs published. The manuscripts, which he had packed away in dynamite boxes. Were discovered years after his death.

Run-on Sentences

Two sentences that run together as if they were a single thought create a *run-on sentence.* There are two kinds of run-on sentences.

- A *fused sentence* has no punctuation at all between the two complete thoughts.
- A *comma splice* has just a comma between them.

> FUSED   Lightning speeds to our eyes at 186,000 miles per second thunder creeps to our ears at 1,087 feet per second.
>
> COMMA SPLICE   We can't hear and see the event at the same time, we sense it twice in different ways.

9f. Avoid using run-on sentences.

The following examples show five ways to correct run-on sentences. Depending on the relationship you want to show between the two ideas, one method may be more effective than another.

- You can make two sentences.

Lightning speeds to our eyes at 186,000 miles per second**.** Thunder creeps to our ears at 1,087 feet per second.

- You can use a comma and a coordinating conjunction.

Lightning speeds to our eyes at 186,000 miles per second**,** **but** thunder creeps to our ears at 1,087 feet per second.

- You can change one of the independent clauses to a subordinate clause.

Lightning speeds to our eyes at 186,000 miles per second, **while** thunder creeps to our ears at 1,087 feet per second.

- You can use a semicolon.

Lightning speeds to our eyes at 186,000 miles per second**;** thunder creeps to our ears at 1,087 feet per second.

SENTENCES

■ You can use a semicolon and a conjunctive adverb.

Lightning speeds to our eyes at 186,000 miles per second**;**
however, thunder creeps to our ears at 1,087 feet per
second.

 REFERENCE NOTE: For a list of conjunctive adverbs, see
page 295.

STYLE
NOTE
You've probably noticed that well-known
writers sometimes use run-ons in their
works. You, too, can use run-ons occasionally
in short stories, journal entries, and other kinds of expressive and creative writing. Run-ons can be especially effective in stream-of-consciousness writing, a style that imitates
the natural flow of a character's thoughts, feelings, and
perceptions.

> The blue light from Cornelia's lampshade drew
> into a tiny point at the center of her brain, it flick-
> ered and winked like an eye, quietly it fluttered
> and dwindled.
>
> Katherine Anne Porter,
> "The Jilting of Granny Weatherall"

Always check your writing for unintentional run-ons. If you
do use run-ons for a stream-of-consciousness effect, make
sure that your meaning will be clear not only to you but
also to your reader.

Unnecessary Shifts in Sentences

9g.   Avoid making unnecessary shifts in sentences.

Shifts in Subject

Sometimes, a shift in subject is necessary to express the
meaning you intend.

EXAMPLE   I wrote to Janine, but she never replied. [The focus in the second clause switches from *I* to *Janine*.]

Often, though, a shift in subject is both awkward and unnecessary. Notice that each of the following sentences is much clearer when the subject refers to the same person in both clauses.

AWKWARD   Athletes should be at the parking lot by 7:00 so that you can leave by 7:15.

BETTER   **Athletes** should be at the parking lot by 7:00 so that **they** can leave by 7:15.

AWKWARD   Grandma goes to the farmers' market every Saturday, where the freshest produce is found.

BETTER   **Grandma** goes to the farmers' market every Saturday, where **she** finds the freshest produce.

Shifts in Verb Tense and Voice

Changing verb tense or voice within a sentence can create an awkward or confusing sentence.

AWKWARD   She walked into the room, and she says, "The lights to your car are on." [shift from past tense to present tense]

BETTER   She **walked** into the room, and she **said**, "The lights to your car are on." [past tense for first and second verb]

AWKWARD   Lyle spent more than four hours at the city library, but no books on his research topic were found. [shift from active to passive voice]

BETTER   Lyle **spent** more than four hours at the city library, but he **found** no books on his research topic.

Often, a shift in voice leads to a shift in subject. Notice that in the second to last example, the shift from active to passive voice results in a shift from the subject *Lyle* to the subject *books*.

REFERENCE NOTE: If you're not sure about the difference between active and passive voice, see pages 170–175.

NOTE In a compound sentence, you can often correct a shift in voice and subject by creating a compound verb. Simply omit the second subject, and place the second verb in the same voice as the first. You may also need to delete a comma when you take out the second subject.

AWKWARD Russell Means starred as Chingachgook in *The Last of the Mohicans,* and an excellent performance was delivered.

BETTER Russell Means **starred** as Chingachgook in *The Last of the Mohicans* and **delivered** an excellent performance.

AWKWARD Teri focused the lens of her camera then the picture was shot.

BETTER Teri focused the lens of her camera then shot the picture.

 QUICK CHECK 4 **Revising to Correct Unnecessary Shifts and Run-on Sentences**

Each of the following items is confusing because it has an unnecessary shift, because it is a run-on sentence, or both. Revise each item for clarity.

1. Dense clouds surrounded the aircraft the pilot had to rely on her instruments.

2. Pilots flying in certain situations must believe the instrument panel rather than their physical sensations because you can easily become disoriented without a point of reference.

3. Flying over snow or water can be tiring, darkness, too, can present problems, especially for inexperienced pilots.

4. For a pilot, boredom was a dangerous state of mind that can lead to an accident.

5. Long flights can be hazardous. Peak mental condition as well as optimum physical health is required.

Revising for Variety

Varying Sentence Beginnings

9h. Generally, varied sentence beginnings hold a reader's attention and improve the overall style of writing.

The following examples show how a writer can revise sentences to open them with a variety of words and word groups—introductory words, phrases, and clauses. Note that when you vary sentence beginnings, you sometimes must reword the sentences for clarity. Be sure to place phrase modifiers close to the words they modify. And remember that including some sentences that begin with the subject and verb is part of having a variety of sentence beginnings.

SENTENCE CONNECTIVES	
SUBJECT FIRST	The seal has a few natural enemies, including sharks, polar bears, and killer whales. The seal's most dangerous enemies, however, are human beings.
COORDINATING CONJUNCTION FIRST	The seal has a few natural enemies, including sharks, polar bears, and killer whales. **But** the seal's most dangerous enemies are humans.
SUBJECT FIRST	Animal-protection laws forbid commercial harvesting of seals on the Pribilof Islands. Seals are hunted in many other parts of the world.
CONJUNCTIVE ADVERB FIRST	Animal-protection laws forbid commercial harvesting of seals on the Pribilof Islands. **However,** seals are hunted in many other parts of the world.
SINGLE-WORD MODIFIERS	
SUBJECT FIRST	The octopus is shy and intelligent and rarely harms people.
SINGLE-WORD MODIFIERS FIRST	**Shy and intelligent,** the octopus rarely harms people.

(continued)

SINGLE-WORD MODIFIERS *(continued)*

SUBJECT FIRST	Octopi usually keep their distance from humans.
SINGLE-WORD MODIFIER FIRST	**Usually,** octopi keep their distance from humans.
SUBJECT FIRST	An octopus may bite a person with its sharp beak if provoked.
SINGLE-WORD MODIFIER FIRST	**Provoked,** an octopus may bite a person with its sharp beak.

PHRASE MODIFIERS

SUBJECT FIRST	A team of determined Norwegian skiers began a 413-mile trek to the North Pole in March 1990.
PREPOSITIONAL PHRASE FIRST	**In March 1990,** a team of determined Norwegian skiers began a 413-mile trek to the North Pole.
SUBJECT FIRST	They used only skis and manually drawn sledges and set a record for reaching the Pole unassisted.
PARTICIPIAL PHRASE FIRST	**Using only skis and manually drawn sledges,** they set a record for reaching the Pole unassisted.
SUBJECT FIRST	They wanted to keep their sledges light, so they brought only enough fuel to melt ice for water.
INFINITIVE PHRASE FIRST	**To keep their sledges light,** they brought only enough fuel to melt ice for water.

CLAUSE MODIFIERS

SUBJECT FIRST	Over one million species of plants, animals, and insects may be wiped out if burning of the Brazilian rain forest continues.
ADVERB CLAUSE FIRST	**If burning of the Brazilian rain forest continues,** over one million species of plants, animals, and insects may be wiped out.
SUBJECT FIRST	Parts of the rain forest are now protected, but about 20 percent of the forest has already been destroyed.
ADVERB CLAUSE FIRST	**Although parts of the rain forest are now protected,** about 20 percent of the forest has already been destroyed.

SENTENCES

Varying Sentence Structure

 Improve your style by varying the structure of
your sentences.

Use a mix of simple, compound, complex, and compound-
complex sentences in your writing.

👉 REFERENCE NOTE: For information about the four types
of sentence structure, see pages 294–296.

Read the following short paragraph, which is made up
of only simple sentences.

> San Francisco is famous for its scenic views.
> The city sprawls over more than forty hills.
> Driving through San Francisco is like riding a
> roller coaster. Atop one of San Francisco's hills is
> Chinatown, a thriving ethnic neighborhood.
> Atop another is Coit Tower, a great lookout
> point. The San Francisco Bay area is a popular
> place to visit. It is where the stately Golden Gate
> Bridge and the picturesque Fisherman's Wharf
> attract a steady stream of tourists.

Now read the revised version of the paragraph. Notice
how the writer has used sentence-combining techniques to
vary the structure of the sentences.

> San Francisco is famous for its scenic views.
> Because the city sprawls over more than forty
> hills, driving through San Francisco is like riding
> a roller coaster. Atop one of San Francisco's hills
> is Chinatown, a thriving ethnic neighborhood;
> and atop another is Coit Tower, a great lookout
> point. The San Francisco Bay area is a popular
> place to visit. Here, the stately Golden Gate
> Bridge and the picturesque Fisherman's Wharf
> attract a steady stream of tourists.

 QUICK CHECK 5 **Revising a Paragraph to Vary
Sentence Beginnings and
Sentence Structures**

Decide which sentences in the following paragraph would
sound better with compound, complex, or compound-

complex structures. Then revise the paragraph, varying sentence beginnings and sentence structures. Try to create clear sentences that fit together smoothly.

> Have you ever heard of kendo? Kendo is an ancient Japanese martial art. It requires skill, concentration, and agility. The contestants fight with long bamboo swords called <u>shinai.</u> Kendo can be dangerous. Each player must wear protective gear that includes a mask, a breastplate, and thick gloves. Each match lasts three to five minutes. The first contestant to score two points wins. Kendo is a graceful, dignified sport. Respect toward one's opponent is important. A contestant can even be disqualified for rudeness.

Revising to Reduce Wordiness

9j. Avoid using unnecessary words in your writing.

Notice how each word in the sentence below is important to the meaning of the sentence.

> At last I knelt on the island's winter-killed grass, lost, dumbstruck, staring at the frog in the creek just four feet away.
>
> Annie Dillard, *Pilgrim at Tinker Creek*

Skilled writers make every word count. They know that conciseness is essential to good style. You can make your own writing more concise by eliminating extra words.

To avoid wordiness in your writing, keep these three points in mind:

- Use only as many words as you need to make your point.
- Choose simple, clear words and expressions over long, complicated ones.
- Don't repeat words or ideas unless you cannot avoid doing so.

The following guidelines suggest some ways to revise wordy sentences.

(1) Take out a whole group of unnecessary words.

WORDY   After descending to the edge of the river, we boarded a small boat that was floating there on the surface of the water.

BETTER   After descending to the edge of the river, we boarded a small boat.

(2) Replace pretentious words and expressions with straightforward ones.

WORDY   The young woman, who was at an indeterminate point in her teenage years, had in her hair a streak of pink dye that could be considered garish.

BETTER   The **teenager** had a streak of **shocking**-pink dye in her hair.

(3) Reduce a clause to a phrase.

WORDY   Su Li, who lives in Washington, D.C., can conveniently visit the Smithsonian.

BETTER   **Living in Washington, D.C.,** Su Li can conveniently visit the Smithsonian.

WORDY   George, who is my childhood friend, lives in Baltimore.

BETTER   George, **my childhood friend,** lives in Baltimore.

(4) Reduce a phrase or a clause to one word.

WORDY   Angelo likes food from the South.
BETTER   Angelo likes **Southern** food.

WORDY   The dance class that has been canceled will be rescheduled.

BETTER   The **canceled** dance class will be rescheduled.

Shoe, by Jeff MacNelly, reprinted by permission: Tribune Media Services.

Here is a list of wordy phrases and their simpler replacements. Avoid such wordy phrases in your writing.

Wordy	Simpler
at this/that point in time	now, then
at which time	when
by means of	by
due to the fact that	because, since
in spite of the fact that	although
in the event that	if
the fact is that	actually, in fact

 QUICK CHECK 6 **Reducing Wordiness**

Some of the following sentences are wordy. Revise each wordy sentence to make it straightforward and concise. If a sentence doesn't need improving, write C.

1. Good writing is precise and straightforward.
2. Have you ever read sentences that seem to ramble on and keep going forever?
3. Redundant sentences are boring and repetitive.
4. Sentences that are longer than it is necessary for them to be may confuse your reader.
5. A sentence with too many clauses that are subordinate becomes a mental maze for the inattentive reader.

 Chapter Review

A. Revising Sentences to Correct Weak Coordination and Faulty Parallelism

Most of the following sentences need revision because of either weak coordination or faulty parallelism. Make any necessary revisions. If a sentence does not need revision, write C.

EXAMPLE   1. Writing a research paper is a much greater challenge than an ordinary essay, so you should plan your research paper well ahead of time.

S E N T E N C E S

> *1. Because writing a research paper is a much greater challenge than writing an ordinary essay, you should plan your research paper well ahead of time.*

1. Riding the roller coaster and to spin the Wheel of Luck were her two greatest pleasures at the carnival.
2. Jessica Mitford wrote *The American Way of Death,* and this best-selling book led eventually to an official investigation of the funeral industry.
3. To milk a goat is more difficult than a cow.
4. It is easy to complain of our petty discomforts and forget that people all over the world may be so much worse off, and so perhaps we should really be grateful.
5. In some West African countries, *griots* were responsible for both providing entertainment in the form of storytelling and to be the village historians.

B. Revising a Paragraph to Eliminate Sentence Fragments and Run-on Sentences

Rewrite the following paragraph by changing the punctuation and capitalization to eliminate sentence fragments and run-on sentences. You should be able to create five complete sentences if you use periods rather than colons or semicolons. (Your revised paragraph will contain fewer than five sentences if you use colons or semicolons.)

EXAMPLE   Cities, like people, change always, it seems, developers are building new buildings. Such as the one on Elm Street.

> *Cities, like people, change. Always, it seems, developers are building new buildings, such as the one on Elm Street.*

A city changes constantly, it is instructive to look back at an old guidebook. And see how many old landmarks are gone. A thirty-year-old guidebook listing places that no longer exist. Makes fascinating reading. For example, take a guidebook for New York City. Dated 1964. Then, when the New York Herald Tribune still existed. Not even the most prophetic columnist could have predicted the kinds of changes. On the way.

C. Revising a Paragraph to Improve Sentence Variety and to Eliminate Wordiness and Unnecessary Shifts

Rewrite the following paragraph to vary sentence beginnings and sentence structure. Also, eliminate wordiness and unnecessary shifts. You will need to move or delete words and phrases, and you may combine sentences.

EXAMPLE
[1] The West Indian island of Hispaniola is shared by two self-ruled and independent nations, which are Haiti and the Dominican Republic.

1. *The West Indian island of Hispaniola is shared by two independent nations: Haiti and the Dominican Republic.*

[6] Haiti, which covers about a third of the island, occupies the western third of the island. [7] Haiti is the smaller of the two nations, but its population is the larger of the two nations. [8] Haiti has two major languages. These two major languages are the languages of Haitian Creole and French. [9] The Dominican Republic has Spanish as its principal language. Haitian cultural influence in the Dominican Republic is strong. [10] One of Hispaniola's chief exports is coffee, and sugarcane is another important export of Hispaniola. Hispaniola is very rural, and more than half of the people of Hispaniola are involved in the farm industry.

SENTENCES

10 SENTENCE COMBINING

✓ Checking What You Know

Combining Sentences

Combine each group of sentences below into one smooth sentence. You may delete unnecessary words, change word order and word forms, and add connective words and punctuation. Do not, however, change the meaning of the original sentences. Be sure to punctuate your combined sentences correctly.

EXAMPLE 1. Oklahoma is home to several Native American nations.
One of these nations is the Cherokee nation.
  1. *Oklahoma is home to several Native American nations, including the Cherokee nation.*

1. Anne Bradstreet wrote poems.
Bradstreet wrote poems privately.
She wrote poems about early American life.
2. The term paper is due Thursday.
The term paper is due by noon on that day.
3. The Olympic athletes marched around the stadium.
The athletes were dressed in sweatsuits.
The sweatsuits were brightly colored.
4. The crowd responded favorably to singer Marian Anderson's concert.

The crowd was cheering and applauding singer
Marian Anderson.

5. Harlem has been a haven for many African American
artists.
Harlem is a large section of New York City.

6. Shakespeare's plays have been admired for centuries.
His plays have also been performed for centuries.
We know little of Shakespeare's life.

7. Jamie has agreed to go dancing with us.
Jamie will be late.

8. The heat wave may end in a few days.
It has caused a drought in the Midwest.

9. The Incas had a highly developed civilization.
The highly developed civilization crumbled under
Spanish attacks.

10. Recycling paper helps save trees.
It is a well-known fact.   ✓

Combining Sentences for Variety

When you revise, you should notice how your sentences
work together to shape each of your paragraphs. In some
cases, a short sentence may be just what you want, but a
long series of short sentences can make writing choppy and
dull.

Read the following passage. Does the writing style help
hold your interest, or does it distract you from the meaning
of the paragraph?

He was stranded. He was on prehistoric Earth.
He was stranded as the result of a sequence of
events. The sequence was complex. It involved his
being blown up. It involved his being insulted.
These things had happened in bizarre regions of
the Galaxy. There were more of these bizarre
regions than he had ever dreamed existed. Life
had now turned quiet. It was very, very, very quiet.

He was still feeling jumpy.
   He hadn't been blown up now for a while. It
had been five years.

The choppy sentences you just read are based on the
following well-crafted sentences by science fiction writer
Douglas Adams. Notice how Adams's smooth, lively style
helps create a humorous tone.

> He was stranded on prehistoric Earth as the re-
> sult of a complex sequence of events that had in-
> volved his being alternately blown up and insulted
> in more bizarre regions of the Galaxy than he had
> ever dreamed existed, and though life had now
> turned very, very, very quiet, he was still feeling
> jumpy.
>   He hadn't been blown up now for five years.
>
> Douglas Adams, *Life, the
> Universe and Everything*

You can make your writing smoother by balancing short
sentences with longer, more detailed ones. Sentence combining helps create this balance. By eliminating repeated
words and ideas, you can make your sentences more precise.

Combining by Inserting Words and Phrases

10a. Combine related sentences by taking a key word
or phrase from one sentence and inserting it into
another sentence.

By combining sentences with this technique, you can eliminate extra words and repeated ideas.

THREE SENTENCES   This simulator gives a realistic experience of flight. It uses computer graphics to do
this. The experience is so real it's amazing.

ONE SENTENCE   Using computer graphics, this simulator gives
an amazingly realistic experience of flight.

or

With computer graphics, this simulator gives an amazingly realistic experience of flight.

NOTE Usually you will have some freedom as to where you insert a word or phrase. Avoid awkward-sounding combinations and ones that confuse the meaning of the original sentences. For example, be sure to revise any combinations like this one: *Amazingly, using computer graphics, this flight simulator gives a realistic experience of flight.* (What *amazingly* modifies is not clear)

Single-Word Modifiers

Sometimes you can take a word from one sentence and insert it directly into another sentence as a modifier. Other times you will need to change the word into an adjective or adverb before you can insert it.

USING THE SAME FORM

ORIGINAL   Timing is essential for performing magic tricks. The magician's timing must be excellent.

COMBINED   **Excellent** timing is essential for performing magic tricks.

ORIGINAL   Magicians guard the secrets of their tricks. They guard them carefully.

COMBINED   Magicians **carefully** guard the secrets of their tricks.

CHANGING THE FORM

ORIGINAL   The famous magician Harry Houdini performed impossible escapes. The escapes only seemed impossible.

COMBINED   The famous magician Harry Houdini performed **seemingly** impossible escapes. [The verb *seemed* becomes the adverb *seemingly*.]

ORIGINAL   He attempted to escape from a sealed crate that had been lowered into a river. He had handcuffs on.

SENTENCES

COMBINED **Handcuffed**, he attempted to escape from a sealed crate that had been lowered into a river. [The noun *handcuffs* becomes the past participle *handcuffed*.]

Prepositional Phrases

You can usually take a prepositional phrase from one sentence and insert it into another without any change in form.

ORIGINAL Our English class is reading "Everyday Use." It is by Alice Walker.

COMBINED Our English class is reading "Everyday Use" **by Alice Walker.**

You can also combine sentences by changing part of a sentence into a prepositional phrase.

ORIGINAL A female narrator tells the story. Her tone is conversational.

COMBINED A female narrator tells the story **in a conversational tone.**

 REFERENCE NOTE: For more information on prepositional phrases, see pages 240–244.

Participial Phrases

A *participial phrase* contains a participle and words related to it. The whole phrase acts as an adjective. Like other modifiers, participial phrases add details to sentences.

EXAMPLE Da-duh, **holding fast to my hand**, became my anchor as they circled around us like a nervous sea, exclaiming, **touching us with calloused hands, embracing us shyly.**

> Paule Marshall, "To Da-duh, in Memoriam"

 REFERENCE NOTE: For more information about participles and participial phrases, see pages 246–249.

Sometimes you can lift a participial phrase directly from one sentence and insert it into another sentence. Other times you will need to change a verb into a participle before you can insert the idea into another sentence.

ORIGINAL   Ants smell, taste, touch, and hear with antennae. The antennae are attached to their heads.

COMBINED   Ants smell, taste, touch, and hear with antennae **attached to their heads.**

ORIGINAL   Weaver ants bind leaves together for nests. They use the silk from their silk-spinning larvae.

COMBINED   **Using the silk from their silk-spinning larvae,** weaver ants bind leaves together for nests.

STYLE NOTE   Be sure to place a participial phrase close to the noun or pronoun you want it to modify. Otherwise, your sentence may end up meaning something you did not intend.

MISPLACED   Hidden under the bench, we found a cat.
IMPROVED   We found a cat **hidden under the bench.**

 REFERENCE NOTE: For more information about how to revise misplaced phrase modifiers, see pages 229–232.

Appositive Phrases

An *appositive phrase* is made up of an appositive and its modifiers. This phrase identifies or explains a noun or pronoun in a sentence. Like a participial phrase, an appositive phrase should be placed directly before or after the noun or pronoun it modifies. It should be set off by a comma (or two commas if you place the phrase in the middle of the sentence).

 REFERENCE NOTE: For more information on punctuating phrases in sentences, see pages 386–392.

EXAMPLE   In Gainesboro, **a hill town with a square of businesses around the Jackson County Courthouse,** I stopped for directions and breakfast.

William Least Heat-Moon, *Blue Highways*

SENTENCES

You can also combine two sentences by changing one of the ideas into an appositive phrase.

TWO SENTENCES Arna Bontemps wrote for the magazine *Opportunity*. Arna Bontemps was a major figure in the Harlem Renaissance.

ONE SENTENCE Arna Bontemps, **a major figure in the Harlem Renaissance,** wrote for the magazine *Opportunity*.

or

A major figure in the Harlem Renaissance, Arna Bontemps wrote for the magazine *Opportunity*.

or

Arna Bontemps, **a writer for the magazine** *Opportunity*, was a major figure in the Harlem Renaissance.

Notice that the last combination emphasizes Bontemps' role in the Harlem Renaissance, while the first two combinations emphasize his work for *Opportunity*. In the last example, the ideas have been rearranged to change the emphasis, and the verb *wrote* has been changed to a noun, *writer*, to form the appositive.

 *QUICK CHECK 1* **Combining by Inserting Single-Word Modifiers and Phrases**

Combine each of the following sets of sentences by inserting adjectives, adverbs, or phrases. You may need to add, delete, or change the forms of some words. Add commas where they are necessary.

1. Ancient peoples believed that dreams carried messages. The messages were important. The messages were about the future.
2. Today, dreams still fascinate people. The people are all over the world.
3. For instance, Sigmund Freud believed that dreams illustrated conflicts. The conflicts were in a person's inner

life. Sigmund Freud was a great psychoanalyst.
4. Carl Jung followed in Freud's footsteps. Carl Jung was Freud's student. Jung was particularly interested in dreams.
5. Nevertheless, other people believe that dreams are meaningless. These people believe that dreams are simply the brain's random activity. This activity might result from eating too much spicy food.

Combining by Coordinating Ideas

10b. Combine sentences that contain equally important words, phrases, or clauses by using coordinating conjunctions (*and, but, nor, for, or, yet*) or correlative conjunctions (such as *both . . . and, either . . . or, neither . . . nor*).

The relationship of the ideas in the sentences determines which connective will work best. When the sentences are joined in one sentence, the coordinate ideas form compound elements.

ORIGINAL   Richard will lend you the new 10,000 Maniacs album. Or maybe Mark will lend you the album.

COMBINED   **Either Richard or Mark** will lend you the new **10,000 Maniacs album.** [compound subject]

ORIGINAL   We could drive across the country. We could take the train.

COMBINED   We could **drive across the country or take the train.** [compound predicate]

ORIGINAL   The baseball player argued forcefully. The umpire refused to listen.

COMBINED   The baseball player argued forcefully**, but the umpire refused to listen.** [compound sentence]

You can also form a compound sentence by linking independent clauses with a semicolon and a conjunctive adverb (*however, likewise, therefore*) or with just a semicolon.

SENTENCES

EXAMPLES   Winston had never made the smallest effort
to verify this guess**;** **indeed**, there was no way
of doing so.

George Orwell, *1984*

You accept risk as part of every new challenge**;** it comes with the territory.

Chuck Yeager, *Yeager: An
Autobiography*

 REFERENCE NOTE: For more information about coordination, see pages 304–306 and 309–313.

©Mell Lazarus. By permission of
Mell Lazarus and Creators Syndicate.

✓ *QUICK CHECK 2*   **Combining by Coordinating
Ideas**

Combine each of the following sets of sentences by forming
a compound element. Be sure to choose a connective that
expresses the correct relationship between the ideas. You
may need to add punctuation, too.

EXAMPLE   **1.** William Least Heat-Moon traveled across
America. He wrote about his trip.
1. *William Least Heat-Moon traveled across
America and wrote about his trip.*

1. William Least Heat-Moon's first name comes from an
English ancestor. His last name was given to him by his
Sioux father.
2. In 1977, Least Heat-Moon left his Missouri home. He
began traveling across the country on back roads.
3. The title of his book *Blue Highways* doesn't refer to the
actual color of roads. It refers to the blue lines that
marked the back roads on his highway map.

4. Least Heat-Moon's trip began in the middle of the nation. His route was shaped like a jagged, sideways heart.

5. Small, oddly named towns made his journey memorable. Friendly, helpful people made his journey memorable.

Combining by Subordinating Ideas

10c. Combine related sentences by placing one idea in a subordinate clause (an *adjective clause*, an *adverb clause*, or a *noun clause*).

Subordination allows you to show the relationship between the ideas or to emphasize one idea.

EXAMPLES   He had a habit of pausing to fix his gaze on part of the congregation as he read, and that Sunday he seemed to be talking to a small group of strangers **who sat in the front row.** [adjective clause]

Andrea Lee, *Sarah Phillips*

My aunt Giorgiana regarded them **as though they had been so many daubs of tube-paint on a palette.** [adverb clause]

Willa Cather, "A Wagner Matinée"

What he had the most of was time. [noun clause]

Juan Sedillo, "Gentleman of Río en Medio"

 REFERENCE NOTE: For more information about subordinating ideas, see pages 306–309. For more information about the different types of subordinate clauses, see pages 264–273.

Adjective Clauses

An *adjective clause* modifies a noun or pronoun. When combining sentences, you can change one sentence into an adjective clause by replacing the subject of the sentence with *who, whose, which,* or *that.* Then you can use the adjective clause to give information about a noun or pronoun in the other sentence. Notice that the revisions that follow have slightly different emphases because the main clauses contain different ideas.

ORIGINAL   The National Air and Space Museum is in Washington, D.C. It contains many exhibits on the history of aeronautics.

REVISED   The National Air and Space Museum, **which contains many exhibits on the history of aeronautics,** is in Washington, D.C. [emphasis in main clause: location of museum]

or

REVISED   The National Air and Space Museum, **which is in Washington, D.C.,** contains many exhibits on the history of aeronautics. [emphasis in main clause: contents of museum]

ORIGINAL   I read about the life of Matthew Henson. He traveled to the North Pole with Robert Peary.

REVISED   I read about the life of Matthew Henson, **who traveled to the North Pole with Robert Peary.** [emphasis in main clause: my reading]

or

REVISED   Matthew Henson, **whose life I read about,** traveled to the North Pole with Robert Peary. [emphasis in main clause: Henson's travels]

To combine sentences by using an adjective clause, first decide which idea you want to emphasize and which you want to subordinate in the sentence. Be sure to keep your main idea in the independent clause.

 REFERENCE NOTE: For more information on punctuating adjective clauses, see pages 386–388.

Adverb Clauses

An *adverb clause* modifies a verb, an adjective, or another adverb in the independent or main clause. To make a sentence into an adverb clause, add a subordinating conjunction like *although, after, because, if, when, where,* or *while* at the beginning. You can then attach the adverb clause to the independent clause. An adverb clause may begin a sentence, end it, or interrupt the main clause. Always place a comma after an adverb clause that begins a sentence.

The conjunction can show a relationship of time, place, cause or reason, purpose or result, or condition. Be sure to choose the subordinating conjunction carefully, so that it shows the proper relationship between the ideas in the adverb clause and the independent clause.

ORIGINAL	The British general Burgoyne attacked a second time. The Americans won a decisive victory.
REVISED	**When the British general Burgoyne attacked a second time,** the Americans won a decisive victory. [time]
ORIGINAL	We should arrive by noon. Martha said that we can beat the crowd that way.
REVISED	Martha said that **if we arrive by noon** we'll beat the crowd. [condition]
ORIGINAL	Yukio and Julia both receive high grades. They work hard.
REVISED	Yukio and Julia both receive high grades **because they work hard.** [cause]

 REFERENCE NOTE: For more complete lists of subordinating conjunctions, see pages 111 and 272. For more information about using adverb clauses to subordinate ideas, see pages 307–308. For more information about the use of commas with subordinate clauses, see pages 267, 386–388, and 390.

Noun Clauses

A *noun clause* is a subordinate clause used as a noun. You can make a sentence into a noun clause by adding a word like *that, how, what, whatever, where, wherever, who,* or *whoever* at the beginning. You may also have to delete or move some words. Then insert the clause into another sentence as if it were an ordinary noun.

S E N T E N C E S

ORIGINAL   Ramón is going to the carnival tonight. Eliza told me this.

REVISED   Eliza told me **that Ramón is going to the carnival tonight.**

ORIGINAL   We are going on a field trip. Do you know where?

REVISED   Do you know **where we are going on a field trip?**

ORIGINAL   The bus driver will wait for them. They're still not here.

REVISED   The bus driver will wait for **whoever's still not here.**

   QUICK CHECK 3   **Combining by Subordinating Ideas**

Combine each of the following pairs of sentences by turning one sentence into a subordinate clause. [Hint: You may have to add, delete, or change some words in the sentences. Add commas where necessary.]

1. Space medicine is one of the most important areas of space study. Space medicine deals with the physical effects of space travel.
2. Doctors learned much about the human body's reactions to space travel. They collected medical data during early space missions.
3. Engineers must consider the effects of acceleration. They must consider how the spacecraft's acceleration will affect the astronauts' bodies.
4. A space shuttle is designed to protect the astronauts against the high-intensity radiation. They encounter this radiation in space.
5. Astronauts must exercise regularly in space. A person's heart and muscles weaken in a weightless condition.

STYLE NOTE

While varied sentences help hold readers' attention, a series of short, simple ones is not necessarily boring. In fact, such a series is often highly effective, creating a plain directness or a break in rhythm (even a jolt) that can strengthen writing. The following passage appears in a short story in which a young man takes a solitary fishing trip. Notice how well the simple sentences describe the stillness of the setting, the solitude, Nick's deliberate movements, and his peaceful sleep.

> Out through the front of the tent he watched the glow of the fire, when the night wind blew on it. It was a quiet night. The swamp was perfectly quiet. Nick stretched under the blanket comfortably. A mosquito hummed close to his ear. Nick sat up and lit a match. The mosquito was on the canvas, over his head. Nick moved the match quickly up to it. The mosquito made a satisfactory hiss in the flame. The match went out. Nick lay down again under the blanket. He turned on his side and shut his eyes. He was sleepy. He felt sleep coming. He curled up under the blanket and went to sleep.
>
> Ernest Hemingway, "Big Two-Hearted River: Part I"

A writer of novels and short stories, Ernest Hemingway is famous for his brief but expressive sentences. Many writers, of nonfiction as well as fiction, know how this style can highlight ideas, create rhythm, and establish mood.

Combining in Different Ways

The words and ideas in separate sentences can often be combined in several ways, by inserting words or phrases, by coordinating ideas, or by subordinating one idea to another. The sentence combining method you use in a given situation will depend on the sense and sound you desire.

If you regularly practice sentence combining during revision, your writing will become smoother and more articulate. The following examples show different combinations of several groups of sentences. You may see still other possibilities.

SENTENCES

SENTENCES

ORIGINAL	Peregrine falcons became scarce. They became scarce in the United States. They became scarce because of the pesticide DDT.
COMBINED	Peregrine falcons became scarce in the United States because of the pesticide DDT.
COMBINED	Because of the pesticide DDT, peregrine falcons became scarce in the United States.
COMBINED	The pesticide DDT caused a scarcity of peregrine falcons in the United States.
ORIGINAL	Scientists have reintroduced peregrine falcons. These scientists are from Cornell University. The falcons are wild. The scientists have reintroduced the falcons to the eastern United States. They did it under controlled conditions.
COMBINED	Scientists from Cornell University have reintroduced wild peregrine falcons, under controlled conditions, to the eastern United States.
COMBINED	Under controlled conditions, Cornell University scientists have reintroduced wild peregrine falcons to the eastern United States.
COMBINED	In the eastern United States, Cornell University scientists have accomplished controlled reintroduction of wild peregrine falcons.
COMBINED	Peregrine falcons have been reintroduced, under controlled conditions set by Cornell University scientists, in the eastern states.
ORIGINAL	Mars is the only planet whose surface can be seen in detail. It can be seen from the earth. The planet is reddish in color. It was named after the ancient Romans' red god of war.
COMBINED	Reddish-colored Mars, named after the ancient Romans' red god of war, is the only planet whose surface can be seen in detail from the earth.
COMBINED	Mars, the only planet whose surface can be seen in detail from the earth, is reddish-colored and takes its name from the ancient Romans' red god of war.
COMBINED	Mars, reddish in color, was named after the ancient Romans' red god of war. It is the only planet whose surface can be seen in detail from the earth.

(continued)

ORIGINAL	*Frankenstein* is an early example of science fiction. The novel describes the scientific creation of human life.
COMBINED	*Frankenstein,* an early science fiction novel, describes the scientific creation of human life.
COMBINED	The novel *Frankenstein,* which describes the scientific creation of human life, is an early example of science fiction.
COMBINED	*Frankenstein* is a novel describing the scientific creation of human life and is an early example of science fiction.
ORIGINAL	Major authors of the early twentieth century often included science fiction in their works. Some critics did not accept the genre as serious literature.
COMBINED	Major authors of the early twentieth century often included science fiction in their works, yet some critics did not accept the genre as serious.
COMBINED	Although major authors of the early twentieth century often included science fiction in their works, some critics did not accept the genre as serious.
COMBINED	While some critics did not accept science fiction as serious literature, major authors of the early twentieth century often included it in their works.
COMBINED	That some critics rejected science fiction as literature did not prevent major authors of the early twentieth century from using it in their works.
COMBINED	That some critics rejected science fiction as literature did not deter major authors of the early twentieth century; many used the genre in their works.

S E N T E N C E S

Combining sentences means experimenting—something a computer is great for. For example, you can use functions like "Copy,"

"Cut," and "Move" to play with the placement of words, phrases, and clauses. When you're revising, try different combinations and print them all. Seeing rearranged wordings on the page helps you decide which one works best for the flow of the paragraph.

 Chapter Review

Combining Sentences

Using the sentence-combining method indicated in parentheses after each group of sentences that follows, combine the sentences into one smooth sentence. You may delete unnecessary words, change word order and word forms, and add connective words and punctuation. Do not, however, change the meaning of the original sentences. Be sure to punctuate your combined sentences correctly.

EXAMPLE
1. The Delaware Aqueduct carries fresh water.
The water is drawn from local reservoirs.
(*participial phrase*)
1. *The Delaware Aqueduct carries fresh water drawn from local reservoirs.*

1. The composer Mozart showed early signs of genius.
He played for the empress of Austria when he was only six.
(*semicolon*)

2. We can never fully appreciate the Greek poet Sappho's poetry.
No poems by Sappho survived intact.
(*adverb clause*)

3. Engineers of the Alaskan pipeline tried to preserve the ecology of the tundra.
The engineers were working with environmentalists.
(*participial phrase*)

4. The minutes ticked away slowly.
The minutes ticked away on the clock.
(*prepositional phrase*)

5. We must take steps to preserve the short-necked tortoise.
   The short-necked tortoise may become extinct.
   (*correlative conjunction*)
6. Somebody left this chair here.
   Do you know why?
   (*noun clause*)
7. Margaret Atwood often refers metaphorically to nature in her poetry.
   Poet Margaret Atwood is from Canada.
   (*single word*)
8. Deep-sea divers must surface slowly to avoid the "bends."
   They know this.
   They have had experience.
   (*adjective clause; noun clause*)
9. The hikers found the trail back to camp.
   The hikers were relieved and exhausted.
   (*participial phrase*)
10. The Chinese poet Tu Fu wrote innovative poetry.
    His poetry is known for its elegance and realism.
    Tu Fu was a melancholy wanderer.
    (*adjective clause; appositive phrase*)

SENTENCES

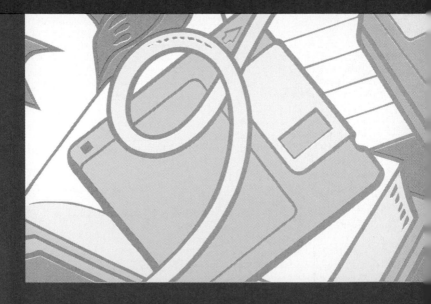

PART FOUR

MECHANICS

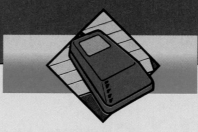

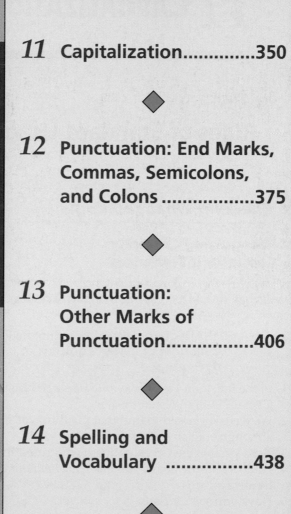

11 CAPITALIZATION

Rules of Standard Usage

 *Checking What You Know*

A. Recognizing Correctly Capitalized Sentences

For each of the following sentences, write the word or words that should be capitalized. If a sentence is correct, write C.

EXAMPLE   1. After Dan finishes shopping, he'll meet us in front of Calvert's grocery.
   1. *Grocery*

1. In the fall, aunt Lisa's play will be staged by the Captain Philip Weston theater.
2. We were surprised to find that the film was in spanish, although english subtitles were provided.
3. Was Artemis the Greek goddess who ruled the hunt?
4. Pablo's favorite board game is *Trivial pursuit* because he always wins.
5. Have you seen *A raisin in the sun* yet?
6. Leon stood at the card counter for a full hour, trying to choose just the right card for Valentine's day.
7. The opening speech will be given by ex-Senator Preston.

8. Alnaba's new brother was delivered at Memorial hospital just before dawn.
9. Come to see our fantastic selection of top-quality stereo equipment at our new location just south of interstate 4 and River Road!
10. Can you name four countries located on the continent of Africa?

B. Proofreading for Correct Capitalization

Proofread the following paragraph for errors in capitalization. In each sentence, change lowercase letters to capitals or capital letters to lowercase as necessary. If a sentence is correct, write C.

EXAMPLE
[1] As humanity has developed more and more of the Earth's wilderness areas, many animal species have become extinct or endangered.
1. earth's

[11] Last year, in a special Ecology course at Charlotte High School, I found out about some endangered North American animals. [12] I learned that conservationists here in the south are particularly concerned about the fate of the Florida panther. [13] All of that classroom discussion didn't have much impact on me, however, until early one Saturday morning last Spring, when I was lucky enough to sight one of these beautiful creatures. [14] My Uncle and I were driving to Big Bass Lake for some fishing, and I saw what looked like a large dog crossing the road some distance ahead of us. [15] Suddenly, Uncle Billy stopped his old ford truck and reached for the field glasses in the glove compartment. [16] As he handed them to me, he said, "look closely, Chris. You probably won't see a panther again any time soon." [17] Standing in the middle of Collingswood avenue, the cat turned and looked straight at us. [18] When those brown eyes met mine, I knew I had the title for my term paper—"Hello And Goodbye." [19] Then the big cat leisurely turned and crossed the road and loped off into the woods east of Sunshine Mall. [20] As the panther disap-

peared back into the wilds of Charlotte county, Uncle Billy said, "May god go with you, pal." ✓

In your reading, you'll notice variations in the use of capitalization. Most writers, however, follow the rules presented in this chapter. In your own writing, following these rules will help you communicate clearly with the widest possible audience.

11a. Capitalize the first word in every sentence.

EXAMPLES   **A**uthor Leslie Marmon Silko was born in Albuquerque, New Mexico, and grew up on the Laguna Pueblo Reservation.
When he missed the bus, my brother asked, "**W**ill you drive me to school?"

(1) Capitalize the first word of a sentence following a colon.

EXAMPLE   The police commissioner issued a startling statement: **I**n light of new evidence, the police department would reopen its investigation of the Brooks burglary.

(2) Capitalize the first word of a direct quotation.

EXAMPLE   When he surrendered in 1877, Chief Joseph declared, "**F**rom where the sun now stands I will fight no more forever."

When quoting from another writer's work, capitalize the first word of the quotation only if the writer has capitalized it in the original work.

EXAMPLE   In his speech of surrender in 1877, Chief Joseph declared that he would "**f**ight no more forever."

 REFERENCE NOTE: For more information about using capital letters in quotations, see pages 412–413.

(3) Traditionally, the first word of a line of poetry is capitalized.

EXAMPLE   I sit and sew—a useless task it seems,
            My hands grown tired, my head weighed-
               down with dreams—
            The panoply of war, the martial tread of men,
            Grim-faced, stern-eyed, gazing beyond the
               ken
            Of lesser souls, whose eyes have not seen
               Death
            Nor learned to hold their lives but as a
               breath—
            But—I must sit and sew.

                          Alice Dunbar-Nelson,
                          "I Sit and Sew"

NOTE Some modern writers, for reasons of style, do not fol-
          low this rule. When you quote from a writer's work,
          always use capital letters exactly as the writer uses
          them.

EXAMPLE   The art of losing isn't hard to master;
            so many things seem filled with the
               intent
            to be lost that their loss is no disaster.

                          Elizabeth Bishop, "One Art"

**(4) Capitalize the first word of a statement or question
inserted in a sentence without quotation marks.**

EXAMPLE   What Jerome wants to know is, **W**ill this new
            project create jobs?

**(5) Capitalize the first word of a resolution following
the word *Resolved*.**

EXAMPLE   *Resolved*, That a salad bar be installed in the
            cafeteria.

11b. Capitalize the first word in the salutation and the
         closing of a letter.

EXAMPLES   **D**ear Maria,   **D**ear Sir or Madame:
            Sincerely,   **Y**ours truly,
            Best regards,

11c. Capitalize the Roman numerals and letters in an outline, as well as the first word in each heading and subheading.

EXAMPLE
    I. Student use of computers
      A. Geography
        1. Maps
        2. Games
        3. Growth and weather patterns
      B. English and journalism
        1. Writing and revising
        2. Charts and graphs

11d. Capitalize the interjection *O* and the pronoun *I*.

The interjection *O* is usually used only for invocations and is followed by the name of the person or thing being addressed. Don't confuse it with the common interjection *oh*, which is capitalized only when it appears at the beginning of a sentence and is always followed by punctuation.

EXAMPLES
    Walt Whitman's tribute to Abraham Lincoln begins, "**O** Captain! my Captain!"
    What **I** meant was—**oh**, never mind.

11e. Capitalize proper nouns and proper adjectives.

A *common noun* is a general name for a person, place, thing, or idea. A *proper noun* names a particular person, place, thing, or idea. *Proper adjectives* are formed from proper nouns.

 REFERENCE NOTE: For more information about proper nouns and common nouns, see pages 88 and 359–360.

    Common nouns are capitalized only if they
- begin a sentence (also, in most cases, a line of poetry)

    or

- begin a direct quotation

    or

- are part of a title

COMMON NOUNS	PROPER NOUNS	PROPER ADJECTIVES
poet	Homer	Homeric epithet
country	Lebanon	Lebanese restaurant
president	Jefferson	Jeffersonian ideals
island	Hawaii	Hawaiian climate
religion	Judaism	Jewish holy day
mountains	the Alps	Alpine flora

In proper nouns made up of two or more words, do *not* capitalize

- articles (*a, an, the*)
- short prepositions (those with fewer than five letters, such as *at, of, for, to, with*)
- the mark of the infinitive (*to*)
- coordinating conjunctions (*and, but, for, nor, or, so, yet*)

EXAMPLES   Army of the Potomac
Queen of Spain
American Society for the Prevention of Cruelty to Animals
Teachers of English to Speakers of Other Languages
Hispanic Association of Colleges and Universities
"Writing to Persuade"

The parts of a compound word are capitalized as if each part stood alone.

EXAMPLES   African American   Central American nations
Chinese checkers   English-speaking tourists

 NOTE Some proper nouns and proper adjectives have lost their capitals after long usage.

EXAMPLES   madras   sandwich
watt   puritan
herculean   quixotic
mogul   vulcanization

Others may be written with or without capitals.

MECHANICS

EXAMPLES   **R**oman (**r**oman) numerals
Venetian (**v**enetian) blinds
plaster of **P**aris (**p**aris)
Gothic (**g**othic) style
Angora (**a**ngora) wool
India (**i**ndia) rubber
Modernist (**m**odernist) writers

When you're not sure whether to capitalize a word, check a dictionary.

(1) Capitalize the names of persons and of animals.

GIVEN NAMES	Patricia	Brian	Toshio	Aretha
SURNAMES	Sánchez	Goldblum	Williams	Ozawa
ANIMALS	Lassie	Rocinante	Socks	Moby-Dick

NOTE Some names contain more than one capital letter. Usage varies in the capitalization of *van, von, du, de la,* and other parts of many multiword names. Always verify the spelling of a name with the person, or check the name in a reference source.

EXAMPLES   **La F**ontaine   **McE**wen
O'Connor   **V**an **D**oren
Yellow **T**hunder **I**bn **E**zra
Villa-**L**obos   van **G**ogh
al-Khansa   de **V**ega

COMPUTER NOTE   The range of correct spellings of personal names can foil even the best spell-checking software. One way to avoid this problem is to customize your spelling checker. If your software allows, add to it any frequently used names that you have difficulty spelling or capitalizing correctly.

Abbreviations such as *Ms., Mr., Dr.,* and *Gen.* should always be capitalized.

EXAMPLES   **Ms.** Gloria Steinem   **Dr.** Antonia Novello
Gen. Colin Powell   **Mr.** Rodríquez

MECHANICS

REFERENCE NOTE: For more about punctuating abbreviations, see pages 380–381 and 395.

Capitalize the abbreviations *Jr.* and *Sr.* following a name and set them off with commas. Also capitalize Roman numerals (I, II, III, etc.), but do *not* set them off with commas.

EXAMPLES   Dr. Martin Luther King, **Jr.**, led the march.
John D. Rockefeller, **Sr.**, made his fortune in the oil-refining industry.
Isabella **I** and Ferdinand **V** of Spain financed Christopher Columbus's voyages.

Capitalize descriptive names and nicknames

EXAMPLES   Pliny the **Y**ounger   the **C**os
Catherine the **G**reat   the **S**alsa **Q**ueen

NOTE Enclose nicknames in quotation marks when they are used along with a full name.

EXAMPLES   Celia Cruz, **"**the **S**alsa **Q**ueen**"**
William **"**the **C**os**"** Cosby

(2) Capitalize geographical names.

TYPE OF NAME	EXAMPLES	
Towns, Cities	Boston Tokyo South Bend	Rio de Janeiro Dar es Salaam Wilkes-Barre
Counties, Townships, Provinces	Marion County Lawrence Township Brooklyn Borough	Lafayette Parish Nottinghamshire Quebec Province
States	Wisconsin New Hampshire Punjab	Oklahoma North Carolina Nuevo León

NOTE Popular place names are usually capitalized.

EXAMPLES   the **A**loha **S**tate
the **C**ity of **B**rotherly **L**ove
the **L**oop (Chicago)
the **V**illage (New York)

MECHANICS

TYPE OF NAME	EXAMPLES	
Regions	the New World the Lake District the East Coast the Pacific Northwest the East the Southwest	the Orient the Panhandle the Midwest the Sunbelt Northern Hemisphere New England

 NOTE Words such as *north, western*, and *southeast* are not capitalized when they indicate direction.

EXAMPLES   **w**estern Iowa   driving **s**outh

 REFERENCE NOTE: The abbreviations of names of states are always capitalized. For more about using and punctuating such abbreviations, see pages 380 and 586–596.

TYPE OF NAME	EXAMPLES	
Countries	Mozambique Costa Rica	United States of America
Continents	North America Africa	Asia Europe
Islands	Catalina Island Greater Antilles	Isle of Pines Florida Keys
Mountains	Blue Ridge Mountains Sierra Nevada	Mount McKinley Humphrey's Peak

 NOTE Since *sierra* is Spanish for "mountain range," *Sierra Nevada Mountains* is redundant. Use *Sierra Nevada* alone.

TYPE OF NAME	EXAMPLES	
Other Land Forms and Features	Cape Cod Mojave Desert Mississippi Valley Dismal Swamp Haleakala Crater San Fernando Valley	Isthmus of Panama Horse Cave Point Sur Bismarck Archipelago Narbona Pass

(continued)

MECHANICS

TYPE OF NAME	EXAMPLES	
Bodies of Water	Pacific Ocean Strait of Hormuz Erie Canal Amazon River Persian Gulf Nord Fiord Guanabara Bay Barton Springs Rio Grande Gulf of Mexico	Great Lakes Saint Lawrence Seaway Lake Huron Dead Sea Firth of Forth Loch Ness Salt Creek Long Island Sound Rosemary Pond

 NOTE Since *río* is Spanish for "river," *Rio Grande River* is redundant. Use *Rio Grande* alone.

TYPE OF NAME	EXAMPLES	

Parks	Pedernaks Falls
	  State Park
	Point Reyes National
	  Seashore
	Hawaii Volcanoes
	  National Park
		Cumbres de Majalca
		  National Park
		Gates of the Arctic
		  National Park
		Mississippi Headwaters
		  State Forest

Roads, Highways, Streets	Route 30 Interstate 55 Pennsylvania Turnpike Cheyenne Court Lantern Lane	Michigan Avenue North Tenth Street Morningside Drive Lake Ponchartrain Causeway

 REFERENCE NOTE: In addresses, abbreviations such as *St., Ave., Dr.,* and *Blvd.* are capitalized. For more about abbreviations, see pages 380–381, 395, and 586–596.

 NOTE The second word in a hyphenated number begins with a small letter.

EXAMPLES   Forty-second Street
Eighty-ninth Street

Words such as *city, island, street,* and *park* are capitalized only when they are part of a name.

MECHANICS

PROPER NOUNS	COMMON NOUNS
a rodeo in **Carson City**	a rodeo in a nearby city
a ferry to **Block Island**	a ferry to a resort island
swimming in **Clear Lake**	swimming in the lake
along **Canal Street**	along a neighborhood street

NOTE Words such as *city, state*, and *county* are often capitalized in official documents such as proclamations. In general usage, however, these words are not capitalized.

| OFFICIAL USAGE | the State of Iowa |
| GENERAL USAGE | the state of Iowa |

QUICK CHECK 1 **Capitalizing Words and Names Correctly**

If a word or words in the following phrases should be capitalized, write the entire phrase correctly. If a phrase is correct, write C.

1. the far west
2. a city north of louisville
3. lock the door!
4. mary mcleod bethune
5. mexican gold
6. She said, "it was not i!"
7. the utah salt flats
8. Yes, but, oh, what a sight it was!
9. III. history of China
10. 210 thirty-eighth avenue north

(3) Capitalize the names of organizations, teams, business firms, institutions, buildings and other structures, and government bodies.

TYPE OF NAME	EXAMPLES
Organizations	American Dental Association Future Farmers of America National Science Foundation Disabled American Veterans Professional Photographers of America Guide Dog Foundation for the Blind

(continued)

MECHANICS

TYPE OF NAME	EXAMPLES	
Teams	Detroit Pistons San Diego Padres Harlem Globetrotters	Miami Dolphins Cedar Hill Hawks Nebraska Cornhuskers

Business Firms	Roth's Optical
	Diesel Engine
	   Specialists
	American Greetings
	   Corporation
		Hip-Hop Music, Inc.
		American Broadcasting
		   Corporation
		La Fiesta Restaurant
		University Square Mall

Institutions	Duke University Mayo Clinic University of California at Los Angeles Habitat for Humanity Southern Christian Leadership Conference	
Buildings and Other Structures	Century Center Rialto Theater the White House Meadowlawn High School the Pyramid of Khufu Washington National Cathedral Lincoln Center for the Performing Arts the Great Wall of China the Golden Gate Bridge Gateway Arch	
Government Bodies	Department of State Congress House of Representatives Atomic Energy Commission Tennessee Valley Authority House of Commons Bundestag United States Marine Corps	

NOTE The names of organizations, businesses, and government bodies are often abbreviated after the first spelled-out use.

EXAMPLES

Parent-Teacher Association	**PTA**
International Business Machines	**IBM**
Federal Bureau of Investigation	**FBI**
Cooperative for American Relief to Everywhere	**CARE**

MECHANICS

NOTE Usually the letters in such abbreviations are not followed by periods, but always check an up-to-date reference source to be sure.

"After working all day on my MBA, I hop into my BMW and race home to watch PBS on my VCR—OK?"

© 1990; reprinted courtesy of Bunny Hoest and Parade Magazine

REFERENCE NOTE: For more about abbreviations, see pages 380–381, 395, and 586–596.

Do not capitalize words such as *democratic, republican,* and *socialist* when they refer to principles or forms of government. Capitalize such words only when they refer to a specific political party.

EXAMPLES The citizens demanded **d**emocratic reforms.
Who will be the **R**epublican nominee for governor?

The word *party* in the name of a political party may be capitalized or not; either way is correct. Within a given composition, however, be consistent in your treatment of the term.

EXAMPLE **D**emocratic **p**arty

or

Democratic **P**arty

 NOTE Do not capitalize words such as *building, hospital, theater, high school, university*, and *post office* unless they are part of a proper noun.

MECHANICS

REFERENCE NOTE: For more on the differences between common nouns and proper nouns, see page 88.

(4) Capitalize the names of historical events and periods, special events, holidays and other calendar items, and time zones.

TYPE OF NAME	EXAMPLES	
Historical Events and Periods	Boston Tea Party Battle of Saratoga Reign of Terror Great Depression War on Poverty March on Washington for Jobs and Freedom	Middle Ages French Revolution Mesozoic Era Holocaust Counter-Reformation Civil Rights Movement Babylonian Captivity
Special Events	Olympics Super Bowl New York Marathon	Ohio State Fair Earth Summit Pan-American Games
Holidays and Other Calendar Items	Wednesday September Kwanzaa National Book Week	Fourth of July Memorial Day Mother's Day Hispanic Heritage Month
Time Zones	Mountain Standard Time (**MST**) Eastern Daylight Time (**EDT**) Greenwich Mean Time (**GMT**)	

 NOTE Do not capitalize the name of a season unless the season is being personified (in which case capitalization is optional) or unless it is used as part of a proper noun.

EXAMPLES The **w**inter was unusually warm.
Overnight, **W**inter crept in, trailing her snowy veil.
We plan to attend the school's **W**inter Carnival.

(5) Capitalize the names of nationalities, races, and peoples.

EXAMPLES   Lithuanian Haitian Jewish Asian
Caucasian Hispanic Bantu Zuni
Croat Romany Mongol Celt

MECHANICS

(6) Capitalize the brand names of commercial products.

EXAMPLES   **B**orden milk
Colonial bread
Zenith television

Notice that the noun that may follow a brand name is not capitalized: a Xerox machine.

(7) Capitalize the names of ships, trains, aircraft, spacecraft, monuments, awards, planets, and any other particular places, things, or events.

TYPE OF NAME	EXAMPLES	
Ships	*Merrimac* *Monitor*	*Cunard Princess* *U.S.S. Forrestal*
Trains	*Orient Express* *Zephyr*	*North Coast Limited* *City of New Orleans*
Aircraft	*Spirit of St. Louis* *Enola Gay*	*Air Force One* *Spruce Goose*
Spacecraft	*Atlantis* *Columbia*	*Apollo 11* *Magellan*
Monuments	Lincoln Memorial Mount Rushmore National Memorial	Statue of Liberty Effigy Mounds National Monument
Awards	Academy Award Medal of Freedom	Pulitzer Prize Springarn Medal
Planets, Stars, Constellations	Jupiter Rigel Big Dipper	Orion Ursa Minor Cassiopeia

NOTE   Do not capitalize the words *sun* and *moon*. Do not capitalize the word *earth* unless it is used along with the names of other heavenly bodies that are capitalized.

EXAMPLES   The **m**oon reflects light from the **s**un.
This orchid grows wild in only one place on **e**arth.
Venus is closer to the **s**un than **E**arth is.

TYPE OF NAME	EXAMPLES	
Other Particular Things, Places, and Events	Underground Railroad Silk Route Hurricane Andrew	Treaty Oak Valkyries Marshall Plan

11f. Do *not* capitalize the names of school subjects, except for names of languages and course names followed by a number.

EXAMPLES   history   art   physics   geometry
           Spanish   Latin   Algebra I   Chemistry II

NOTE   As a rule, nouns identified by a number or letter are capitalized.

EXAMPLES   Room 31   School District 18
           Chapter 4   Plate 4
           Figure 1   Parlor B

EXCEPTIONS   The word *page* is usually not capitalized, nor are plural nouns followed by two or more numbers or letters.

EXAMPLE   For comparison, see figures 4 and 5 on page 127.

Do not capitalize the class names *senior, junior, sophomore,* and *freshman* unless they are part of a proper noun.

EXAMPLES   The juniors are planning a surprise for Senior Day.
           The Freshman Follies was a big success.

 QUICK CHECK 2   **Capitalizing Words and Names Correctly**

Write the following words and phrases, using capital letters where they are needed. If a word or phrase is correct, write C.

1. st. patrick's cathedral
2. *city of new orleans* (train)
3. the federal reserve bank
4. the normandy invasion

MECHANICS

5. classes in auto mechanics
6. cherokee history
7. jones and drake, inc.
8. on labor day
9. early summer
10. gold medal flour

11g. Capitalize titles.

(1) Capitalize a title belonging to a particular person when it comes before the person's name.

EXAMPLES   **G**eneral Davis   **D**r. Ramírez
                 President Kennedy

☞ **REFERENCE NOTE:** See pages 356–357 and 586–587 for information on abbreviating titles before names.

In general, do not capitalize a title used alone as a subject or object or following a name. Some titles, however, are capitalized according to tradition. If you are unsure of whether or not to capitalize a title, check in a dictionary.

EXAMPLES   Who is the **g**overnor of Kansas?
                 Sherian Grace Cadoria, a **b**rigadier **g**eneral, is the highest-ranking African American woman in the U.S. Armed Forces.
                 The **S**peaker of the **H**ouse rose to greet the **Q**ueen of England.

A title is usually capitalized when it is used alone in direct address.

EXAMPLES   Have you reached your decision, **G**overnor?
                 We're honored to welcome you, **M**s. **M**ayor.
                 Please come in, **S**ir [or sir].

STYLE NOTE

For special emphasis or clarity, writers sometimes capitalize a title used alone or following a person's name.

EXAMPLES   The **G**overnor was in the last car in the parade.
                 Did the **P**resident veto the bill?

MECHANICS

Do not capitalize *ex-, -elect, former,* or *late* when they are used with a title.

EXAMPLES   **ex-Governor Walsh**   **the president-elect**

(2) Capitalize words showing family relationships when used with a person's name but *not* when preceded by a possessive.

EXAMPLES   **A**unt Amy   my **a**unt
            Uncle Hector   your **u**ncle
            Grandma Díaz   Al's **g**randmother

NOTE   A word showing a family relationship is capitalized when used in place of a person's name.

EXAMPLE   May I borrow the car, **M**om?

(3) Capitalize the first and last words and all important words in titles of books, periodicals, poems, stories, essays, speeches, plays, historical documents, movies, radio and television programs, works of art, musical compositions, and cartoons.

Unimportant words in a title include
- articles: *a, an, the*
- short prepositions (fewer than five letters): *of, to, in, for, from, with,* and so on
- coordinating conjunctions: *and, but, for, nor, or, so, yet*

TYPE OF NAME	EXAMPLES
Books	*I Know Why the Caged Bird Sings* *The Way to Rainy Mountain* *One Hundred Years of Solitude*
Periodicals	*Car and Driver* *Essence* *Louisville Courier-Journal & Times*
Poems	"Tonight I Can Write" *I Am Joaquín* "Most Satisfied by Snow" "The Raven"
Stories	"In Another Country" "Billy Budd" "The Catch in the Shadow of the Sunrise"
Essays and Speeches	"By Any Other Name" "The Lost Worlds of Ancient America" "I Have a Dream" "The Gettysburg Address"

(continued)

MECHANICS

TYPE OF NAME	EXAMPLES	
Plays	*Song of Sheba* *Watch on the Rhine* *The Importance of Being Earnest*	*Into the Woods* *Macbeth*
Historical Documents	Declaration of Independence Mayflower Compact Treaty of Versailles	
Movies	*Children of a Lesser God* *No Place to Be Somebody* *Come See the Paradise*	
Radio and TV Programs	"Adventures in World Music" *A Different World* *Star Trek: The Next Generation*	
Works of Art	*Three Dancers* [painting] *The Kiss* [sculpture] March of Humanity [mural]	*Double Dutch on the Golden Gate Bridge* [story quilt]
Musical Compositions	"Lift Every Voice and Sing" *Into the Light*	*Three Places in New England* "Tears in Heaven"
Cartoons	"For Better or Worse" "The Far Side"	"Where I'm Coming From" "Jump Start"

NOTE The first word of a subtitle is always capitalized.

EXAMPLES *Utamara: The Musical*
"From Jump Street: The Story of Black Music"
Frida: A Biography of Frida Kahlo

Always capitalize the first element in a hyphenated compound used in a title. Capitalize the second element only if it is a noun or a proper adjective or if it has equal force with the first element.

EXAMPLES *Seventeenth-Century Poetry Revisited*
The Non-Muslim Culture of Modern Egypt

Do not capitalize the second element if it is a participle that modifies the first element or if the two elements make up a single word.

MECHANICS

EXAMPLES   Spanish-**s**peaking   Economy-**s**ized
                 A-**s**harp   Re-**c**reate
                 Self-**s**upporting   Life-**s**ustaining

NOTE   The article *the* is often written before a title but is not capitalized unless it is part of the official title. The official title of a book is found on the title page. The official title of a newspaper or periodical is found on the masthead, which usually appears on the editorial page.

EXAMPLES   the *Austin American-Statesman*
                the *Odyssey*
                the *Philadelphia Inquirer*

                The Atlantic
                The Wall Street Journal
                The Man in the Iron Mask

Frank & Ernest reprinted by permission of NEA, Inc.

REFERENCE NOTE: For information about which titles should be italicized and which should be enclosed in quotation marks, see pages 408–410 and 416–418.

(4) Capitalize the names of religions and their followers, holy days and celebrations, holy writings, and specific deities and venerated beings.

TYPE OF NAME	EXAMPLES	
Religions and Followers	Amish Christianity Muslim Judaism	Roman Catholic Hinduism Shintoism Presbyterian
Holy Days and Celebrations	Epiphany Ramadan Holy Week Rosh Hashanah	Easter Passover Christmas Potlatch

(continued)

MECHANICS

TYPE OF NAME	EXAMPLES	
Holy Writings	Bible Koran I Ching Talmud	Rig Veda Genesis Book of Mormon the Pentateuch
Specific Deities and Venerated Beings	Allah Brahma God	Jehovah the Prophet (Mohammed) the Messiah

The words *god* and *goddess* are not capitalized when they refer to the deities of ancient mythology. The names of specific mythological deities are capitalized, however.

EXAMPLE   The Greek **g**od of the sea was Poseidon.

NOTE   Some writers capitalize all pronouns that refer to a deity. Others capitalize such pronouns only if necessary to prevent confusion.

EXAMPLE   Through Moses, God commanded the pharaoh to let **H**is people go. [*His* is capitalized to show that it refers to *God*, not *pharaoh* or *Moses*.]

 QUICK CHECK 3   **Capitalizing Names and Titles Correctly**

Write the following items, using capital letters where they are needed. If an item is correct, write C.

1. the *washington post*
2. ex-senator Margaret Chase Smith
3. *I'll fly away* (TV program)
4. captain of the fencing team
5. emancipation proclamation
6. the first chapter in *the grapes of wrath*
7. the teachings of islam
8. the late Bessie Smith
9. Come with me, dad.
10. the new testament

MECHANICS

✓ *Chapter Review*

Capitalizing Words and Phrases Correctly

For each of the following sentences, write the words that should be capitalized. If a sentence is correct, write C.

EXAMPLE　　**1.** The rotary club has invited representative William Bashone to speak at tonight's annual banquet.
　　　　　　　1. *Rotary Club; Representative*

1. According to Zack Johnson, the company's representative, you shouldn't buy just any car; you should buy a saturn.
2. One of the earliest cars made by Henry Ford was called the Model T; it had a four-cylinder, twenty-horsepower engine.
3. On our vacation we toured several states in the south.
4. Johnson's bake shop and deli is just north of state street on highway 143.
5. Before you can take this computer course, you must pass algebra II.
6. Aren't they planning a parade to celebrate Martin Luther King, jr., day?
7. Because we cheered so loudly at the special olympics, ms. Andrews made Bill and me honorary cheerleaders for her special education class.
8. On the television program *Meet the press*, a journalist predicted that the president would veto any tax increase.
9. The british poet Ted Hughes was married to Sylvia Plath, who was an american poet.
10. The only man in American history who was not elected to be vice-president or president, yet held both positions, is ex-president Gerald Ford.
11. My mother asked me to walk to the supermarket and buy a quart container of farmingbury milk and two pounds of pinto beans.
12. When we toured eastern Tennessee, we visited the Oak Ridge Laboratory, where atomic research was carried out during World War II.

MECHANICS

13. The Spanish-american Club has planned a festival for late summer; it will be held at the north end of the city.
14. If you are looking for great apples, follow route 14 until you see signs for Peacock's Orchard.
15. In a controversial debate on the Panama canal, the United States voted to relinquish its control of the canal to the Panamanian government.
16. When my Aunt Janice visited England last summer, she toured buckingham palace and tried to catch a glimpse of queen Elizabeth.
17. Mayor-elect Sabrena Willis will speak to the public about her proposals to upgrade the city's bilingual education program.
18. Earl and Jamie were lucky to get tickets to see the Indigo girls at the Erwin center.
19. When spring arrives, I know it's time to start thinking about looking for a summer job.
20. Although the east room of the White house is now used for press conferences, it was once a place where Abigail Adams aired the president's laundry.

SUMMARY STYLE REVIEW

Names of Persons

Mrs. Martin A. LaForge, Sr.	a neighbor
Louise Brown	a girl in my class
Mr. Peter Echohawk	a math teacher

Geographical Names

Sioux City	a city in Iowa
Orange County	a county in Florida
Brazil	a country in South America
Staten Island	an island in New York Harbor
Allegheny Mountains	a mountain range
Pacific Ocean	across the ocean
Forty-third Street	a one-way street
Sequoia National Park	a national park
in the East, North, Midwest	heading east, north, south

Organizations, Teams, Business Firms, Institutions, Buildings, Government Bodies

New York Philharmonic	a symphony orchestra
San Antonio Spurs	a basketball team

(continued)

SUMMARY STYLE REVIEW *(continued)*

Organizations, Teams, Business Firms, Institutions, Buildings, Government Bodies *(continued)*

Something from the Oven	a bakery
Madison High School	a large high school
the Pyramid of the Sun	a pyramid in Mexico
Supreme Court	a district court
Department of the Interior	a department of government

Historical Events and Periods, Special Events, Calendar Items

the Korean War	a veteran of the war
the Stone Age	a prehistoric age
the Super Bowl	a championship game
Father's Day	a national holiday
April, July, October, January	spring, summer, autumn, winter

Nationalities, Races, Peoples

Cambodian	a nationality
Caucasian	a race
Ibo	a people of western Africa

Brand Names

Stutz Bearcat	an antique automobile
Pac-Man	a video game

Other Particular Places, Things, Events, Awards

Niña	a ship
Metroliner	a train
Galileo	a spacecraft
Spirgarn Medal	an award
the Milky Way	a galaxy
Earth, Venus, Saturn	from the earth
Suite 402	the presidential suite
the Coronado Memorial	a memorial in Arizona
Senior Prom	a senior in high school
Silver Star	a medal for heroism

Specific Courses, Languages

Bookkeeping I	after bookkeeping class
Spanish	a foreign language
Geometry II	a geometry test

Titles

Mayor Dixon	a mayor
President of the United States	president of the club

(continued)

MECHANICS

SUMMARY STYLE REVIEW *(continued)*	
Titles *(continued)*	
the Duke of Edinburgh	a duke's title
Aunt Rosa	my aunt
The Piano Lesson	a play
the *Oakland Tribune*	a daily newspaper
Holy Bible	a religious book
"Kubla Khan"	a poem
"The Secret Sharer"	a short story
the Bill of Rights	a document
Robin Hood: Prince of Thieves	a movie
Roc	a television program
La Giocanda	a work of art
"America the Beautiful"	a musical composition
"Wizard of Id"	a cartoon

Names of Religions, Their Followers, Holy Days, Celebrations, Holy Writings, Specific Deities

Islam	the religious faith of Muslims
Ash Wednesday	the first day of Lent
Hanukkah	a Jewish festival
the Holy Bible	a holy book
God	Zeus, a Greek god

12 PUNCTUATION

End Marks, Commas, Semicolons, and Colons

✓ Checking What You Know

A. Correcting Sentences by Changing Punctuation

Add, delete, or replace end marks, commas, semicolons, or colons to correct each of the following sentences.

EXAMPLE   **1.** Do you think that it will rain today Brian.
           1. *Do you think that it will rain today, Brian?*

1. Gov Jameston, a well-known Democrat does not plan to run for another term.
2. This year I am taking courses in English, Spanish algebra and history
3. When I joined the staff of the newspaper I was taught to write short powerful headlines
4. The essay, that Ms. Hughes assigned yesterday, is due next Monday.
5. "I like everything about my new car its design, color, and smooth ride," Cari said.
6. Bravo, what a great solo.

MECHANICS

375

7. Geometry which I took last year was not an easy subject for me.
8. Peg asked, "Have you read for example *Animal Farm* by George Orwell"?
9. Please send this package to Mrs Rose Sanchez 116 East Elm Street Allentown P.A. 18001.
10. The letter was dated June 16 1993 and was mailed from Washington D.C.

B. Proofreading a Paragraph for Correct Punctuation

Add, delete, or replace commas, semicolons, or colons to correct each sentence in the following paragraph.

[11] One of the most dangerous assignments for a pilot is to fly over the cold barren stretches of snow and ice north of the Arctic Circle. [12] Ellen Paneok, an Inupiat pilot should know. [13] Even before she learned to drive a car Paneok was flying over the tundra far from her hometown of Kotzebue, in Alaska. [14] Traveling in the Arctic a bush pilot must be alert to the dangers of: fatigue, vertigo, and the northern lights. [15] Caught in dense fog or a snowstorm a pilot can easily lose his or her bearings and become a victim of vertigo. [16] Furthermore, the pilot, who stares at the northern lights too long, can wind up buried in a snowbank. [17] Paneok therefore keeps a sharp lookout for objects on the ground. [18] A glimpse of a caribou, a patch of brush, a jutting ice dome etc. will help her regain her sense of direction and will also break the monotony. [19] Soaring over the tundra she provides many rural people with produce, and transportation. [20] Paneok believes that the rewards of flying outweigh the risks; for the beauty of Alaska, and the needs of her fellow Alaskans make the risk worthwhile. ✔

NOTE In speaking, the tone and pitch of your voice, the pauses in your speech, and your gestures and expressions all help to make your meaning clear. In writing, marks of punctuation signal these verbal and nonverbal cues. However, if the meaning of a sentence is unclear in the first place, punctuation will not usually clarify it. Whenever you find yourself struggling to punctuate a sentence correctly, take a closer look at your arrangement of phrases or your choice of words. Often you can eliminate the punctuation problem by rewriting the sentence.

End Marks

Sentences

12a. A statement (or declarative sentence) is followed by a period.

EXAMPLES   October is Hispanic Heritage Month in the United States**.**

Felipe asked whether Edgar Allan Poe was primarily a poet, an essayist, or a short-story writer**.**

12b. A question (or interrogative sentence) is followed by a question mark.

EXAMPLES   Did you get the leading role**?**

Can you tell me when your first show is**?**

(1) Do not use a question mark after a declarative sentence containing an indirect question.

INDIRECT QUESTION   Katie wonders who will win the award**.**

QUESTION   Who will win the award**?**

(2) Polite requests are often put in question form even when they aren't actually questions. In that case, they may be followed by either a period or a question mark.

EXAMPLES   Would you please take a moment to complete this brief questionnaire**?**

or

Will you please take a moment to complete this brief questionnaire**.**

MECHANICS

REFERENCE NOTE: Requests in question form are often used in business letters. For more information on writing business letters, see pages 573–580.

(3) A question mark should be placed inside the closing quotation marks when the quotation itself is a question. Otherwise, a question mark should be placed outside the closing quotation marks.

EXAMPLES   To avoid answering a personal question, simply reply, "Why do you ask?" [The quotation is a question.]
Did Mr. Shields actually say, "Your reports are due in three days"? [The quotation is not a question, although the sentence as a whole is.]

12c.   An imperative sentence is followed by either a period or an exclamation point.

EXAMPLES   Turn the music down, please. [request]
Turn the music down. [mild command]
Turn that music down right this minute! [strong command]

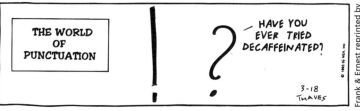

THE WORLD OF PUNCTUATION

— HAVE YOU EVER TRIED DECAFFEINATED?

3-18
THAVES

Frank & Ernest reprinted by permission of NEA, Inc.

!?!!?!!?!!?!!?!!?!!?!!?!!?!!?!!?!!?!

 NOTE   When an imperative sentence is stated as a question but actually expresses a command, it is usually followed by a period or an exclamation point rather than a question mark.

EXAMPLES   May we get through, please. [request]
Won't you come join us at our table. [request]
Will you let us through! [command]

12d. An exclamation is followed by an exclamation point.

EXAMPLES   I can't believe that**!**
What a bargain that used car is**!**

(1) An exclamation mark should be placed inside the closing quotation marks when the quotation itself is an exclamation. Otherwise, it should be placed outside the quotation marks.

EXAMPLES   "Down in front**!**" yelled the crowd.
Ms. Chen couldn't have said, "No home-work"**!**

(2) An interjection at the beginning of a sentence is usually followed by a comma but may be followed by an exclamation point.

USUAL   Hey**,** don't do that**!**
INFREQUENT   Hey**!** Don't do that**!**

    Notice in the examples above that an exclamation point may be used after a single word (especially an interjection) as well as after a sentence.

NOTE   As a rule, when you use a typewriter or word processor, place two spaces after the end mark of a sentence.

STYLE NOTE   Sometimes (most often in dialogue), a writer will use more than one end mark to express (1) intense emotion or (2) a combination of emotions.

EXAMPLES   Marvin shouted, "Pass me the ball**!!**" [intense emotion]
"You did what**?!**" gasped Brenda. [combination of curiosity and surprise]

Using such double punctuation is acceptable in most informal writing. However, in formal writing, such as essays and business letters, use only one end mark at a time.

REFERENCE NOTE: For information on how sentences are classified according to purpose, see pages 297–298. For more information about the placement of end marks with closing quotation marks, see pages 413–414.

Other Uses of the Period

Abbreviations

12e. An abbreviation is usually followed by a period.

TYPES OF ABBREVIATIONS	EXAMPLES		
Personal Names	Susan B. Anthony S. I. Hayakawa I. M. Pei J.R.R. Tolkien		
Organizations and Companies	Assn. Co.	Corp. Inc.	Ltd.
Titles Used with Names	Dr. Jr.	Mr. Mrs.	Ms. Ph. D.
Time of Day	A.M. *(or* a.m.*)*	P.M. *(or* p.m.*)*	
Years	B.C. *(written after the date)* A.D. *(written before the date)*		
Addresses	Ave. Blvd.	Dr. Pkwy.	Rd. St.
States	Ark. Calif.	Fla. Penn.	S. Car. N. Mex.

 NOTE Two-letter state codes, which are not followed by periods, are used only when the ZIP code is included.

EXAMPLE   Springfield, **MA** 01101

 REFERENCE NOTE: For a complete list of state abbreviations, see pages 590–591.

When an abbreviation ending with a period is the last word in a sentence, do not add another period. Do add a question mark or an exclamation point if one is needed.

EXAMPLES   Ms. Rojas is scheduled to speak at 7:00 P.M.
Melba, have you met Hershel Heinz, Jr.?

Some abbreviations, including the abbreviations for most units of measurement, are written without periods.

EXAMPLES   AM/FM, CORE, FBI, GI, IOU, MTV, OK, PC,
ROTC, SOS, cc, ft, lb, kw, ml, psi, rpm

Do use a period with the abbreviation for *inch (in.)*, so that it will not be confused with *in,* the word.

NOTE   As a rule, an abbreviation is capitalized only if the words that it stands for are capitalized. If you're not sure whether to use periods with an abbreviation or whether to capitalize it, check a dictionary.

Shoe, by Jeff MacNelly, reprinted by permission:
Tribune Media Services.

 REFERENCE NOTE: For a more complete discussion of abbreviations, see pages 586–596. For information on capitalizing abbreviations, see pages 356–362.

Outlines, Lists, Numbers

12f.   Each letter or number introducing an item in an outline or a list is followed by a period.

EXAMPLE   The Life of Zora Neale Hurston
I. Childhood in Eatonville
    A. Incorporated black town
    B. Early exposure to folklore
II. College years

MECHANICS

EXAMPLE   Items on this week's student council agenda
             include
             1. suggestions for fundraising
             2. decorations for Jazz Appreciation week
             3. upcoming student council elections

 REFERENCE NOTE: For information on capitalizing items
in an outline, see page 354.

12g. Use a period as a decimal point in numbers.

EXAMPLES   **18.76% $6.95   .75** miles

☑ *QUICK CHECK* 1   **Checking for Correct Use of
                        the Period and Other End
                        Marks**

Each of the following sentences lacks one or more end
marks. Identify words or abbreviations that should be followed by end marks, and name the types of end marks required. If quotation marks are needed, tell whether they
should precede or follow the end mark.

1. Wow Did you see that liftoff
2. He yelled across the field, "Hurry
3. Mrs Tan, is your correct address 5208 W Yarrow St
   Williamsburg, Pa
4. Have a 14-ft. length of chain delivered from Nick's
   Lumber Co by 1:00 PM
5. Didn't you hear her say "I'm not ready yet

Commas

Items in a Series

12h. Use commas to separate items in a series.

EXAMPLES   The basketball coach recommended that she
             practice dribbling, shooting, weaving, and
             passing. [words]

We can meet before English class, during
lunch, or after school. [phrases]
After school I must make sure that my room is
clean, that my little brother is home from his
piano lesson, and that the garbage has been
emptied. [clauses]

**(1) When *and, or,* or *nor* joins the last two items in a
series, you may omit the comma before the conjunction.
Never omit the final comma, however, if such an
omission would make the sentence unclear.**

CLEAR   My cat has orange, yellow and white stripes.
[The meaning of this sentence is clear without a comma before the conjunction *and*.]

UNCLEAR   Phyllis, Ken and Matt formed a rock band. [It
looks as though Phyllis is being addressed.]

CLEAR   Phyllis, Ken, and Matt formed a rock band.
[Phyllis is clearly a member of the band.]

Some writers prefer always to use the comma before
the *and* in a series. Follow your teacher's instructions on
this point.

NOTE   Some words—such as *bread and butter* and *law and
order*—are paired so often that they may be considered a single item.

EXAMPLE   For lunch we had soup, salad, bread and
butter, and milk.

**(2) If all the items in a series are linked by *and, or,* or
nor, do not use commas to separate them.**

EXAMPLES   Tyrone **and** Earlene **and** Lily won awards for
their sculptures.
Should we walk **or** ride our bikes **or** take the
bus?

**(3) Do not place a comma before the first item or after
the last item in a series.**

INCORRECT   I enjoy, gymnastics, basketball, and wrestling,
more than any other sports.

CORRECT   I enjoy gymnastics, basketball, and wrestling
more than any other sports.

MECHANICS

(4) Short independent clauses may be separated by commas.

EXAMPLE   I wash, you dry, and Anthony puts the dishes away.

👉 **REFERENCE NOTE:** Independent clauses in a series are usually separated by semicolons. For more about this use of the semicolon, see pages 397–399.

NOTE The abbreviation *etc.* (meaning "and so forth") at the end of a series is always followed by a comma unless it falls at the end of a sentence.

EXAMPLES   Randy bought hamburger, buns, onions, etc., for the cookout.
For the cookout Randy bought hamburger, buns, onions, etc.

12i. Use a comma to separate two or more adjectives preceding a noun.

EXAMPLE   Lucia is an intelligent, thoughtful, responsible student.

When the last adjective before the noun is thought of as part of the noun, the comma before the adjective is omitted.

EXAMPLES   Let's play this new video game. [*Video game* is thought of as one unit.]
I've finally found a decent, affordable used car. [*Used car* is thought of as one unit.]

You can use two tests to determine whether an adjective and a noun form a unit.

TEST 1:   Insert the word *and* between the adjectives. If *and* fits sensibly between the adjectives, use a comma. In the first example above, *and* cannot be logically inserted: *new and video game*. In the second sentence, *and* sounds sensible between the first two adjectives (*decent and affordable*) but not between the second and third (*affordable and used*).

TEST 2:   Change the order of the adjectives. If the order of the adjectives can be reversed sensibly, use a comma. *Affordable, decent used car* makes sense, but *used decent car* and *video new game* do not.

NOTE If one word in a series modifies the word following it, do *not* separate the two words with a comma.

EXAMPLE Does your mother like that **dark green** carpet? [*Dark* modifies *green*.]

Independent Clauses

12j. Use a comma before *and, but, for, or, nor, so,* and *yet* when they join independent clauses.

EXAMPLES I read about Athol Fugard's *Master Harold and the Boys,* and now I want to see the play.
Amy followed the recipe carefully, for she had never made paella before.

NOTE Always use a comma before *yet, so,* or *for* joining independent clauses. The comma may be omitted before *and, but, or,* and *nor* if the independent clauses are very short and if the sentence is not confusing or unclear without it.

EXAMPLES The phone rang and I answered it. [clear without comma]
We can go in the morning or we can leave now. [clear without comma]
The teacher called on Maria but John began to answer. [awkward without comma]
The teacher called on Maria, but John began to answer. [clear with comma]

Don't confuse a compound sentence with a simple sentence that has a compound verb.

SIMPLE SENTENCE My sister had been accepted at Howard University but decided to attend Grambling University instead. [one independent clause with a compound verb]

COMPOUND SENTENCE My sister had been accepted at Howard University, but she decided to attend Grambling University instead. [two independent clauses]

MECHANICS

Punctuation

Also, keep in mind that compound subjects and compound objects are not separated by commas.

EXAMPLES What he is saying today and what he said yesterday are two different things. [two subordinate clauses serving as a compound subject]

Television crews covered the Daytona 500 and the Indianapolis 500. [compound object]

☞ REFERENCE NOTE: For more information on compound subjects and compound verbs, see pages 282–283.

Nonessential Clauses and Phrases

12k. Use commas to set off nonessential clauses and nonessential participial phrases.

A *nonessential* (or *nonrestrictive*) clause or participial phrase is one containing information that isn't needed to understand the main idea of the sentence.

NONESSENTIAL CLAUSES
Lydia Cabrera, **who was born in Cuba,** wrote many books about African Cuban culture.

Did the Senate hearings, **which were televised,** attract a large viewing audience?

NONESSENTIAL PHRASES
Lee, **noticing my confusion,** rephrased her question.

Willie Herenton, **defeating the incumbent in 1991,** became the first African American mayor of Memphis.

Each nonessential clause or phrase in the examples above can be left out without changing the main idea of the sentence.

EXAMPLES Lydia Cabrera wrote many books about African Cuban culture.

Did the Senate hearings attract a large viewing audience?

Lee rephrased her question.

Willie Herenton became the first African American mayor of Memphis.

An *essential* (or *restrictive*) clause or phrase is one that can't be left out without changing the meaning of the sentence. Essential clauses and phrases are *not* set off by commas.

ESSENTIAL CLAUSES	The juniors **who were selected for Boys State and Girls State** were named.
	Material **that is quoted verbatim** should be placed in quotation marks.
ESSENTIAL PHRASES	Those **participating in the food drive** should bring their donations by Friday.
	The election **won by Willie Herenton** took place in October 1991.

Notice how the omission of the essential clause or phrase affects the main idea of the sentence.

EXAMPLES	The juniors were named.
	Material should be placed in quotation marks.
	Those should bring their donations by Friday.
	The election took place in October 1991.

NOTE Adjective clauses beginning with *that* are nearly always essential.

Some clauses and participial phrases may be either essential or nonessential. The presence or absence of commas tells the reader how the clause or phrase relates to the main idea of the sentence.

NONESSENTIAL CLAUSE	Una's cousin, **who wants to be an astronaut,** attended a space camp in Huntsville, Alabama, last summer. [Una has only one cousin. Her only cousin attended the space camp.]
ESSENTIAL CLAUSE	Una's cousin **who wants to be an astronaut** attended a space camp in Huntsville, Alabama, last summer. [Una has more than one cousin. The one who wants to be an astronaut attended the space camp.]
NONESSENTIAL PHRASE	Your cat, **draped along the back of the couch,** seems contented. [You have only one cat. It seems contented.]
ESSENTIAL PHRASE	Your cat **draped along the back of the couch** seems contented. [You have more

MECHANICS

than one cat. The one on the back of the couch seems contented.]

 REFERENCE NOTE: See **Chapter 7: Clauses** for more information on clauses and pages 247–249 for more information on participial phrases.

 QUICK CHECK 2 **Correcting Sentences by Adding Commas**

For the following sentences, write each word that should be followed by a comma, and add the comma. If a sentence is correct, write *C*.

1. The photograph showed a happy mischievous little boy.
2. Barbara will bring potato salad to the picnic and Marc will bring the cold cuts.
3. Alain Leroy Locke was a Rhodes scholar who taught philosophy and created one of the foremost collections of African art and mentored many black writers.
4. The White River Bridge which closed today for resurfacing will not be open for traffic until mid-October.
5. All contestants submitting photographs for the contest must sign a release form.

Introductory Elements

12l. Use a comma after certain introductory elements.

(1) Use commas after one-word adverbs such as *first, yes,* and *no* or after any mild exclamation such as *well* or *why* at the beginning of a sentence.

EXAMPLES   **Well,** I guess so.
              First, tell us what you think.
              Yes, I heard your question.

(2) Use a comma after an introductory participial phrase.

EXAMPLES   **Looking poised and calm,** Jill walked to the podium.
              Exhausted after the five-mile hike, the scouts took a break.

NOTE Be sure that an introductory participial phrase modifies the subject of the sentence; otherwise, the phrase is misplaced.

MISPLACED   Pecking at the new feed, we watched the chickens. [Were *we* pecking at the new feed?]

REVISED   We watched the chickens **pecking at the new feed.**

REFERENCE NOTE: For more about correcting misplaced modifiers, see pages 229–232.

Don't confuse a gerund phrase used as the subject of a sentence with an introductory participial phrase.

EXAMPLES   **Following directions** can sometimes be difficult. [The gerund phrase *following directions* is the subject of the sentence.]
Following directions, I began to assemble the bike. [*Following directions* is an introductory participial phrase modifying *I*.]

(3) Use a comma after two or more introductory prepositional phrases.

EXAMPLE   **In the first round of the golf tournament,** I played one of the best golfers in the state.

A single introductory prepositional phrase does not require a comma unless the sentence is awkward without it or unless the phrase is parenthetical.

EXAMPLES   **At the track meet** our school's team placed first. [The sentence is clear and does not need a comma after the introductory phrase.]
At the track, meet me in front of the snack bar. [The comma is needed to avoid reading "track meet."]
By the way, I need to borrow a quarter. [The comma is needed because *by the way* is parenthetical.]

REFERENCE NOTE: See pages 391–392 for more information on using commas with parenthetical elements. For more information on all types of phrases, see **Chapter 6: Phrases.**

(4) Use a comma after an introductory adverb clause.

An introductory adverb clause may appear at the beginning of a sentence or before any independent clause in the sentence.

EXAMPLES   **After I had locked the car door,** I remembered that the keys were still in the ignition.

Fortunately, I had a spare set of keys with me; **if I hadn't,** I would have had to walk home.

 NOTE An adverb clause that follows an independent clause is usually not set off by a comma.

EXAMPLE   Thousands of homes in the Philippines were destroyed **when Mt. Pinatubo erupted in 1991.**

Interrupters

12m. Use commas to set off elements that interrupt a sentence.

(1) Appositives and appositive phrases are usually set off by commas.

An *appositive* is a noun or pronoun placed beside another noun or pronoun to identify or explain it. An *appositive phrase* consists of an appositive and its modifiers.

EXAMPLES   My favorite book by Claude McKay, ***Banjo,*** was first published in 1912.
Is that he, **the one with the red hair?**

Sometimes an appositive is so closely related to the word or words near it that it should not be set off by commas. Such an appositive is called a **restrictive appositive.**

EXAMPLES   my nephew **Jim**
the young American gymnast **Lanna Apisukh**
the saying **"Haste makes waste"**

 REFERENCE NOTE: See pages 256–258 for more information on appositives and appositive phrases.

(2) Words used in direct address are set off by commas.

EXAMPLES   **Mom,** have you called Mrs. Johnson yet?
Your essay, **Theo,** was well organized.
Will you answer the question, **Monica?**

(3) Compound comparisons are set off by commas.

EXAMPLE   Jamaica Kincaid is as well-known as, **if not
better-known than,** Derek Walcott.

(4) Parenthetical expressions are set off by commas.

Parenthetical expressions are remarks that add incidental
information or that relate ideas to each other.

Commonly Used Parenthetical Expressions		
after all	I believe (hope, etc.)	naturally
at any rate	incidentally	nevertheless
by the way	in fact	of course
consequently	in general	on the contrary
for example	in the first place	on the other
for instance	meanwhile	hand
however	moreover	that is
		therefore

EXAMPLES   **Incidentally,** I won't be home for supper.
Simón Bolívar liberated much of South
America from Spanish rule; he went on,
moreover, to become the most powerful
man on the continent.
It's too late to call now, **I believe.**

 REFERENCE NOTE: Parentheses and dashes are sometimes used to set off parenthetical expressions. See
pages 430 and 431–433.

    Some of these expressions are not always used paren-
thetically. When they are not used parenthetically, don't set
them off with commas.

EXAMPLES   **By the way,** she is in my vocal music class.
[parenthetical, meaning "incidentally"]
You can tell **by the way** she sings that she en-
joys the class. [not parenthetical, meaning
"by the manner in which"]

MECHANICS

A contrasting expression introduced by *not* is parenthetical and must be set off by commas.

EXAMPLE Margaret Walker**, not Alice Walker,** wrote the novel *Jubilee*.

 REFERENCE NOTE: Some parenthetical expressions, such as *however, consequently, moreover,* and *therefore*, may also be used as conjunctive adverbs. For more about conjunctive adverbs, see pages 294–295 and 398–399.

In many cases, your intention determines the punctuation you use. If you want your reader to pause, set the parenthetical expression off with commas; if not, leave it unpunctuated. Sometimes, the placement of the expression in a sentence determines the punctuation.

EXAMPLES They are **after all** the top-ranked team in the country. [no pause]
They are**, after all,** the top-ranked team in the country. [pause]
After all, they are the top-ranked team in the country. [comma required by placement of expression]

 If you write using a computer, you may want to create a file of the parenthetical expressions listed on page 391. Refer to this file as you proofread your writing, and be sure that you've punctuated these expressions correctly. If your word-processing software has a "Search" function, use the function to speed up your proofreading. The computer will search for and highlight each occurrence of whatever expression you select.

 QUICK CHECK 3 **Correcting Sentences by Adding Commas**

For each of the following sentences, write each word that should be followed by a comma, and add the comma. If a sentence is correct, write *C*.

1. Well as a matter of fact your lateness is your own fault since you knew what time the bus would be leaving.

MECHANICS

2. Looking poised and aloof the girl began to move to the flamenco music.
3. Zimbabwe's stone ruins once a stronghold for an ancient empire attest to the skill of those early stonemasons.
4. If no one hears a tree fall does it make any noise?
5. It's the phone that's ringing Suzanne not the doorbell.

Commas Used for Clarity

12n. Use a comma between words or phrases that might otherwise confuse a reader.

(1) Use a comma after an introductory adverb that might be confused with a preposition.

EXAMPLE   **Above, an eagle soared majestically in the cold mountain air.** [comma needed to prevent reading *above an eagle*]

(2) Use a comma between a verbal and a noun that follows it if there is any possibility of misreading.

EXAMPLE   **Before leaving, you should turn out the lights.** [comma needed to prevent reading *before leaving you*]

(3) Use a comma in an elliptical construction that replaces an independent clause.

    An ***elliptical construction*** is a word group from which some words have been left out.

EXAMPLES   **The sea was calm; the moonlight, bright.** [comma takes the place of *was*]
                   Ernest Hemingway is known for using few words; Henry James, for using many. [comma takes the place of *is known*]

(4) Use a comma to separate most words that are repeated.

EXAMPLE   **What seats there were, were already taken.**

MECHANICS

NOTE Do not use a comma between repeated words that are part of a verb phrase.

EXAMPLE   When I left Germany, I told my host family that I **had had** a lovely time.

(5) Use a comma between contrasting clauses in folk sayings and other interdependent sentences.

EXAMPLES   The bigger they are, the harder they fall.
            The more poetry we read, the better I like it.

NOTE Do *not* use a comma between short contrasting phrases.

EXAMPLES   The sooner the better.
            The more the merrier.

Conventional Uses

12o. Use a comma in certain conventional situations.

(1) Use a comma to separate items in dates and addresses.

EXAMPLES   On Friday, October 23, 1991, my niece Leslie
            was born.
            Please address all inquiries to 92 Keystone
            Crossings, Indianapolis, IN 46240, until
            June 22.

Notice that no comma separates the month from the day (October 23), the house number from the street name (92 Keystone Crossings), or the ZIP Code from the two-letter state code (IN 46240). Notice also that a comma separates the last item in a date (1991) or in an address (IN 46240) from the words that follow it.

No comma is needed when

■ items in an address or a date are joined by a preposition

EXAMPLE   The play is at the Melrose Theater **on Broad
           Avenue in Midland Heights.**

■ the day is given before the month

EXAMPLE   On **15 June 1924** Congress approved a law
           making all Native Americans U.S. citizens.

■ only the month and the year are given

EXAMPLE   Will our new school be open by **August 1996?**

(2) Use a comma after the salutation of a friendly letter and after the closing of any letter.

EXAMPLES   Dear Rosa,   Sincerely yours,

 REFERENCE NOTE: For information on punctuating the salutation of a business letter, see page 574.

(3) Use a comma after a personal name followed by an abbreviation such as *Jr., Sr., RN*, or *M.D.*, or after a business name followed by an abbreviation such as *Ltd.* or *Inc.*

EXAMPLES   Frank Tisdale, CPA   Baker-Henson, Ltd.
            Coretta Jones, M.D.   May Flowers, Inc.

Used within a sentence, such an abbreviation is followed by a comma as well.

EXAMPLE   Is Juan Fuentes, Jr., your cousin?

(4) Use a comma in numbers of more than three digits. Place the comma between groups of three digits, counting from the left. If a number includes a decimal, count starting from the left of the decimal.

EXAMPLES   17,012 nails $3,245.15   1,000,000 miles

NOTE   Do *not* use commas in ZIP codes, telephone numbers, house numbers, and four-digit years (1929).

Unnecessary Commas

12p. Do not use unnecessary commas.

Using too many commas can be confusing. Use a comma only if a rule requires one or if the meaning is unclear without one.

INCORRECT   The teacher in the room across the hall, is Cam's aunt. [*The teacher in the room across the hall* contains the sentence's subject, *teacher,* and should not be treated as an introductory element.]

CORRECT   The teacher in the room across the hall is Cam's aunt.

INCORRECT   Sam woke up, and fed the dog. [*Fed* is part of a compound verb and should not be separated from the subject, *Sam.*]

CORRECT   Sam woke up and fed the dog.

 REFERENCE NOTE: For a summary of comma uses, see pages 404–405.

STYLE NOTE   In the past, many writers used all (or most) of the punctuation that convention allowed them. Nowadays, most writers—especially fiction writers—prefer a simpler style, and they use punctuation only when it is necessary to prevent misreading. Compare the punctuation in the sentences below.

> At first, as he spoke, there was a slight rushing movement of this group in the direction of the intruder, who at the moment was also near at hand, and now, with deliberate and stately step, made closer approach to the speaker.
>
> Edgar Allan Poe, "The Masque of the Red Death"

> Even when you watch the process of coal extraction you probably only watch it for a short time, and it is not until you begin making a few calculations that you realize what a stupendous task the "fillers" are performing.
>
> George Orwell, *The Road to Wigan Pier*

Based on their use of punctuation, can you tell which of these writers is more modern? Would you change the punctuation of one or both of these sentences to make the meaning clearer? What would you change?

 QUICK CHECK 4 | **Correcting Sentences by Adding or Deleting Commas**

Rewrite each of the following sentences by adding or deleting commas as necessary. If a sentence is correct, write *C*.

1. Address inquiries to Manager Able Industries Inc. 6,235 South Main Street Salt Lake City Utah.
2. This technique has, been technically possible for the last fifty years.
3. A shipment of 1,250 of their latest model is expected to arrive on 28 August.
4. All the coins I had had been lost.
5. From the hilltop we could see the stars; below the town was dark.

Semicolons

12q. Use a semicolon between independent clauses that are closely related in thought and are not joined by *and, but, for, nor, or, so,* or *yet.*

EXAMPLES The rain had finally stopped; a few rays of sunshine were pushing their way through breaks in the clouds.

"Tart words make no friends; a spoonful of honey will catch more flies than a gallon of vinegar."

Benjamin Franklin, *Poor Richard's Almanack*

Do not join independent clauses unless there is a close relationship between the main ideas of the clauses.

NONSTANDARD For Ramón, oil painting is a difficult medium to master; when he was younger, he had enjoyed taking photographs.

STANDARD For Ramón, oil painting is a difficult medium to master. When he was younger, he had enjoyed taking photographs.

MECHANICS

12r. Use a semicolon between independent clauses joined by a conjunctive adverb or a transitional expression.

A *conjunctive adverb* or a *transitional expression* indicates the relationship of the independent clauses that it joins.

EXAMPLES The snowfall made traveling difficult; **nevertheless,** we arrived home safely.
Denisa plays baseball well; **in fact,** she would like to try out for a major-league team.

Commonly Used Conjunctive Adverbs		
accordingly	however	moreover
besides	indeed	nevertheless
consequently	instead	otherwise
furthermore	meanwhile	therefore

Commonly Used Transitional Expressions		
as a result	for instance	in other words
for example	in fact	that is

NOTE When a conjunctive adverb or a transitional expression is used *between* independent clauses, it is preceded by a semicolon and followed by a comma. When used *within* a clause, a conjunctive adverb or a transitional expression is set off by commas.

EXAMPLES Most members of Congress favor the new tax bill; **however,** the president does not support it.
Most members of Congress favor the new tax bill; the president, **however,** does not support it.

REFERENCE NOTE: For more information about conjunctive adverbs and transitional expressions, see pages 294–295.

12s. Use a semicolon (rather than a comma) before a coordinating conjunction to join independent clauses that contain commas.

EXAMPLE   During the seventeenth century—the era of such distinguished prose writers as Sir Thomas Browne, John Donne, and Jeremy Taylor—the balanced compound sentence using commas and semicolons reached a high degree of perfection and popularity; but the tendency today is to use a fast-moving style with shorter sentences and fewer commas and semicolons. [commas within the first clause]

12t. Use a semicolon between items in a series if the items contain commas.

EXAMPLE   The president of the club has appointed the following members to chair the standing committees: Richard Stokes, planning; Rebecca Hartley, membership; Salvador Barrios, financial; and Ann Jeng, legal.

 QUICK CHECK 5   **Using Semicolons Correctly**

Add semicolons where they are needed in the following sentences.

1. The great American humorist Will Rogers was proud of his Cherokee heritage he often referred to it in his talks and writings.

2. William Penn Adair Rogers was born in 1879 in Oologah, Indian Territory, which is now Oklahoma, and he spent his childhood on his father's ranch, a prosperous holding of about sixty thousand acres.

3. As a youth, Will Rogers liked to learn and practice rope tricks he often could be found roping instead of attending to his chores.

4. Rogers was captivated by professional roping performers at the Chicago World's Fair in 1893 in fact, that experience probably marked the start of his interest in show business.

5. Rogers' stage shows, combining his roping with humorous comments, were popular they led to starring roles in musicals, the legendary Ziegfeld Follies, and movies.

Colons

12u.   Use a colon to mean "note what follows."

(1) Use a colon before a list of items, especially after expressions such as *as follows* and *the following*.

EXAMPLES   The magazine article profiles **the following** famous women of nineteenth-century America: Mary Baker Eddy, Clara Barton, Maria Mitchell, Mary Church Terrell, Susan B. Anthony, and Sarah Winnemucca.

Prior to 1722, the Iroquois Confederation consisted of five Native American nations: Mohawk, Oneida, Onondaga, Cayuga, and Seneca.

 NOTE   Do not use a colon before a list that directly follows a verb or a preposition.

EXAMPLES   The emergency kit included safety flares, jumper cables, and a flashlight. [The list directly follows the verb *included*.]
Each student taking the math test was provided with two sharpened pencils, paper, and a ruler. [The list directly follows the preposition *with*.]

(2) Use a colon before a quotation that lacks a speaker tag such as *he said* or *she remarked*.

EXAMPLE   Dad's orders were loud and clear: "Everybody up and at 'em."

(3) Use a colon before a long, formal statement or quotation.

EXAMPLE   Patrick Henry concluded his revolutionary speech before the Virginia House of Burgesses with these ringing words: "Is life so dear, or peace so sweet as to be purchased at the price of chains and slavery? Forbid it, Almighty God! I know not what course others may take, but as for me, give me liberty or give me death!"

REFERENCE NOTE: For more information about using long quotations, see pages 414–415 and 419–421.

(4) Use a colon between independent clauses when the second clause explains or restates the idea of the first.

EXAMPLES   Lois felt that she had done something worthwhile: She had designed and sewn her first quilt.

Thomas Jefferson had many talents: He was a writer, a politician, an architect, and an inventor.

12v. Use a colon in certain conventional situations.

(1) Use a colon between the hour and the minute.

EXAMPLES   5:20 P.M.   8:45 in the
                    12:01 A.M.   morning

(2) Use a colon between chapter and verse in referring to passages from the Bible.

EXAMPLES   Proverbs 10:1   Deuteronomy 5:6–21
                    Mark 3:10

NOTE Modern Language Association (MLA) documentation style recommends using a period rather than a colon in biblical citations.

EXAMPLE   Deuteronomy 5.6–21

Follow the documentation style that your teacher requires.

(3) Use a colon between a title and subtitle.

EXAMPLES   *Another View: To Be Black in America* [book]
Superman IV: The Quest for Peace [movie]
Impression: Sunrise [painting]
Star Trek: The Next Generation [television show]

(4) Use a colon after the salutation of a business letter.

EXAMPLES   Dear Ms. Rodríquez: To Whom It May
                                 Concern:

                  Dear Sir or Madam: Dear Service Manager:

MECHANICS

NOTE Use a comma after the salutation of a friendly letter.

EXAMPLE   Dear Mom and Dad**,**

 QUICK CHECK 6   **Using Colons Correctly**

Rewrite each of the following sentences by adding or deleting colons where necessary.

1. Major leaders in the women's suffrage movement included the following women Carrie Chapman Catt, Susan B. Anthony, Lucretia Mott, and Elizabeth Cady Stanton.

2. I think I'll entitle my autobiography *Into the Fire The Life of Sam Kettle.*

3. My task was simple Locate the whereabouts of the Lost Dutchman Mine.

4. By 5 00 that afternoon, I had memorized twelve verses, beginning with Genesis 1 1.

5. Medal of Honor winners include: Sergeants José Mendoza López and Macarío García.

✓ Chapter Review

A. Correcting Sentences by Changing Punctuation

Rewrite the following sentences by adding, deleting, or replacing end marks, commas, semicolons, and colons as necessary. If a sentence is correct, write *C.*

EXAMPLE   **1.** Sally asked, "Where do you want to go after the recital"?

       1. *Sally asked, "Where do you want to go after the recital?"*

1. Who was it who said: "I only regret that I have but one life to give for my country?"

2. Startled, we heard a high-pitched, whining, noise just outside the window.

3. Any student, who has not signed up for the contest by three o'clock, will not be eligible to participate.

4. My friend Esteban, running up the stairs two at a time, yelled out the good news.

MECHANICS

5. "Why does the telephone always ring just as soon as I sit down to work," she asked?

6. My parents are trading in their car for a spiffy two-door model with a sunroof bucket seats and air conditioning.

7. I have drilled practiced trained and exercised for weeks, and now I am too tired to compete.

8. "Well Coach I can promise you that I'll be ready for the game next week," Kit said.

9. James King an Iroquois guide used to conduct tours of the Somers Mountain Indian Museum in Somers Connecticut.

10. Mr. Elliot's favorite books are *Atlas Shrugged*, by Ayn Rand, *East of Eden*, by John Steinbeck, and *Beloved*, by Toni Morrison.

B. Proofreading a Letter for the Correct Use of Punctuation

Add, delete, or replace end marks, commas, semicolons, or colons to correct each sentence in the following letter.

EXAMPLE   [1]Dear Toni:
            1. *Dear Toni,*

[11] As she had promised our friend, Takara, and her family were waiting for us at the Osaka airport on Monday June 16. [12] I'm so glad that you introduced us and that I could come to visit such a kind generous, and friendly family [13] Wow I love their house; it's totally different from any home that I've ever seen before and my favorite part of it is the garden [14] In the middle of the house and down one step a large rectangular courtyard lies open to the sun and air; the garden is in the courtyard. [15] Rocks not plants and trees dominate the space, and clean white sand instead of grass covers the ground [16] I wonder who carefully rakes the sand every day leaving small rows of lines covering the ground? [17] Takara told me that the sand represents the ocean the lines are like waves, and the rocks stand for islands. [18] Sitting in the garden I believe she is right for the garden is as peaceful as any deserted beach. [19] My

flight by the way will be arriving in Portland on July 18 at
4.05; if you're free would you please meet me at the airport.
[20] Sincerely yours.

Ramona

SUMMARY OF COMMA USES	
12h	Use commas to separate items in a series.
12i	Use a comma to separate two or more adjectives preceding a noun.
12j	Use a comma before *and, but, or, nor, for, so,* and *yet* when they join independent clauses.
12k	Use commas to set off nonessential clauses and nonessential participial phrases.
12l	Use a comma after certain introductory elements. (1) after interjections and after introductory words such as *yes* and *no* (2) after an introductory participial phrase (3) after two or more introductory prepositional phrases (4) after an introductory adverb clause
12m	Use commas to set off elements that interrupt a sentence. (1) appositives and appositive phrases (2) words used in direct address (3) compound comparisons (4) parenthetical expressions
12n	Use a comma between words or phrases that might otherwise confuse a reader. (1) after an introductory adverb that might be confused with a preposition. (2) between a verbal and a noun (3) in elliptical constructions (4) between repeated words (5) between contrasting clauses in folk sayings

(continued)

MECHANICS

SUMMARY OF COMMA USES *(continued)*

12o Use a comma in certain conventional situations.
 (1) to separate items in dates and addresses
 (2) after the salutation of a friendly letter and the closing of any letter
 (3) after a name followed by an abbreviation such as *Jr., Sr.,* or *M.D.*
 (4) in numbers of more than three digits

12p Do not use unnecessary commas.

13 PUNCTUATION

Other Marks of Punctuation

✓ *Checking What You Know*

A. Proofreading Sentences for Correct Punctuation

The following sentences contain errors in the use of dashes, parentheses, brackets, italics (underlining), quotation marks, apostrophes, and hyphens. Rewrite each sentence correctly. [Note: A sentence may contain more than one error.]

EXAMPLE　　**1.** "This job", the employment director said, requires some experience with computers; dont apply for it unless you know BASIC.".

　　　　　　1. *"This job," the employment director said, "requires some experience with computers; don't apply for it unless you know BASIC."*

1. She learned the word daube from working the crossword puzzle in The New York Times.

2. At his press conference, the mayor stated, "He (the mayor's brother in-law) was not guilty of anything more serious than poor judgment."

MECHANICS

3. Denmark, Liberia, Korea, Uruguay, and France, those are the countries that our new exchange students come from.

4. Our flight will land in *Rio de Janeiro* by 8:00 P.M.; moreover, our hotel and car rental reservations have already been confirmed.

5. Franklin Delano Roosevelt's presidency 1933–1945 was the longest one in American history.

6. Did you hear about the student councils latest decision that the class song must be chosen by a three fourths majority?

7. Last year Garth Brooks's The Dance do you know that song? was chosen overwhelmingly as the best country-and-western song.

8. The guide added, "Rosa Bonheur a French artist painted Buffalo Bill sitting on his favorite horse.

9. Nancy asked, "Can you remember whether there are two cs or two s's in occasion"?

10. For my book report in American history, Im reading Only Yesterday, a nonfiction book about life in the 1920s.

B. Proofreading Paragraphs for Correct Punctuation

The following paragraphs of conversation contain errors in the use of dashes, parentheses, italics (underlining), quotation marks, apostrophes, and hyphens. Rewrite each paragraph to correct the errors.

EXAMPLE   [1] "The Renaissance Festival will open at 10:30 in the morning; therefore, we should be in line for tickets by 9:30, Janice said.

   1. *"The Renaissance Festival will open at 10:30 in the morning; therefore, we should be in line for tickets by 9:30," Janice said.*

[11] What in the world please dont think me too uninformed is a Renaissance festival"? Leroy asked.

[12] "Its a fair that celebrates Europes Renaissance, which lasted from about A.D. 1300 to around A.D. 1600," Janice said.

MECHANICS

[13] "Well, I'm ready to go; I know what to expect because Ive seen the movies Camelot and The Princess Bride," Leroy said.

[14] "Even so, youll be amazed Janice said, because youll see people dressed up as kings and queens, jesters, peasants, knights and ladies, wizards, and even dragons."

[15] "I suppose Id better mind my ps and qs with wizards and dragons around"! Leroy exclaimed.

[16] "Oh, all the wizards's manners are good, and the fierce looking dragons actually are friendly," Janice said. [17] "And there are many other sights to see, too: jousts, mazes, elephants and camels, games of strength, music, and all kinds of crafts".

[18] Leroy asked, "Isnt there any Renaissance food?

[19] "Plenty!" Janice said. "My favorites are bagels, which are sold from traveling carts; soup served in bread bowls, which are freshly baked; and apple and pineapple fritter's." [20] "I've been to several Renaissance fairs, including big ones in Texas and Missouri; but of course, I think theyre all great."

✔

Italics

Italics are printed characters that slant to the right. To indicate italics in handwritten or typewritten work, use underlining.

PRINTED   *Pride and Prejudice* **was written by the British author Jane Austen.**

HANDWRITTEN   <u>Pride and Prejudice</u> was written by the British author Jane Austen.

COMPUTER NOTE

If you use a personal computer, you may be able to set words in italics. Most word-processing software and many printers are capable of producing italic type.

13a. Use italics (underlining) for titles of books, plays, long poems, periodicals, newspapers, works of art, films, television series, long musical compositions, recordings, comic strips, computer software, trains, ships, aircraft, spacecraft, and court cases.

TYPE OF NAME	EXAMPLES	
Books	*The Scarlet Letter* *Invisible Man*	*Fifth Chinese Daughter*
Plays	*The Crucible*	*A Raisin in the Sun*
Long poems	*I Am Joaquín*	the *Epic of Gilgamesh*
Periodicals	*Reader's Digest* *Ebony*	*Newsweek* *Seventeen*
Newspapers	*The Wall Street Journal* *The Boston Globe*	*Austin American-Statesman*

NOTE The article *the* before the title of a book, periodical, or newspaper is not italicized nor capitalized unless it is part of the official title. The official title of a book appears on the title page. The official title of a periodical or newspaper is the name on the masthead, usually found on the editorial page.

EXAMPLE I found this information in *The New York Times.*

TYPE OF NAME	EXAMPLES	
Works of Art	*The Kiss*	*The Starry Night*
Films	*Rain Man* *It's a Wonderful Life*	*Stand and Deliver* *Out of Africa*
TV Series	*Jeopardy!* *American Playhouse*	*Star Trek: The Next Generation*
Long Musical Compositions	*Liverpool Oratorio* *The Planets*	*Hiawatha's Wedding Feast*
Recordings	*Achtung Baby* *Unforgettable*	*Sketches of Spain* *The Broadway Album*

MECHANICS

(continued)

TYPE OF NAME	EXAMPLES	
Comic Strips	*Peanuts* *Calvin and Hobbes*	*Doonesbury* *Cathy*
Computer Software	*WordPerfect* *Quicken*	*Paintbrush* *Lotus 1-2-3*
Trains, Ships	*Century Limited*	*Queen Mary*
Aircraft, Spacecraft	*Solar Challenger* *Graf Zeppelin*	*Apollo 11* *Landsat-1*
Court Cases	*Plessy* v. *Ferguson*	*Bailey* v. *Alabama*

 NOTE Usually, only the names of the parties involved in a court case are italicized. The abbreviation *v.* (*versus*) is not italicized.

 REFERENCE NOTE: For examples of titles that are not italicized but that are enclosed in quotation marks, see pages 416–418.

13b. Use italics (underlining) for words, letters, and symbols referred to as such and for foreign words that have not been adopted into English.

EXAMPLES   Should the use of *their* for *there* be considered a spelling error or a usage error?
The teacher couldn't tell whether I had written a script *S* or an *&*.
Some U.S. coins were stamped with the inscription *e pluribus unum.*
Domesticated cats (*Felis domesticus*) have
been popular pets since ancient times.

 NOTE English has borrowed numerous words and expressions from other languages. Many of these words are
now a part of English vocabulary and are not italicized.

EXAMPLES   pizza (Italian)   rodeo (Spanish)
shalom (Hebrew)   karate (Japanese)
au revoir (French)   non sequitur (Latin)

If you are not sure whether to italicize a foreign expression, look in a current dictionary.

MECHANICS

13c.   Use italics (underlining) sparingly for emphasis.

EXAMPLES   Tardiness will *not* be tolerated in this class.
Jason insisted that *his* was the best stereo.

NOTE   Be careful not to overuse italics, or the emphasis will be lost. Try to express your ideas so that your words carry the emphasis without the help of italics or underlining.

STYLE NOTE   In written dialogue, the use of italics (underlining) is especially important.
Because italic type shows emphasis, you can change the meaning of a sentence by changing the word or words you italicize. Read the following sentences aloud and compare their meanings.

"Are *you* the head baseball coach?" asked Rhonda.
"Are you the head *baseball* coach?" asked Rhonda.
"Are you the *head* baseball coach?" asked Rhonda.

   QUICK CHECK 1   **Revising Sentences by Adding Italics (Underlining)**

For each of the following sentences, add italics (underlining) where needed.

1. Does the library have a copy of Ashanti to Zulu: African Traditions?
2. There was an article in Omni about Arthur C. Clarke's 2001: A Space Odyssey and the similarities to our own space flights; the article also reviewed Clarke's 2010: Odyssey Two.
3. Can you tell me the name of the symbol over the second n in the Spanish word niño?
4. While reading a history book called The Rise and Fall of Nazi Germany, I used my dictionary to look up the definitions of the terms Anschluss and Luftwaffe.
5. I don't like that karate game; Super Mario Brothers is still my favorite.

MECHANICS

Quotation Marks

13d. Use quotation marks to enclose a *direct quotation*—a person's exact words.

Be sure to place quotation marks both before and after a person's exact words.

EXAMPLES   After his surrender in 1877, Chief Joseph said, "The earth is the mother of all people, and all people should have equal rights upon it."

"The track meet is canceled because of the unusually cold weather," announced Coach Griffey.

Do not use quotation marks to enclose an *indirect quotation* (a rewording of a direct quotation).

DIRECT QUOTATION   Aaron said, "I can type ninety-five words a minute."

INDIRECT QUOTATION   Aaron said that he can type ninety-five words a minute.

(1) A direct quotation begins with a capital letter.

EXAMPLE   The poet Emily Dickinson wrote in a letter to Thomas Wentworth Higginson, her literary advisor, "If I feel physically as if the top of my head were taken off, I know *that* is poetry."

However, when the quotation is only a part of a sentence, do not begin it with a capital letter.

EXAMPLE   In her essay "On the Mall," Joan Didion describes shopping malls as "toy garden cities in which no one lives. . . ."

(2) When the expression identifying the speaker divides a quoted sentence, the second part begins with a small letter.

EXAMPLE   "I really have to leave now," said Gwen, "so that I will be on time." [Notice that each part of a divided quotation is enclosed in quotation marks.]

MECHANICS

When the second part of a divided quotation is a new sentence, it begins with a capital letter.

EXAMPLE   "Teddy Roosevelt was the first U.S. President to express concern about the depletion of the nation's natural resources," explained Mr. Fuentes. "He established a conservation program that expanded the national park system and created many wildlife sanctuaries."

NOTE   When a direct quotation of two or more sentences is *not* divided, only one set of quotation marks is used.

EXAMPLE   "Teddy Roosevelt was the first U.S. President to express concern about the depletion of the nation's natural resources. He established a conservation program that expanded the national park system and created many wildlife sanctuaries," Mr. Fuentes explained.

(3) A direct quotation is set off from the rest of the sentence by a comma, a question mark, or an exclamation point, but not by a period.

EXAMPLES   "I nominate Pilar for class president," said Erin.
"What is the capital of Thailand?" asked Mr. Klein.
"This chili is too spicy!" Brian exclaimed.

NOTE   If the quotation is only a word or a phrase, do not set it off with commas.

EXAMPLE   When Clara tried to keep the crystal vase from falling off the shelf and knocked over the china plates in the process, she truly understood what the expression "clumsy as an ox" meant.

(4) When used with quotation marks, the other marks of punctuation are placed according to the following rules:

■ Commas and periods are always placed inside the closing quotation marks.

EXAMPLE   "On the other hand," he said, "your decision may be correct."

MECHANICS

- Semicolons and colons are always placed outside the closing quotation marks.

EXAMPLES   My neighbor said, "Of course I'll buy a magazine subscription"; it was lucky that I
asked her on payday.
Edna St. Vincent Millay uses these devices in
her poem "Spring": alliteration, slant
rhyme, and personification.

- Question marks and exclamation points are placed inside the closing quotation marks if the quotation itself is a question or an exclamation. Otherwise, they are placed outside.

EXAMPLES   "Dad, will you please call the doctor tomorrow morning?" I asked.
"Move those golf clubs right now!" yelled
my mother.
Did Langston Hughes write the line "My soul
has grown deep like the rivers"?
I'm sick of hearing "This is so boring"!

Notice that in the last two examples given above, the end mark belonging with each quotation has been omitted. In a question or an exclamation that ends with a quotation, only the question mark or exclamation point is necessary. The punctuation is placed outside the closing quotation marks.

(5) When quoting a passage that consists of more than one paragraph, put quotation marks at the beginning of each paragraph and at the end of only the last paragraph in the passage.

EXAMPLE   "The water was thick and heavy and the
color of a mirror in a dark room. Minnows
broke the surface right under the wharf. I
jumped. I couldn't help it.
    "And I got to thinking that something
might come out of the water. It didn't have a
name or a shape. But it was there."

Shirley Ann Grau,
"The Land and the Water"

NOTE A long passage quoted from a printed source is often set off from the rest of the text. The entire passage may be indented or set in smaller type. The passage is sometimes single-spaced instead of double-spaced. Modern Language Association (MLA) guidelines call for the passage to be indented ten spaces and double-spaced. When a quotation is set off in any of these ways, no quotation marks are necessary.

EXAMPLE

In this passage from <u>West with the Night</u>, Beryl Markham recalls her exciting solo flight from England to Nova Scotia:

> I find the land. Visibility is perfect now and I see land forty or fifty miles ahead. If I am on my course, that will be Cape Breton. Minute after minute goes by. The minutes almost materialize; they pass before my eyes like links in a long slow-moving chain, and each time the engine cuts, I see a broken link in the chain and catch my breath until it passes.

(6) Use single quotation marks to enclose a quotation within a quotation.

EXAMPLES   The teacher requested, "Jorge, please explain what Emerson meant when he said, 'To be great is to be misunderstood.'" [Notice that the period is placed inside the single quotation mark.]

The teacher asked, "Jorge, do you understand what Emerson meant when he said, 'To be great is to be misunderstood'?" [The question mark is placed inside the double quotation marks, not the single quotation mark, because the entire quotation of the

MECHANICS

mark, because the entire quotation of the teacher's words is a question.]

(7) When writing *dialogue* (a conversation), begin a new paragraph every time the speaker changes, and enclose the speaker's words in quotation marks.

EXAMPLE

"But what kind of authentic and valuable information do you require?" asked Klapaucius.

"All kinds, as long as it's true," replied the pirate. "You never can tell what facts may come in handy. I already have a few hundred wells and cellars full of them, but there's room for twice again as much. So out with it; tell me everything you know, and I'll jot it down. But make it snappy!"

"A fine state of affairs," Klapaucius whispered in Trurl's ear. "He could keep us here for an eon or two before we tell him everything we know. Our knowledge is colossal!!"

"Wait," whispered Trurl, "I have an idea."

Stanislaw Lem, "The Sixth Sally"

NOTE   Be sure always to reproduce quoted material exactly as it appears in the original. If the original contains an error, write *sic* in brackets immediately after the error.

EXAMPLE   The article began, "Careful poofreading [*sic*] is the key to avoiding embarrassing mistakes."

13e.   Use quotation marks to enclose titles of short works, such as short stories, poems, essays, articles, songs, episodes of television series, and chapters and other parts of books.

TYPE OF NAME	EXAMPLES	
Short Stories	"The Open Boat"	"The Tell-Tale Heart"
Poems	"Guitarreros"	"Thanatopsis"
Essays	"On the Mall"	"The Creative Process"

(continued)

TYPE OF NAME	EXAMPLES
Articles	"Old Poetry and Modern Music" "How to Improve Your Grades"
Songs	"On Top of Old Smoky" "Wind Beneath My Wings"
TV Episodes	"The Flight of the Condor" "Tony's Surprise Party"
Chapters and Parts of Books	"The World Was New" "The Colonies' Struggle for Freedom"

 REFERENCE NOTE: For examples of titles that are italicized, see pages 409–410.

Neither italics nor quotation marks are used for the titles of major religious texts or for the titles of legal or historical documents.

RELIGIOUS TEXTS	New Testament Koran Rig-Veda Talmud
LEGAL AND HISTORICAL DOCUMENTS	Declaration of Independence Treaty of Ghent Bill of Rights Constitution Code of Hammurabi
EXCEPTION	The names of court cases are usually italicized.
EXAMPLES	*Marbury* v. *Madison* *Brown* v. *Board of Education of Topeka*

STYLE NOTE

Sometimes, especially in a research paper, you may need to punctuate a title contained in another title. The following guidelines will help you punctuate such titles correctly.

■ Use quotation marks to enclose a minor title that appears in a longer italicized title.

MECHANICS

EXAMPLE   **"*In Another Country*" and Other Stories**

■ Use single quotation marks for a minor title that appears within a longer title enclosed in quotation marks.

EXAMPLE   **"An Analysis of Donne's 'Meditation 17'"**

■ Use italics for a major title contained in a longer title enclosed in quotation marks.

EXAMPLE   **"George Orwell and *1984*"**

NOTE   In general, do not use italics or quotation marks for the titles of your own papers. However, you may need to use these marks of punctuation if your title is also the title of another work or if it contains such a title.

EXAMPLES   Katherine Mansfield and the Art of the Short Story [contains no other title]
A Farewell to Arms [same title as the novel]
Color Imagery in *Macbeth* [contains the title of a play]
"A Good Man Is Hard to Find": An Analysis [contains the title of a short story]

13f.   Use quotation marks to enclose slang words, invented words, technical terms, and dictionary definitions of words.

EXAMPLES   Chloe reached for a high note and hit a **"clinker."**
The newspaper reporter described the Halloween festival as **"spooktacular."**
Although I am not familiar with computer language, I do know that to **"boot"** a disk does not mean to kick it.
The verb *recapitulate* means **"to repeat briefly"** or **"to summarize."**

NOTE   Avoid using slang words in formal speaking and writing. When using technical terms, be sure to explain their meanings. If you are not sure whether a word is appropriate or its meaning is clear, consult an up-to-date dictionary.

QUICK CHECK 2   **Proofreading a Dialogue for Correct Punctuation**

In the following dialogue, correct any errors in the use of quotation marks and other marks of punctuation. Also correct any errors in the use of capitalization, and regroup sentences to form a new paragraph each time the speaker changes.

[1] I think The Weeping Woman would be a good title for my new song Tomás told Jim. can you guess what it's about [2] Well, I once read a magazine article titled La Llorona the Weeping Woman about a popular Mexican American legend, Jim replied. [3] That's the legend I'm talking about Tomás exclaimed I first heard it when I was a little boy growing up in southern California. [4] I think Jim commented, People in the music business would call the song a tear-jerker because it tells a sad story about a poor, wronged woman who goes crazy, drowns her children, and kills herself; then she returns as a ghost to look for them forever. [5] Didn't your mother ever say, Don't believe those horrible stories, Tomás asked Jim

Ellipsis Points

13g. Use three spaced periods called *ellipsis points* (. . .) to mark omissions from quoted material and pauses in a written passage.

ORIGINAL   Sitting here tonight, many years later, with more time than money, I think about those faces that pass before my eyes like it was yesterday. They remind me of the chances and temptations to become an outlaw. I sure came through a tough mill. I see those men as they stood in those old days of the Golden West—some of them in the springtime of their manhood, so beautiful and strong that it makes you wonder, because their hearts are as black as night, and they are cruel, treacher-

MECHANICS

> ous and merciless as a man-eating tiger of the
> jungle.
>
> Andrew García,
> *Tough Trip Through Paradise*

(1) If the quoted material that comes before the ellipsis points is not a complete sentence, use three ellipsis points with a space before the first point.

EXAMPLE   In his autobiography, *Tough Trip Through Paradise,* Andrew García reflects, "Sitting here tonight, . . . I think about those faces that pass before my eyes like it was yesterday."

(2) If the quoted material that comes before or after the ellipsis points is a complete sentence, use an end mark before the ellipsis points.

EXAMPLE   García observes, "I see those men as they stood in those old days of the Golden West— some of them in the springtime of their manhood. . . ." [The period is placed before the ellipsis points.]

(3) If one sentence or more is omitted, ellipsis points follow the end mark that precedes the omitted material.

EXAMPLE   Recalling his youth, Andrew García writes, "Sitting here tonight, many years later, with more time than money, I think about those faces that pass before my eyes like it was yesterday. . . . I sure came through a tough mill." [The period precedes the ellipsis points.]

(4) To show that a full line or more of poetry has been omitted, use an entire line of spaced periods.

ORIGINAL   I dream of Hanoi:
Co-ngu Road
ten years of separation
the way back sliced by a frontier of hatred.

I want to bury the past
to burn the future
still I yearn
still I fear
those endless nights
waiting for dawn.

Nguyen Thi Vinh,
"Thoughts of Hanoi"

WITH OMISSION   I dream of Hanoi:

· · · · · · · · · · · · ·

ten years of separation

· · · · · · · · · · · · · · · · ·

still I yearn
still I fear
those endless nights
waiting for dawn.

Notice that each line of periods is as long as the line of poetry above it.

(5) To indicate a pause in a written passage, use three ellipsis points with a space before the first point.

EXAMPLE   "Well . . . I can't really say," hedged the company's representative.

Apostrophes

Possessive Case

The *possessive case* of a noun or a pronoun shows ownership or relationship.

OWNERSHIP   the **performers'** costumes
               Ellen **Zwilich's** music
               Grandmother's recipe
               your responsibility
RELATIONSHIP   the **team's** coach
               ten **dollars'** worth
               my best **friend's** sister
               our cousins

MECHANICS

13h. Use an apostrophe in forming the possessive of nouns and indefinite pronouns.

(1) To form the possessive of a singular noun, add an apostrophe and an *s*.

EXAMPLES   a bird's nest   Ross's opinion
the principal's office   everyone's
                          responsibility

NOTE When forming the possessive of a singular noun ending in an *s* sound, add only an apostrophe if the noun has two or more syllables and if the addition of *'s* will make the noun awkward to pronounce. Otherwise, add *'s*.

EXAMPLES   for conscience' sake   Ms. Schwartz's car
Hercules' strength   the witness's
                            testimony

(2) To form the possessive of a plural noun ending in *s*, add only the apostrophe.

EXAMPLES   the girls' gym   the Joneses' house
the players' uniforms the volunteers'
                         efforts

The few plural nouns that do not end in *s* form the possessive by adding an apostrophe and an *s*.

EXAMPLES   men's fashions   children's toys

NOTE Do not use an apostrophe to form the plural of a noun. Remember that an apostrophe indicates ownership or relationship, not number.

INCORRECT Carl Lewis has won six Olympic gold medal's.
CORRECT Carl Lewis has won six Olympic gold **medals.**

(3) Do not use an apostrophe with possessive personal pronouns or with the possessive pronoun *whose*.

Possessive Personal Pronouns

my, mine	our, ours
your, yours	their, theirs
his, her, hers, its	

INCORRECT	The books were her's.
CORRECT	The books were **hers**.

INCORRECT	The leopard can't change it's spots.
CORRECT	The leopard can't change **its** spots.

INCORRECT	Marjorie is the girl who's mother I met.
CORRECT	Marjorie is the girl **whose** mother I met.

👉 **REFERENCE NOTE:** Do not confuse the possessive pronouns *its, your, their, theirs,* and *whose* with the contractions *it's, you're, they're, there's,* and *who's.* See pages 82, 126, and 424–425. For more information about possessive pronouns, see pages 92, 133–139 and 195–196.

(4) To form the possessive of an indefinite pronoun, add an apostrophe and an *s.*

EXAMPLES   Each one**'s** time is recorded separately.
He seems to need to be the center of everybody**'s** attention.

Indefinite Pronouns in the Possessive Case

another's	everybody's	no one's	somebody's
anybody's	everyone's	one's	someone's
anyone's	nobody's	other's	

NOTE In such forms as *anyone else* and *somebody else,* the correct possessives are *anyone else's* and *somebody else's.*

👉 **REFERENCE NOTE:** For a list of indefinite pronouns, see page 94.

(5) Form the possessive of only the last word in a compound word, in the name of an organization or business firm, or in a word group showing joint possession.

EXAMPLES   father-in-law**'s** gloves
Taylor, Sanders, and Weissman**'s** law office
Roz and Denise**'s** screenplay
Uncle Bert and Aunt June**'s** chihuahua

👉 **REFERENCE NOTE:** For more information about compound nouns, see page 89.

MECHANICS

When a possessive pronoun is part of a word group showing joint possession, each noun in the word group is also possessive.

EXAMPLE　　Chen's, Ramona's, and **my** project
Jason's and her friendship

(6) Form the possessive of each noun in a word group showing individual possession of similar items.

EXAMPLES　　Baldwin's and Ellison's writings
the doctor's and dentist's fees

(7) When used in the possessive form, words indicating time, such as *minute, hour, day, week, month,* and *year,* and words indicating amounts in cents or dollars require apostrophes.

EXAMPLES　　a week's vacation　　four weeks' vacation
a dollar's worth　　five dollars' worth

Contractions

13i.　Use an apostrophe to show where letters, words, or numbers have been omitted in a contraction.

A *contraction* is a shortened form of a word, word group, or figure in which an apostrophe takes the place of the letters, words, or numbers that are omitted.

EXAMPLES　I am . . . . **I'm**　they had . . . . . **they'd**
let us . . . . **let's**　where is . . . . **where's**
of the clock . . **o'clock**　we are . . . . **we're**
she would . . . . **she'd**　you will . . . . **you'll**
1992 . . . . **'92**　Pat is . . . . **Pat's**

The word *not* can be shortened to *n't* and added to a verb, usually without any change in the spelling of the verb.

EXAMPLES　is not . . . . **isn't**　has not . . . . . . **hasn't**
do not . . . . **don't**　should not . **shouldn't**
does not . . . . **doesn't**　were not . . . . **weren't**
EXCEPTIONS will not . . . . . . **won't**　cannot . . . . **can't**

Do not confuse contractions with possessive pronouns.

MECHANICS

CONTRACTIONS	POSSESSIVE PRONOUNS
It's [*It is*] late.	**Its** wing is broken.
It's [*It has*] been an exciting week.	
Who's [*Who is*] in charge?	**Whose** ticket is this?
Who's [*Who has*] been keeping score?	
You're [*You are*] a good student.	**Your** shoe is untied.
They're [*They are*] in the library.	**Their** house is for sale.
There's [*There is*] no one at home.	Those dogs are **theirs**.

NOTE Contractions are acceptable in informal writing and speaking situations. However, in formal writing it is better to avoid using contractions, especially those in which the apostrophe replaces the word *not* (as in *shouldn't*) or the first two numbers in a year (as in *'94*).

13j. Use an apostrophe to show where letters have been omitted in dialect, archaic speech, or poetry.

DIALECT I **b'lieve** that there dog is **fixin'** to bite you.

ARCHAIC SPEECH Arthur is king **o'er** all the land.

POETRY Down dropt the breeze, the sails dropt down,
'**Twas** sad as sad could be;
And we did speak only to break
The silence of the sea!

Samuel Taylor Coleridge,
The Rime of the Ancient Mariner

Plurals

13k. Use an apostrophe and an s to form the plurals of all lowercase letters, some uppercase letters, and some words referred to as words.

EXAMPLES There are two *r*'s and two *s*'s in *embarrassed*.
Try not to use so many *I*'s in your cover letter.
[Without the apostrophe, the plural of the pronoun *I* would spell *Is*.]

MECHANICS

After the happy couple said their *I do*'s, everyone cheered.

You may add only an *s* to form the plurals of such items—except lowercase letters—if the plural forms will not cause misreading.

EXAMPLE Compact discs (**CDs**) were introduced more than ten years ago.

Use apostrophes consistently.

EXAMPLE On her report card were three **A**'s and three **B**'s. [Without the apostrophe, the plural of *A* would spell *As*. The apostrophe in the plural of *B* would normally be unnecessary, but it is included for consistency.]

NOTE To form the plural of an abbreviation that ends with a period, add *'s*.

EXAMPLES B.A.'s M.F.A.'s

To form the plurals of abbreviations not followed by periods, add either *'s* or *s*.

EXAMPLES VCR'**s** *or* VCR**s**
RN'**s** *or* RN**s**

 REFERENCE NOTE: For more information about forming these kinds of plurals and the plurals of numbers, see pages 457–458.

 QUICK CHECK 3 **Proofreading for Errors in the Use of Apostrophes**

For the following sentences, correct each error in the use of apostrophes.

1. Havent you and you're sister ever visited your sister and brother-in-law's ranch?
2. No, not yet; its something weve been wanting to do for a long time.
3. Ill bet; Id be saying so long to this towns city streets and be out there in a flash.
4. Well, its not all fun and games; they're day does start at four o clock in the morning, so a visit isnt just a weeks vacation.

5. Yikes! Im just fixin to get to sleep by then; maybe Texas's wilds are better left to you and your's.

Hyphens

13l. Use a hyphen to divide a word at the end of a line.

When dividing a word at the end of a line, remember the following rules:

■ Do not divide a one-syllable word.

INCORRECT	The treaty that ended the war was sign-ed in Paris in 1783.
CORRECT	The treaty that ended the war was signed in Paris in 1783.

■ Divide a word only between syllables.

INCORRECT	Shashona wrote a story about the enda-ngered gray wolf.
CORRECT	Shashona wrote a story about the endan-gered gray wolf.

NOTE When you are not sure about a word's syllabication, that is, the division of a word into syllables, look in a dictionary.

■ Divide an already hyphenated word at the hyphen.

INCORRECT	Among Elena's drawings were two self-por-traits.
CORRECT	Among Elena's drawings were two self-portraits.

■ Do not divide a word so that one letter stands alone.

INCORRECT	Most of the buildings there are made of a-dobe.
CORRECT	Most of the buildings there are made of adobe.

■ In general, divide words containing double consonants between the double consonants.

INCORRECT	The sign says, "Until further notice, swimm-ing in the creek is prohibited."

MECHANICS

CORRECT The sign says, "Until further notice, swimming in the creek is prohibited."

■ In general, do not divide a proper noun or a proper adjective.

INCORRECT My cousin and I are extremely proud of our Polish heritage.

CORRECT My cousin and I are extremely proud of our
Polish heritage.

13m. Use a hyphen with compound numbers from
twenty-one to ninety-nine and with fractions
used as modifiers.

EXAMPLES six hundred **twenty-five**
a **three-fourths** quorum [*Three-fourths* is an
adjective modifying *quorum.*]
three fourths of the audience [*Three fourths*
is not a modifier. *Fourths* is a noun modified
by the adjective *three.*]

NOTE Be sure to use a hyphen in ZIP Codes having more
than five numbers.

EXAMPLE Austin, TX 78746-6487

13n. Use a hyphen with the prefixes *ex-, self-,* and *all-,*
with the suffix *-elect,* and with all prefixes before
a proper noun or proper adjective.

EXAMPLES **ex-**mayor   **pre-**Columbian
self-improvement **mid-**Atlantic
governor-**elect**   **trans-**Siberian
all-star   **pro-**American

☞ REFERENCE NOTE: For more guidelines on adding prefixes and suffixes to words, see pages 449–453.

NOTE Use hyphens with some figures and letters.

EXAMPLES mid-1990s   T-shirt

13o. Hyphenate a compound adjective when it
precedes the noun it modifies.

EXAMPLES a **well-designed** engine   an engine that is
well designed

a **world-famous** skier　　a skier who is
world famous

Do not use a hyphen if one of the modifiers is an adverb ending in -*ly*.

EXAMPLE　　a **partly finished** research paper

NOTE　Some compound adjectives are always hyphenated, whether they precede or follow the words they modify.

EXAMPLES　an **up-to-date** dictionary
a dictionary that is **up-to-date**

a **well-informed** debater
a debater who is **well-informed**

If you are unsure about whether a compound adjective is hyphenated, look up the word in a dictionary.

13p. Use a hyphen to prevent awkwardness or confusion.

EXAMPLES　　**de-emphasize** [prevents awkwardness of two identical vowels]
anti-inflammatory [prevents awkwardness of two identical vowels]
re-cover an ottoman [prevents confusion with *recover*]
a re-creation of the event [prevents confusion with *recreation*]

Other Marks of Punctuation

Dashes

13q. Use a dash to indicate an abrupt break in thought. If the sentence continues, use a second dash after the interruption.

EXAMPLES　　The poor condition of this road—it really needs to be paved—makes this route unpopular.

MECHANICS

The real villain turns out to be—but I don't
want to spoil the ending for those of you
who have not yet seen the movie.

"One with mustard, and one—I believe—without."

13r.   Use a dash to mean *namely, in other words, that
is,* and similar expressions that come before an
explanation.

EXAMPLES   Amanda joined the chorus for only one reason—she loves to sing.
Very few people in this class—three, to be
exact—have completed their projects.

13s.   Use dashes to set off an appositive or a
parenthetical expression that contains commas.

EXAMPLES   Several of the British Romantic poets—
Shelley, Keats, and Byron, for example—
lived remarkable lives.
However, poets such as Blake—and
Wordsworth, for that matter—were at
least as creative as the others but had
more conventional lives.

MECHANICS

13t. Use a dash to set off an introductory list or group of examples.

EXAMPLES   Tent, blankets, large cooler, and plenty of food—have we forgotten anything?

Idiosyncratic punctuation, unusual capitalization, and striking imagery—these are hallmarks of Emily Dickinson's poetry.

 NOTE   When you type or use a word processor, indicate a dash with two hyphens.

EXAMPLE   Several of our neighbors--nine, to be precise--have signed the petition opposing the building of an incinerator in our community.

Parentheses

13u. Use parentheses to enclose informative or explanatory material of minor importance.

EXAMPLES   Harriet Tubman (ca. 1820–1913) is remembered for her work in the Underground Railroad.

A *roman à clef* (literally, "novel with a key") is a novel about real people to whom the novelist has assigned fictitious names.

The common housefly (*Musca domestica*) is a pest found almost everywhere on earth.

On our vacation to the South, we visited Natchitoches (nak'-ə-täsh), Louisiana.

Be sure that the material enclosed in parentheses can be omitted without losing important information or changing the basic meaning and construction of the sentence.

IMPROPER USE OF PARENTHESES   George Eliot (whose real name was Mary Ann Evans) was one of many women in nineteenth-century England who wrote under a masculine pseudonym. [The information in parentheses clarifies that George Eliot was a woman. Each parenthesis should be replaced by a comma.]

MECHANICS

Follow these guidelines for capitalizing and punctuating parenthetical sentences.

(1) A parenthetical sentence that falls within another sentence

■ should not begin with a capital letter unless it begins with a word that should always be capitalized
■ should not end with a period but may end with a question mark or an exclamation point

EXAMPLES   The Malay Archipelago **(see the map on page 350)** includes the Philippines.
Legendary jazz musician Louis "Satchmo" Armstrong **(have you heard of him?)** was born in Louisiana.

(2) A parenthetical sentence that stands by itself

■ should begin with a capital letter
■ should end with a period, a question mark, or an exclamation point before the closing parenthesis

EXAMPLES   The Malay Archipelago includes the Philippines. **(See the map on page 350.)**
Legendary jazz musician Louis "Satchmo" Armstrong was born in Louisiana. **(That's a coincidence! My hero, Harry Connick, Jr., was born there, too.)**

 NOTE   When parenthetical material falls within a sentence, punctuation should never come before the opening parenthesis but may follow the closing parenthesis.

INCORRECT   The first professional baseball team, the Cincinnati Red Stockings, (the Reds), was formed in 1869.
CORRECT   The first professional baseball team, the Cincinnati Red Stockings **(the Reds),** was formed in 1869.

13v.   In a formal research paper, use parentheses to identify the source of quoted or paraphrased material.

EXAMPLES   In *Mules and Men,* Hurston reported how she underwent a whole ceremony to get the

MECHANICS

"Black Cat Bone" or bitter bone of invisibility (272).
Hurston was attacked for the picture of
African American life presented in *Mules
and Men.* The novel's portrayal is another
connection between her anthropology and
her fiction (Howard, "Being Herself" 156).

13w. Use parentheses to enclose letters or numbers
that identify items in a series.

EXAMPLE   According to this article, we should (a)
choose the clothes we want to pack, (b) see
what will fit in our suitcases, and (c) reduce
that amount by at least one third.

 NOTE Parentheses are used to set off the area code from
the rest of the telephone number: (800) 555-1212.

Brackets

13x. Use brackets to enclose an explanation within
quoted or parenthetical material.

EXAMPLES   The newspaper article stated that "at the
time of that Democratic National Convention
[in Chicago in 1968] there were many protest
groups operating in the United States." [The
information in brackets has been added by
the user of the quotation.]
Hilda Doolittle (more commonly known as
H.D. [1886-1961]) is best remembered for her
Imagist poetry. [The information in brackets
falls within parenthetical information.]

Use brackets and the Latin word *sic* to indicate that an
error existed in the original of a quoted passage.

EXAMPLE   According to one critic, "The publication of
The Golden Apples in 1948 [*sic*] established
Eudora Welty as a major figure in twentieth-
century American literature." [The publication date should be 1949.]

Slashes

13y. Use a slash between words to indicate that either term can be used.

EXAMPLES   Aunt Jean's fiancé calls himself an attorney/sculptor.

The goat and/or the chickens must have gotten into the garden.

Please ask everyone what he/she would like for lunch.

Notice that there are no spaces before or after the slash.

STYLE NOTE   *And/or* and *he/she* constructions can make your writing clumsy. Whenever possible, avoid these constructions by (1) choosing the more accurate term or (2) revising the sentence.

EXAMPLES   The goat **or** the chickens must have gotten into the garden.

Please ask what everyone would like for lunch.

13z. Within a paragraph, use a slash to mark the end of a line quoted from poetry or from a verse play.

EXAMPLES   The narrator in Elizabeth Bishop's "First Death in Nova Scotia" vividly recalls her child's-eye view of a funeral: "Arthur's coffin was / a little frosted cake, / and the red-eyed loon eyed it / from his white, frozen lake."

Who that has read Shakespeare's *Macbeth* can forget the witches' eerie incantation: "Double, double, toil and trouble; / Fire burn and cauldron bubble"?

Notice that in verse excerpts quoted in paragraphs, the slash has a space on either side of it.

NOTE The slash is also commonly used in writing fractions and ratios.

FRACTIONS   3/4 c   7 2/3 lb   15 7/10 mi
RATIOS   55 mi/hr   250 ft/sec

 QUICK CHECK 4   **Revising Sentences by Adding Hyphens, Dashes, Parentheses, Brackets, and Slashes**

Revise the following sentences by adding hyphens, dashes, parentheses, brackets, and slashes where they are needed.

1. Les Brown be sure to watch his show is a tremendous motivational speaker who encourages people to make positive changes in their lives.
2. The citizen who spoke before the town's planning committee stated, "The project under proposal the halfway house will provide benefits both to the residents of the house and to our community."
3. Providing visuals pictures, charts, maps, or graphs can often help an audience understand technical information more easily.
4. Use two thirds cup of wheat germ, a quarter of a cup of raisins currants may be substituted for raisins and or a cup of nuts.
5. You can give me a call at 504 936-7232 or reach me at the Lion Building; the ZIP Code is 10102 2354.

✓ *Chapter Review*

A. **Proofreading Sentences for Correct Punctuation**

The following sentences contain errors in the use of dashes, parentheses, brackets, italics (underlining), quotation marks, apostrophes, slashes, and hyphens. Rewrite the sentences to correct the errors. [Note: There may be more than one error in a sentence. You may have to add punctuation where it is needed or delete incorrect punctuation.]

MECHANICS

EXAMPLE   **1.** Did you say "that you want to join us"?
           1. *Did you say that you want to join us?*

1. Ed and Jim's essays were both titled Kwanzaa: A Special Time for African Americans.
2. "Among the writers in America today, he Galway Kinnell has earned his reputation as an outstanding poet," noted the critic in Newsweek.
3. The circus audience applauded and cheered as the acrobats performed the perfectly-timed stunt.
4. Paula said in a desperate tone, "I know Janine's directions stated, "Turn right when you get to the gas station. "Unfortunately, I'm not sure which gas station she meant.
5. William Butler Yeats 1865-1939, an Irish poet who won the Nobel Prize for literature, was once a member of the Irish Parliament.
6. I couldn't get along in school without the following items: a college dictionary and-or a thesaurus and a pocket calculator.
7. My driver's license wo'nt expire for another two weeks.
8. "Well, I dont know," Lauren said. "Where do you think all this soot comes from?"
9. Several people I respect think Raintree County by Ross Lockridge, Jr., is the greatest American novel.
10. Heres my telephone number; call me if your willing to trade shifts at work.

B. Proofreading Paragraphs for Correct Punctuation

The following paragraphs of conversation contain errors in the use of dashes, parentheses, italics (underlining), quotation marks, apostrophes, and hyphens. Rewrite each paragraph to correct the errors.

EXAMPLE   [1] "You may like mystery, comedy, and science fiction movies; but my favorite movies are those about real peoples lives, Ben said."

1. *"You may like mystery, comedy, and science fiction movies; but my favorite movies are those about real people's lives,"* Ben said.

[11] Tell me we've got time some of your all time favorites, then," Tani said.

[12] "I recently saw Mountains of the Moon for the first time. I really learned a lot about the life of Sir Richard Burton from it," Ben replied.

[13] Whats his claim to fame"? Tani asked.

[14] "Sir Richard Burton was a man of many talent's: He was an explorer, an author, a scholar, a linguist, and a diplomat."

[15] "Did the movie try to show all those talents?" Tani asked. That would seem difficult to do."

[16] "The movie is mostly an African adventure; its about Burtons search for the source of the Nile River," Ben said. [17] "Some of my other favorites include Gandhi, about the Indian independence leader; Amadeus, about Mozarts life; and *The Spirit of St. Louis,* a really old film about Charles Lindbergh."

[18] "I'll bet three-fourths of our friends have never heard of most of the movies youve seen," Tani said.

[19] "The downtown video store the one owned by Ross' brother has them all," Ben said.

[20] "Biographical movies well researched ones, anyway are a good way to learn about famous people," Tani said.

14 SPELLING AND VOCABULARY

Improving Your Spelling and Vocabulary; Forming New Words; Choosing the Appropriate Word

Improving Your Spelling

Using the following techniques will improve your spelling.

1. **Pronounce words carefully.** Most people spell "by ear"—that is, by how a word sounds. Therefore, it makes sense that correct pronunciation will lead to better spelling.

    EXAMPLES ath•lete [not *ath•e•lete*]
    ac•ci•den•tal•ly [not *ac•ci•dent•ly*]
    can•di•date [not *can•i•date*]

 REFERENCE NOTE: When you are not sure about the correct pronunciation of a word, look it up in a current dictionary. The pronunciation of the word will usually be given in parentheses after the main entry. Use the pronunciation key in your dictionary to help you pronounce the word correctly.

2. **Spell by syllables.** A *syllable* is a word part that can be pronounced by itself.

   EXAMPLES   **per•ma•nent** [three syllables]
                    op•ti•mis•tic [four syllables]
                    oc•ca•sion•al•ly [five syllables]

3. **Use a dictionary.** By using a dictionary, you will become familiar with the correct pronunciations and divisions of words. In fact, using a dictionary to check the spelling of one word may help you spell other words. For example, checking the spelling of *democracy* may help you spell other words ending in *-cracy,* such as *theocracy, autocracy,* and *aristocracy.*

STYLE NOTE   Dictionaries vary in the way in which they order, label, and cross-reference variant spellings. Usually, you'll find an explanation of the editors' reasoning in a guide preceding the main entries. When you check the spelling of a word, make sure that its use isn't limited by a label such as *British* or *chiefly British.*

BRITISH	cheque	colour	connexion
	grey	metre	practise
AMERICAN	check	color	connection
	gray	meter	practice

Also check for labels such as *obsolete* (*megrim* for *migraine*) or *archaic* (*immerge* for *immerse*). In general, unlabeled optional spellings, such as *tornadoes/tornados,* are equally correct.

4. **Proofread for careless spelling errors.** Always reread what you have written so that you can eliminate careless spelling errors, such as transposed letters (*thier* for *their*), missing letters (*familar* for *familiar*), and the misuse of similar-sounding words (*affect* for *effect*).

5. **Keep a spelling notebook.** Divide each page into four columns.

MECHANICS

COLUMN 1   Write correctly any word you find troublesome.

COLUMN 2   Write the word again, dividing it into syllables and marking the stressed syllable(s). (You will likely need to use a dictionary.)

COLUMN 3   Write the word again, circling the part(s) that cause you trouble.

COLUMN 4   Jot down any comments that will help you remember the correct spelling.

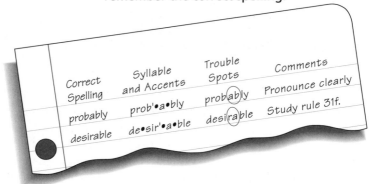

Correct Spelling	Syllable and Accents	Trouble Spots	Comments
probably	prob'•a•bly	probably	Pronounce clearly
desirable	de•sir'•a•ble	desirable	Study rule 31f.

NOTE In some names, diacritical marks (marks that show pronunciation) are as essential to correct spelling as the letters themselves. If you're not sure about the spelling of a name, check with the person or consult a reference source.

EXAMPLES
Abolfat'h	Hélène
Bashō	Inés
Da 'Shawn	Jesús
Ésteban	Kenkabô
Fasséké	Lagerlöf
François	Muñoz Marín
García Márquez	Sohráb
Gómez	

COMPUTER NOTE If you have access to word-processing software that checks spelling, use it whenever possible to help you proofread your writing. Keep in mind, however, that a computer can only identify misspellings. It can't, for example, tell the difference between *too* and *two,* both of which are correctly spelled.

Understanding Word Structure

Many English words are made up of two or more word parts. Learning how to spell the most frequently used parts—and how to combine them with each other—can help you spell thousands of words correctly. Learning what these word parts mean can help you build your vocabulary (see pages 458–461).

Roots

The *root* of a word is the part that carries the word's core meaning. Many roots come from ancient Latin and Greek words. For example, the root *-vis-* or *-vid-* comes from the Latin word *videre,* meaning "to see." The English words in which this root appears—such as *evident, invisible, supervisor, provident, vision,* and *visor*—all have something to do with seeing.

 NOTE Some word parts borrowed from other languages have alternate spellings. The spelling used in a particular English word is influenced by how the word sounds. If you try pronouncing "televidion," for example, you'll see why *-vis-,* not *-vid-,* is the form used in *television.*

COMMONLY USED ROOTS		
ROOTS	**MEANINGS**	**EXAMPLES**
LATIN		
-ag-, -act-	drive, do, impel	agitate, action, enact
-agr-	field	agriculture, agrarian
-am-, -ami-	love, friend	amorous, amiable
-aqu-	water	aquatic, aquarium
-aud-, -audit-	hear	audible, auditorium
-bene-	well, good	benefit, benediction
-brevi-	short, brief	abbreviate, brevity
-cand-	white, glowing	candle, incandescent

(continued)

MECHANICS

COMMONLY USED ROOTS *(continued)*		
ROOTS	**MEANINGS**	**EXAMPLES**
-capit-	head	capital, decapitate
-cent-	hundred	century, percent
-cid-	kill	suicide, homicide
-cogn-	know	recognize, cognition
-cred-	belief, trust	incredible, credit
-crypt-	hidden, secret	crypt, cryptic
-culp-	fault, blame	culpable, culprit
-duc-, -duct-	lead	educate, conductor
-equ-	equal	equation, equanimity
-err-	wander, stray	erratic, aberration
-fac-, -fact-, -fect-, -fic-	do, make	facile, manufacture, defective, efficient
-fid-	belief, faith	fidelity, infidel
-fin-	end, limit	final, infinite
-frag-, -fract-	break	fragment, fracture
-fus-	pour	transfuse, effusive
-gen-	birth, kind, origin	generate, generic, generous
-jac-, -ject-	lie, throw	adjacent, eject
-jud-	judge	prejudice, adjudicate
-junct-	join	junction, disjunctive
-jur-	swear	jury, perjury
-jus-	right, law	just, justice
-leg-, -lig-, -lect-	choose, read	eligible, legible, lectern
-loc-	place	locale, locate
-loqu-, -loc-	talk, speech	colloquial, eloquent, locution
-magn-	large	magnitude, magnify
-mal-	bad	malady, dismal
-man-, -manu-	hand	manicure, manual
-mit-, -miss-	send	remit, emissary
-mort-	die, death	mortuary, immortal
-omni-	all	omnipotent, omniscient
-ped-	foot	pedal, quadruped
-pend-, -pens-	hang, weigh	pendant, pensive
-pon-, -pos-	place, put	exponent, position
-port-	carry, bear	transport, portable
-prim-	first, early	primary, primitive
-punct-	point	punctuation, punctilious
-rect-	right, straight	correct, rectify
-reg-	rule	regulate, irregular
-rupt-	break	rupture, interrupt
-sang-	blood	sanguine, consanguinity

(continued)

MECHANICS

COMMONLY USED ROOTS *(continued)*		
ROOTS	**MEANINGS**	**EXAMPLES**
-scrib-, -script-	write	prescribe, manuscript
-sent-, -sens-	feel	sentiment, sensitive
-sequ-, -secut-	follow	sequel, consecutive
-son-	sound	sonic, sonar
-spir-	breath, breathe	expire, inspiration
-strict-, -string-	bind, tight	constrict, stringent
-tract-	pull, draw	tractor, extract
-uni-	one	unity, universe
-ven-, -vent-	come	intervene, supervene
-verb-	word	verbal, adverb
-vid-, -vis-	see	television, evident
-vit-	life	vitality, vitamin
GREEK		
-arch-	ancient, rule	archaeology, monarch
-auto-	self	automatic, autonomy
-bibli-	book	bibliography, bibliophile
-bio-	life	biology, symbiotic
-chron-	time	chronological, synchronize
-cycl-	circle, wheel	cyclone, bicycle
-dem-	people	democracy, epidemic
-gen-	kind, race	gender, genesis
-gram-	write, writing	grammar, epigram
-graph-	write, writing	autograph, geography
-log-, -logue-	study, word	logic, epilogue
-micr-	small	microbe, microscope
-mon-	one, single	monogamy, monologue
-neo-	new	neologism, neolithic
-pan-	all, entire	panorama, pandemonium
-phil-	like, love	philanthropic, philosophy
-phon-	sound	phonograph, euphony
-poly-	many	polygon, polygamy
-proto-	first	prototype, protoplasm
-pseudo-	false	pseudonym
-psych-	mind	psychology, psychosomatic
-soph-	wise, wisdom	philosophy, sophomore
-tele-	far, distant	telegram, telepathy

Prefixes

A *prefix* is one or more than one letter or syllable added to the beginning of a word to create a new word with a different meaning.

COMMONLY USED PREFIXES		
PREFIXES	**MEANINGS**	**EXAMPLES**
OLD ENGLISH		
a-	in, on, of, up, to	ashore, aside
be-	around, about	beset, behind
for-	away, off, from	forget, forgo
mis-	badly, not, wrongly	misfire, misspell
over-	above, excessive	oversee, overdo
un-	not, reverse of	untrue, unfold
LATIN AND LATIN-FRENCH		
a-, ab-, abs-	from, off, away	averse, abrupt, abstain
ante-	before	antedate, antecedent
bi-	two	bimonthly, bisect
circum-	around	circumnavigate, circumference
co-, col-, com-, con-, cor-	with, together	coexist, collide, compare, convene, correspond
contra-	against	contradict, contrast
de-	away, from, off, down	defect, desert, decline
dif-, dis-	away, off, opposing	differ, dismount, dissent
ex-, e-, -ef-	away from, out	excise, emigrate, efface
in-, im-	in, into, within	induct, impose
in-, im-, il-, ir-	not	incapable, impious, illegal, irregular
inter-	between, among	intercede, international
intro-, intra-	inward, to the inside, within	introduce, intravenous, intramural
non-	not	nonentity, nonessential
post-	after, following	postpone, postscript
pre-	before	prevent, preposition
pro-	forward, in place of, favoring	proceed, pronoun, pro-American
re-	back, backward, again	revoke, recede, recur
retro-	back, backward	retroactive, retrospect
semi-	half	semiannual, semicircular
sub-, suf-, sum-, sup-, sus-	under, beneath	subjugate, suffuse, summon, suppose, suspect
super-	over, above, extra	supersede, supervise, superfluous
tra-, trans-	across, beyond	traffic, transport

(continued)

MECHANICS

COMMONLY USED PREFIXES *(continued)*		
PREFIXES	**MEANINGS**	**EXAMPLES**
GREEK		
a-	lacking, without	amorphous, apolitical
anti-	against, opposing	antipathy, antithesis
cata-	down, thoroughly, against	catastrophe, catalog, catapult
dia-	through, across, apart	diagonal, diameter, diagnose
eu-	good, pleasant	eulogy, euphemism
hemi-	half	hemisphere, hemicycle
hyper-	excessive, over	hyperactive, hypertension
para-	beside, beyond	parallel, paradox
peri-	around	periscope, perimeter
syn-, sym-, syl-, sys-	together, with	synchronize, sympathy, syllable, system

Suffixes

A *suffix* is one or more than one letter or syllable added to the end of a word to create a new word with a different meaning.

COMMONLY USED SUFFIXES		
NOUN SUFFIXES	**MEANINGS**	**EXAMPLES**
OLD ENGLISH		
-dom	state, rank, condition	freedom, martyrdom, wisdom
-er	doer, maker	hunter, writer
-hood	state, condition	childhood, falsehood
-ness	quality, state	softness, shortness
LATIN, FRENCH, GREEK		
-age	act, state	passage, marriage
-ance, -ancy	act, condition, quality	acceptance, vigilance, hesitancy
-ard, -art	one that does (esp. excessively)	coward, braggart
-ate	rank, office	primate, delegate
-ation, -ition	action, result, state	occupation, starvation, condition

(continued)

MECHANICS

COMMONLY USED SUFFIXES *(continued)*		
NOUN SUFFIXES	**MEANINGS**	**EXAMPLES**
-cy	state, condition	accuracy, normalcy
-ee	one receiving action	employee, refugee
-eer	doer, worker at	racketeer, engineer
-ence	act, condition, fact	conference, patience, evidence
-er	doer, native of	baker, westerner
-ery, -ry	skill, action, collection	surgery, rivalry, finery
-ess	feminine	princess, lioness
-et, -ette	little, feminine	islet, majorette
-ion	action, result, state	union, fusion, dominion
-ism	act, manner, doctrine	baptism, barbarism, socialism
-ist	doer, believer	monopolist, capitalist
-ity	state, quality, condition	possibility, amiability, civility
-ment	means, result, action	refreshment, disappointment, acknowledgment
-or	doer, office, action	director, juror, error
-tion	action, condition	selection, relation
-tude	quality, state	fortitude, multitude
-ty	quality, state	novelty, surety
-ure	act, result, state	signature, erasure, composure
-y	quality, action	jealousy, inquiry
ADJECTIVE SUFFIXES	**MEANINGS**	**EXAMPLES**
OLD ENGLISH		
-en	made of, like	wooden, golden
-ful	full of, marked by	thankful, masterful
-ish	suggesting, like	smallish, childish
-less	lacking, without	helpless, hopeless
-like	like, similar	childlike, dreamlike
-ly	like, characteristic of	friendly, cowardly
-some	apt to, like	tiresome, lonesome
-ward	in the direction of	backward, homeward
-y	showing, suggesting	hilly, sticky, wavy
LATIN, FRENCH, GREEK		
-able	able, likely	capable, changeable

(continued)

MECHANICS

COMMONLY USED SUFFIXES *(continued)*		
ADJECTIVE SUFFIXES	**MEANINGS**	**EXAMPLES**
-ar	of, pertaining to	lunar, solar
-ate	having, characteristic of	animate, collegiate
-escent	becoming, growing	obsolescent, adolescent
-esque	in the style of, like	picturesque, statuesque
-fic	making, causing	terrific, soporific, horrific
-ible	able, likely, fit	edible, flexible, possible, divisible
-ose	marked by, given to	comatose, bellicose
-ous	marked by, given to	religious, furious
-some	characterized by	burdensome, troublesome
ADJECTIVE OR NOUN SUFFIXES	**MEANINGS**	**EXAMPLES**
-al	doer, pertaining to	rival, animal, autumnal
-an, -ain	one belonging to, pertaining to	human, European, barbarian
-ant	actor, agent, showing	servant, observant, radiant
-ary	belonging to, one connected with	primary, adversary, auxiliary
-ent	doing, showing, actor	confident, adherent
-ese	of a place or style, style	Chinese, journalese
-ic	dealing with, caused by, person or thing showing	classic, choleric, workaholic
-ile	marked by, one marked by	juvenile, servile
-ine	marked by, dealing with, one marked by	marine, canine, divine
-ite	formed, showing, one marked by	favorite, composite
-ive	belonging or tending to, one belonging to	detective, native
-ory	having the nature of	sensory, advisory

MECHANICS

(continued)

COMMONLY USED SUFFIXES *(continued)*		
VERB SUFFIXES	**MEANINGS**	**EXAMPLES**
OLD ENGLISH -en	cause to be, become	deepen, darken
LATIN, FRENCH, GREEK -ate	become, cause, treat	populate, activate, vaccinate
-esce	become, grow, continue	convalesce, acquiesce
-fy	make, cause, cause to have	glorify, identify, fortify
-ish	do, make, perform	punish, finish
-ize	make, cause to be	sterilize, motorize

Spelling Rules

ie and *ei*

14a. Write *ie* when the sound is long *e,* except after *c.*

EXAMPLES believe   field   conceit
          ceiling   receive niece
          chief   piece   relieve
          thief   yield   deceive

EXCEPTIONS either   leisure neither   seize
            weird   sheik   protein

14b. Write *ei* when the sound is not long *e.*

EXAMPLES forfeit freight eight   neighbor   weigh
          reign   foreign their   sovereign height

EXCEPTIONS ancient view friend mischief
            conscience

NOTE Rules 14a and 14b apply only when the *i* and the *e* are in the same syllable.

MECHANICS

Frank & Ernest reprinted
by permission of NEA, Inc.

-cede, -ceed, and *-sede*

14c. The only English word ending in *-sede* is
supersede. The only words ending in *-ceed* are
exceed, proceed, and *succeed.* All other words
with this sound end in *-cede.*

EXAMPLES   ac**cede**   con**cede**   inter**cede**
           pre**cede**   re**cede**   se**cede**

Adding Prefixes

14d. When adding a prefix, do not change the spelling
of the original word.

EXAMPLES   dis + satisfy = **dis**satisfy
           im + mature = **im**mature
           mis + spell = **mis**spell
           re + adjust = **re**adjust

👉 REFERENCE NOTE: For a listing of prefixes, see pages
444–445.

Adding Suffixes

14e. When adding the suffix *-ness* or *-ly,* do not
change the spelling of the original word.

EXAMPLES   plain + ness = plain**ness**
           casual + ly = casual**ly**

MECHANICS

gentle + ness = gentle**ness**
final + ly = final**ly**

EXCEPTION For most words ending in *y,* change the *y* to *i*
before adding -*ness* or -*ly.*

empty + ness = empt**iness**
busy + ly = bus**ily**
heavy + ness = heav**iness**
ready + ly = read**ily**

One-syllable adjectives ending in *y* generally follow
rule 14e.

EXAMPLES   dry + ness = dry**ness**
shy + ly = shy**ly**

REFERENCE NOTE: For a listing of suffixes, see pages
445–448.

 QUICK CHECK 1   **Proofreading for Spelling
Errors**

Proofread each of the following sentences, and correct each
misspelled word.

1. At last, the road work is finaly finished, and freight
   shipments can go directly downtown instead of taking a
   ten-mile detour.
2. Neither the mischeif he got into nor the damage he
   caused ever seemed to weigh too heavily on the
   puppy's conscience.
3. Their everyday troubles forgotten, the audience plainly
   was enjoying the wriness of the comedian's humor.
4. If you continue to procede in this diligent way, I am
   sure that you will succeed in my class as well as in college.
5. Unless we recieve payment by Friday, you will forfeit
   your deposit.

14f.   Drop the final silent *e* before a suffix beginning
with a vowel.

EXAMPLES   care + ing = car**ing**
dose + age = dos**age**
simple + er = simpl**er**

MECHANICS

love + able = lov**able**

EXCEPTIONS Keep the final silent *e*

- in a word ending in *ce* or *ge* before a suffix beginning with *a* or *o:* peac**eable;** coura-**geous**
- in *dye* and in *singe* before -*ing:* dy**eing,** sing**eing**
- in *mile* before -*age:* mil**eage**

NOTE When adding -*ing* to words that end in *ie,* drop the *e* and change the *i* to *y*.

EXAMPLES die + ing = d**ying**
lie + ing = l**ying**

14g. Keep the final silent *e* before a suffix beginning with a consonant.

EXAMPLES hope + ful = hop**eful**
love + ly = lov**ely**
care + less = car**eless**
place + ment = plac**ement**
life + like = lif**elike**
state + hood = stat**ehood**

EXCEPTIONS awe + ful = aw**ful**
whole + ly = whol**ly**
argue + ment = arg**ument**
nine + th = nin**th**
judge + ment = judg**ment**
true + ly = tru**ly**
wise + dom = wis**dom**
due + ly = du**ly**
acknowledge + ment = acknowledg**ment** *or*
acknowledg**ement**

14h. For words ending in *y* preceded by a consonant, change the *y* to *i* before any suffix that does not begin with *i*.

EXAMPLES thirsty + est = thirst**iest**
plenty + ful = plent**iful**
modify + ing = modif**ying**
accompany + ment = accompan**iment**

MECHANICS

14i. For words ending in *y* preceded by a vowel, keep the *y* when adding a suffix.

EXAMPLES   gray + est = gray**est**
obey + ing = obey**ing**
play + ed = play**ed**
enjoy + ment = enjoy**ment**

EXCEPTIONS day—**daily**   lay—**laid**
pay—**paid**   say—**said**

14j. Double the final consonant before a suffix that begins with a vowel if the word *both* (1) has only one syllable or has the accent on the last syllable *and* (2) ends in a single consonant preceded by a single vowel.

EXAMPLES   thin + est = thi**nnest**
occur + ence = occu**rrence**
rap + ing = ra**pping**
refer + ed = refe**rred**

EXCEPTIONS
- For words ending in *w* or *x,* do not double the final consonant.

  new + er = new**er**
  relax + ing = relax**ing**
  bow + ed = bow**ed**
  tax + able = tax**able**

- For words ending in *c,* add *k* before the suffix instead of doubling the *c.*

  picnic + k + ed = picnic**ked**
  politic + k + ing = politic**king**

Do not double the final consonant unless the word satisfies both of the conditions.

EXAMPLES   **prevent + ing = preventing** [has accent on the last syllable but does not end in a single consonant preceded by a single vowel]
mellow + er = mellower [ends in a single consonant preceded by a single vowel but does not have accent on the last syllable]

MECHANICS

When a word satisfies both conditions but the addition of the suffix causes the accent to shift, do not double the final consonant.

EXAMPLES   refer + ence = refe**rence**
           prefer + able = prefe**rable**

EXCEPTIONS   excel—excel**lent,** excel**lence,** excel**lency**

NOTE   The final consonant of some words may or may not be doubled. Either spelling is acceptable.

EXAMPLES   cancel + ed = cance**led** *or* cance**lled**
           travel + er = trave**ler** *or* trave**ller**

If you are not sure whether you should double the final consonant, follow rule 14j or consult a dictionary.

QUICK CHECK 2   **Spelling Words with Suffixes**

Spell each of the following words, adding the suffix given.

1. mile + age
2. graze + ing
3. vie + ed
4. freeze + able
5. true + ly

6. dirty + est
7. survey + or
8. pay + ed
9. dim + er
10. cow + ed

Forming the Plurals of Nouns

14k.   Remembering the following rules will help you spell the plural forms of nouns.

(1) For most nouns, add -*s.*

	SINGULAR		
SINGULAR	player	beagle	ship
	island	senator	Jefferson
PLURAL	players	beagles	ships
	islands	senators	Jeffersons

NOTE   Don't confuse singular nouns ending in -*nce* with plural nouns ending in -*nts.*

EXAMPLES   If you need **assistance,** ask one of the sales **assistants.**

MECHANICS

In a microwave, for **instance**, some foods take only **instants** to cook.

Patients who have to wait hours to see a doctor may run out of **patience**.

(2) For nouns ending in *s, x, z, ch,* or *sh,* add -*es*.

SINGULAR	class	tax	waltz
	match	brush	Chávez
PLURAL	class**es**	tax**es**	waltz**es**
	match**es**	brush**es**	Chávez**es**

(3) For nouns ending in *y* preceded by a vowel, add -*s*.

SINGULAR	monkey	journey	alloy
	decoy	tray	McKay
PLURAL	monkey**s**	journey**s**	alloy**s**
	decoy**s**	tray**s**	McKay**s**

(4) For nouns ending in *y* preceded by a consonant, change the *y* to *i* and add -*es*.

SINGULAR	fly	country	comedy
	trophy	cavity	theory
PLURAL	fl**ies**	countr**ies**	comed**ies**
	troph**ies**	cavit**ies**	theor**ies**

EXCEPTION   For proper nouns, add -*s*.
Kennedy—Kennedy**s**
Gregory—Gregory**s**

(5) For some nouns ending in *f* or *fe*, add -*s*. For others, change the *f* or *fe* to *v* and add -*es*.

SINGULAR	gulf	roof	belief
	leaf	shelf	knife
PLURAL	gulf**s**	roof**s**	belief**s**
	lea**ves**	shel**ves**	kni**ves**

For proper nouns, add -*s*.

EXAMPLES   Tallchief—Tallchief**s**
Wolfe—Wolfe**s**

NOTE If you are not sure how to spell the plural of a word ending in *f* or *fe*, look in a dictionary.

(6) For nouns ending in *o* preceded by a vowel, add -*s*.

SINGULAR	studio	radio	cameo
	stereo	igloo	Ignacio
PLURAL	studios	radios	cameos
	stereos	igloos	Ignacios

(7) For nouns ending in *o* preceded by a consonant, add -*es*.

SINGULAR	torpedo	tomato	hero
	veto	potato	
PLURAL	torpedoes	tomatoes	heroes
	vetoes	potatoes	

For some common nouns ending in *o* preceded by a consonant, especially those referring to music, and for proper nouns, add only an -*s*.

SINGULAR	taco	photo	piano	solo
	alto	Ibo	Suro	
PLURAL	tacos	photos	pianos	solos
	altos	Ibos	Suros	

NOTE For some nouns ending in *o* preceded by a consonant, you may add either -*s* or -*es*.

SINGULAR	motto	tornado	mosquito
	zero	banjo	
PLURAL	mottos	tornados	mosquitos
	zeros	banjos	

or

mottoes	tornadoes	mosquitoes
zeroes	banjoes	

If you are ever in doubt about the plural form of a noun ending in *o* preceded by a consonant, check the spelling in a dictionary.

(8) The plurals of a few nouns are formed in irregular ways.

SINGULAR	tooth	goose	woman
	mouse	foot	child
	man	ox	
PLURAL	teeth	geese	women
	mice	feet	children
	men	oxen	

MECHANICS

(9) For a few nouns, the singular and the plural forms are the same.

SINGULAR	sheep	deer	trout	salmon
AND PLURAL	moose	species	Sioux	Japanese
	aircraft	corps	scissors	pliers
	trousers	series	shears	binoculars

(10) For most compound nouns, form the plural of only the last word of the compound.

SINGULAR	notebook	bookshelf	baby sitter
	ten-year-old		
PLURAL	notebook**s**	bookshel**ves**	baby sitter**s**
	ten-year-old**s**		

(11) For compound nouns in which one of the words is modified by the other word or words, form the plural of the noun modified.

SINGULAR	sister-in-law	runner-up	mountain goat
	eyetooth	bill of sale	musk ox
PLURAL	sister**s**-in-law	runner**s**-up	mountain goat**s**
	eye**teeth**	bill**s** of sale	musk ox**en**

NOTE Some compound nouns have two acceptable plural forms.

SINGULAR	attorney general	court-martial
	notary public	
PLURAL	attorney general**s**	court-martial**s**
	notary public**s**	

or

attorney**s** general	court**s**-martial
notar**ies** public	

Check an up-to-date dictionary whenever you are in doubt about the plural form of a compound noun.

(12) For some nouns borrowed from other languages, the plural is formed as in the original languages.

SINGULAR	alga	datum
	alumna [female]	ellipsis
	alumnus [male]	genus
	analysis	hypothesis

	bacterium	radius
	basis	phenomenon
PLURAL	alg**ae**	data
	alumn**ae** [female]	ellips**es**
	alumn**i** [male]	gen**era**
	analys**es**	hypothes**es**
	bacter**ia**	rad**ii**
	bas**es**	phenomen**a**

Overboard copyright 1992 Universal
Press Syndicate. Reprinted with
permission. All rights reserved.

A few nouns borrowed from other languages have two
plural forms. For each of the following nouns, the plural
form preferred in English is given first.

SINGULAR	index	appendix	formula	cactus
PLURAL	index**es**	appendix**es**	formula**s**	cactus**es**

or

	indi**ces**	appendi**ces**	formul**ae**	cact**i**

NOTE Whenever you are in doubt about which spelling to
use, remember that a dictionary lists the most frequently used spelling first.

(13) To form the plurals of figures, most uppercase
letters, signs, and words used as words, add an *-s* or
both an apostrophe and an *-s*.

SINGULAR	8	1990	C	&	*and*
PLURAL	8**s**	1990**s**	C**s**	&**s**	*and***s**

or

	8**'s**	1990**'s**	C**'s**	&**'s**	*and***'s**

REFERENCE NOTE: For information on when to spell out
numbers, see pages 596–598.

MECHANICS

To prevent confusion, add both an apostrophe and an -*s* to form the plural of all lowercase letters, certain uppercase letters, and some words used as words.

EXAMPLES   The word *Mississippi* contains four *s*'s and four *i*'s. [Without an apostrophe, the plural of *s* would look awkward, and the plural of *i* could be confused with *is*.]

Sebastian usually makes straight A's. [Without an apostrophe, the plural of *A* could be confused with *As*.]

Because I mistakenly thought Evelyn Waugh was a woman, I used *her*'s instead of *his*'s in my paragraph. [Without an apostrophe, the plural of *her* would look like the possessive pronoun *hers* and the plural of *his* would look like the word *hiss*.]

 REFERENCE NOTE: For more information about forming these kinds of plurals, see page 426.

A list of three hundred commonly misspelled words appears on pages 462–465.

  QUICK CHECK 3   **Spelling Plurals**

Spell the plural form of each of the following nouns.

1. scarf
2. dish
3. agency
4. radio
5. 500

6. foot
7. bass
8. basis
9. *z*
10. point of honor

Improving Your Vocabulary

An effective vocabulary increases the power and persuasiveness of what you write and say. Moreover, studies have shown that a large vocabulary is an important indicator of your success in high school, in college, and in your future career. Because of this correlation, college entrance examinations place great emphasis on vocabulary, and many job tests have sections devoted to word knowledge.

Using the following techniques will help you to improve your vocabulary.

1. Adding to Your Word Bank. When you find new words in your reading or in school, write these words and their definitions in a notebook. Consult a dictionary to be sure you have understood the meaning of each word.

2. Using Context Clues. Frequently, you can figure out the meaning of unfamiliar words by analyzing how these words are used. Determining the meaning of new words in this way is known as using **context clues.** The **context** of a word is made up of the phrases and sentences that surround it.

The following chart shows examples of some of the most common types of context clues.

TYPES OF CONTEXT CLUES	
TYPE OF CLUE	**EXPLANATION**
Definitions and Restatements	Look for words that define or restate the meaning of a word. ■ Vonelle studied *ethnology,* that is, the science dealing with the cultures of various people.
Examples	A word may be accompanied by an example that illustrates its meaning. ■ His acts of *benevolence* were well-known, especially his generous donations to children's hospitals.
Synonyms	Look for clues that an unfamiliar word is similar in meaning to a familiar word. ■ Rosita has always been so dependably prompt that she has been given a special award by her employer for her consistent *punctuality.*
Comparisons	Sometimes an unknown word may be compared with a more familiar word. ■ Registration procedures for the *symposium* will be similar to those of other conferences.

(continued)

TYPES OF CONTEXT CLUES *(continued)*	
TYPE OF CLUE	**EXPLANATION**
Contrast	An unfamiliar word may sometimes be contrasted with a more familiar word. ■ Everyone from the largest *metropolis* to the smallest village participated in the nationwide peace effort.
Cause and Effect	Look for clues that indicate an unfamiliar word is related to the cause, or is the result of, an action, feeling, or idea. ■ Since the instructions were given in the wrong order, it's not surprising that most of the students looked quite *flummoxed.*

3. Determining Meanings from the General Context. Sometimes context clues are subtle. You may need to read an entire passage to understand the meaning of an unfamiliar word. In such a case, you must infer the meaning of the unfamiliar word by drawing on your own knowledge of the general topic or by making connections between the unfamiliar word and the other information provided in the material.

4. Using Word Parts. In general, English words are of two kinds: those that can be divided into smaller parts (*unthinkable, displeased*) and those that cannot (*youth, money*). Words that stand alone and are complete by themselves are **base words.** Words that can be divided are made up of two or more word parts. The three types of word parts are

■ roots
■ prefixes
■ suffixes

Learning the meanings of some of the most commonly used word parts can often help you determine the meanings of unfamiliar words. Refer to the word parts listed on pages 441–448 whenever you come upon a word you don't know. Determine the meaning of each part of the word; then try making up your own definition. Check in a current

MECHANICS

dictionary to find the actual definition of the word. With practice, you will get better at deciphering new words.

Forming New Words

New words are constantly added to the English language. The most common way new words are formed is by a process of combination. *Affixes,* prefixes or suffixes, are usually added to a base word or to a word root to make a new word. Sometimes, however, two base words can be combined or put together with a hyphen to make a new word. Here are some of the most common ways new words are made.

METHODS OF FORMING NEW WORDS		
PROCESS	**DESCRIPTION**	**EXAMPLES**
combining	combining two base words to make a compound; combining a word with an affix	doorway, high-rise, unfold, wonderful
shortening	omitting part of an original word to shorten it or to change it to another part of speech	telephone → phone burglar → burgle nuclear → nuke
blending	shortening and combining two words	breakfast + lunch = brunch smoke + fog = smog
shifting	changing the meaning or usage of a word	host (n.) → host (v.) farm (n.) → farm (v.)

Calvin & Hobbes copyright 1993 Watterson. Reprinted with permission of Universal Press Syndicate. All rights reserved.

MECHANICS

Choosing the Appropriate Word

Synonyms are words that have the same or nearly the same meaning. However, synonyms often have subtle shades of differences in meaning. Use a dictionary or a thesaurus to make sure you understand the exact differences in meanings between synonyms.

Many words have two kinds of meaning: *denotative* and *connotative*. The **denotative** meaning of a word is the meaning given by a dictionary. The **connotative** meaning of a word is the feeling or tone associated with it. For example, the words *smirk* and *grin* both mean "to smile." However, the word *grin* has a more positive connotation than *smirk,* which suggests an affected, insincere, or annoying smile. When you read, listen, or speak, be aware of both the denotative and connotative meanings of words.

300 Spelling Words

The following list contains three hundred commonly misspelled words. The words are grouped so that you can study them ten at a time. To master any words that give you difficulty, follow the five-step procedure given at the beginning of this chapter (see pages 438–440). If you are not sure of the exact meaning of a word, look the word up in a dictionary and add it to your word bank.

accidentally	amateur	arctic
accommodate	analyze	argument
accurate	announce	arrangement
acknowledgment	anonymous	assassinate
acquaintance	apologize	association
across	appearance	athletics
aerial	appreciate	atomic
aisle	approaching	attach
all right	appropriate	attention
always	approval	attitude

auxiliary
awful
awkward
bachelor
background
banana
bargain
beggar
beginning
believe

benefited
bicycle
biscuit
bookkeeper
bracelet
breathe
bruise
bulletin
bureau
business

calendar
campaign
candidate
catastrophe
cellophane
cemetery
ceremony
challenge
chaperon
classroom

college
colonel
colossal
column
commission
committee
comparatively
compel
competition
completely

complexion
concentrate
conscience
conscientious
contemptible
convenience
copies
cordially
corps
correspondence

corroborate
courageous
courteous
criticism
criticize
cylinder
decide
decision
defense
definitely

dependent
descendant
descent
description
desirable
develop
dictionary
different
dining
dinosaur

disappear
disappoint
discipline
discuss
disease
dissatisfied
divided
doesn't
economical
efficient

eighth
elementary
eligible
embarrass
emphasize
endeavor
environment
equipment
especially
etiquette

exaggerate
excellent
excitement
exercise
exhausted
existence
expense
experienced
extraordinary
familiar

fascinating
fatigue
February
feminine
fiery
financial
foreign
forfeit
fourth
fragile

generally
genius
government
governor
grammar
grateful
guarantee
guard
gymnasium
handkerchief

happened
harass
haven't
height
heroes
hindrance
hoping
horizon
hospital
humorous

imitation
immediately
incident
inconvenience
indispensable
inevitable
influence
initial
interpreted
interrupted

irrelevant
irresistible
jewelry
laboratory
leisure
license
lightning
likelihood
literacy
loneliness

losing
luxurious
maintenance
maneuver
marriage
matinee
meant
medicine
medieval
mentioned

microphone
minimum
mischievous
missile
misspelled
movable
municipal
necessary
neighbors
nickel

ninety
ninth
nonsense
noticeable
nuclear
nuisance
occasionally
occur
occurred
omitted

opinion
opportunity
optimistic
pamphlet
parallel
parliament
particularly
pastime
permanent
permissible

perseverance
personally
personnel
perspiration
persuade
playwright
pleasant
pneumonia
possess
possibility

potato
practice
preference
prejudice
privilege
probably
procedure
professor
pronunciation
propaganda

propeller
prophecy
psychology
pursue
questionnaire
realize
receive
recognize
recommend
referral

rehearse
reign
relief
repetition
representative
restaurant
rhythm
satisfactorily
schedule
scissors

seize
semester
separate
sergeant
shiny
siege
similar
sincerely
souvenir
straight

strategy	tariff	twelfth
subtle	television	tyranny
successful	temperament	undoubtedly
sufficient	temperature	unforgettable
suppress	thoroughly	unfortunately
surprised	tomorrow	unnecessary
suspension	tournament	vacuum
syllable	traffic	valuable
sympathy	tragedy	villain
synonym	transferred	weird

PART FIVE

COMPOSITION

467

15 THE WRITING PROCESS

In this chapter you'll read not only about writing but about thinking, because it's impossible to separate the two. You'll learn about the basic stages of the writing process, as shown in the following diagram.

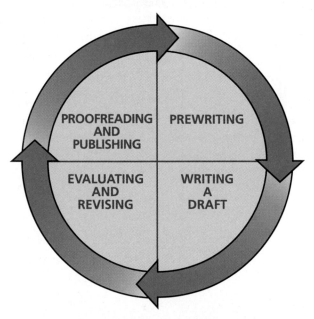

As you can see, the diagram does not show writing as a straight line from your ideas to the finished product. As a writer, you'll always have, and need, the freedom to jump forward, go back, or start over again.

Finding Ideas for Writing

Writing starts with getting an idea and collecting information about it. "Easily said," you may be thinking, "not so easily done." Well, there are practical helps: prewriting techniques for stirring up ideas. In the following pages you will find examples and explanations of several of these techniques.

Keeping a Writer's Journal

A *journal*—a daily log of happenings—is a great way to keep a record of experiences, observations, feelings, opinions, original ideas, and unanswered questions. You can put anything you want into your journal: newspaper and magazine articles, interesting quotations, songs, poems, photos, dreams. Here are some suggestions for getting started.

1. Use a notebook, scrapbook, or file folder.
2. Try to add something to your journal every day, and date your entries. Consider writing at the same time every day, early in the morning or late at night perhaps. (But you can jot down notes any time on anything, and insert them later.)
3. Don't worry about punctuation, grammar, or usage.
4. Use your imagination. Be creative. Write original poems or song lyrics if you want. Jot down story ideas.
5. For paste-in entries, write notes beside them. Why did you like a particular poem, quotation, or cartoon?

Kudzu by Marlette. By permission of Marlette and Creators Syndicate.

Freewriting

When you're *freewriting,* you jot down whatever comes to mind. You can freewrite anywhere—in your journal, or on a loose sheet of paper.

1. Write for three to five minutes. Keep writing until your time is up.
2. Start with any topic or word, such as *photography* or *sports cars* or *honesty.*
3. Don't worry about using complete sentences or proper punctuation. Your thoughts may be disorganized. You may repeat yourself. That's perfectly okay.
4. Occasionally, choose one key word or phrase from your freewriting and use it as a starting point for more writing. This *focused freewriting,* or *looping,* allows you to "loop" from what you've already written to something new.

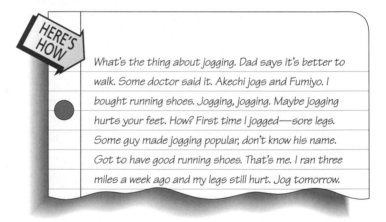

HERE'S HOW

What's the thing about jogging. Dad says it's better to walk. Some doctor said it. Akechi jogs and Fumiyo. I bought running shoes. Jogging, jogging. Maybe jogging hurts your feet. How? First time I jogged—sore legs. Some guy made jogging popular, don't know his name. Got to have good running shoes. That's me. I ran three miles a week ago and my legs still hurt. Jog tomorrow.

Brainstorming

Another way to generate ideas is through *brainstorming,* or using free association. You can brainstorm alone or with others by using the following steps:

1. Write a word, phrase, or topic on your paper or on the board.
2. Without any careful thought, begin listing every related word or idea that enters your mind. One person can write for a group.

3. Don't stop to evaluate the ideas. Anything goes, even jokes and ideas that seem to be off the topic.

Clustering

Clustering is another free-association technique. Like brainstorming, it is used to break up a large subject into its smaller parts or to gather information, but it also shows connections. Clustering is sometimes called *webbing* or *making connections.*

1. Write a subject in the center of a sheet of paper. Draw a circle around it.
2. In the space around the circle, write all the words or ideas that come to mind. Circle each addition, and then connect it to the original circled subject with a line.
3. Create offshoots by adding and connecting related ideas. Then circle each related idea and connect it to the appropriate circle.

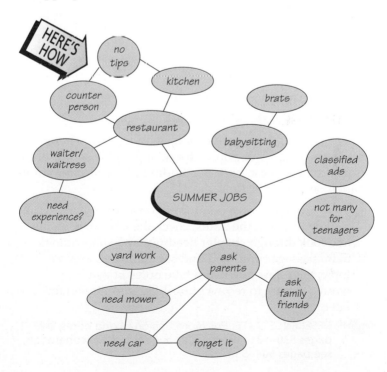

COMPOSITION

Asking Questions

One good way to gather information is to use the reporter's *5W-How?* questions: *Who? What? Where? When? Why?* and *How?* Although not every question applies to every situation, the *5W-How?* questions are a good basic approach. You can also ask the same *5W-How?* question more than once, about various aspects of your topic.

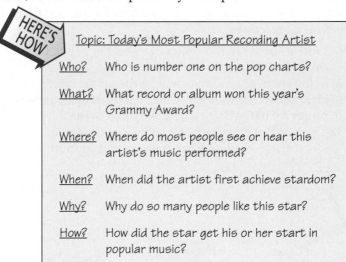

Topic: Today's Most Popular Recording Artist

Who?   Who is number one on the pop charts?

What?   What record or album won this year's Grammy Award?

Where? Where do most people see or hear this artist's music performed?

When?   When did the artist first achieve stardom?

Why?   Why do so many people like this star?

How?   How did the star get his or her start in popular music?

Reading with a Focus

When you read to gather information, you should be clearly focused. Once you've found a possible source of information, use these hints for finding and collecting information on a specific topic.

1. First, give the source of information a "once-over." Look for key words in the index, check the table of contents, and look through chapter headings and subheadings.
2. Skim passages until you find something about your topic; then slow down and take notes in your own words. Be sure to record publishing information for later use.

 REFERENCE NOTE: For more tips on taking notes, see pages 530–531. For more about citing source materials, see pages 544–552.

Listening with a Focus

Your ears are another powerful prewriting tool, but they can't do the work all by themselves. It pays to *prepare* to listen.

Listening for information may include listening to a tape recording, a radio or television program, a speech, or an expert during a personal or telephone interview.

1. Think ahead. Make an outline of information you need, or prepare questions to ask.
2. In an interview, concentrate on the question the person is answering. Don't let your mind wander to the next question.
3. Take notes even if you are also recording. However, don't try to write every word—use phrases and abbreviations, and listen for main ideas and significant details.

Imagining

Creative people have active imaginations. Many famous scientists, artists, and writers looked at something ordinary, then wondered, "Well, that's interesting, but what if . . . ?" You can take this *"What if?"* approach and apply it to any subject. Here are some sample "What if?" questions.

- *What if I could change my circumstances?* (What if I were an only child, or what if I were *not* an only child? What if I had lived during the Middle Ages?)
- *What if a familiar thing in our world no longer existed?* (What if we had no music? What if we had no public schools?)
- *What if major social changes were made overnight?* (What if racial prejudice no longer existed? What if everyone earned the same amount of money?)

Observing

You can gather great writing material just by observing, but you need to remember that observation is purposeful and deliberate. It's important to use all five of your senses—sight, hearing, smell, taste, and touch. Here are some examples showing how one writer used his observation skills on a camping trip.

COMPOSITION

HERE'S
HOW

	SIGHT:	trout leaping high out of the water; campers struggling to win a tug of war; moonlit nights around the campfire
	HEARING:	roar of the river water; chatter of crickets; crackling fire; campers' shouting and laughter
	SMELL:	tangy odor of wet leaves and grass; musty smell of wet swimsuits drying; savory odor of fish frying
	TASTE:	toasted marshmallows; tart lemonade from a bottle in an ice-filled tub
	TOUCH:	rough, splintery firewood; shoulders aching from carrying backpacks; dry, crackling leaves underfoot

Analyzing a Subject

When you're preparing to write, you need to *analyze* your subject—to break it into its different parts. For example, you may be interested in transportation, but that subject is too broad. You need to find and explore a narrower, more manageable topic for the length of paper you plan.

Broad subject: transportation

More narrow subject: urban transportation

Topic: mass transit systems

More narrow topics: their history in U.S.
                       new and experimental systems

Considering Purpose, Audience, and Tone

Purpose. With all the different kinds of writing, you would think the purposes for writing are limitless. Well, yes and no.

It's true that every writer writes for a very specific reason. But even though each writer has a particular intent for writing, a main idea he or she wants to express, each specific reason falls within four basic purposes for writing.

WHY PEOPLE WRITE	
To express themselves	To get to know themselves better; to find some kind of meaning or purpose in their own lives
To inform, to explain, or to explore	To give other people information that they need or want; to provide an explanation; to explore an idea or problem or situation
To persuade	To convince other people to do something or believe something that the writer would like them to do or believe
To create literary works	To be creative with language; to communicate or portray something in a unique and expressive way

Probably everything written fits one of these purposes, but it's also true that much writing has a combination of purposes. Someone may write about a strong opinion both to persuade others and to know her own values better. Someone else may write a story both to be creative and to share special knowledge.

Just as you can have various reasons for writing, you can use various forms. The following chart shows some of the possibilities.

MAIN PURPOSE	FORMS OF WRITING
Self-Expressive	Journal, letter, personal essay
Expository: Informative, Explanatory, or Exploratory	Technical or scientific report, newspaper or magazine article, biography, autobiography, travel essay, brochure
Persuasive	Persuasive essay, letter to the editor, pamphlet, advertisement, political speech, poster
Literary works	Short story, poem, play

Audience. You don't talk the same way to everyone, nor do you write the same way for everyone. You adjust your writing for your *audience.* Ask yourself the following questions to find out more about your audience.

AUDIENCE CHECKLIST

- Who is my audience?
- How much does my audience already know about the topic?
- Do I need to give background information or explain technical terms?
- What strong feelings might my audience have about the topic?
- What kind of language should I use? Should my attitude be formal or informal? Should the writing be simple or complex?
- How can I make my message interesting and meaningful to this particular audience?

Tone. When you are speaking to someone, your tone of voice tells your listener how you feel about your subject, as well as how you feel about the listener. Your writing also takes on a *tone.* Tone in writing is created by choice of words, choice of details, and sentence structure.

- **Word Choice.** Generally, the use of contractions and colloquial language creates a more personal, friendly tone, while the use of polysyllabic words and impersonal language creates a less personal, more serious tone. You also create a tone depending on whether you use objective, unemotional words or words with emotional connotations (the "old goat" or "the elderly gentleman").

- **Choice of Details.** As you've seen in your reading, a list of facts creates a rather serious tone, while a set of personal examples or reminiscences creates a friendlier, perhaps even playful, tone.
- **Sentence Length and Structure.** Long, involved sentences, for example, can produce a serious and weighty tone. A series of very short, clipped sentences and even sentence fragments can be used to create an urgent tone.

 *Prewriting*

Arranging Ideas

By the time you have gathered enough information to begin writing, you're likely to have your notes in various forms: on notepaper, on 3" x 5" cards, on photocopies. How do you bring order to this chaos?

Arranging your ideas is an important part of planning. The following chart shows four common ways of arranging ideas.

ARRANGING IDEAS		
TYPE OF ORDER	**DEFINITION**	**EXAMPLES**
Chronological	Narration: Order that presents events as they happen in time	Story; narrative poem; explanation of a process; history; biography; drama
Spatial	Description: Order that describes objects according to location	Descriptions (near to far; left to right; top to bottom; and so on)

(continued)

ARRANGING IDEAS (*continued*)		
TYPE OF ORDER	**DEFINITION**	**EXAMPLES**
Importance	Evaluation: Order that gives details from least to most important or the reverse	Persuasive writing; descriptions; explanations; evaluative writing
Logical	Classification: Order that relates items and groups	Definitions; classifications; comparisons and contrasts

REFERENCE NOTE: For more information on arranging ideas, see pages 496 and 499–504.

Charts

Charts are a practical, graphic way to arrange your prewriting notes. They group related bits of information, allowing you to "see" the overall arrangement clearly. Here's a chart for a student's paper on the inhabitants of Mexico before the Spanish conquest.

MAJOR CULTURES OF MEXICO IN 1500		
PEOPLE	LOCATION	CHARACTERISTICS
Aztecs	Central Mexico	centralized government; large, efficient army; 365-day solar calendar; advanced engineering and architectural skills
Mayas	Yucatán peninsula	written language; base-20 mathematical system; 365-day calendar; sophisticated artistry, especially sculpture

(continued)

MAJOR CULTURES OF MEXICO IN 1500 (continued)		
PEOPLE	LOCATION	CHARACTERISTICS
Mixtecs	Southwest Mexico	fine stone and metal work; beautiful carvings in wood; painted polychrome pottery
Zapotecs	Southern Oaxaca and Isthmus of Tehuantepec	priestly hierarchy; ancestor worship; artistic heritage influenced by the early Mayan civilization

Time Lines

Another graphic way to organize notes is a *time line*—a chart showing information in chronological order. The following time line shows the periods of dominance of the four major cultural groups in Mexico.

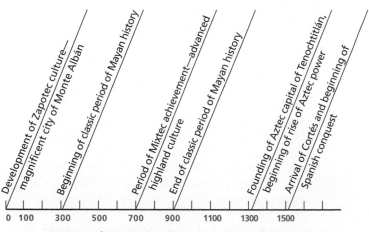

Stages of Pre-Columbian Cultures of Mexico

Take advantage of software that allows you to create graphic displays such as diagrams, tables, and flow charts. Even without graphic software, you can create simple column charts and time lines on the computer, rearranging information easily if you need to add or cut details or change groupings.

☞ **REFERENCE NOTE:** For information on creating prewriting plans and formal outlines, see pages 508–510 and 532–533.

 ## *Writing a First Draft*

There is no magic formula, no *one* right way, to write a first draft. Your prewriting notes may be rough, or you may create a detailed outline. You may prefer to write quickly, or you may write slowly, carefully shaping each sentence. Whatever your writing style, consider these suggestions:

- Use your prewriting notes or outline as a guide.
- Write freely. Concentrate on expressing your ideas.
- Include any new ideas that come to you as you write.
- Don't worry about making errors in grammar, usage, and mechanics. You can fix them later.

Here's a first draft of a paragraph on dogs and politics.

Dogs and politics go together like ham and eggs. Apparently there's something about a dog that makes its politician-owner more human, lovable, and electable. A first rule of politics would seem to be—own a dog. You've just got to own a dog. In 1944 the opponents of President Franklin D. Roosevelt claimed that Fala, FDR's Scottie [check breed], had been brought back from Alaska on a U.S. Navy destroyer sent especially for the purpose. The story was a lie, and Roosevelt's "Fala speech" of September [?] seriously hurt Thomas E. Dewey, his

COMPOSITION

opponent. So a second rule is never to criticize someone else's dog. When Richard M. Nixon ran into trouble over the gift of a dog [was that all?] in his 1952 vice-presidential campaign, Nixon responded with his famous "Checkers speech"— Checkers being the dog in question. This speech, delivered eight years to the day after FDR's Fala speech, saved Nixon [how?]. Who can doubt that other dogs will arrive in the future to help other threatened politicians?

Evaluating and Revising

Evaluating means deciding what changes need to be made. *Revising* involves making the changes.

Evaluating

Evaluating your writing—looking critically at what you have written—is one of the most important steps in the writing process. What seems to be good about your first draft? What changes will make it better?

Self-Evaluation. Seeing what needs improvement in your writing can be difficult, but the following techniques will help.

TIPS FOR SELF-EVALUATION

1. **Reading Carefully.** Read your paper several times. First concentrate on *content* (what you say), next on *organization* (how you've arranged your ideas), and then on *style* (how you've used words and sentences).

2. **Listening Carefully**. Read your paper aloud, "listening" to what you've written. What looked all right on paper may sound awkward or unclear when read aloud.

3. **Taking Time.** If possible, put your paper aside for a while. A day or two (or even a few hours) will give you some mental distance from it and help you to see flaws you didn't notice before.

Peer Evaluation. Every writer needs an editor—a person who can read critically and with a different viewpoint. You can get an editor (or editors) of your own through peer evaluation. Members of a peer-evaluation group read and comment on each other's papers. Sometimes you'll be the writer whose work is being evaluated, and sometimes you'll be evaluating someone else's writing. Here are some guidelines to help you with both of these roles.

PEER-EVALUATION GUIDELINES
Guidelines for the Writer 1. Tell the evaluator what bothers you most about your own paper. Point out anything that has caused you difficulty. 2. Don't be defensive. Keep an open mind and make good use of the evaluator's comments.
Guidelines for the Peer Evaluator 1. Be sure to tell the writer what's right as well as what's wrong. 2. Make suggestions for improvement. If you see a weakness, give the writer some suggestions to correct it. 3. Concentrate on content and organization. Don't worry about mechanical errors such as spelling or punctuation. 4. Be sensitive to the writer's feelings. Make sure that your comments are constructive—that means offering solutions, not criticism.

Luann reprinted with special permission of North America Syndicate, Inc.

Revising

Even if you identify some problems with your writing, you may have trouble deciding how to fix them. The four basic ways to revise are to **add, cut, replace,** and **reorder.** The following chart shows how these techniques can be applied.

GUIDELINES FOR EVALUATING AND REVISING

EVALUATION GUIDE	REVISION TECHNIQUE
CONTENT	
1 Is the writing interesting?	**Add** examples, an anecdote, dialogue, or additional details. **Cut** repetitious or boring details.
2 Does the writing achieve the writer's purpose?	**Add** explanations, descriptive details, arguments, or narrative details.
3 Are there enough details?	**Add** more details, facts, or examples to support your ideas.
4 Are there unrelated ideas that distract the reader?	**Cut** irrelevant or distracting information.
5 Are unfamiliar terms explained or defined?	**Add** definitions or other explanations of unfamiliar terms. **Replace** unfamiliar terms with familiar ones.
ORGANIZATION	
6 Are ideas and details arranged in an effective order?	**Reorder** ideas and details to make the meaning clear.
7 Are the connections between ideas and sentences clear?	**Add** transition words to link ideas: *therefore, for example, because,* and so on.
STYLE	
8 Is the meaning clear?	**Replace** vague or unclear wording. Use words and phrases that are precise and easy to understand.
9 Does the writing contain clichés or overworked phrases?	**Cut** or **replace** with specific details and fresh comparisons.
10 Does the language fit the audience and purpose?	**Replace** formal words with less formal words and phrases to create an informal tone. To create a more formal tone, **replace** slang and contractions.
11 Do sentences read smoothly?	**Reorder** to vary sentence beginnings and sentence structure.

COMPOSITION

A computer is a real timesaver during revision. Most writers who use computers revise more thoroughly because they can draft different versions of a passage. Be sure to evaluate your work and mark revisions on a *hard copy,* or printout, so you can see your writing as a whole on paper.

Here is the revised paragraph on dogs and politics. To understand the changes, look at the chart of Symbols for Revising and Proofreading on page 488. Notice how the writer has answered the questions noted on the draft.

Dogs and politics go together like ~~ham~~ *fireworks* **replace**
and the Fourth of July⊙
~~and eggs~~. Apparently there's something

about a dog that makes its politician-

owner more human, lovable, and elect-

able. A first rule of politics would seem to

be ∧*to* own a dog, ~~You've just got to own a~~ **replace/reorder**

~~dog.~~ In 1944 the opponents of President **cut**

Franklin D. Roosevelt claimed that Fala,
sh terrier
FDR's Scottie ~~[check breed]~~, had been **replace/cut**

brought back from Alaska on a U.S. Navy

destroyer sent especially for the purpose.
untrue∧
The story was ~~a lie~~, and Roosevelt's "Fala **replace**
23
speech" of September ~~[?]~~ seriously hurt **replace**
the chances of
∧Thomas E. Dewey, his opponent. ~~So a~~ **add/cut**
~~discovered in the presidential elections of 1944~~ ≡ **add**
second rule is never to criticize someone

else's dog. When Richard Nixon ran into

trouble over the gift of a dog [was that
all?] *(among other things)* **replace**

in his 1952 vice-presidential cam- **cut**

paign, he responded with his famous

"Checkers speech"—Checkers being the

cuddly little
dog in question. This speech, delivered **add**

eight years to the day after FDR's Fala

speech, saved Nixon [how?]. Who can *'s nomination* **replace**

doubt that other dogs will arrive in the *wag into view* **replace**

future to help other threatened

politicians?

Proofreading and Publishing

Proofreading

When you *proofread,* you catch and correct any remaining
errors in grammar, usage, and mechanics (spelling, capitalization, punctuation). If you've put your paper aside for a
while, you'll find it easier to spot these mistakes. Here are
some techniques for proofreading:

- Focus on one line at a time. Use a sheet of paper to cover
  all the lines below the one you're proofreading. Or try beginning at the bottom line and working your way to the
  top. That way you'll be forced to concentrate on mechanics, not content.
- Consider peer proofreading. Exchange papers with a
  classmate and proofread each other's papers.
- When in doubt, look it up. For spelling, use a college dictionary. For grammar, usage, and punctuation, refer to the
  appropriate pages in a handbook like this one.

The following guidelines are designed to help you handle a few of the most common errors.

COMPOSITION

GUIDELINES FOR PROOFREADING

1. Is each sentence a complete sentence? (See pages 279–285.)

2. Does every sentence end with the appropriate punctuation mark? (See pages 377–435.)

3. Does every sentence begin with a capital letter? Are all proper nouns and proper adjectives capitalized when necessary? (See pages 352–370.)

4. Does every verb agree in number with its subject? (See pages 120–133.)

5. Are verb forms and tenses used correctly? (See pages 145–170.)

6. Are subject and object forms of personal pronouns used correctly? (See pages 187–196.)

7. Does every pronoun agree with its antecedent in number and gender? Are pronoun references clear? (See pages 133–140 and 204–209.)

8. Are frequently confused words (such as *there* and *their*, *imply* and *infer*) used correctly? (See pages 2–83.)

9. Are all words spelled correctly? Are the plural forms of nouns correct? (See pages 438–458.)

10. Is the paper neat and in correct manuscript form? (See pages 584–599.)

A word processing spelling checker, which finds misspelled words, is an obvious proofreading aid. However, beware: Your sentence may need *chord* instead of *cord*, *you're* instead of *your*, or *principal* instead of *principle*. The computer won't catch these errors, since it determines misspellings in terms of individual words, not context. When you do find a spelling error or other word error (such as British *Islands* instead of *Isles*), use the computer's SEARCH/REPLACE function to find and correct every instance of that error.

Publishing

Your readers should always be on your mind, and the publishing stage is the time you can finally reach out to them. Here are a few suggestions for sharing your writing.

- Submit your writing for publication in the school newspaper or magazine. Or, send it to your local newspaper. Most newspapers publish letters to the editors, and many accept feature stories.
- Look for writing contests. A few are specifically for high school students. Some offer prizes or certificates. Ask your teacher or counselor for information.
- Compile a class anthology of each student's favorite piece of writing. Donate it to your school library. If possible, make a copy for each contributor.

As you make a final copy of your paper for publication, follow the guidelines for manuscript style on pages 584–599.

COMPOSITION

Shoe, by Jeff MacNelly, reprinted by permission: Tribune Media Services.

SYMBOLS FOR REVISING AND PROOFREADING

SYMBOL	EXAMPLE	MEANING OF SYMBOL
cap ≡	Spence college	Capitalize a lowercase letter.
lc /	our Best quarterback	Lowercase a capital letter.
∧	the on Fourth of July	Insert a missing word, letter, or punctuation mark.
/	a endurence	Change a letter.
	Ohio the capital of Iowa	Change a word.
	hoped for to go	Leave out a word, letter, or punctuation mark.
	on that occassion	Leave out and close up.
	today's home work	Close up space.
	nieghbor	Change the order of letters.
tr	the counsel general of the corporation	Transpose words. (Write tr in nearby margin.)
¶	¶ "Wait!" I shouted.	Begin a new paragraph.
⊙	She was right⊙	Add a period.
∧,	Yes that's true.	Add a comma.
#	center field	Add a space.
⊙:	the following items :	Add a colon.
∧;	Evansville, Indiana; Columbus, Ohio	Add a semicolon.
=	self=control	Add a hyphen.
∨	Mrs. Ruizs office	Add an apostrophe.
stet	a very tall building	Keep the crossed-out material. (Write stet in nearby margin.)

16 PARAGRAPH AND COMPOSITION STRUCTURE

A *paragraph* is usually defined as a group of sentences that develop a main idea. A *composition,* in turn, can be described as a group of paragraphs that develop a main idea. Indeed, paragraphs and compositions (essays) are remarkably similar. Understanding how a paragraph works—what it is made of and how it is built—is a good preparation for understanding the larger structure of a composition.

Paragraphs That Develop Main Ideas

Not all paragraphs develop a main idea or even consist of a series of sentences. In essays as well as in advertisements and newspaper articles, a paragraph may be a single sentence that serves as a transition or that presents a single quotation. This chapter, though, deals with paragraphs that develop main ideas. Each paragraph usually has a topic sentence and several supporting sentences.

 NOTE All of the model paragraphs in this chapter were written as parts of longer works. The paragraphs are taken out of context so that you can study the form and structure of each one.

The Topic Sentence

A *topic sentence* is a specific, limiting statement about the subject of a paragraph.

In the following paragraph, Dr. Martin Luther King, Jr., states his topic—that *a just law may be unjustly applied*—in the first sentence.

> Sometimes a law is just on its face and unjust in its application. For instance, I have been arrested on a charge of parading without a permit. Now, there is nothing wrong in having an ordinance which requires a permit for a parade. But such an ordinance becomes unjust when it is used to maintain segregation and to deny citizens the First-Amendment privilege of peaceful assembly and protest.
>
> Martin Luther King, Jr.,
> "Letter from Birmingham Jail"

Location of a Topic Sentence

You'll often find the topic sentence as the first or second sentence of a paragraph (sometimes following a catchy, inviting first sentence). But a topic sentence can be any place in a paragraph. To create surprise or to summarize ideas, a writer sometimes places the topic sentence at or near the end of a paragraph.

Importance of a Topic Sentence

Not all paragraphs have or need topic sentences. Paragraphs that relate sequences of events or actions in stories, for example, frequently don't contain topic sentences. In the writing that you do in school, however, you'll find that topic sentences are useful. They provide a focus for your reader, and they keep you from straying from the topic as you develop the rest of your paragraph.

Supporting Sentences

Supporting sentences give details to support or develop a paragraph's main idea. Supporting sentences often consist of sensory details, facts or statistics, examples, or anecdotes. A paragraph may be developed with one type of detail or with a combination of types.

Sensory Details

Sensory details are images of sight, sound, taste, smell, and texture that bring the subject to life for readers. In the following paragraph, notice how sensory details help you to see and hear the children as well as to smell the evening's refreshments.

> The weeks until graduation were filled with heady activities. A group of small children were to be presented in a play about buttercups and daisies and bunny rabbits. They could be heard throughout the building practicing their hops and their little songs that sounded like silver bells. The older girls (nongraduates, of course) were assigned the task of making refreshments for the night's festivities. A tangy scent of ginger, cinnamon, nutmeg and chocolate wafted around the home economics building as the budding cooks made samples for themselves and their teachers.
>
> Maya Angelou, *I Know
> Why the Caged Bird Sings*

Facts and Statistics

A *fact* is something that can be proven true by concrete evidence: *Archbishop Desmond Tutu, a South African civil rights leader, received the Nobel Prize for peace in 1984.* A **statistic** is a fact based on numbers: *The United States border with Mexico is 1,952 miles long.* To verify the accuracy of facts or statistics, you can check in reference materials. In the following paragraph, the writer uses statistics to illustrate the popularity of pencils.

> You'd think that the pencil would just fade away, what with pattering keyboards and ubiquitous ballpoint pens. Pencil popularity, however,

COMPOSITION

seems here to stay—more than 2½ billion pencils are produced in America every year. The U.S. government uses 45 million of them a year, and the New York Stock Exchange more than a million. Perhaps it's because the pencil's an old-fashioned hard worker—one standard pencil can leave a 35-mile trail, or about 45,000 words. At least forty materials from twenty-eight countries go into one.

Mary Blocksma,
Reading the Numbers

Examples

Examples are specific instances or illustrations of a general idea. The following paragraph uses specific examples to support the writers' main idea about the modern interest in mazes.

Since the 1970s, there has been a revolution in innovative puzzle mazes. Greg Bright's puzzle maze at Longleat had curving paths, wooden bridges, a complete lack of symmetry, and, above all, immense size. Stuart Landsborough's wooden mazes triggered off a maze craze in Japan, resulting in the construction of over two hundred three-dimensional wooden mazes during the 1980s. Our own puzzle innovations have encompassed traditional, interactive and color mazes, within a diverse range of landscape settings.

Adrian Fisher and Georg
Gerster, *Labyrinth: Solving
the Riddle of the Maze*

Anecdotes

An *anecdote,* a little story that is usually biographical or autobiographical, can also be used to support or prove a main idea. In the following paragraph, for example, the writer uses an anecdote to help support a point about General Stonewall Jackson's ability to ignore the suffering of his men.

He had a strange quality of overlooking suffering. He had a young courier, and during one of the battles Jackson looked around for him and he wasn't there. And he said, "Where is Lieutenant So-and-so?" And they said, "He was killed, General." Jackson said, "Very commendable, very commendable," and put him out of his mind. He would send men stumbling into battle where fury was, and have no concern about casualties at the moment. He would march men until they were spitting cotton and white-faced and fell by the wayside. He wouldn't even stop to glance at one of them, but kept going.

> Geoffrey C. Ward et al., "Men at War: An Interview with Shelby Foote," *The Civil War*

The Clincher Sentence

A *clincher sentence* is a final sentence that emphasizes or summarizes the main idea or that draws a conclusion. In the following paragraph, for example, the writer uses a clincher sentence to summarize and emphasize his main idea about Native American cultures. Notice that the topic sentence at the beginning of the paragraph also expresses the main idea.

In the past forty years, however, anthropologists have done some very thorough digging into the life of the North American Indians and have discovered a bewildering variety of cultures and societies beyond anything the schoolbooks have taught. There were Indian societies that dwelt in permanent settlements, and others that wandered; some were wholly democratic, others had very rigid class systems based on property. Some were ruled by gods carried around on litters, some had judicial systems, to some the only known punishment was torture. Some lived in caves, others in tepees of bison skins, others in cabins. There were tribes ruled by warriors or by women, by sacred elders or by councils. . . . There were tribes who worshiped the bison or a matriarch or the maize they lived by. There were tribes that had never heard of war, and there were tribes debauched by centuries of fighting. In short, there was a great diversity of Indian nations, speaking over five hundred languages.

Alistair Cooke,
Alistair Cooke's America

Unity

Unity simply means that the paragraph "hangs together." In other words, all the supporting sentences work together to develop the main idea. Unity can exist whether the main idea is stated in a topic sentence or is implied (suggested). In paragraphs that relate a series of actions or events, the main idea is often implied rather than stated.

All Sentences Relate to the Stated Main Idea

In the following paragraph, the topic sentence states the main idea—that animals' eyes tell a lot about them. Each of the sentences that follow the main idea gives the reader some specific information about what you can see in animals' eyes.

You can tell a lot about an animal's way of life by looking at its eyes. If it relies a lot on sight, its eyes will be relatively big. If it is a hunting animal, like the tiger, its eyes will be placed toward the front of its head, so that the fields of view of the two eyes overlap. This allows it to judge distance accurately for pouncing on prey. Animals with many predators, like the rabbit, usually have eyes at the sides of their heads. They can spot a predator coming from almost every angle, but they are not very good at judging distance.

Tony Seddon and Jill Bailey,
The Living World

COMPOSITION

All Sentences Relate to an Implied Main Idea

The following paragraph doesn't have a topic sentence, but all the sentences support an implied main idea—American women began experimenting with shorter hairstyles during the early 1900s.

One of the first women to commit the shocking act of cutting her hair was the famous American ballroom dancer Irene Castle. In 1913 she popularized a very short hairstyle called the Castle Clip, worn with a string of pearls around her forehead. It wasn't until after World War I, though, that most women found the courage to bob their hair and exchange their hairpins for the new spring-clip "bobby pin." The shortest cuts of the 1920s flapper age were the "boyish bob" and the "shingle," for which the hair was actually shaved at the back of the neck. For women who wanted their short hair frizzy-curly rather than sleek, there was a new hair treatment called a permanent wave.

Lila Perl, *From Top Hats to Baseball Caps, From Bustles to Blue Jeans: Why We Dress the Way We Do*

All Sentences Relate to a Sequence of Events

The writer of the following paragraph achieves unity through the sequence of events and actions. You won't find a topic sentence in this paragraph, but you will find that all sentences relate to the experience of entering an emerald mine on a tire attached to a steel cable.

First came a drizzle. Then groundwater poured from the walls, and I was plunging through a waterfall. The darkest darkroom doesn't begin to compare to the pitch-black inside the mine shaft. I couldn't look upward at the patch of daylight above for fear of drowning. After about three minutes—an eternity—the unseen operator threw on

COMPOSTIION

> the brake, jerking me to a stop two feet above the mud. To no one in particular, I sighed, "Welcome to the glamorous world of emeralds."
>
> Fred Ward, "Emeralds,"
> *National Geographic*

Coherence

In a *coherent* paragraph, the relationship between ideas is clear—the paragraph flows smoothly. You can go a long way toward making paragraphs coherent by paying attention to two things: (1) the order you use to arrange your ideas, and (2) the connections you make between ideas.

Order of Ideas

The chart below lists four basic ways of arranging ideas.

WAYS OF ORDERING IDEAS	
Chronological Order	Arrange events in the order they occur.
Spatial Order	Arrange details in the order that the eye sees them.
Order of Importance	Arrange ideas or details according to how important they are.
Logical Order	Arrange ideas or details into related groups.

 REFERENCE NOTE: See the section **Strategies of Development** on pages 499–504 for more information about arranging ideas.

Connections Between Ideas

Arranging ideas in an order that makes sense helps to make paragraphs coherent, but *direct references* and *transitional words and expressions* can also help. These words and phrases act as connectors between and among ideas so that the paragraph is clear to readers.

Direct References. Referring to a noun or pronoun that you've used earlier in the paragraph is a *direct reference.* You can make direct references by

1. using a noun or pronoun that refers to a noun or pronoun used earlier
2. repeating a word used earlier
3. using a word or phrase that means the same thing as one used earlier

In the following paragraph, the superscript numbers are keyed to the list above to indicate the type of direct reference the writer is using.

> Pepé drank from the water bag, and *he*[1] reached into the flour sack and brought out a black string of jerky. *His*[1] white teeth gnawed at the *string*[2] until the tough *meat*[3] parted. *He*[1] *chewed*[3] slowly and *drank*[2] occasionally from the water *bag.*[2] *His*[1] little eyes were slumberous and tired, but the muscles of *his*[1] face were hard-set. The earth of the trail was black now. *It*[1] gave up a hollow sound under the walking hoofbeats.
>
> John Steinbeck, "Flight"

Transitional Expressions. Words and phrases that make a transition from one idea to another are called *transitional expressions.* These words and phrases include conjunctions, which connect and show relationships, as well as prepositions that indicate chronological or spatial order.

Transitional words and phrases are underlined in the following paragraph about a woman who was paralyzed as a result of a diving accident. Notice how the underlined words help to show relationships of time and space.

> <u>At first</u>, when Marca Bristo was injured, she couldn't see what she could do <u>beyond</u> that time. <u>Later</u>, as she mastered coping with life in a wheelchair, she decided to fight for more opportunities for disabled people. <u>Then</u> she became executive

director of Access Living, an organization that works to remove any barriers that prevent disabled people from becoming independent and taking part in society. <u>Eventually</u>, she co-founded the National Council on Independent Living and <u>afterward</u> prepared a report that resulted in the Americans with Disabilities Act.

The following chart includes some frequently used transitional expressions grouped according to the relationships they indicate. The chart also indicates how the expressions are most often used.

TRANSITIONAL WORDS AND PHRASES		
Comparing Ideas/Classification and Definition		
also	another	similarly
and	moreover	too
Contrasting Ideas/Classification and Definition		
although	in spite of	on the other hand
but	instead	still
however	nevertheless	yet
Showing Cause and Effect/Narration		
as a result	consequently	so that
because	since	therefore
Showing Time/Narration		
after	eventually	next
at last	finally	then
at once	first	thereafter
before	meanwhile	when
Showing Place/Description		
above	before	here
across	beyond	in
around	down	inside

(continued)

TRANSITIONAL WORDS AND PHRASES *(continued)*		
Showing Place/Description		
into	over	to
next	there	under
Showing Importance/Evaluation		
first	mainly	then
last	more important	to begin with

Strategies of Development

Depending on your main purpose, you can choose from among the four strategies of development shown in the chart that follows. Remember that you can have more than one purpose (and more than one strategy of development) in a paragraph. For example, writers often combine description and narration in the same paragraph.

STRATEGIES OF DEVELOPMENT	
Description	Looking at individual features of a particular subject
Narration	Looking at changes in a subject over a period of time
Classification	Looking at a subject in relation to other subjects
Evaluation	Judging the value of a subject

Calvin & Hobbes copyright 1992 Watterson. Reprinted with permission of Universal Press Syndicate. All rights reserved.

COMPOSITION

Description

In a *description* you use sensory details (details of sight, sound, taste, touch, and smell) for support. You'll often use *spatial order* to organize a description, but depending on your subject or purpose, you might also use *order of importance* or *chronological order.* The writer of the following paragraph uses spatial order to describe a store in Nameless, Tennessee.

> The old store, lighted only by three fifty-watt bulbs, smelled of coal oil and baking bread. In the middle of the rectangular room, where the oak floor sagged a little, stood an iron stove. To the right was a wooden table with an unfinished game of checkers and a stool made from an apple-tree stump. On shelves around the walls sat earthen jugs with corncob stoppers, a few canned goods, and some of the two thousand old clocks and clockworks Thurmond Watts owned. Only one was ticking; the others he just looked at.
>
> William Least Heat-Moon,
> *Blue Highways*

Narration

The strategy of *narration* examines changes over time. You may use narration *to tell a story, to explain a process,* or *to explain causes and effects.* You usually use **chronological order** to present ideas and information in paragraphs of narration.

Telling a Story. Writers use the strategy of narration to tell stories, either true or fictional. In this paragraph, the writer tells part of a Native American story.

> The Youngman Started Out to Look for Wood. It was not long Before he Saw Wood that would Make a Beautiful Warm Fire, and he Began to Busy himself Gathering the Wood. Suddenly he Felt the Presence of the Owl. The Owl Reached Down and Put the Youngman in its Ear. The Youngman

Strung his Bow and Fitted One of his Arrows, Letting it Fly from his Bow Deep Into the Ear of the Owl. And the Youngman was Free.

> Hyemeyohsts Storm,
> *Seven Arrows*

Explaining a Process.   Explaining a process—telling how something works or telling how to do something— also requires the strategy of narration. In the following paragraph, for example, the writer explains how to perform the "Violin with Cord Elastic Strings" clown trick.

You enter with a violin and prepare to play some lovely music. Taking out a pocket handkerchief, you fold it carefully and place it on your *right* shoulder as a violin rest. You then put the violin under your chin on your *left* shoulder (or vice versa if you are left-handed). Drawing the bow back on the [elastic-cord] strings, you suddenly send the bow flying offstage into the wings like an arrow! Dismayed, you produce a second bow and repeat the action, launching this bow offstage as well. You investigate the violin and discover the elastic strings, reacting with either embarrassment or delight (perhaps even leading into a full demonstration of target practice with "violin and arrow").

> Turk Pipkin, *Be a Clown!*

Explaining Causes and Effects.   You also use narration when you explain causes and effects. For example, the following writer explains how the Civil War helped to promote the development of the blues as a musical form.

Primitive blues-singing actually came into being because of the Civil War, in one sense. The emancipation of the slaves proposed for them a normal human existence, a humanity impossible under slavery. Of course, even after slavery the average Negro's life in America was, using the more ebullient standards of the average American white

COMPOSITION

man, a shabby, barren existence. But still this was the black man's first experience of time when he could be alone. The leisure that could be extracted from even the most desolate sharecropper's shack in Mississippi was a novelty, and it served as an important catalyst for the next form blues took.

LeRoi Jones, *Blues People*

Classification

The strategy of ***classification*** examines a subject and its relationship to other subjects. You can classify a subject by dividing it into its parts, defining it, or comparing and contrasting it with something else. In paragraphs that classify, writers usually use ***logical order:*** grouping related ideas together.

Dividing.   Classifying by *dividing* means looking at the parts of a subject in order to understand the subject as a whole. In the following paragraph, the writers divide dinosaurs into two groups in order to explain their characteristics.

To begin with, dinosaurs fell into two groups: the bird-hipped ones, or *ornithischians,* and the reptile-hipped ones, or *saurischians.* (*Ornith-* is Greek for "bird," and *saur-* is Greek for "reptile.") The bird-hipped dinosaurs were almost all herbivores, or plant-eaters, while the reptile-hipped group contained both meat-eaters (carnivores) and plant-eaters.

Tom and Jane D. Allen with
Savannah Waring Walker,
Dinosaur Days in Texas

Defining.   To *define,* you first identify a subject as a part of a larger group or class. Then you discuss some features that make the subject different from other members of the class. In the following paragraph, the writer defines *pikas.*

Pikas are mountain-dwelling mammals that are tiny relatives of rabbits and hares. Pikas are only about six inches long and have short, rounded ears. They live in colonies in rocky areas. They prepare for winter by gathering grass and spreading it out to dry in the sun. Then they make little haystacks near their dens, and eat the dried grass throughout the winter.

Comparing and Contrasting. You also use the strategy of classification when *comparing* subjects (telling how they're alike), when *contrasting* them (telling how they're different), or when both comparing and contrasting. The following paragraph compares and contrasts the ears of dogs and wolves.

A dog's skull is generally somewhat smaller and rounder than a wolf's and its brain is about twenty percent smaller. Wolves and all the other kinds of wild dogs have upstanding ears, which act as sound funnels. Like antennas, they gather sound waves from the air and direct them down the ear canals into the inner ear. Most domestic dogs have lop ears: at rest their ears hang limply down, although they can be pricked up to listen to interesting sounds. . . . For all of the dogs, both wild and domestic, the ears are not only organs of hearing but also organs of expression. The position of a dog's ears can communicate a great deal about its mood.

Alvin and Virginia Silverstein,
Dogs: All About Them

Evaluation

Evaluation means judging the value of something. You often evaluate a subject in order to inform readers or to persuade them to think or act differently. An evaluation should be supported with reasons showing *why* you made the judgment about the subject. A good way to arrange reasons is by *order of importance:* You emphasize a point by listing it first or last in the paragraph.

The following paragraph is part of a review of recent movies. Notice the reasons the writer gives for the evaluation of the three movies.

> "Movies are better then ever" can usually be regarded as nothing more than a slogan to sell tickets, but now there are some movies that may make it a slogan to believe. After several years of movies of doubtful mentality, the early 1990s gave us some surprisingly intelligent, beautifully filmed, thought-provoking films, such as *Dances with Wolves*, *Fried Green Tomatoes,* and *Cinema Paradiso.* These go back to the artistry of the best movies of the past and go against the tendency to film everything in closeup, with the eventual (or immediate) transfer to videotape in mind. Movies should be movies, made as these were for large screens, and should give audiences something to admire and think about as these do. Not all movies are better than ever, but some are. Let's hope it's a trend.

STYLE NOTE   In your reading, you've probably discovered that what a professional writer considers a paragraph can range from a single word to a page or more of writing. In general, the paragraph length that a writer uses depends on the writer's purpose and audience. For example, a reporter writing a front-page news story will likely use a series of short paragraphs and will put the most crucial information at the beginning of the article. This style and arrangement allows busy readers to glance at the article and get the gist of the news quickly. On the other hand, a feature article in the Sunday paper will likely contain longer, more detailed paragraphs. Relaxing on the weekend, people have time to enjoy reading a detailed account of some entertaining or informative topic.

The Composition

You've been writing compositions for years, but you may have called them essays or reports. You've written them for different classes as assignments and on tests, and you'll continue to write them in school and for job, college, and scholarship applications. This section focuses on aspects of composition form.

Peanuts reprinted by permission of UFS, Inc.

COMPOSTIION

The Thesis Statement

When you write a composition, you have something specific to say about your topic. This is your thesis, and the sentence that you write to express this main idea is the *thesis statement*. The *thesis statement* of a composition is like the topic sentence of a paragraph; it helps you control the direction of your writing. The entire composition will support the ideas in the statement. Your thesis is not your topic (*youth football*) but what you want to say about it (*youth football causes serious, unnecessary injuries*). In some essays, a thesis is implied rather than stated, but in your school compositions a thesis statement aids your writing, and your teacher may require it.

Location, Length, and Aim

The thesis statement often appears in the introduction, where it introduces or summarizes the composition's main idea or ideas. Some thesis statements go further—they state what the writer will prove in the composition. Sometimes the thesis statement may appear later in the composition or not at all (in the case of an implied thesis statement). Depending on your topic, purpose, and writing approach or style, the statement can be long or short, one sentence or more.

Preliminary and Revised Thesis Statements

While planning your composition, you will develop a preliminary thesis statement to guide your first draft. Later, during revision, you can revise that statement to make it more interesting.

PRELIMINARY   Under nearly ideal conditions, scientists observed the total solar eclipse over Hawaii on July 11, 1991.

REVISED   When the morning sun grew dark over Hawaii on July 11, 1991, the eclipse shed light on mysteries that have baffled astronomers for centuries.

HINTS FOR WRITING AND USING A THESIS STATEMENT

1. **Use your prewriting notes.** Before you begin to write, you'll gather a great deal of information about your topic. Look over this information carefully. What one idea unifies the facts and details you have?

2. **State both your topic and your main idea.** Your thesis statement needs to make clear two things: your topic and your main idea. For example, think about this thesis statement: *If you want to be among the nearly eight million teens who are employed part time, the following tips on landing a job may boost your chances of success.* The topic is the teen part-time job market. The main idea is how to improve your chances of finding a part-time job.

3. **Change your thesis statement if you need to.** To begin with, reword your thesis statement until it says clearly what you want it to say. Remember that if you get a different idea or decide to change the focus of your composition, you can always write a new thesis statement.

4. **Use your thesis statement to guide your writing.** Keep your thesis statement in front of you as you write, and be sure that all your ideas and details support it.

Development and Organization

In the prewriting stage (see pages 469–480), you gather information on your topic and decide on the thesis of your composition. Then you create a prewriting plan by choosing a *strategy of development* to *order* your material.

The four strategies of paragraph development—*narration, description, classification,* and *evaluation* (page 499) are also used for the larger structure of a composition. In a composition, however, you develop several ideas and paragraphs as well as each paragraph's details and sentences.

NOTE Because a composition is longer and more complex than a paragraph, you often use more than one strategy of development. An essay *evaluating* a school floor plan, for example, may also involve *classification* by dividing information into classroom design, grounds, and so on.

COMPOSTIION

The Early Plan

The *early plan*—sometimes called a *rough outline* or *informal outline*—gives you a general idea of the kinds and order of information you want to include in your composition. Two steps in developing an early plan are *grouping* and *ordering*.

Grouping and Ordering. Organizing often involves *grouping* information so that you can discuss similar ideas together. The following steps help in making and grouping notes.

- Sort related ideas and details into separate groups.
- Make a separate list of details that don't fit into any group. (At some later stage you may find a use for them.)
- Give each group of details a separate label.

Here's an example of grouping for a composition on teens finding part-time jobs. Notice that the plan isn't detailed. Instead, it breaks the job-hunt into three broad categories, or groups.

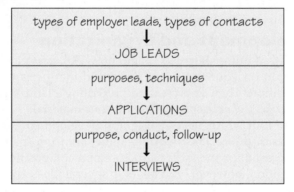

 REFERENCE NOTE: For information on using charts as early plans, see pages 478–479.

After you have grouped your details, you will order them. *Ordering* involves arranging details within groups and then arranging the groups. The four basic types of order—chronological, spatial, logical, and order of importance (p. 496) apply to compositions as well as paragraphs.

REFERENCE NOTE: For different examples of ordering in paragraphs, see pages 500–504.

The Formal Outline

Structured outlines sometimes grow out of early plans. A *formal outline* has numerals and letters to identify headings and subheadings; these headings and subheadings are indented to show levels of subordination. A formal outline may be a *topic outline*, which uses single words and phrases, or a *sentence outline,* which uses only complete sentences. Formal outlines may be used for planning, but they are more often written after the composition is complete to provide an overview or summary for the reader.

 REFERENCE NOTE: For more information on formal outlines, see pages 532–533.

Here's a formal topic outline for a composition about teens finding part-time jobs. The full paper follows. Notice that the introduction and the conclusion are not part of the outline.

Title: It Takes Work to Get Work

Thesis Statement: If you want to be among the nearly eight million teens who are employed part time, the following tips on finding and landing a job may boost your chances of success.

I. Job leads
  A. Employer leads
    1. Signs
    2. Newspaper ads
    3. Employment agencies
  B. Contacts
    1. Potential employers
    2. Friends
    3. Family members
    4. Business acquaintances
    5. School counselor
II. Job applications
  A. Purpose
  B. Techniques

    1. First impression
    2. Skills and accomplishments
III. Job interviews
  A. Purpose
  B. Conduct
    1. Grooming/dress
    2. Preparation
    3. Directness/honesty
  C. Follow-up

COMPUTER NOTE

Your word-processing software may have an "Outline" feature that automatically inserts the correct Roman numeral, letter, or Arabic numeral at each level of your outline. With the "Outline" feature on, the number of indents before a line signals the computer to insert the appropriate label.

A COMPOSITION MODEL

It Takes Work to Get Work

INTRODUCTION

Thesis statement

"You're hired!" These are exciting words to any anxious teen entering the job market for the very first time. If you want to be among the nearly eight million teens who are employed part time, the following tips on finding and landing a job may boost your chances of success.

BODY

Major point: job leads

The first step is to find out what part-time jobs are available in your area. Some job leads come directly from employers: signs in store and restaurant windows, "help wanted" ads in the newspaper, and listings at employment agencies. Other leads can be developed by contacting potential employers yourself or by making use of contacts, such as friends, family members, business acquaintances, and your school counselor. The more leads you have, the more likely you are to find the job you want.

Major point: job applications

Once you have a list of job leads, start applying for some jobs. In most cases, the first thing you'll be asked to do is fill out a job application. This is what an employer uses to decide whom to interview. It's your first chance to show that you are qualified for the job.

Here are some ways to use the job application to make a good first impression. First of all, neatness counts; use a pen and write clearly. Make sure you use standard English, and avoid slang words. Spell words correctly, and use good grammar. Finally, answer all questions honestly and clearly.

Above all, don't sell yourself short. Most job applications have a space to list special skills and accomplishments. Be honest, but don't be shy. Does the job involve selling? Maybe you've sold ads for your school annual. Do you speak a second language? Many businesses need bilingual employees. Are you on the honor roll? Many employers know that people who work hard at school will also work hard at a job. Do you have job skills from completing courses in typing, computers, bookkeeping, or shop? Let your potential employer know.

Major point: job interviews

After reviewing all the job applications, employers will choose some candidates to interview. An interview is the employer's chance to find out more about you and your chance to find out more about the job.

Arrive for the interview alert, well-groomed, neatly dressed, and about five minutes early. Have your Social Security card and a pen and pad of paper with you. During the interview, look the interviewer in the eye, smile, and remember to use the interviewer's name (always Ms., Mrs., or Mr.—never first names). Be direct and honest, and be ready to answer questions. (Prepare yourself by going to the library to consult employment booklets that list some of the most commonly asked interview questions.) When the interview is over, express your interest in the job and thank the interviewer for his or her time.

Major point:
following up

Finally, that evening, type or neatly write a brief letter expressing your interest in the job and reminding the interviewer of the attributes that make you the perfect person for the job. Thank the interviewer for considering you. Address the envelope to the interviewer and mail the letter the next day.

CONCLUSION

It may take a little time to prepare for and follow through with your job search, but it's worth the effort. You'll be glad you did it right when you finally hear the words "You're hired!"

The Introduction

The *introduction* of an article or composition may vary a great deal—from one sentence to several paragraphs. However, there are three things an introduction needs to accomplish:

- catch the audience's attention (otherwise they may not read on)
- set the tone or show the writer's attitude toward the topic (humorous, serious, critical, and so forth)
- present the thesis (sometimes at the beginning, but often at the end, of the introduction)

Techniques for Writing Introductions

The following techniques represent some of the options writers have for getting the reader's attention.

1. **Begin with an interesting or dramatic quotation.** A writer used this technique in a biographical sketch of American photographer Eliot Porter.

> "Color," Eliot Porter used to say when asked to reveal the secret behind his photographs. "Color is the only thing I'm really concerned about. Color and patterns. That's all."
>
> Eliot Porter, quoted in *Life*

2. **Begin with an anecdote.** Starting with an anecdote, a brief story, can immediately involve your reader, especially if the anecdote is humorous or mysterious. This introduction relates an anecdote about a letter that a pioneer in the development of computers wrote to a poet. The article goes on to explain how scholars are now using computers to determine whether William Shakespeare actually wrote all the works attributed to him.

> In 1842 literature and science met with a thud. Alfred Tennyson had just published his poem "The Vision of Sin." Among the appreciative letters he received was one from Charles Babbage, the mathematician and inventor who is known today as the father of the computer. Babbage wrote to suggest a correction to Tennyson's "otherwise beautiful" poem—in particular to the lines "Every moment dies a man, / Every moment one is born."

COMPOSTIION

"It must be manifest," Babbage pointed out, "that, were this true, the population of the world would be at a standstill." Since the population was in fact growing slightly, Babbage continued, "I would suggest that in the next edition of your poem you have it read: 'Every moment dies a man, / Every moment $1^{1}/_{16}$ is born.'" Even this was not strictly correct, Babbage conceded, "but I believe $1^{1}/_{16}$ will be sufficiently accurate for poetry."

Edward Dolnick,
"The Ghost's Vocabulary"

3. **Open with an extended example.** Like an anecdote, a detailed **example,** or specific instance, draws readers into the composition by placing them in the scene. Notice how this writer uses an extended example to create immediacy in the introduction to an article about a new course for people who care for elderly patients.

There they were, a roomful of nurses feeding each other crackers that crumbled on their chest, juice that dribbled down their chin, and spoons laden with orange Jell-O that tasted like grandma's punishment for sassing.

The women giggled at the awkward experience of being a dependent adult. It's silly at first, then strange, frighteningly confining and, well, downright demeaning after decades of independence.

You try it tonight, too. Get in some pajamas with no back. Turn the heat down. Remove your glasses. And have someone feed you on their schedule, not yours. See if you pull back as unfamiliar fingers near your face. See if they place proper portions in your mouth when you want, in the order you want, without you feeling like an infant. Try to capture the moving straw with your mouth before it catches on your nose.

For atmosphere, line the room with linoleum and spritz blasts of bleach. Turn on two or three loud TV's nearby, each to a different program (but one must be "Jeopardy"). Have the children ring the doorbell and run around with paper megaphones paging people. Experience the need to request everything, even a bedpan. Sip tepid tea. See how good the institutional life is. See how long you're interested in eating. Oh, don't forget your pills in that dinky paper cup. And imagine your reply to the cheery query, "Well, how are we today?"

> Andrew H. Malcolm,
> "Nurses Get a Taste of an
> Elderly Patient's Life"

4. **Begin with an unusual or enlightening fact.** Some new or unusual fact will often entice your audience to read on and learn more about your topic. For example, an article about a most unusual bird begins this way:

The hoatzin is an odd bird. Not only does it eat leaves—far more than any other bird—but it digests them like a cow or a sheep, grinding the leaves up in its specialized, muscular crop. Up close the hoatzin smells bad, and it flies poorly.

> "Geographica,"
> *National Geographic*

5. **Begin with a question or a challenge.** When you start with a question or a challenge, you immediately involve your readers. Even if they know the answer, they'll want to know what you have to say about the subject.

Can an ape master anything like human language? Although primatologists have reported such abilities, the high priests of linguistics have scoffed. The animals, they said, displayed a gift for mimicry, reinforced by rewards of food and play, rather than true understanding.

> Frederic Golden,
> "Clever Kanzi"

COMPOSITION

6. **Take a stand on some issue.** When you are writing persuasion, you can begin with a statement that expresses a strong or even controversial opinion. This will make your readers want to read on to see how you will support your opinion. This introduction is from an article about the harmful effects of European explorations on Native Americans. It was written shortly before the five hundredth anniversary of Columbus's voyage to the New World. Notice that the writer does not hold back her strong criticism of Columbus Day.

> Columbus Day, never on Native America's list of favorite holidays, became somewhat tolerable as its significance diminished to little more than a good shopping day. But this next long year of Columbus hoopla will be tough to take amid the spending sprees and horn blowing to tout a five-century feeding frenzy that has left Native people and this red quarter of Mother Earth in a state of emergency. For Native people, this half millennium of land grabs and one-cent treaty sales has been no bargain.
>
> Suzan Shown Harjo,
> "I Won't Be Celebrating
> Columbus Day"

7. **Begin with an outrageous or comical statement.** An outrageous or comical statement will let your readers know to expect a humorous or satirical composition. Most readers are attracted to humor and will want to keep reading.

> The first rule of car-buying is one that I learned long ago from my father, namely: Never buy any car that my father would buy.
>
> Dave Barry,
> "Car-Buying: The Compleat
> Guide," *The Washington
> Post Magazine*

8. **Begin with a simple statement of your thesis.** Often a well-written thesis statement is all you need to catch your reader's attention.

> There's something about the desert that doesn't like man, something that mocks his nesting instinct and makes his constructions look feeble and temporary. Yet it's just that inhospitableness that endears the arid rockiness, the places pointy and poisonous, to men looking for its discipline.
>
> William Least Heat-Moon,
> *Blue Highways*

COMPOSITION

The Body

The *body* of a composition is the part that develops the main idea of your thesis statement. One or more paragraphs express the major points of the thesis and support or prove it with details. These paragraphs should connect with one another and relate directly to the thesis statement. You can achieve these goals if the body has *unity, coherence,* and *emphasis.*

Unity

In a composition, *unity* means that every paragraph and every detail supports a single main idea. Each paragraph should relate to the thesis statement of the composition. And each detail in a paragraph should relate to the main point of the paragraph.

Coherence

To achieve *coherence,* an ordered flow of ideas within and between sentences and paragraphs, you can use three techniques. The first two—*transitional expressions* and *direct references*—are demonstrated on pages 497–499. The third, *a short transition paragraph,* applies to compositions.

For example, the following paragraph is purely a transition; it does not develop an idea. Within an essay by Zora Neale Hurston about how it feels to be an African

COMPOSTIION

American, the paragraph is a bridge between paragraphs explaining the advantages of being a person of color and paragraphs describing feelings of difference.

> I do not always feel colored. Even now I often achieve the unconscious Zora of Eatonville before the Hegira. I feel most colored when I am thrown against a sharp white background.
>
> Zora Neale Hurston, "How It Feels to Be Colored Me"

Emphasis

To *emphasize* is to stress, and in most compositions you have some ideas that you want to stress because you think they are more important. You can emphasize ideas

- by giving them extra space: writing more about major points (or one point) than about others
- by repetition: repeating key words or phrases; using parallel sentence structures to introduce main ideas
- by order: placing the most important points first or last

 REFERENCE NOTE: For more information about parallel structure, see pages 311–313.

The Conclusion

Compositions need *conclusions* that allow readers to feel that the ideas are tied together and are complete. The following techniques are some options writers have for creating effective conclusions.

1. **Refer to the introduction.** The model composition on pages 510–512 neatly wraps up ideas in the conclusion by referring to the introduction.

> You'll be glad you did it right when you finally hear the words "You're hired!"

2. **Offer a solution or make a recommendation.** When you've taken a stand on an issue, you can stress your point by offering a solution or by recommending a course of action in the conclusion.

> People do get the government they deserve, and our low voter turnout shows that we deserve no better than what we have. We need a grassroots campaign nationwide to educate and convince people that voting is not only a right and a privilege but also a serious responsibility. Complaining to each other about the mess the country's in is no answer. Putting the responsibility where it belongs—on all of us—is.

3. **Restate your thesis.** Another good way to wind up your composition is to restate your thesis. Use different words to say the same thing to bring your composition to an end that echoes the beginning. For example, look at the conclusion of the model research paper on pages 535–542.

4. **Summarize your major points.** Another satisfying ending is a summary of the major points of a composition. For instance, the main points of an article on emeralds are briefly included in this conclusion.

> Gems satisfy primal needs—the lure of instant wealth, some sort of desire, perhaps, to join with the secrets of the earth. They fulfill our longing for beauty. They are our link to mysteries we can appreciate but cannot explain. Gems are as near the eternal as anything we can ever own.
>
> Fred Ward, "Emeralds," *National Geographic*

5. **Point out consequences or areas for future research.** The following conclusion points out possibilities for future research in Native American languages.

> Maya was long considered the only true writing system to have developed in the New World. Now we know that another written language, perhaps belonging to the Olmec people, developed more or less independently. Some 400 glyphs are

COMPOSTIION

discernible on the stela. Simply on the basis of their variety Grube speculates that the La Mojarra language may have fewer signs than Maya, and may thus represent an even more phonetic, less logographic system. But unless many more carved stones are found in Veracruz, the glyphs will probably never be read.

> David Roberts,
> "The Decipherment of
> Ancient Maya"

6. **End with an appropriate quotation.** A striking quotation like the one in the following paragraph sums up the main point and can make a strong ending.

Being a stranger in a strange land is never easy. "All the English-speaking kids should learn a foreign language. Then they'd know how hard it is for us sometimes," says 17-year-old Sufyan Kabba, a Maryland high-school junior, who left Sierra Leone last year. But here they are, part of the nation's future, young Yankees who in the end must rely on the special strength of children: adaptability.

> Connie Leslie, Daniel Glick,
> and Jeanne Gordon,
> "Classrooms of Babel"

The Title

The title of your composition should serve not only to grab a reader's attention but also to briefly summarize your main ideas. In general, try to create a title that's both catchy and pointed. However, don't contradict your composition's tone or purpose. For example, a cute or slangy title is inappropriate for a formal research paper.

You may want to give your composition a tentative title as you're writing, but plan to evaluate the title when you're finished. Your final draft may suggest a more fitting, engaging title.

FRAMEWORK FOR A COMPOSITION

Introduction ● ● ● ● ● ● ● ▶
Catches the reader's interest
Establishes the tone
Presents the thesis statement

Body ● ● ● ● ● ● ● ● ● ● ● ▶
States the major points
Supports the major points
with details

Conclusion ● ● ● ● ● ● ● ● ▶
Reinforces the main idea in
the thesis statement
Ties the ideas together
Leaves the reader with a
sense of completion

COMPOSITION

17 THE RESEARCH PAPER

Your factual writing usually involves some form of research or exploration: listening, observing, reading, or experimenting. Often you present this information in compositions that are *informal reports;* they don't contain footnotes or a detailed list of your information sources. A research paper, however, is a *formal report;* it presents the results of your research and tells readers exactly where you found your information. A research paper

- covers a topic in depth
- presents information from a number of sources
- documents the sources using a specific, consistent format

 *Prewriting*

Exploring Research Subjects

In exploring subjects for a research paper, begin with your own interests: You will be thinking and reading about your final topic and working hard on it for some time, so it makes sense to choose a subject that interests you. Most people think of the library when they think of research, but the library is only one place to start your exploration.

COMPOSITION

SOURCES FOR RESEARCH SUBJECTS

- **Family and friends:** Does someone you know have an interesting job or hobby—a legislator? a musician?

- **Heroes:** Whom do you admire and wish you knew more about—an inventor? a film director? a president? a writer?

- **Places near and far:** What trip was an especially memorable experience? What place have you always wanted to see—a city? a landmark? a landform? a country?

- **Current events:** When you watch the television news or open a newspaper, which events and subjects grab your attention—environmental disasters? civil rights?

- **Library and media:** What subjects arouse your curiosity as you browse through books, magazines, and the card catalog; turn the pages of the *Readers' Guide to Periodical Literature;* or check out television listings and videotapes—opera? modern warfare? American pioneers?

Selecting a Topic

Your first idea may be a very broad subject, such as "great scientists" or "the American Civil War." You then must narrow your focus to a specific aspect that intrigues you, one that can be covered in a composition.

To limit a topic, you can analyze it on your own, or you can look for subtopics in the card catalog, the *Readers' Guide,* encyclopedias, and specialized dictionaries. Whatever your process, you must constantly try to *be more specific.*

Subject:	I'm interested in African American literature
<u>Be more specific:</u>	Zora Neale Hurston is great.
<u>Be more specific:</u>	She was an anthropologist <u>and</u> a novelist.
<u>Be more specific:</u>	I could research the links between her work as an anthropologist and her fiction.
Limited topic:	How Hurston's study of anthropology and her fiction are related

Finally, your choice of topic must suitable for a research paper. Keep the following requirements in mind.

CHECKLIST FOR A SUITABLE TOPIC

1. **Available sources of information.** Be sure you can find five or six good sources. You may not be able to find enough sources for very new or technical topics.

2. **Objectivity and facts.** Your interest leads to a topic, but your experience isn't the basis of a formal report. You could write about how sonar detection of fish works, but not about your fishing trips using the equipment.

3. **Audience interest.** Almost any topic can be interesting, but think ahead. If your topic isn't universally appealing ("the Smoot-Hawley Tariff Act of 1930") or is so appealing that it's widely known ("the disappearance of dinosaurs"), what unusual approach can you take? What could intrigue your readers?

Beginning Your Research

Considering Purpose, Audience, and Tone

Purpose. For a formal paper, it is crucial that you understand and remember your goals. Your *purpose* is to inform readers through research, and that involves an original *synthesis* (combination) of information. You will not just compile a list of facts and expert opinions; you need to make sense of what you discover as well.

Audience. Your audience is usually your classmates and teacher, but you might plan your report for another specific audience, such as a local organization or publication. See page 476 for help in tailoring approach and content to your audience.

Tone. The *tone* of your report will be formal, which means using

■ *third-person point of view.* Do not use the word *I.*

- *relatively formal language.* Formal language usually does not include slang, colloquial expressions, or contractions.

Asking Research Questions

A first step toward your research is asking general questions about your topic. (You may raise other issues as your research continues.) Two possible techniques for generating questions are *brainstorming* and the *5W-How?* questions (see pages 470–471 and 472). Below are some examples of general questions about the relationship between Zora Neale Hurston's anthropological research and her fiction.

Did Zora Neale Hurston write any fiction before becoming an anthropologist? If so, did it differ from her later fiction?

What did Hurston focus on as an anthropologist?

Do elements of her studies appear in her fiction, and, if so, how? folk tales? characters?

Did Hurston herself ever suggest links between her academic studies and her fiction?

Did Hurston's childhood experiences influence her writing?

Getting an Overview and Finding Sources

You can use general reference works like encyclopedias and biographical dictionaries to get an overview of your topic. In the process, you may get ideas for other research questions, and you may find helpful references to other information sources.

If your topic is narrowly focused ("weather forecasting by supercomputer"), you may not find an encyclopedia entry for it, but you can look for related or larger topics ("meteorology," "supercomputers").

If you already have a solid background in your topic, you can eliminate general reference works and go directly to the types of sources listed in the following chart.

COMPOSITION

SOURCES OF INFORMATION	
LIBRARY	
RESOURCES	**INFORMATION**
Card catalog or on-line catalog	Books, recordings, audiotapes, and videotapes (Print and audiovisual listings are in separate catalogs in some libraries.)
Readers' Guide to Periodical Literature or an on-line index	Magazine and journal articles, indexed by subject and author (*InfoTrac®* is one well-known computerized index.)
Indexes to news-papers, essays, and articles	Articles from major newspapers, such as *The New York Times;* possibly local newspapers (Newspapers are frequently on microfilm or microfiche.)
Specialized reference books	Encyclopedias of special subjects, such as the *Encyclopedia of Anthropology;* almanacs; atlases; biographical refer-ences like *Current Biography*
Vertical file	Pamphlets and clippings, often on subjects of local interest, arranged by subject
Microfilm or microfiche	Indexes to major newspapers, back issues of some newspapers and magazines
COMMUNITY	
RESOURCES	**INFORMATION**
Colleges, historical societies, museums	Libraries, exhibits, experts, special collections, records, conferences
Local, state, and federal offices	Statistics, politicians' voting records, recent or pending legislation, suveys, reports, pamphlets, experts
Newspaper offices	Clippings, files on local events and history (Call to see if research is permitted.)

 REFERENCE NOTE: For more help on using the library, see pages 558–562. For more information on using reference materials, see pages 563–570.

Calvin & Hobbes copyright 1989 Watterson.
Reprinted with permission of Universal Press
Syndicate. All rights reserved.

Making Source Cards. When you find possible sources, it's important to keep accurate and complete information on them. Your *Works Cited list*—the list of sources at the end of your report—must contain specific information because some of your readers may want to consult your sources.

The best method of collecting accurate information is to put each source on a 3" x 5" card. Sample *source cards* (sometimes called *bibliography cards*) are shown on page 528. In the long run you'll save time by doing your source cards in final format, prepared in the exact style required for the Works Cited list. (Many more examples of proper style are shown in *Sample Entries for the List of Works Cited,* pages 549–552.)

GUIDELINES FOR SOURCE CARDS

1. **Assign each source a number.** Later, when you're taking notes, it will save time to write a number instead of the author and title.

2. **Record full publishing information.** Record everything you might need: subtitles, translators, and volume and edition numbers. Too much information is always better than too little. Do the job right and avoid backtracking. (For examples of the types of information you will need, see the sample Works Cited entries on pages 549–552.)

3. **Note the call number or location.** This information will help you relocate the source quickly.

COMPOSITION

Sample Source Cards

Book

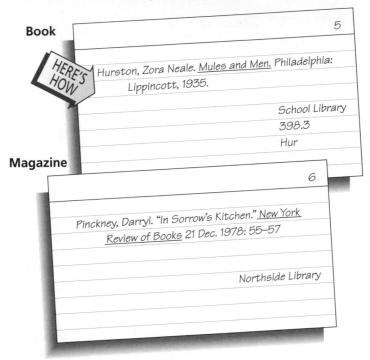

```
                                                              5

   HERE'S    Hurston, Zora Neale. Mules and Men. Philadelphia:
   HOW            Lippincott, 1935.

                                              School Library
                                              398.3
                                              Hur
```

Magazine

```
                                                          6

   Pinckney, Darryl. "In Sorrow's Kitchen." New York
        Review of Books 21 Dec. 1978: 55–57

                                          Northside Library
```

STYLE NOTE The style for documenting sources shown in this chapter is the one recommended by the Modern Language Association of America (MLA), an organization of language scholars. Your teacher may ask you to use a different style. Whichever style you use, it is important to include all the information required.

Evaluating Sources. Before using a source, you need to evaluate its usefulness to you. One good way to evaluate a source is to use the "4R" test.

1. *Relevant.* Does the source's information relate directly to your limited topic? For a book, check the table of con-

tents and index. Skim magazine articles. Some nonprint sources include summaries, and you may also find excerpted reviews and summaries in *Book Review Digest.*

2. *Reliable.* Can you trust it? A respected scholar or a respected magazine, such as *The Atlantic Monthly* or *Scientific American,* is usually reliable for accuracy. Look for authors who are quoted frequently or appear in most bibliographies on your topic.

3. *Recent.* Be sure you aren't using outdated information, especially for rapidly changing topics. For any topic, look for the most recent work about it. If the author is thorough, you'll learn which older sources of information are still being consulted.

4. *Representative.* If you are working on a controversial topic, you must represent different points of view. Your task as a researcher is to study, balance, and interpret the views on all sides.

Using Primary and Secondary Sources. A *primary source* is firsthand, original information: a letter, an autobiography, an interview with a person who participated in the experience being researched, a work of literature, historical documents. A *secondary source* is information derived from, or about, primary sources or other secondary sources: an encyclopedia, a documentary film, a biography, history books, or an interview with a historian.

For example, if you are writing about post-Revolutionary America, the Articles of Confederation and Thomas Jefferson's letters are primary sources. A biography of Jefferson is a secondary source (as your completed paper will be).

Although secondary sources are essential to your paper and often provide excerpts from primary sources, don't use them exclusively when primary sources are available. At the same time, don't assume that all primary sources are exempt from evaluation. Memory may be faulty or selective in an autobiography, and emotions may override facts in a letter. Read and research as widely as possible, so that you have a good basis for deciding what's accurate and what's slanted or biased.

COMPUTER NOTE

If you are writing with a computer, you can start putting your source cards into a working reference list at any time. As your research continues, you can delete sources that aren't helpful, add others, and easily keep the list in alphabetical order. (See page 549, item 3, for alphabetizing guidelines.) When you've finished writing the paper, you can print the list and use it as the first draft of your final Works Cited list.

Recording and Organizing Information

Taking Notes

Read, or listen to, the material (or a complete section of it) before you begin taking notes. Then go back over the information, using 4" x 6" cards to record your notes. Later, when you're organizing your report, cards make it easy to arrange and rearrange information. Here are more specific tips about note cards. A sample note card follows.

GUIDELINES FOR NOTE CARDS

1. **Use a separate card or a half-sheet of paper for each source and item of information.** Organizing note cards is difficult if they combine different sources or information.

2. **Record the source number in the upper right corner.** Write the number you have previously assigned each source. This step is important; it's a shorthand system to show exactly where you got the information.

3. **Write a label, or heading, in the upper left corner.** By identifying the main idea of your note, you will not later have to reread each card to discover its basic content.

4. **Write the page number(s) at the end of your note.** Record the page numbers from which each piece of information comes. In your paper, page references will be required for the documentation.

Direct Quotations. Resist the urge to quote too much. Quote an author directly only when you want to be sure of technical accuracy or when the author's words are especially interesting or well phrased. Copy the statement exactly (including punctuation, capitalization, and spelling) and enclose it in quotation marks.

Summaries and Paraphrases. In most of your notes, you will record the author's ideas and facts *in your own words.* A **summary** is highly condensed—typically one fourth to one third the length of the original. A **paraphrase** is a restatement in your own words that is more detailed.

Whether you summarize or paraphrase, you must use your own words and sentence structure. Try setting the passage aside and writing ideas from memory. Also, use lists and phrases—not complete sentences.

SAMPLE NOTE CARD

early use of folk tales	5

Arna Bontemps (a black writer and Hurston's friend) says many of folk tales in <u>Mules and Men</u> were part of Hurston's storytelling before anthropology at Barnard. Some early short stories confirm his memory of hearing the tales when she first came to NY.

pp. 166–67

NOTE   Remember that you must give credit when you use another writer's *words or ideas* in your paper. Not to do so is *plagiarism,* an extremely serious offense. Even a summary or paraphrase—if it is someone else's original idea—must be credited. When in doubt about plagiarism, give credit.

Writing a Thesis Statement

Once you have gathered your information, you need to reread your notes to have a sense of it as a whole. Now you can clarify your report's main ideas and write a preliminary, or working, thesis statement.

The **_thesis statement_** is a sentence or two stating both your topic and what you will say about it. While you may change or reword your thesis statement as your writing progresses, such a summary helps keep you on track as you work.

SAMPLE THESIS STATEMENTS

Zora Neale Hurston's work in anthropology affected her fiction—its events, characters, and language.

In the 1950s, Senator Margaret Chase Smith of Maine had the qualifications to be president, but a woman was considered unelectable at the time.

The great Apache chief Cochise was quite different in real life from the Cochise shown in the movies.

☞ REFERENCE NOTE: See page 506 for more help with writing thesis statements.

Big Nate reprinted by permission of UFS, Inc.

Developing an Outline

To create your writing plan, start by sorting your note cards into stacks according to their labels. These stacks may immediately suggest the main sections of your report, as well as the ideas you want to emphasize. Then you can decide on the best sequence for your ideas and supporting details.

NOTE Look carefully at stacks with only a few note cards. A small stack may indicate that an idea should be either omitted or more fully developed.

COMPOSITION

Your working outline can be rough in form, as long as it is sufficiently detailed to give shape and direction to your draft. But for your completed paper, your teacher may request a final, *formal outline* like the one below. Such an outline serves as a table of contents and is prepared *after* you've finished the report.

FOLKLORE INTO FICTION:
THE WRITINGS OF ZORA NEALE HURSTON

I. Childhood in Eatonville
   A. Incorporated black town
   B. Early exposure to folklore
II. College years
   A. Morgan College and Howard University
   B. Early stories using folk tales and Eatonville
   C. Study of anthropology
      1. Ruth Benedict at Barnard College
      2. Franz Boas at Columbia University
         a. Decision to become social scientist
         b. Grant to collect southern folklore
III. Connections between anthropology and fiction
   A. Plots and characters
   B. Dialect and idiom
   C. Portrayal of black life

Writing a First Draft

Structuring the Report

The research report is longer than most papers you write, with several special elements. Use the chart below to get an overview of a report's main parts.

COMPOSITION

ELEMENTS OF A RESEARCH REPORT	
Formal outline (optional)	Your teacher may ask you to include a final outline of the content of your report.
Title	Your title, often on a separate title page, should be both attention-catching and informative. Ask your teacher about format.
Introduction	Your introduction should draw readers into your report with interesting details, an anecdote, or a striking quotation.
Thesis statement	The statement of your thesis should appear early in your report, usually in or at the end of the introduction. The thesis statement might be more than one sentence.
Body	Paragraphs in the body of your report should develop and support the main ideas presented in your thesis statement.
Conclusion	The conclusion should briefly restate your thesis in different words, summarize your main points, or both. The conclusion should bring your paper to a convincing end.
Citations	Throughout the paper, you should include brief references in parentheses (or footnotes if your teacher recommends them) to credit sources for specific information.
Works Cited list	In a list at the end of the report, you should include all the sources you have cited. The list should appear on a separate sheet of paper and should provide complete publication information for each source.

The following model shows how one writer used research findings to develop an original paper. Notice how the author incorporates facts, quotations, and summaries of ideas. You will see source information in parentheses throughout the paper; these *citations* are fully explained on pages 544–547.

A MODEL RESEARCH PAPER

COMPOSITION

Folklore into Fiction:
The Writings of Zora Neale Hurston

INTRODUCTION
Interesting
anecdote/
Summary of
article, author
named

In her essay "In Search of Zora
Neale Hurston," Alice Walker, the author
of The Color Purple, describes a senti-
mental visit that she made to the all-
black city of Eatonville, Florida. The goal
of her 1973 journey was to find the
grave of Zora Neale Hurston, a writer
Walker greatly admired. Hurston, a
major figure of the Harlem Renaissance,
died in poverty in 1960. Walker found
no grave or marker in Eatonville,
Hurston's hometown. Instead, she
learned that her literary idol had been
buried in an unmarked grave in a segre-
gated cemetery in Fort Pierce, Florida.
She commissioned a headstone, which
now stands at the site. The stone reads
as follows:

ZORA NEALE HURSTON
"A GENIUS OF THE SOUTH"
NOVELIST   FOLKLORIST
ANTHROPOLOGIST
1901   1960

Background
information

It is significant that Alice Walker,
poet, novelist, and winner of the Pulitzer
Prize for fiction, would add "folklorist"
and "anthropologist" to her description
of the neglected author. For Zora Neale
Hurston was more than a gifted novelist. She was also a perceptive student of
her own culture, an author of two no-
table books of folklore, and a member of

the American Folklore Society, the American Ethnological Society, and the American Anthropological Society

Thesis statement (Hurston, <u>Dust Tracks</u> 171). Hurston's work as an anthropologist is, in fact, directly related to her creative writing. The connection is clear in many elements of her fiction.

BODY
Eatonville childhood Hurston's life story begins in Eatonville, Florida, not far from Orlando. Eatonville was originally incorporated as an all-black town—a unique situation that had an impact throughout

Important details Hurston's life. Her hometown was also her earliest training ground (although she could hardly have realized it at the time) in black southern folklore, the place where she heard the local story-

Direct quotation tellers tell their big "lies" (Hurston, <u>Dust Tracks</u> 197).

Young Zora, whose father was a Baptist preacher, received little formal education and worked at menial jobs. However, she read whenever and whatever she could, and her great goal was to become well educated.

College years Paying her own way, Hurston was able to study at Morgan College and Howard University. By that time she was already a writer. She used many of the folk tales she had heard on neighbors' front porches and recreated her home-

Specific examples town in her fiction. At Howard she wrote "John Redding Goes to Sea," which had "black folk beliefs" about witches' curses and screech owls

Authors and pages cited (Ikonné 185–86). Another early short story, "Spunk," was set in an "unnamed village that is obviously Eatonville" (Hemenway 41, 77–78).

COMPOSITION

Then came a turning point in her life. In 1925 she was admitted to prestigious Barnard College in New York City—its first black student (Howard, "Being Herself" 101–02). At Barnard,

Study of anthropology

Hurston studied anthropology under Ruth Benedict. Just before she graduated, Franz Boas of Columbia University, another eminent anthropologist, read one of her term papers. Boas invited Hurston to study with him and gave her another way to look at the Eatonville tales she loved to tell. According to Lillie Howard, "She learned to view the good old lies and racy, sidesplitting anecdotes . . . as invaluable folklore, creative material that continued the African oral tradition . . ." ("Hurston" 135). Hurston decided then to become a serious social scientist. In 1927 Boas recommended her for the first of several grants she was to receive, and she headed south to gather folklore.

Author named in text, more than one title in Works Cited

Clearly, Hurston's attraction to her culture's stories and to writing fiction were always intertwined. Anthropology simply made her natural attention to black folklore and culture more systematic and intensive; as she said, "research is formalized curiosity" (qtd. in Chamberlain).

Writer's conclusion/transitional statement

Direct quotation within another source

Connections between anthropology and fiction

After she began doing fieldwork, she alternated between anthropological and creative writing. Her study of Eatonville folk tales and New Orleans hoodoo (voodoo) in 1927 and 1928 resulted in the book of folk tales <u>Mules and Men</u>, and she wrote her first novel, <u>Jonah's Gourd Vine</u>, soon after. Many critics have noted that all of Hurston's novels

COMPOSITION

Plots and characters

Examples

showed the effects of her study of anthropology, and one of the most obvious connections between the two appears in her fiction's plots and characters.

Just one example of how Hurston's research worked into the plot of <u>Jonah's Gourd Vine</u> is the "bitter bone" that An' Dangie uses in a ritual to make Hattie invisible (200). In <u>Mules and Men</u>, Hurston reported how she underwent a whole ceremony to get the "Black Cat Bone," or bitter bone, of invisibility (272).

In later books, too, these connections occur. A field trip to Haiti and Jamaica in 1936 produced <u>Tell My Horse</u>, another study of voodoo. A year after its appearance she published the novel <u>Moses, Man of the Mountain</u>, which has been described as a blend of "fiction, folklore, religion, and comedy" (Howard, "Hurston" 140). In it, Moses is a "hoodoo man," an idea that also appears in <u>Jonah's Gourd Vine</u> (231).

Dialect and black idiom

Dialect and black idiom are also important parts of both Hurston's scientific work and her creative writing. She worked into her fiction the words she heard and researched in the field. According to her biographer, Robert Hemenway, the long sermon that is the climax of <u>Jonah's Gourd Vine</u> "was taken almost verbatim from Hurston's field notes" (197). The novel, in fact, contains so many folk sayings that Robert Bone has claimed "they are too nonfunctional, too anthropological" (127).

Most critics have agreed with Darryl Pinckney that Hurston's "ear for the

COMPOSITION

vernacular of folk speech is impeccable" (56). Even a critic in 1937 who found Hurston's dialect "less convincing" than another writer's suggested that Hurston's dialect might be more realistic (Thompson). Her excellent ear and her "skill at transcribing" (Young 220) made the language in her first novel something new and therefore somewhat hard to read:

Long quotation, indented; quotation marks for dialogue

> "Iss uh shame, Sister. Ah'd cut down dat Jonah's gourd vine in uh minute, if Ah had all de say-so. You know Ah would, but de majority of em don't keer whut he do, some uh dese people stands in wid it. De man mus' is got roots uh got piece uh dey tails buried by his door-step. . . ." (Jonah's 230)

However, some black writers of Hurston's time disapproved of her "playing the minstrel" in her fiction's use of southern black dialect—and in other ways as well. Zora Neale Hurston was in fact a controversial figure within the Harlem Renaissance. She was attacked for her novels' picture of black life, and this portrayal is another connection between her anthropology and her fiction (Howard, "Being Herself" 156).

Portrayal of black life

Background: Harlem Renaissance

Hurston came to New York when the Harlem Renaissance was in full bloom. This literary movement of the 1920s included such noted writers as Langston Hughes, Countee Cullen, Jean Toomer, and Arna Bontemps. They, too, were celebrating blackness and bringing it to the public, but they saw their mission as "a guiding elite" for other blacks who were not as liberated (Pinckney 55). They didn't want to support a stereotyped image in art. Sterling Brown even attacked Hurston's nonfiction. He said that "<u>Mules and Men</u> should be more bitter" (qtd. in Howard, "Hurston" 139).

Paraphrase

Hurston, on the other hand, believed she was serving an unmet need. African American folklore had always fascinated the American public; but it had been presented mostly by white writers (such as Joel Chandler Harris), and to her these white representations seemed either patronizing or inadequate (Wilson 109). She wanted to put African American folklore in its true social context.

Moreover, Hurston felt her picture of blacks in <u>Jonah's Gourd Vine</u> and in <u>Their Eyes Were Watching God</u>, generally regarded as her finest novel, was thoroughly realistic. She felt that the Harlem Renaissance writers were unfairly criticizing her fiction because it didn't have a political message. She said they believed ". . . Negroes were supposed to write about the Race Problem," while her intent in <u>Jonah's Gourd Vine</u> was "to tell . . . a story about a man" (<u>Dust Tracks</u> 214).

Several sources used as support

Hurston did not intend to be a reformer if it meant falsifying what she saw as a scientist and wanted to achieve as an artist. Through her fieldwork she knew intimately the everyday, "normal life of Negroes in the South," and that's what she focused on in much of her fic-

COMPOSITION

tion (Thompson). Also, her study of many cultures showed her that folk tales functioned, in part, the same way all over the world, as "communal tradition in which distinctive ways of behaving and coping with life were orally transmitted" (Pinckney 56). Hurston thought the tales were sophisticated and important and should be shown as they were. Margaret Wilson sums up Hurston's anthropological and fictional beliefs this way: "She saw people as people" (110).

So even though critics like Richard Wright, Alain Locke, and Sterling Brown objected to the "minstrel image" of blacks in a novel such as <u>Their Eyes Were Watching God</u>, other critics saw both a realistic, vibrant main character (Janie) and Hurston's "fullest description of the mores [customs and values] in Eatonville" (Hemenway 241–42; Pinckney 56). Perhaps Hurston would have been more "race conscious" if she had not grown up in and studied Eatonville, a wholly self-governing black town; but that does not negate the reality of what she observed and transformed into fiction (Wilson 109; Pinckney 56).

For better or worse, Hurston's fictional world—its plots, characters, language, and picture of life—grew out of the folklore she had heard as a child and then studied as a professional. Like the fine anthropologist she was, Zora Neale Hurston the writer intended to get that world down on paper, and to get it down right.

Writer's addition in brackets

Two sources cited at once

CONCLUSION Restatement of thesis

Clincher statement

Works Cited

Bone, Robert. <u>The Negro Novel in America</u>. New Haven: Yale UP, 1958.

Chamberlain, John. "Books of the Times." <u>New York Times</u> 7 Nov. 1942: 13.

Hemenway, Robert E. <u>Zora Neale Hurston: A Literary Biography</u>. Urbana: U of Illinois P, 1977.

Howard, Lillie P. "Zora Neale Hurston." <u>Dictionary of Literary Biography</u>. 1987 ed.

---. "Zora Neale Hurston: Just Being Herself." <u>Essence</u> Nov. 1980: 100+.

Hurston, Zora Neale. <u>Dust Tracks on a Road: An Autobiography</u>. Philadelphia: Lippincott, 1942.

---. <u>Jonah's Gourd Vine</u>. Philadelphia: Lippincott, 1934, 1971.

---. <u>Moses, Man of the Mountain</u>. Philadelphia: Lippincott, 1939.

---. <u>Mules and Men</u>. Philadelphia: Lippincott, 1935.

---. <u>Tell My Horse: Voodoo and Life in Haiti and Jamaica</u>. Philadelphia: Lippincott, 1938.

Ikonné, Chidi. <u>From Du Bois to Van Vechten: The Early New Negro Literature, 1903–1926</u>. Westport: Greenwood, 1981.

Pinckney, Darryl. "In Sorrow's Kitchen." <u>New York Review of Books</u> 21 Dec. 1978: 55–57.

Thompson, Ralph. "Books of the Times." <u>New York Times</u> 6 Oct. 1937: 23.

Walker, Alice. "In Search of Zora Neale Hurston." <u>Ms</u>. Mar. 1975: 74+.

Wilson, Margaret F. "Zora Neale Hurston: Author and Folklorist." <u>Negro History Bulletin</u> Oct.-Nov.-Dec. 1982: 109–10.

Young, James O. <u>Black Writers of the Thirties</u>. Baton Rouge: Louisiana State UP, 1973.

COMPOSITION

Using Quotations

Even though much of what you put in your report will be summarized or paraphrased, you'll find that good quotations, especially short ones, can add interest and authority to your writing. You can work quotations smoothly into your paper in several ways.

GUIDELINES FOR USING QUOTATIONS

1. Quote a whole sentence, introducing it in your own words.

EXAMPLE   Margaret Wilson sums up Hurston's belief this way: "She saw people as people" (110).

2. Quote part of a sentence within a sentence of your own.

EXAMPLE   The long sermon "was taken almost verbatim from Hurston's field notes" (Hemenway 197).

3. Quote just one word or a few words within a sentence of your own.

EXAMPLE   Eatonville was where she heard the local storytellers tell their "lies" (Hurston, <u>Dust Tracks</u> 197).

4. Use ellipses (three spaced periods) to indicate omissions from quotations. You may want to alter a quotation to shorten it or make it fit grammatically into your text. Use ellipses to indicate words deleted within a quotation or any deletion that leaves a quotation that appears to be a complete sentence but is only part of the original sentence.

EXAMPLE   According to Lillie Howard, "She learned to view the good old lies . . . as invaluable folklore . . ." ("Hurston" 136).

5. Set off longer quotations as "blocks." If a quotation will be more than four typed lines, start a new line, indent the entire quotation ten spaces from the left, and do not use quotation marks. Double-space a long quotation just like the rest of your report. For an example, see the blocked quotation on page 000. [Note: The example uses quotation marks because it is *dialogue* in the original source.]

COMPOSITION

COMPOSITION

Documenting Sources

Deciding which information you must *document,* or give credit for, in a research paper sometimes requires thought. That thought process can start with noticing what is or is not documented when you read reports of research. The following guidelines will also help you stay clear of documentation pitfalls.

WHAT TO DOCUMENT

1. In general, don't document information that appears in several sources or facts that appear in standard reference books. For example, a statement like "*Their Eyes Were Watching God* is generally considered Hurston's finest novel" needs no documentation because it clearly relies on several sources. The main facts of her life that are available in encyclopedias and other standard references also do not need to be credited.

2. Document the source of each direct quotation (unless it's very widely known, such as Patrick Henry's "Give me liberty or give me death!").

3. Document any original theory or opinion other than your own. Since ideas belong to their authors, you must not present the ideas of other people as your own.

4. Document the source of data or other information from surveys, scientific experiments, and research studies.

5. Document unusual, little known, or questionable facts and statistics.

Parenthetical Citations

A *parenthetical citation* gives source information in parentheses in the body of a research paper. There are two main issues concerning the handling of these citations: (1) What are the content and correct form of the citation? (2) Exactly where does the citation go?

The content and form of parenthetical citations are fairly easy once you understand one basic principle: *The citation should provide just enough information to lead the reader to the full source listing on the Works Cited page.*

COMPOSITION

Since the Works Cited list is alphabetized by authors' last names, an author's last name and the page numbers are usually enough for a parenthetical citation. There are some exceptions of course; information about some of them is given below.

- A nonprint source such as an interview or audiotape will not have a page number.
- A print source of fewer than two pages (such as a one-page letter or article) will not require a page number.
- If you name the author in your sentence, you need give only the page number (for print sources of more than one page) in parentheses:

> According to her biographer, Robert Hemenway, the long sermon that is the climax of <u>Jonah's Gourd Vine</u> "was taken almost verbatim from Hurston's field notes" (197).

- If the author has more than one work in the Works Cited list, you will also have to give a short form of the title so readers will know which work you are citing:

> (Hurston, <u>Dust Tracks</u> 171).

Sources vary, of course, and you'll sometimes have to refer to published style guidelines for correct form. The chart that follows shows the form for nine kinds of citations.

BASIC CONTENT AND FORM FOR PARENTHETICAL CITATIONS

These examples assume that the author or work has not already been named in a sentence introducing the source's information.

Works by One Author

Author's last name and a page reference	(Hemenway 197)

Separate Passages in a Single Work

Author's last name and multiple page references	(Hemenway 41, 77–78)

More Than One Work by the Same Author

Author's last name and the full title or a shortened version	(Hurston, <u>Dust Tracks</u> 197)

(continued)

BASIC CONTENT AND FORM FOR PARENTHETICAL CITATIONS *(continued)*

Works by More Than One Author

All authors' last names or first author's last name and et al. ("and others") if over three	(Brooks and Warren 24) (Bell, Parker, and Guy-Sheftall 51) (Anderson et al. 313)

Multivolume Works

Author's last name plus volume and page	(Cattell 2: 214–15)

Works with a Title Only

Full title (if short) or a shortened version	("Old Eatonville" 2) (World Almanac 809)

Classic Literary Works Published in Many Editions

Prose: give page numbers and then supply other identifying information, such as chapter numbers, after a semicolon.	(Swift, Gulliver's Travels 62; pt. 2, ch. 4)
Poems and plays: omit page numbers and give divisions, such as book, act, scene, and lines, separated by periods	(Shakespeare, Hamlet 3.4.107–08) [Note the use of Arabic numbers, not Roman numerals.]

Indirect Sources

Abbreviation *qtd. in* [quoted in] before the source	(qtd. in Howard 161)

More than One Work in the Same Citation

Citations separated with semicolons	(Bone 127; Pinckney 56)

Biblical References

Name of book (abbreviated), chapter, and verse	(Gen. 1.2) [Note that the names of books of the Bible are neither underlined nor enclosed in quotation marks.]

To determine where to place a citation, you can follow the general rules given below. You'll also find it helpful to look at the model paper to see how citations appear there.

PLACEMENT OF CITATIONS

1. Place the citation as close as possible to the material it documents, preferably at the end of a sentence.

2. Place the citation *before* the punctuation mark of the sentence, clause, or phrase you are documenting.

   EXAMPLE   Her best work appeared after she had abandoned the narrow academic approach (Hemenway 215).

3. For a quotation that ends a sentence, put the citation after the quotation mark but before the end punctuation mark.

   EXAMPLE   Most critics have agreed with Darryl Pinckney that Hurston's "ear for the vernacular of folk speech is impeccable" (56).

4. For an indented quotation, put the citation *two spaces after* the final punctuation mark. (See the indented quotation on page 539 for an example of this style.)

STYLE NOTE

Your teacher may want you to use a documentation style different from the parenthetical citation system just discussed. The other common system uses numbered footnotes or endnotes. Footnotes and endnotes are identical except that a *footnote* is placed at the bottom of the page where you use the source information, while *endnotes* are listed all together at the end of the report.

For either type, you place the note number in the body of your report where a parenthetical citation would otherwise occur. The first note for a source gives full information; following notes are shortened. You will need guidelines to prepare notes. One example follows.

EXAMPLE

Note number in body of report

The long sermon "was taken almost verbatim from Hurston's field notes."[3]

Note (full form)

[3]Robert E. Hemenway, <u>Zora Neale Hurston: A Literary Biography</u> (Urbana: U of Illinois P, 1977) 197.

COMPOSITION

Peanuts reprinted by permission of UFS, Inc.

COMPUTER NOTE

When writing your first draft, do not stop your forward progress by striving for perfectly formatted citations. You can revise later. The computer makes editing, adding, and deleting citations much less time consuming, since you do not have to retype the complete paper to print out a revised version.

Some word processing programs also include a footnote/endnote feature that automatically numbers notes and places them properly on the page or at the paper's end. Specialized software even automatically puts citation information into styles such as MLA.

List of Works Cited

The *Works Cited* list contains all the sources, print and nonprint, that you credit in your report. (The term *Works Cited* is a broader title than *Bibliography*, which refers to print sources only.) You may have used other sources, such as general reference works, but if you didn't need to credit them, you don't include them in a Works Cited list. (However, some teachers want a list of Works Consulted—all the sources you examined, whether cited or not—instead of, or in addition to, the Works Cited list. Ask to be sure.)

GUIDELINES FOR PREPARING THE LIST OF WORKS CITED

1. Center the words *Works Cited* on a new sheet of paper.

2. Begin each entry on a separate line. Position the first line of the entry even with the left margin and indent the second and all other lines five spaces. Double-space all entries.

3. Alphabetize the sources by the author's last name. If there is no author, alphabetize by title, ignoring *A, An,* and *The* and using the first letter of the next word.

4. If you use two or more sources by the same author, include the author's name only in the first entry. For all other entries, use three hyphens followed by a period (---.) in place of the author's name. Order the entries alphabetically by title.

You can use the following sample entries, which reflect MLA style, are a reference for preparing your Works Cited list. Notice that you supply page numbers only for articles in periodicals or for other works that are part of a whole work, such as one essay in a collection of essays.

SAMPLE ENTRIES FOR THE LIST OF WORKS CITED

Standard Reference Works

When the author of an entry is given in a standard reference work, that person's name is written first. Otherwise, the title of the book or article appears first. Page and volume numbers aren't needed if the work alphabetizes entries. For common reference works, only the edition year is needed.

ENCYCLOPEDIA ARTICLE
Hurston, Zora Neale. <u>Encyclopedia Americana</u>. 1991 ed.

ARTICLE IN A BIOGRAPHICAL REFERENCE BOOK
Howard, Lillie P. "Zora Neale Hurston."<u>Dictionary of
    Literary Biography</u>. 1987 ed.

(continued)

COMPOSITION

SAMPLE ENTRIES FOR THE LIST OF WORKS CITED *(continued)*

Books

ONE AUTHOR
Huggins, Nathan Irvin. <u>Harlem Renaissance</u>. New York: Oxford UP, 1971.

TWO AUTHORS
Logan, Rayford W., and Irving S. Cohen. <u>The American Negro: Old World Background and New World Experience</u>. Boston: Houghton, 1970.

THREE AUTHORS
Bell, Roseann, Bettye Parker, and Beverly Guy-Sheftall. <u>Sturdy Black Bridges: Visions of Black Women in Literature</u>. Garden City: Anchor, 1979.

FOUR OR MORE AUTHORS
Anderson, Robert, et al. <u>Elements of Literature: Fifth Course</u>. Austin: Holt, 1989.

NO AUTHOR SHOWN
<u>American Statistics Index</u>. Washington: Congressional Information Service, 1992.

EDITOR OF A COLLECTION OF WRITINGS
Locke, Alain, ed. <u>The New Negro: An Interpretation</u>. New York: Boni, 1925.

TWO OR THREE EDITORS
Meier, August, and Elliott Rudwick, eds. <u>The Making of Black America: Essays in Negro Life and History</u>. New York: Atheneum, 1969.

TRANSLATION
Niane, D. T. <u>Sundiata: An Epic of Old Mali</u>. Trans. G. D. Pickett. London: Longman, 1965.

Selections within Books

FROM A BOOK OF WORKS BY ONE AUTHOR
Hughes, Langston. "April Rain Song." <u>The Dream Keeper and Other Poems</u>. New York: Knopf, 1932. 8.

FROM A BOOK OF WORKS BY SEVERAL AUTHORS
Hemenway, Robert. "Zora Neale Hurston and the Eatonville Anthropology." <u>The Harlem Renaissance Remembered: Essays Edited with a Memoir</u>. Ed. Arna Bontemps. New York: Dodd, 1972. 190–214.

(continued)

SAMPLE ENTRIES FOR THE LIST OF WORKS CITED *(continued)*

FROM A COLLECTION OF LONGER WORKS (NOVELS, PLAYS)
Edmonds, Randolph. <u>Bad Man</u>. <u>The Negro Caravan</u>. Ed.
   Sterling A. Brown, Arthur P. Davis, and Ulysses Lee.
   New York: Arno, 1969. 507–34. [<u>Bad Man</u> is a play.
   <u>The Negro Caravan</u> is a collection.]

Articles from Magazines, Newspapers, and Journals

FROM A WEEKLY MAGAZINE
Hughes, Langston. "The Negro Artist and the Racial
   Mountain." <u>Nation</u> 23 June 1926: 692–94.

FROM A MONTHLY OR QUARTERLY MAGAZINE
Howard, Lillie. "Zora Neale Hurston: Just Being Herself."
   <u>Essence</u> Nov. 1980: 100+. [The + sign indicates that
   the article isn't printed on consecutive pages.]

WITH NO AUTHOR SHOWN
"The Battle for Malcolm X." <u>Newsweek</u> 26 Aug. 1991: 52–54.

FROM A DAILY NEWSPAPER, WITH A BYLINE
Chamberlain, John. "Books of the Times." <u>New York
   Times</u> 7 Nov. 1942: 13.

FROM A DAILY NEWSPAPER, WITHOUT A BYLINE
"Zora Hurston, 57, Writer, Is Dead." <u>New York Times</u>
   5 Feb. 1960: 27.

UNSIGNED EDITORIAL FROM A DAILY NEWSPAPER, NO CITY IN TITLE
"The Last Hurrah." Editorial. <u>Star-Ledger</u> [Newark, NJ]
   29 Aug. 1991: 30.

FROM A SCHOLARLY JOURNAL
Beal, Frances. "Slave of a Slave No More." <u>Black Scholar</u>
   6 (1975): 2–10.

Other Sources

PERSONAL INTERVIEW
Wilson, August. Personal interview. 27 Aug. 1990.

TELEPHONE INTERVIEW
Brooks, Gwendolyn. Telephone interview. 3 Nov. 1991.

PUBLISHED INTERVIEW
Walker, Alice. Interview. <u>Interviews with Black Writers</u>.
   Ed. John O'Brien. New York: Liveright, 1973.
   185–211.

(continued)

COMPOSITION

SAMPLE ENTRIES FOR THE LIST OF WORKS CITED *(continued)*

RADIO OR TELEVISION INTERVIEW
Morrison, Toni. <u>All Things Considered</u>. Natl. Public Radio.
WNYC, New York. 16 Feb. 1986.

UNPUBLISHED LETTER
Hurston, Zora Neale. Letter to Mary Holland. 13 June
1955. Historical Collection. U of Florida, Gainesville.

PUBLISHED LETTER
Singer, Ben. Letter. <u>Atlantic</u>. Dec. 1983: 4.

UNPUBLISHED THESIS OR DISSERTATION
Ward, Hazel Mae. "The Black Woman as Character: Images
in the American Novel, 1852–1953." Diss. U of
Texas, Austin, 1977.

CARTOON
Frascino, Edward. Cartoon. <u>New Yorker</u> 2 Sep. 1991: 46.

COMPUTER SOFTWARE
Tobias, Andrew. <u>Managing Your Money</u>. Computer software. MECA, 1986.

SPEECH OR LECTURE
King, Rev. Martin Luther, Jr. "I Have a Dream." Lincoln
Memorial. Washington, 28 Aug. 1963.

RECORDING
Robeson, Paul. "Going Home." Rec. 9 May 1958. <u>Paul
Robeson at Carnegie Hall</u>. Vanguard, VCD-72020, 1986.

FILM, FILMSTRIP, OR VIDEOTAPE
<u>The Color Purple</u>. Dir. Steven Spielberg. With Danny
Glover, Whoopi Goldberg, Margaret Avery, and Oprah
Winfrey. Warner Bros., 1985. [The title, director, dis-
tributor, and year are standard information. You may
add other information, such as performers.]

 Evaluating and Revising

You may use the following chart both to assess your work
and to take steps to improve it. Check also to be sure that
you have included every element of the report, such as an
outline, that your teacher specified.

COMPOSITION

EVALUATING AND REVISING RESEARCH REPORTS

EVALUATION GUIDE	REVISION TECHNIQUE
1 Is the report developed with sufficient primary and secondary sources that meet the "4R" test (pages 528–529)?	**Add** facts, examples, opinions of experts, and primary sources if possible. **Cut** outdated or questionable information.
2 Is a thesis statement included early in the report?	**Add** a sentence or two stating your main idea to the introduction of your report.
3 Is the report suitable for and appealing to its audience?	**Add** needed definitions, background information, and explanations. **Add** interesting, unusual, or surprising details.
4 Is the tone of the report appropriate?	**Replace** words or phrases that are too informal for a research report.
5 Are facts and ideas stated mostly in the writer's own words?	**Cut** unnecessary quotations. **Replace** words, phrases, and sentences that do not use your own wording.
6 Is all information in the report related directly to the topic and thesis?	**Cut** unnecessary material.
7 Is every source of information credited when necessary?	**Add** documentation for quotations, others' ideas, and facts or ideas that aren't common knowledge.
8 Does all documentation follow the format recommended by your teacher?	**Replace** as necessary to follow the MLA format or another professional fomat.

Look closely at the revision techniques the writer uses in the paragraph below. Notice that the writer is aiming for clarity and conciseness.

> In later books, too, these connections occur. ~~By 14 April 1936 she was in the Caribbean, collecting material for her second book of folklore, Tell My Horse (1938)" (Howard, Hurston 139). Hurston had been working for the WPA Federal Theater Project before that.~~ *A field trip to Haiti and Jamaica in 1936 produced Tell My Horse, another story of voodoo.* **replace** **cut**
>
> A year after ~~Tell My Horse~~ *its appearance* she published the novel Moses, Man of the Mountain, which has been described as a blend of "fiction, folklore, religion, and comedy" (Howard *Hurston* 140). In it, Moses is a "hoodooman," *an* ~~pretty wild~~ idea *that also appears in Jonah's Gourd Vine* (231). **replace** **add/replace** **cut/add**

Proofreading and Publishing

Proofreading

Checking the mechanics of your documentation (parenthetical citations and list of Works Cited) is a very important part of proofreading a research paper. Remember that your documentation is there for readers' use: accuracy is required because they may want to find one of your sources. Keep the charts of sample documentation (pages 545–546 and 549–552) beside you as you proofread.

Publishing

A research report is a substantial piece of work, a paper to be proud of and to *use*. Try one of the following suggestions for publishing your paper.

- During your research, you may discover persons or groups especially interested in your subject. For example, there is an organization called Preserve Eatonville Community, Inc., which might appreciate a copy of the report on Zora Neale Hurston for its files. If you come across anyone or any group similarly involved with your subject, consider sending them a copy of your report.

- Make your report a part of your writing portfolio. Since schools and employers frequently request writing samples, save your report as an example of your writing and research skills for a college or job application.

- You might make your report the basis of a videotape documentary, or you could make an audiotape of the report, adding sound effects or background music. Play the tape for your family, your class, or a club or other organization.

COMPOSITION

PART SIX

RESOURCES

RESOURCES

Using Libraries and Reference Works; Preparing Letters, Forms, and Manuscripts

The Library/Media Center

The Librarian

Librarians are professionals trained to locate information; they can show you how to use the library's resources effectively. Also, a librarian may be able to find information for you by borrowing sources from other libraries.

Finding Books in the Library

The Call Number

In most libraries, books are assigned *call numbers* to identify books and to indicate where they're shelved. Call numbers are assigned according to one of two classification systems: the *Dewey decimal system* or the *Library of Congress system.*

The Dewey Decimal System. In the Dewey decimal system, nonfiction books and some works of literature are grouped by subject into ten general subject areas, each assigned a range of numbers. Your library's reference desk will have a complete list of numbered codes for the ten sunject areas. Within this range, subgroups of numbers identify more specific categories. Some libraries use the prefix *R* before the call number to indicate that the title is located in the reference section and is for library use only.

The Dewey decimal system groups books of fiction in alphabetical order according to the authors' last names. Works of fiction by the same author are arranged alphabetically by the first important word of the title (excluding *A, An,* and *The*). Collections of short stories may be grouped separately from novels.

NOTE Authors' names that begin with *Mc* are alphabetized as *Mac.* Names beginning with *St.* are alphabetized as *Saint.*

The Library of Congress System. The Library of Congress system uses code letters to identify subject categories. The first letter of a book's call number tells the general category. The second letter tells the subcategory. The librarian can provide you with a complete list of letter codes for Library of Congress categories and subcategories.

The Card Catalog

The *card catalog* is a cabinet of drawers filled with alphabetically arranged cards: *title cards, author cards,* and *subject cards.* You may also find cross-reference cards that advise you where to look for additional information. Catalog cards may give publication facts, list the number of pages, tell whether the book contains illustrations or diagrams, and provide cross-references to related topics.

RESOURCES

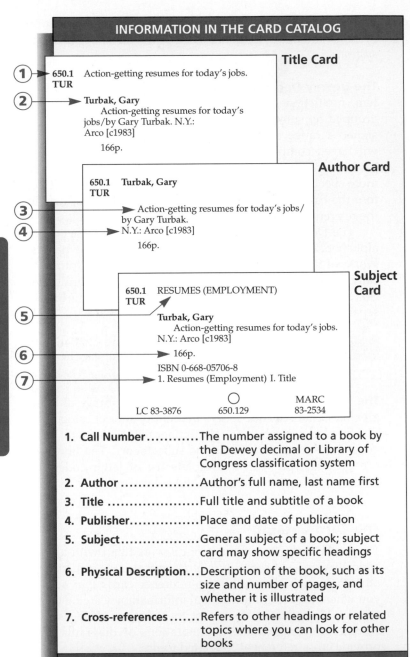

INFORMATION IN THE CARD CATALOG

Title Card

(1) 650.1 TUR   Action-getting resumes for today's jobs.

(2) Turbak, Gary
    Action-getting resumes for today's jobs/by Gary Turbak. N.Y.: Arco [c1983]

    166p.

Author Card

650.1 TUR   Turbak, Gary

(3) Action-getting resumes for today's jobs/ by Gary Turbak.
(4) N.Y.: Arco [c1983]

    166p.

Subject Card

650.1 TUR   RESUMES (EMPLOYMENT)

(5) Turbak, Gary
    Action-getting resumes for today's jobs. N.Y.: Arco [c1983]

(6) 166p.

    ISBN 0-668-05706-8
(7) 1. Resumes (Employment) I. Title

    LC 83-3876   650.129   MARC 83-2534

1. **Call Number** .... The number assigned to a book by the Dewey decimal or Library of Congress classification system

2. **Author** .... Author's full name, last name first

3. **Title** .... Full title and subtitle of a book

4. **Publisher** .... Place and date of publication

5. **Subject** .... General subject of a book; subject card may show specific headings

6. **Physical Description** ... Description of the book, such as its size and number of pages, and whether it is illustrated

7. **Cross-references** .... Refers to other headings or related topics where you can look for other books

RESOURCES

The On-line Catalog

The *on-line catalog* is a computerized version of the card catalog. To view a catalog listing on a library's computer, you use the keyboard to type in an author's name, a title, or a subject. The computer screen then displays the information available under this heading in the card catalog. The on-line catalog can locate information quickly and may tell you if a book you are looking for is checked out or if it is available at another library.

Using Reference Materials

The *Readers' Guide*

When you need to find a magazine article, use the **Readers' Guide to Periodical Literature.** It indexes articles, poems, and stories from more than one hundred magazines.

Throughout the year, paperback editions of the *Readers' Guide* are published. Each issue lists materials published two to four weeks previously. The paperback issues are then bound into a single hardcover volume at the end of the year.

As the following sample entry shows, magazine articles are listed by subject and by author but not by title. The

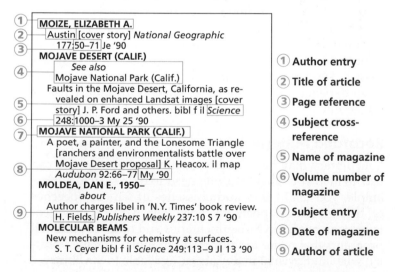

① **MOIZE, ELIZABETH A.**
② Austin [cover story] *National Geographic*
③ 177:50–71 Je '90
MOJAVE DESERT (CALIF.)
④ See also
Mojave National Park (Calif.)
Faults in the Mojave Desert, California, as revealed on enhanced Landsat images [cover
⑤ story] J. P. Ford and others. bibl f il *Science*
⑥ 248:1000–3 My 25 '90
⑦ **MOJAVE NATIONAL PARK (CALIF.)**
A poet, a painter, and the Lonesome Triangle
[ranchers and environmentalists battle over
Mojave Desert proposal] K. Heacox. il map
⑧ *Audubon* 92:66–77 My '90
MOLDEA, DAN E., 1950–
about
Author charges libel in 'N.Y. Times' book review.
⑨ H. Fields. *Publishers Weekly* 237:10 S 7 '90
MOLECULAR BEAMS
New mechanisms for chemistry at surfaces.
S. T. Ceyer bibl f il *Science* 249:113–9 Jl 13 '90

① Author entry
② Title of article
③ Page reference
④ Subject cross-reference
⑤ Name of magazine
⑥ Volume number of magazine
⑦ Subject entry
⑧ Date of magazine
⑨ Author of article

RESOURCES

Readers' Guide also gives *"see"* and *"see also"* references. A key at the front of the *Readers' Guide* explains the meanings of the abbreviations used in entries.

The Vertical File

The *vertical file* is a file cabinet containing a variety of up-to-date materials. Libraries generally keep current pictures, pamphlets, newspaper clippings, and catalogs in folders in the vertical file. Organized by subject, these materials often consist of government, business, or educational publications. Ask the librarian to help you use the vertical file to find current materials.

Microforms

To save space, many libraries photographically reduce periodicals and newspapers and store them on *microforms.* The two most common kinds of microforms are *microfilm* (a roll or reel of film) and *microfiche* (a sheet of film). The librarian can tell you if your library uses microforms, where they are kept, and how to use them.

Computers

Large volumes of printed and visual materials can be stored on optical storage devices. In some libraries, you can access reference information in *databases*—collections of information that are stored on a computer for easy retrieval. The kind of information you can find on a computer depends on what database systems the library has or can access.

Recorded Materials

Your library may have audiovisual materials that you can use to help you whenever you need to do research. For example, you might find audiocassettes of famous speeches or of well-known poets reading their works. On videotapes, you might find documentaries and other educational programs that relate to your research topic. Ask the librarian what audiovisual materials are available in the library.

Reference Works

In the library you will find a special, separate area called the *reference section*. Reference works contain information organized so it is easy to find. Ask your librarian to tell you about the types of reference works in your library.

Common Reference Books

BOOKS OF SYNONYMS	
EXAMPLES	**DESCRIPTION**
Roget's International Thesaurus	uses a categorized index system of synonyms; words grouped into categories and subcategories
Funk & Wagnalls Standard Handbook of Synonyms, Antonyms, & Prepositions *The New Roget's Thesaurus in Dictionary Form* *Webster's New Dictionary of Synonyms*	list entries alphabetically, as in a dictionary

ENCYCLOPEDIAS	
EXAMPLES	**DESCRIPTION**
Academic American Encyclopedia *Collier's Encyclopedia* *The Encyclopedia Americana* *The Encyclopaedia Britannica* *The World Book Encyclopedia*	multivolume works; articles arranged alphabetically by subject; may contain an index or an annual supplement
Lincoln Library of Essential Information *The New Columbia Encyclopedia* *The Random House Encyclopedia*	single-volume works; articles are briefer and less comprehensive in coverage than in multivolume encyclopedias

RESOURCES

GENERAL BIOGRAPHICAL REFERENCE BOOKS	
EXAMPLES	**DESCRIPTION**
Biography Index	tells where to find books and periodicals with biographical information about prominent people
OTHER BIOGRAPHICAL REFERENCE BOOKS	
EXAMPLES	**DESCRIPTION**
Current Biography Yearbook	monthly issues, bound at year end; often has photographs
The International Who's Who Webster's New Biographical	profiles of famous people from many nationalities; give details about their births, careers, and accomplishments
Who's Who in America Dictionary Who's Who Among Black Americans	profiles of famous people, their lives, and their major accomplishments
The Dictionary of American Biography	profiles famous deceased Americans; multiple volumes
The Dictionary of National Biography	profiles famous deceased Britons; multiple volumes

LITERARY BIOGRAPHIES	
EXAMPLES	**DESCRIPTION**
American Authors 1600–1900 *American Women Writers* (series) Magill's *Cyclopedia of World Authors* *Dictionary of Literary Biography* *Twentieth Century Authors* *British Authors of the Nineteenth Century*	profiles of authors; usually have details about dates of authors' births or deaths, titles of major works and dates when they were published, awards or honors received

| SPECIAL FIELD BIOGRAPHIES ||
EXAMPLES	DESCRIPTION
American Men and Women of Science *Baker's Biographical Dictionary of Musicians* *Biographical Dictionary of American Sports* (series) *A Biographical Dictionary of Film* Vasari's *Lives of the Most Eminent Painters, Sculptors, and Architects*	profiles of individuals who are famous for their distinctions or accomplishments in a specific field or career

| ATLASES ||
EXAMPLES	DESCRIPTION
Goode's World Atlas *Hammond Medallion World Atlas* *National Geographic Atlas of the World* *The New York Times Atlas of the World*	primarily, provide maps; may also give statistics about industries, raw materials, exports and imports, or climates of various countries or regions of the world

| HISTORICAL ATLASES ||
EXAMPLES	DESCRIPTION
The American Heritage Pictorial Atlas of United States History *Atlas of World Cultures* Heyden's *Atlas of the Classical World* *Rand McNally Atlas of World History* *Rand McNally World Facts & Maps* *Shepherd's Historical Atlas*	give graphic representations of significant historical changes, such as the rise and fall of empires, movement of peoples, and spread of world cultures

RESOURCES

RESOURCES

| ALMANACS AND YEARBOOKS ||
EXAMPLES	DESCRIPTION
The World Almanac and Book of Facts	summary of year's notable events; index in front
Information Please Almanac: Atlas & Yearbook	less formal and complete than *World Almanac;* articles may be more comprehensive
The International Year Book and Statesmen's Who's Who *The Stateman's Yearbook*	facts about international organizations, nations of the world, and sketches of world leaders
Statistical Abstract of the United States	statistics on many topics, such as population, health and nutrition, education

| INDEXES AND BIOGRAPHIES ||
EXAMPLES	DESCRIPTION
Art Index *Biography Index* *General Sciences Index* *The National Geographic Magazine Cumulative Index* *The New York Times Index* *Social Sciences Index* *General Sciences Index*	guides to articles found in periodicals or other information sources
A Biographical Guide to the Study of Western American Literature *Three Centuries of English and American Plays: A Checklist* *World Historical Fiction Guide*	lists of books or articles; grouped by subject, author, or time period; annotated bibliographies may include descriptions and notes
Gale Directory of Databases	information on current electronic databases and on-line services including product descriptions and telephone numbers of producers

BOOKS OF QUOTATIONS

EXAMPLES	DESCRIPTION
Bartlett's *Familiar Quotations* Flesch's *The New Book of Unusual Quotations* *The Oxford Dictionary of Quotations* *A New Dictionary of Quotations on Historical Principles from Ancient and Modern Sources*	famous quotations; usually indexed by subject; some are arranged by author or time period; often provide author, date, and source of quotation

REFERENCES TO LITERATURE

EXAMPLES	DESCRIPTION
Granger's Index to Poetry	tells where to find specific poems; entries indexed by subject, by title, and by first line
Subject Index to Literature	tells where to find short stories and poems in collections or anthologies; entries indexed by subject

OTHER LITERATURE REFERENCE GUIDES

EXAMPLES	DESCRIPTION
Benét's Reader's Encyclopedia	contains information—such as plots, main characters, and so on—about works of literature; also gives summaries of poems, descriptions of operas
Book Review Digest *Book Review Index* *Brewer's Dictionary of Phrase and Fable* *Essay and General Literature Index* *An Index to One-Act Plays* *Play Index* *Short Story Index*	guides to book reviews, essays, short stories, plays, poems, and other literary works that may be found in periodicals or in collections or anthologies

RESOURCES

LITERATURE AND AUTHOR DIRECTORIES

EXAMPLES	DESCRIPTION
The Cambridge History of American Literature *Harper's Dictionary of Classical Literature and Antiquities* *The Oxford Companion to American Literature* *The Oxford Companion to English Literature* *American Authors and Books*	contain information about authors and their major works; may include brief critiques of best-known works by specific authors or plot outlines of selected works; may offer information on literary movements or genres

CURRENT EVENTS RESOURCES

EXAMPLES	DESCRIPTION
Social Issues Resources Series (SIRS) (audiotapes, videotapes, reprints of newspaper and magazine articles, photographs, letters, and posters)	up-to-date information on a number of important subjects, such as crime or family issues, scientific discoveries, or documents from the National Archives

SPECIAL REFERENCES FOR SPECIFIC SUBJECTS

EXAMPLES	DESCRIPTION
The Encyclopedia of American Facts and Dates *The Encyclopedia of Religion* *The International Encyclopedia of the Social Sciences* *Facts on File* (series of books and yearbooks) *The New Grove Dictionary of Music and Musicians* (series) *McGraw-Hill Encyclopedia of Science & Technology* *The Sports Encyclopedia* *Webster's New Geographical Dictionary*	contain information related to specific topics or of interest to researchers in specific fields; may include short biographies of major figures or evaluations of a person's major contributions to the field

| COLLEGE REFERENCE BOOKS ||
EXAMPLES	DESCRIPTION
Barron's Index of College Majors	arranged by state; highlights majors offered at each school
Barron's Profile of American Colleges *The Insider's Guide to the Colleges* *Peterson's Guide to Two-Year Colleges* *Peterson's Guide to Four-Year Colleges*	profile most accredited, four-year colleges; include articles on choosing a college, taking entrance exams, preparing applications; give information about student life, application deadlines, and financial aid
College Admissions Data Handbook	four volumes; arranged by regions; covers mostly same information as *Barron's Index*
The Directory of Educational Institutions	divided into regional volumes; includes community and junior colleges; has index of programs and index of schools
Peterson's Colleges with Programs for Learning Disabled Students	profiles two- and four-year colleges with programs designed for students with learning disabilities
Technical, Trade, and Business School Data Handbook	covers business schools that offer programs in secretarial science, business administration, accounting

RESOURCES

| COLLEGE ENTRANCE EXAM GUIDES ||
EXAMPLES	DESCRIPTION
Barron's Basic Tips on the SAT *Barron's How to Prepare for the American College Testing Program* *Official Guide to the ACT Assessment*	contain specific information relating to performing well on college entrance exams

COLLEGE FINANCIAL GUIDES	
EXAMPLES	**DESCRIPTION**
Peterson's College Money Handbook *Meeting College Costs* *The College Cost Book* *Directory of Financial Aids for Women* *Directory of Financial Aids for Minorities*	contain information about grants, scholarships, and loans that may be available through colleges and universities

CAREER GUIDES	
EXAMPLES	**DESCRIPTION**
The Encyclopedia of Careers and Vocational Guidance *The Dictionary of Occupational Titles* *Occupational Outlook Handbook* *Career Opportunities Series* *Guide to Federal Jobs*	contain information—such as job descriptions, projected figures for employment for specific occupations, and job-related education requirements—about various industries and occupations

RESOURCES

The Dictionary

Types of Dictionaries

Unabridged Dictionaries

An *unabridged dictionary* is the most comprehensive source for finding information about words. Unabridged dictionaries offer more entries and usually give more information than abridged dictionaries. Unabridged dictionaries may include fuller word histories or longer lists of synonyms or antonyms.

The Oxford English Dictionary (*OED*) is the largest unabridged dictionary. The *OED* gives the approximate date of a word's first appearance in English and gives a quotation to show how the word was used at that time. The *OED* also traces the changes in spelling and meaning that a word has had over the centuries.

Abridged Dictionaries

Abridged or *college dictionaries* are among the most commonly used reference books in the United States. Abridged dictionaries do not contain as many entries or as much information about entry words as unabridged dictionaries. However, abridged dictionaries are revised frequently, so they give the latest information on meanings and uses of words. Besides word entries, most abridged dictionaries contain other useful information, such as tables of commonly used abbreviations, selected biographical entries, or tables of signs and symbols.

Specialized Dictionaries

A *specialized dictionary* contains entries that relate to a specific subject or field. For example, there are specialized dictionaries for terms used in art, music, sports, gardening, mythology, and many other subjects.

Contents of a Dictionary Entry

1. **Entry word.** The boldfaced entry word shows how the word is spelled and how it is divided into syllables. The entry word may also show capitalization and provide alternate spellings.
2. **Pronunciation.** The pronunciation is shown by the use of accent marks and either diacritical marks or phonetic respelling. A pronunciation key, often located at the bottom of the dictionary page, explains the sounds represented by these symbols. Accent marks show which syllables receive greater stress.
3. **Part-of-speech labels.** These labels (usually in abbreviated form) indicate how the entry word should be

RESOURCES

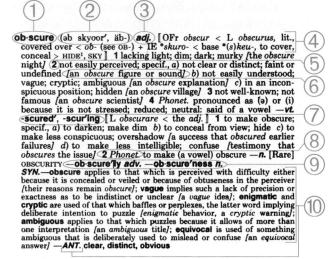

From the entry "obscure" from *Webster's New World Dictionary, 3rd Edition*. Copyright © 1988 by Simon and Schuster, Inc. Reprinted by permission of New World Dictionaries, a division of Simon & Schuster, New York.

used in a sentence. Some words may be used as more than one part of speech. In this case, a part-of-speech label is given before each numbered (or lettered) series of definitions.

4. **Etymology.** The etymology is the origin and history of a word. It tells how the word (or its parts) came into English and traces the word from its earliest known form in the language it came from.

5. **Definitions.** If there is more than one meaning for a word, the definitions are numbered or lettered. Most dictionaries list definitions in order of frequency of use, but some order definitions according to the date when the word came to have each meaning. Read your dictionary's introduction to be sure you know how a word's definitions are listed.

6. **Examples.** Phrases or sentences may demonstrate how the defined word is to be used.

7. **Other forms.** Your dictionary may show spellings for other forms of the word. Full or partial spellings of plural forms of nouns, different tenses of verbs, or the comparison forms of adjectives and adverbs may be given.

8. **Special usage labels.** These labels may show that a definition is limited to certain forms of speech (such as [archaic] or [slang]). Or the labels may indicate that a definition is used only in a certain field, such as *Law*, *Med.* (medicine), or *Chem.* (chemistry). Your dictionary will have a key for abbreviations used.

9. **Related word forms.** These are various forms of the entry word, usually created by adding suffixes or prefixes.

10. **Synonyms and antonyms.** Synonyms and antonyms may appear at the end of some word entries. You may also find synonyms (printed in capital letters) included within the list of definitions.

Letters and Forms

The Appearance of a Business Letter

Business letters follow certain standards of format.

- Use plain paper (8½" x 11").
- Type your letter if possible (single-spaced with an extra line between paragraphs). Otherwise, write legibly in black or blue ink.
- Center your letter on the page with equal margins, usually one inch, on all sides.
- Use only one side of the paper. If you need a second page, leave a one-inch margin at the bottom of the first page and carry over at least two lines to the second page.
- Avoid markouts, erasures, or other careless marks. Check for typing errors and misspellings.

Writing Business Letters

The Parts of a Business Letter

A business letter contains six parts:

(1) the heading   (4) the body
(2) the inside address   (5) the closing
(3) the salutation   (6) the signature

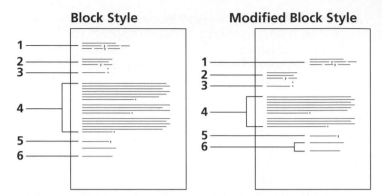

Block Style   **Modified Block Style**

There are two styles used frequently for business letters. With the *block form,* every part of the letter begins at the left-hand margin, and paragraphs are not indented. In the *modified block form,* the heading, the closing, and the signature are aligned along an imaginary line just to the right of the center of the page. The other parts of the letter begin at the left-hand margin. All paragraphs are indented.

The Heading. The heading usually consists of three lines:

- your street address (or post office box number)
- your city, state, and ZIP Code
- the date that you wrote the letter

The Inside Address. The inside address shows the name and address of the person or organization you are writing. If you're writing to a specific person, use a courtesy title (such as *Mr., Ms., Mrs.,* or *Miss*) or a professional title (such as *Dr.* or *Professor*) in front of the person's name. After the person's name, include the person's business or job title (such as *Owner* or *Sales Manager*) followed by the name of the company or organization and the address.

The Salutation. The salutation is your greeting. If you are writing to a specific person, begin with *Dear,* followed by a courtesy title or a professional title and the person's last name. End the salutation with a colon.

If you don't have the name of a specific person, you can use a general salutation, such as *Dear Sir* or *Madam* or

Ladies and Gentlemen. You can also use a department or a position title with or without the word *Dear.*

The Body. The main part of your letter (the body) contains your message. If the body of your letter contains more than one paragraph, leave a space between paragraphs.

The Closing. You should end your letter in a courteous manner. Closings often used in business letters include *Sincerely, Yours truly, Respectfully yours,* and *Regards.* Capitalize only the first word of the closing.

The Signature. Your signature should be written in ink, directly below the closing. Sign your full name. Do not use a title. If you type your letter, type your name neatly below your signature.

GUIDELINES FOR THE CONTENTS OF A BUSINESS LETTER

Business letters usually follow a few simple guidelines.

- *Use a courteous, positive, and professional tone.* Maintain a respectful, constructive tone—even if you're angry. Rude or insulting letters are counterproductive.

- *Use formal, standard English.* Avoid slang, dialect, contractions, or abbreviations. Business letters are usually formal in tone and use of language.

- *State your purpose clearly and quickly.* Assume that the person reading your letter is busy. Tell why you are writing in the first or second sentence of the letter.

- *Include all necessary information.* Provide all the information your reader needs to understand and respond appropriately to your letter.

Types of Business Letters

Request or Order Letters

Occasionally you may require something that you can obtain by writing a *request letter.* For example, you might write to a college to request a catalog of courses offered, or you might write to a state's tourism agency to request a brochure about a travel destination. An *order letter* is a special kind of request letter that is written to order merchandise by mail, especially when you do not have a printed order form.

Here is the body of a sample request letter.

> Please send me a catalog of courses as well as an application form for admission to Stanville College. I am a junior in high school and beginning to consider my choices among colleges.
>
> Along with the catalog and application, please also send a list of the admissions requirements for both the School of Liberal Arts and the School of Engineering.

When you are writing a request or order letter, follow these guidelines.

1. State your request clearly.
2. If you're asking for information, enclose a self-addressed, stamped envelope.
3. If you're asking an individual for a special request, make sure your request is reasonable and that you have allowed enough time for the person to answer you well in advance of the time you must have the information.
4. If you're ordering something, include all important details, such as the size, color, style, catalog number, and price. You might include information about the magazine or newspaper in which you saw the item advertised. Compute correctly if there are costs involved, including any necessary sales tax or shipping charges.

Complaint or Adjustment Letters

The purpose of a *complaint* or *adjustment letter* is to report a problem and to request a satisfactory resolution of the difficulty.

Here is the body of a sample adjustment letter.

> On October 25, I bought a silk button-down shirt at your store for $42.26. The shirt was charged to my mother's account. Since the size I wanted was not in stock, the shirt was later delivered to my home. When the shirt arrived, on October 28, the package had split open and the shirt was stained.
>
> I am returning the shirt and would like the full amount of $42.26 credited to my mother's account. The account is under the name of Sabrina Tallwood. Her account number is 55-432-6591-2.

When you are writing a complaint or adjustment letter, follow these suggestions.

1. Register your complaint as soon as possible after noticing the problem.
2. Explain exactly what is wrong. Necessary information might include
   - what product or service you ordered or that you expected
   - why you are not satisfied (damaged goods, incorrect merchandise, or bad service)
   - how you were affected (lost time or money)
   - what you want the individual, company, or organization to do about it
3. Keep the tone of your letter calm and courteous. Despite your possible frustration about the mistake or error, you will be much more effective if you are cool-headed and communicate clearly about the problem.

Appreciation or Commendation Letters

An *appreciation* or *commendation letter* is written to compliment or to express appreciation to a person, a group, or an organization. For example, you might write to a state

RESOURCES

legislator to compliment the way he or she handled a difficult situation. Or you might write to a television network to tell how much you like a particular program and to encourage the network not to cancel it.

Here is the body of a sample appreciation letter.

> On Tuesday, June 13, I watched the first show in your series about the problems facing today's teens. I wanted to let you know that I especially appreciate your broadcast of "Teenagers in the 90's."
>
> As a teenager, I considered your portrayal of some of the problems we face very accurate. Instead of focusing only on the dilemmas of modern adolescence, your program gave helpful—and hopeful—suggestions about where teens like me might find information, resources, or support as we deal with these crucial concerns.
>
> Many parents, such as my own, rarely hear about these issues from an unbiased source. I hope your network will continue to broadcast programs such as this one that help to increase people's understanding of one another's concerns. We need more programs like yours that contribute to frank and open talks about serious issues.

Letters of Application

You write a *letter of application* to provide a selection committee or a possible employer with enough information to determine whether you are a good candidate for a position. This position may be a job, a membership in an organization, or a scholarship.

Here is a sample job application letter.

321 Fifth Street
Riverside, MO 64168
May 26, 1994

Personnel Director
Value Insurance Company
41 Bank Street
Riverside, MO 64168

Dear Personnel Director:

Please consider me an applicant for the summer stenographer position advertised in Sunday's <u>Herald</u>.

I am seventeen years old and a junior at Central High School. My course of study has included business classes such as typing, bookkeeping, and business English. I can take dictation and can type either from shorthand notes or recordings at a rate of about fifty words a minute.

Last summer I was employed as a stenographer for the Ace Company. I did billing and performed other tasks as well as stenographic work. I feel at home in an office and enjoy responsibility.

I will gladly supply you with references who can tell you about my qualifications for this position.

I am available for a personal interview at your convenience. My telephone number is 555-7023. I can be reached most evenings after 5:00 p.m.

Very truly yours,

Veronica Harjo

Veronica Harjo

RESOURCES

When you are writing a letter of application, remember the following points.

1. Identify the job or position you are applying for. Mention how you heard about it.
2. Depending on the position you are applying for, you might include
   - your age, grade in school, or grade-point average
   - your experience or your activities, awards, and honors

- personal qualities or characteristics that make you a good choice for the position
- the date or times you are available
3. Offer to provide references. Your references should include two or three responsible adults (usually not relatives) who have agreed to recommend you. Be prepared to supply their addresses and telephone numbers.

The Personal Résumé

A *résumé* is a summary of your background and experience. For many positions, you submit a résumé with your letter of application. There are many different ways to arrange the information on a résumé. Whatever way you select, be sure your résumé looks neat and businesslike.

JOHN L. ZENO		1632 Garden View Drive Allentown, PA 18103 Telephone: (215) 555-6160
EDUCATION:	Junior, St. Timothy High School Major studies: College preparatory courses in business and foreign languages Grade-point average: 3.0 (B)	
WORK EXPERIENCE:	Summer 1991	Camp counselor Camp Holiday Beaver Lake, PA
	Summer 1990	Volunteer office worker YMCA Allentown, PA
SKILLS:	Shorthand: Typing: Business machines:	120 words a minute 70 words a minute dictating, calculating, and duplicating machines
	Languages:	Can speak and translate Spanish fluently
	Extracurricular activities:	Vice President, Future Business Leaders of America; member, Spanish Club
REFERENCES:	Mary Francis Tate, Teacher St. Timothy High School Allentown, PA	(215) 555-1019
	Mr. Glen Ramos, Director Camp Holiday Beaver Lake, PA	(215) 555-4593

Addressing an Envelope

First impressions are important, and the first impression that a prospective employer may have of you is the envelope you send your letter and résumé in.

- Send your business letter in a plain business envelope.
- Write or type your name and address in the upper left-hand corner of the envelope.
- Write or type the name and address of the person or organization to whom you are writing (the addressee) on the center of the envelope. The addressee's name and address should exactly match the inside address on the letter.
- Use the two-letter postal-service abbreviations for state names, and be sure to include correct ZIP Codes.

```
Veronica Harjo
321 Fifth Street
Riverside, MO  64168


            Personnel Director
            Value Insurance Company
            41 Bank Street
            Riverside, MO  64168
```

RESOURCES

 REFERENCE NOTE: For a list of state name abbreviations, see pages 590–591.

Completing Printed Forms and Applications

As you enter the work force or begin applying to colleges, you'll be asked to fill out a variety of forms and applications. The person or organization who receives your form or application will be able to help you best if you fill the form out neatly and completely. Use the guidelines on page 583 when you fill out applications and other forms. An example of a complete job application appears on the following page.

Application for Employment

Personal Information

1. Social Security Number   034-38-3151   Date   5/20/94
2. Name _____Cohen_____Sarah_____Lynn_____
            Last   First   Middle
3. Present Address   10226 Zenith Lane   Omaha   Nebraska 68154
4. Permanent Address same as above
5. Phone No.   (402) 555-3376   6. Date of Birth   9/19/76
7. Referred by   Mrs. Bernstein

Employment Desired

8. Position _Salesclerk_   can start 6/8/94   desired $5.25/hr
                             Date you   Salary
9. Are you employed now?_ yes
   If so, may we inquire of your present employer ___yes___
10. Ever applied to this company before? _no_
                                   Where   When

Education

11. Name and Location of Last School   Lincoln High School Omaha, NE
    Years Attended   91-present   Date Graduated   N/A
    Subjects Studied   Academic

Former Employers
(List below last two employers, beginning with most recent.)

12. Date   Name and Address   Salary   Position   Reason
    Month/Year of Employer   for Leaving

6/91–	Mrs. Richard Lance	$4.25/hr	Yardwork	None
	1225 N. Washington, Omaha, NE			
3/89–7/91	Minneapolis Tribune	$2.50/hr	Paper	Moved to
	Minneapolis, MN		Carrier	Nebraska

References: List the names of three persons not related to you, whom you have known at least one year.

Name	Address	Business	Years Acquainted
13. Dr. Yolanda Torres	208 De Kalb	Veterinarian	1
	Omaha, NE 61851		
14. Mr. Howard Dannenberg	535 S. Fifth St.	Nurse (Retired)	1
	Omaha, NE 61854		
15. Mrs. Gretchen Musich	104 York Lane	Beautician	1
	Omaha, NE 61853		

Signature: *Sarah L. Cohen*   **Date:** 5/20/94

GUIDELINES FOR COMPLETING FORMS

1. Always read the entire form to make sure you understand exactly what items of information you are being asked to supply.

2. Type neatly or print legibly, using a pen or pencil as directed.

3. Include all information requested. If a question does not apply to you, write *N.A.* or *not applicable* rather than leave the space blank.

4. Keep the form neat and clean. Avoid crossing out your writing or smearing the ink.

5. When you have completed the form, proofread it carefully to correct any spelling, grammar, punctuation, or factual errors.

6. Submit the form to the correct person or mail it to the correct address.

Writing Social Letters

Sometimes, the best way to communicate with friends is through the mail. When you want to thank someone formally, to congratulate someone, to send an invitation, or to respond to an invitation extended to you, you should write a social letter.

Social letters are much less formal in style than business letters. For example, a social letter doesn't include an inside address, and most social letters use the modified block form.

Types of Social Letters

Thank-you Letters

The purpose of a thank-you letter is to express appreciation for a gift or a favor. Try to say more than just "thank you": Offer details about how the person's gift or efforts were helpful or appreciated.

Invitations

An invitation should contain specific information—such as the occasion, the time and place, and so on—about a planned event.

Letters of Regret

If you have been invited to a party or another social function and will be unable to attend, it's polite to send a letter of regret. A written reply is especially appropriate if you were sent a written invitation that included the letters *R.S.V.P.* (In French, these letters are an abbreviation for "please reply.")

Manuscript Style

You think your ideas are important, and you want your readers to think so, too. Make their first impression a good one by giving your manuscript a professional look, by using abbreviations and numbers correctly, and by avoiding sexist language.

Materials and Arrangement

Use the following guidelines as you make a final copy of your paper.

Handwritten Papers

- Use regular $8\frac{1}{2}$" x 11" lined paper. Do not use ragged-edged paper torn from a spiral-bound notebook.
- Use blue or black ink.
- Write legibly: Dot your *i*'s, cross your *t*'s, and distinguish among *o*'s, *a*'s, and *e*'s.
- Use only one side of a sheet of paper.
- Do not skip lines unless your teacher tells you to do so.

Typewritten Papers

- Use regular $8\frac{1}{2}$" x 11" typing paper. Avoid very thin (onionskin) paper and erasable paper.
- Use a fresh black ribbon.

■ Double-space between lines.

Word-Processed Papers

■ Use letter-sized sheets or continuous-feed paper that separates cleanly along the edges.
■ Make sure that the printer you use can produce clear, dark, letter-quality type.
■ Check with your teacher to be sure that the typeface you plan to use is acceptable.
■ Double-space between lines.

Word-processing software and printers can help you format your paper in some or all of these ways:

■ producing italic and bold type
■ centering heads
■ numbering pages
■ generating black-and-white or color graphics
■ setting up tables, charts, and graphs

RESOURCES

General Guidelines

Set up your pages to make them clear and readable. Whether you are preparing a handwritten, typed, or word-processed paper, use the following format.

■ Leave one-inch margins at the top, sides, and bottom of each page.
■ Indent the first line of each paragraph five spaces from the left margin.
■ Number all pages (except the first page) in the upper right-hand corner, one-half inch from the top.
■ Follow your teacher's instructions for placement of your name, the date, your class, and the title of your paper.
■ Make corrections neatly. You may make a few corrections with correction fluid, but they should be barely noticeable. To insert a word or a short phrase, use a caret mark (∧) and add the word(s) immediately above it.

- Use charts, graphs, tables, and illustrations effectively. Place such materials close to the text they illustrate. Label and number each one. The standard labels are *Table* (for tables) and *Figure* or *Fig.* (for photographs, drawings, maps, graphs, charts, and the like). Give each table or figure a number and a title. Whenever necessary, give the source of the material.

If a table or chart is too wide to fit on the page vertically, position the table or chart sideways (broadside). Position the bottom of the graphic along the left-hand margin of the page so that the reader need only turn the page ninety degrees to the left to read the graphic.

Abbreviations

An **abbreviation** is a shortened form of a word or phrase. Only a few abbreviations are appropriate in the text of a formal paper written for a general (nontechnical) audience. Many other abbreviations are used to save space in tables, notes, and bibliographies.

Personal Names

Abbreviate given names only if the person is most commonly known that way.

EXAMPLES   Susan **B.** Anthony   **S. I.** Hayakawa
                W.E.B. Du Bois

 NOTE   Leave a space between two such initials, but not between three or more.

Titles

(1) Abbreviate social titles whether used before the full name or before the last name alone.

EXAMPLES   **Mr.**   **Mrs.**   **Ms.**
              Sr.   **Sra.**   **Dr.**

(2) Abbreviate civil and military titles used before full names or before initials and last names. Spell them out before last names alone.

EXAMPLES   **Prof.** R. B. Adams   **Professor** Adams
             Sen. Daniel K. Inouye   **Senator** Inouye

COMMON CIVIL AND MILITARY TITLES	
CIVIL	**MILITARY**
Amb., Ambassador	Adm., Admiral
Atty. Gen., Attorney General	Brig. Gen., Brigadier General
Dist. Atty., District Attorney	Capt., Captain
Gov., Governor	Col., Colonel
Lt. Gov., Lieutenant Governor	Ens., Ensign
Pres., President	Gen., General
Prof., Professor	Lt., Lieutenant
Rep., Representative	Maj., Major
Sen., Senator	Pfc., Private, First Class
Supt., Superintendent	Pvt., Private
Treas., Treasurer	Sgt., Sergeant

(3) Abbreviate titles and academic degrees that follow proper names.

EXAMPLES   Henry Lewis Gates, **Jr.**   Maria Sandoz, **D.V.M.**

NOTE Use such abbreviations only after a person's full name, not after the last name alone. With the exception of numerals such as *III* or *IV,* abbreviations of titles and degrees used after a name are set off by commas.

EXAMPLES   The story "Before the End of Summer" by Grant Moss, **Jr.,** first appeared in The New Yorker.
Maria Sandoz, **D.V.M.,** announces the opening of her practice for the treatment of domestic animals.
Leland Powers III, **M.F.A.,** will address the monthly meeting of the Society for Art Appreciation.

Do not include the titles *Mr., Mrs., Ms.,* or *Dr.* when you use a title or degree after a name.

EXAMPLE   **Dr.** Rowena Jefferson *or* Rowena Jefferson, **M.D.** [*not* Ms. Rowena Jefferson, M.D.]

COMMON TITLES AND DEGREES	
B.A. or A.B.	Bachelor of Arts
B.S. or S.B.	Bachelor of Science
CPA	Certified Public Accountant
D.D.S.	Doctor of Dental Surgery
D.V.M.	Doctor of Veterinary Medicine
J.D.	Doctor of Laws
M.A. or A.M.	Master of Arts
M.B.A.	Master of Business Administration
M.D.	Doctor of Medicine
M.F.A.	Master of Fine Arts
M.S. or S.M.	Master of Science
Ph.D.	Doctor of Philosophy
R.N.	Registered Nurse

Company Names

Spell out most company names in text. They may be abbreviated in tables, notes, and bibliographies.

TEXT	Chandra Brothers Printing Company
TABLES, NOTES, ETC.	Chandra Bros.

NOTE The abbreviations *Inc.* and *Ltd.* are set off by commas. These abbreviations may be omitted in text as well as in tables, notes, and bibliographies.

EXAMPLE   Among the newspapers published by Knight-Ridder, **Inc.,** [or Knight-Ridder] are the *Miami Herald* and the *Philadelphia Inquirer.*

COMMON PARTS OF COMPANY NAMES	
Bro., Bros., Brothers	Inc., Incorporated
Co., Company	Ltd., Limited
Corp., Corporation	& (ampersand), and

Agencies and Organizations

After spelling out the first use, abbreviate the names of agencies, organizations, and other things commonly known by their initials.

EXAMPLES   Jennifer Lawson is the programming chief for the Public Broadcasting Service (**PBS**). Lawson, a former film producer, plans to expand **PBS**'s coverage of the work of independent producers.

The North Atlantic Treaty Organization (**NATO**) was formed in 1950. **NATO**'s original mission was to unify military leadership among sixteen Western nations to defend those nations from the possiblity of Soviet (or other) attacks.

NOTE Abbreviations pronounced letter by letter (such as *PBS*) are called *initialisms.* Those pronounced as words (such as *NATO*) are called *acronyms.* Both types of abbreviations are usually capitalized and do not use periods.

INITIALISMS	ACT, American College Test CIA, Central Intelligence Agency ESL, English as a second language MTV, Music Television NYSE, New York Stock Exchange SAT, Scholastic Aptitude Test
ACRONYMS	AWOL, absent without leave CAD, computer aided design CORE, Congress of Racial Equality DOS, disk operating system NOW, National Organization for Women ZIP (as in ZIP Code), zoning improvement plan

RESOURCES

 REFERENCE NOTE: For information on forming plurals of abbreviations, see page 426.

Geographical Terms

States. In text, spell out the names of states and other political units whether they stand alone or follow any other geographical term. Abbreviate them in tables, notes, and bibliographies.

EXAMPLES   Federico Peña, who was born in **Texas,** served two terms as mayor of Denver, **Colorado.**

On our vacation to **Mexico,** we visited Guadalajara, the capital of **Jalisco.**

EXCEPTION   Always include the traditional abbreviation
for the District of Columbia, *D.C.,* with the
city name *Washington* to distinguish it
from the state of Washington.

In tables, notes, and bibliographies, use the first of the two
forms shown in the following table. Use the second form
only in addresses that include the ZIP Code.

ABBREVIATIONS FOR POLITICAL UNITS		
POLITICAL UNIT	**TRADITIONAL**	**POSTAL SERVICE**
Alabama	Ala.	AL
Alaska	Alaska	AK
Arizona	Ariz.	AZ
Arkansas	Ark.	AR
California	Calif.	CA
Colorado	Colo.	CO
Connecticut	Conn.	CT
Delaware	Del.	DE
District of Columbia	D.C.	DC
Florida	Fla.	FL
Georgia	Ga.	GA
Guam	Guam	GU
Hawaii	Hawaii	HI
Idaho	Idaho	ID
Illinois	Ill.	IL
Indiana	Ind.	IN
Iowa	Iowa	IA
Kansas	Kans.	KS
Kentucky	Ky.	KY
Louisiana	La.	LA
Maine	Maine	ME
Maryland	Md.	MD
Massachusetts	Mass.	MA
Michigan	Mich.	MI
Minnesota	Minn.	MN
Mississippi	Miss.	MS
Missouri	Mo.	MO
Montana	Mont.	MT
Nebraska	Nebr.	NB
Nevada	Nev.	NV
New Hampshire	N.H.	NH

(continued)

RESOURCES

ABBREVIATIONS FOR POLITICAL UNITS *(continued)*		
POLITICAL UNIT	**TRADITIONAL**	**POSTAL SERVICE**
New Jersey	N.J.	NJ
New Mexico	N.Mex.	NM
New York	N.Y.	NY
North Carolina	N.C.	NC
North Dakota	N.Dak.	ND
Ohio	Ohio	OH
Oklahoma	Okla.	OK
Oregon	Oreg.	OR
Pennsylvania	Pa.	PA
Puerto Rico	P.R.	PR
Rhode Island	R.I.	RI
South Carolina	S.C.	SC
South Dakota	S.Dak.	SD
Tennessee	Tenn.	TN
Texas	Tex.	TX
Utah	Utah	UT
Vermont	Vt.	VT
Virgin Islands	V.I.	VI
Virginia	Va.	VA
Washington	Wash.	WA
West Virginia	W.Va.	WV
Wisconsin	Wis.	WI
Wyoming	Wyo.	WY

RESOURCES

Countries. In text, spell out the names of countries. Such names may be abbreviated in tables, notes, and bibliographies.

TEXT	TABLES, NOTES, ETC.
France	Fr.
Germany	Ger.
Jamaica	Jam.
Mexico	Mex.
People's Republic of China	P.R.O.C.
United Kingdom	U.K.
United States	U.S.

STYLE
NOTE

United States may be abbreviated to *U.S.* when it is used as an adjective in text. However, it is never incorrect to spell it out.

EXAMPLE   The **U.S.** (*or* **United States**) proposal is being considered by the other members of the Security Council.

Addresses. In text, spell out every word in an address. In letter and envelope addresses, the two-letter state code may be used when followed by a ZIP Code. Addresses may be abbreviated in tables, notes, and bibliographies.

TEXT	TABLES, NOTES, ETC.
Avenue	Ave.
Building	Bldg.
Boulevard	Blvd.
Drive	Dr.
Highway	Hwy.
North, South, East, West	N., S., E., W. (before street names)
Parkway	Pkwy.
Road	Rd.
Route	Rte.
Street	St.

EXCEPTION   Some cities use the abbreviations *NW, NE, SE,* and *SW* after the street name.

EXAMPLE   The Israeli embassy in Washington, D.C., is located at 3541 International Drive **NW.**

NOTE   In text, spell out references to the points of the compass.

EXAMPLE   Travel north [*not* N] from Main Street.

Time

Eras. Abbreviate the two most frequently used era designations, A.D. and B.C. The abbreviation A.D. stands for the Latin phrase *Anno Domini,* meaning "in the year of the Lord." It is used with dates in the Christian era. When used with a specific year number, A.D. precedes the number. When used with the name of a century, it follows the name.

EXAMPLES   The son of a samurai, the acclaimed haiku
            poet Matsuo Bashō was born in A.D. 1644.
            Bashō perfected the art of haiku in the
            seventeenth century A.D.

The abbreviation *B.C.*, which stands for "before Christ,"
is used for dates before the Christian era. It follows either a
specific year number or the name of a century.

EXAMPLES   Queen Hatshepsut reigned as pharaoh of
            Egypt from about 1500 to 1480 B.C.
            Egypt underwent a religious revolution in the
            fourteenth century B.C., when the pharaoh
            Amenhotep IV introduced a doctrine of
            monotheism.

Months and Days. In text, spell out the names of months
and days whether they appear alone or in dates. Both may
be abbreviated in tables, notes, and bibliographies.

TEXT		TABLES, NOTES, ETC.	
Months	**Days**	**Months**	**Days**
January	Sunday	Jan.	Sun.
February	Monday	Feb.	Mon.
March	Tuesday	Mar.	Tues.
April	Wednesday	Apr.	Wed.
May	Thursday	May	Thurs.
June	Friday	June	Fri.
July	Saturday	July	Sat.
August		Aug.	
September		Sept.	
October		Oct.	
November		Nov.	
December		Dec.	

Time of Day. Abbreviate the designations for the two
halves of the day measured by clock time.

The abbreviation *A.M.* stands for the Latin phrase *ante
meridiem,* meaning "before noon." The abbreviation *P.M.*
stands for *post meridiem,* meaning "after noon." Both abbreviations follow the numerals designating the specific time.

EXAMPLE   The meeting, originally scheduled for 9:00 A.M.,
           has been postponed until 3:30 P.M.

RESOURCES

<table>
<tr><td>STYLE NOTE</td><td>Do not use *A.M.* or *P.M.* with numbers spelled out as words or as substitutes for the words *morning, afternoon,* or *evening.*</td></tr>
</table>

INCORRECT	The meeting has been rescheduled for three-thirty P.M.
CORRECT	The meeting has been rescheduled for 3:30 P.M. [*or* three-thirty in the afternoon]
INCORRECT	Writing in *The Pillow Book,* Sei Shōnagon considers the early A.M. the most beautiful time of the day in winter.
CORRECT	Writing in *The Pillow Book,* Sei Shōnagon considers the early **morning** the most beautiful time of the day in winter.

Also, do not use the words *morning, afternoon,* or *evening* with numerals followed by *A.M.* or *P.M.*

INCORRECT	The armistice that ended World War I went into effect at 11:00 A.M. on the morning of November 11, 1918.
CORRECT	The armistice that ended World War I went into effect at 11:00 A.M. on November 11, 1918.

Other Abbreviations

Common Latin Expressions. In text, spell out the English equivalents of common Latin expressions. In tables, notes, or bibliographies, use abbreviations for the Latin expressions.

TEXT	TABLES, NOTES, ETC.
about	c. *or* ca. *or* circ. (used with approximate dates)
compare	cf.
for example	e.g.
and others	et al.
and so forth	etc.
that is	i.e.
versus	vs. *or* v.

Parts of Books. In text, spell out the words *volume, part, unit, chapter,* and *page.*

EXAMPLE   As shown in the time line in **Volume 2, Chapter 12, page 51,** the genre of magical realism developed in Latin America during the 1950s and 1960s.

 NOTE   With the exception of the word *page,* the names of parts of books identified by a number are usually capitalized.

 REFERENCE NOTE: For guidelines to the use of abbreviated forms for book parts in parenthetical citations and Works Cited lists, see **Chapter 17: The Research Paper.**

School Subjects. In text, spell out the names of school subjects.

EXAMPLE   Dr. Wu has taught **Chemistry II** [*not* Chem. II] since 1987.

 REFERENCE NOTE: See **Chapter 11: Capitalization** for information on capitalizing the names of school subjects.

Units of Measurement. In text, spell out the names of units of measurement whether they stand alone or follow a spelled-out number or a numeral. When they follow numerals, units of measurement may be abbreviated in tables and notes.

TEXT	TABLES, NOTES, ETC.
Traditional	
Fahrenheit	F
foot, feet	ft
gallon(s)	gal
inch(es)	in.
mile(s)	mi
ounce(s)	oz
pint(s)	pt
pound(s)	lb
quart(s)	qt
tablespoon(s)	tbsp *or* T
teaspoon(s)	tsp *or* t
yard(s)	yd

(continued)

RESOURCES

TEXT	TABLES, NOTES, ETC.
Metric	
Celsius	C
centimeter(s)	cm
gram(s)	g
kilogram(s)	kg
liter(s)	l or L
milliliter(s)	ml
meter(s)	m
millimeter(s)	mm

Symbols

In text, spell out the words for the symbols % (percent), + (plus), – (minus), = (equals), and ¢ (cents).

EXAMPLE   In our county, the sales tax is currently seven **cents** (*not* 7¢) on the dollar.

STYLE NOTE   The dollar sign ($) may be used whenever it precedes numerals. Do not substitute the symbol for the words *money* or *dollars.*

EXAMPLES   Barry bought a used car for $1950 [*not* $one thousand nine hundred fifty].

Anita received a lot of money [*not* $] for her birthday.

Few people can imagine a billion dollars [*not* a billion $].

 REFERENCE NOTE: See pages 596 (below) through 598 for information on using figures or words for numbers.

Numbers

(1) Spell out a *cardinal number*—a number that states how many—if it can be expressed in one or two words. Otherwise, use numerals.

EXAMPLES	**thirteen** seniors	**forty-four** days
	one thousand books	**two-thirds** of them
	546 seniors	**365** days
	1,645 books	**1¹/₂** (*or* **1.5**) miles

Cardinal numbers from twenty-one to ninety-nine are hyphenated in compounds.

Do not spell out some numbers and use numerals for others in the same context. If any of the numbers require numerals, use numerals for all of them.

INCONSISTENT	The Congress of the United States is composed of one hundred senators and 435 representatives.
CONSISTENT	The Congress of the United States is composed of **100** senators and **435** representatives.

However, when it is necessary to distinguish between numbers appearing beside each other, spell out one number and use numerals for the other.

EXAMPLE   We bought **seven 15**-pound sacks.

For large round numbers, you may use words or a combination of words and numerals.

EXAMPLES   seven billion dollars *or* $7 billion
21,500,000 *or* 21.5 million

(2) Spell out any number that begins a sentence.

EXAMPLE   **Four hundred twenty-one** students participated in the contest.

If a number appears awkward when spelled out, revise the sentence so that it does not begin with the number.

AWKWARD	Two hundred twenty-three thousand six hundred thirty-one votes were cast in the election.
IMPROVED	In the election, **223,631** votes were cast.

(3) Spell out an *ordinal number*—a number that expresses order.

EXAMPLES   Junko Tabei, the **first** [*not* 1st] woman who climbed Mount Everest, was born in Japan in 1940.
Of the fifty states, Wyoming ranks **fiftieth** [*not* 50th] in population.

(4) Use numerals to express numbers in conventional situations such as those listed in the chart that follows.

TYPE OF NUMBER	EXAMPLES	
Names	Elizabeth II	Enrique Silva III
Identification	Room 12 Model 19–A	pages 246–315
Numbers	Channel 4 lines 3–19	State Road 541
Measurements and Statistics	72 degrees ratio of 6 to 1 84 feet by 12 feet	1½ yards 32.7 ounces 14 percent
Dates	April 5, 1994 *or* 5 April 1994 [*not* April 5th, 1994] the 1990's *or* the 1990s in 1800 in 1991–1992 *or* in 1991–92 from 1990 to 1995 *or* 1990–1995 *or* 1990–95 [*not* from 1990–1995 *or* from 1990–95]	
Addresses	345 Lexington Drive Tampa, FL 33628–4533	
Times of Day	8:20 P.M. (*or* p.m.)	7:35 A.M. (*or* a.m.)

NOTE   Spell out a number used with *o'clock.*

EXAMPLE   **ten** o'clock

Nonsexist Language

Nonsexist language is language that applies to people in general, both male and female. For example, you might use the nonsexist terms *humanity, human beings,* and *people* instead of the gender-specific term *mankind.*

In the past, many skills and occupations excluded either men or women. Expressions like *seamstress, stewardess,* and *mailman* reflect those limitations. Now that most jobs are held by both men and women, language is adjusting to reflect this change.

When you are referring to humanity as a whole, use nonsexist expressions rather than gender-specific ones. Here are some widely used nonsexist terms that you can use to replace the older, gender-specific ones.

GENDER-SPECIFIC	NONSEXIST
businessman	executive, businessperson
chairman	chairperson, chair
deliveryman	delivery person
fireman	firefighter
foreman	supervisor
housewife	homemaker
mailman	mail carrier
manmade	synthetic, manufactured
manpower	workers, human resources
may the best man win	may the best person win
policeman	police officer
salesman	salesperson, salesclerk
steward, stewardess	flight attendant
watchman	security guard

If the antecedent of a pronoun may be either masculine or feminine, use both masculine and feminine pronouns to refer to it.

EXAMPLES **Anyone** who is going on the field trip needs to bring **his or her** lunch.
Any qualified **person** may submit **his or her** application.

 REFERENCE NOTE: For more information on indefinite pronouns whose antecedents may be either masculine or feminine, see pages 135–136.

✓ Quick Check Answer Key

Chapter 1
Parts of Speech

p. 90 *QUICK CHECK* 1

1. abstract   4. concrete
2. concrete   5. concrete
3. abstract

p. 95 *QUICK CHECK* 2

1. himself, everyone, who, one, him
2. Everybody, one
3. mine, you, several
4. Those, some, who
5. What, that

p. 100 *QUICK CHECK* 3

Adjective	Word Modified
1. four	cups
this	recipe
2. (Your); new; spacious; sunny; ideal	apartment
3. powerful	image
many; Native American	cultures
4. Neither; enjoyable	film
5. space	program
which	astronaut

p. 104 *QUICK CHECK* 4

1. was—linking (judge); would have tried—trans. (case)
2. was—intrans.; left—intrans.
3. Do ride—trans. (motorcycle); is—linking (safe)
4. tastes—linking (good); prefer—trans. (cereal)

5. sounded—trans. (alarm); scrambled—intrans.

p. 106 *QUICK CHECK* 5

Adverb	Word Modified
1. now	understand (when)
2. too	costly (extent)
3. professionally	tap-danced (how)
very	young (extent)
4. so	late (extent)
5. often; back	bring (when *or* to what extent; where)
delicately	carved (how)

p. 113 *QUICK CHECK* 6

1. until—subordinating
2. not only, but also—correlative
3. but—coordinating
4. For; with; with
5. Before; of

p. 115 *QUICK CHECK* 7

1. adverb   4. adjective
2. verb   5. preposition
3. noun

Chapter 2
Agreement

p. 124 *QUICK CHECK* 1

1. all—are
2. Most—stress
3. each—Does
4. Both—show
5. class—begins; all—are

p. 129 *QUICK CHECK* 2

1. crew—are

2. flight—is
3. one third—was
4. Red beans and rice—is
5. walks, jogging—serves

p. 133 *QUICK CHECK 3*

1. make   4. hang
2. recounts   5. are
3. doesn't

p. 140 *QUICK CHECK 4*

1. his or her   4. her
2. their   5. its
3. he or she

Chapter 3
Using Verbs

p. 150 *QUICK CHECK 1*

1. led   4. sat
2. taught   5. crept
3. told

p. 152 *QUICK CHECK 2*

1. come   4. chosen
2. did   5. drove
3. begun

p. 153 *QUICK CHECK 3*

1. burst   4. spread
2. C   5. hit
3. hurt

p. 156 *QUICK CHECK 4*

1. lie   4. rises
2. set   5. lay
3. sit

p. 163 *QUICK CHECK 5*

1. will stop—will have stopped
2. would have asked—had asked
3. made—make
4. happened—had happened
5. studied—has studied

p. 175 *QUICK CHECK 6*

1. C
2. Every member of the committee had heard the proposal.
3. Your brother should have washed the dishes.
4. Before Friday, the coach will have named a replacement.
5. C

p. 178 *QUICK CHECK 7*

1. imperative   4. subjunctive
2. indicative   5. indicative
3. subjunctive

p. 182 *QUICK CHECK 8*

1. to have protected—to protect
2. Deciding—Having decided
3. to have gone—to go
4. singing—having sung
5. to live—to have lived

Chapter 4
Using Pronouns

p. 191 *QUICK CHECK 1*

1. they—subject
2. I—subject
3. he—subject
4. she—predicate nominative
5. we—predicate nominative

p. 194 *QUICK CHECK 2*

(Answers may vary.)
1. him, her   4. her
2. me   5. them
3. him

p. 196 *QUICK CHECK 3*

1. present participle—it
2. gerund—his *or* present participle—him
3. present participle—ribbons

shooter—she
4. designing a new filing system—task
5. persimmon tree, mango tree, and hawthorn—leaves

Chapter 7
Clauses

p. 265 *QUICK CHECK* 1

1. subordinate clause
2. independent clause
3. subordinate clause
4. independent clause
5. independent clause

p. 267 *QUICK CHECK* 2

1. which was written by Richard Wright—*Native Son*—subject
2. that I caught yesterday—fish—direct object
3. to whom we should go for help—people—object of a preposition
4. who enjoy Native American art—those—subject
5. whose colt grazed nearby—mare—modifier

p. 269 *QUICK CHECK* 3

1. whatever you say—object of a preposition
2. whoever wants one—indirect object
3. That Jill was worried—subject
4. that we could leave now—direct object
5. where the pirates buried their treasure—predicate nominative

p. 274 *QUICK CHECK* 4

1. When we have a fire drill—

must go—when
2. so that they can escape their enemies—need—why
3. if (you are) not completely satisfied—Return—condition
4. than I (do)—better—extent
5. while the doctor was busy—Reading—when

Chapter 8
Sentence Structure

p. 280 *QUICK CHECK* 1

1. fragment   4. sentence
2. sentence   5. fragment
3. fragment

p. 285 *QUICK CHECK* 2

1. litter, mother—were
2. (you)—stand, tell
3. All—was lost
4. Ms. Odoski—Could have been
5. entrance—is

p. 290 *QUICK CHECK* 3

1. homes—direct object
2. her—direct object; qualified—objective complement
3. Sam—direct object; chairperson—objective complement; him—indirect object; gavel—direct object
4. cousin, me—indirect objects; records—direct object; posters—direct object
5. voice—direct object

p. 293 *QUICK CHECK* 4

1. is—Icy—predicate adjective
2. Was—author—predicate nominative
3. feel—concerned—predicate adjective

4. does taste—spicy—predicate adjective
5. is—Great Sphinx—predicate nominative

p. 298 *QUICK CHECK* 5

1. interrogative—equations?
2. exclamatory—record!
3. imperative—pepper.
4. declarative—hydrogen.
5. imperative or exclamatory—now!

Chapter 9
Sentence Style

p. 309 *QUICK CHECK* 1
(Answers may vary.)

1. which
2. If
3. but
4. consequently
5. Either . . . or

p. 313 *QUICK CHECK* 2
(Answers may vary.)

1. Sports fans may disagree over whether going to baseball games or to football games is more fun, but few people can ignore the importance of sports in America.
2. C
3. Some sports fans argue endlessly and angrily about whether football or baseball is truly the American pastime.
4. Baseball backers may insist that baseball is the more important game, since it requires intelligence and dexterity.
5. On the other hand, football fans may praise a

quarterback's speed, skill, and agility.

p. 317 *QUICK CHECK* 3
(Answers may vary.)

1. One colorful figure of the Old West, Andrew García, tells of his exploits in his auto-biography *Tough Trip Through Paradise*.
2. C
3. Like many of the outlaws García knew, Reynolds died a violent death.
4. Although tempted to become an outlaw himself, García eventually settled down and began writing his exciting account of his life.
5. García didn't live to see his memoirs published. The manuscripts, which he had packed away in dynamite boxes, were discovered years after his death.

p. 321 *QUICK CHECK* 4
(Answers may vary.)

1. Dense clouds surrounded the aircraft, and the pilot had to rely on her instruments.
2. Pilots flying in certain situations must believe the instrument panel rather than their physical sensations because a person can easily become disoriented without a point of reference.
3. Flying over snow or water can be tiring; darkness, too, can present problems, especially for inexperienced pilots.
4. For a pilot, boredom is a

dangerous state of mind that can lead to an accident.

5. Because long flights can be hazardous, pilots must be in peak mental condition as well as optimum physical health.

p. 324   *QUICK CHECK* 5

(Answers may vary.)

Have you ever heard of kendo? Kendo is an ancient Japanese martial art requiring skill, concentration, and agility. The contestants fight with long bamboo swords called *shinai.* Because kendo can be dangerous, each player must wear protective gear that includes a mask, a breastplate, and thick gloves. Each match lasts three to five minutes, and the first contestant to score two points wins. Kendo is a graceful, dignified sport. Respect toward one's opponent is important, and a contestant can even be disqualified for rudeness.

p. 327   *QUICK CHECK* 6

(Answers may vary.)

1. C
2. Have you ever read sentences that seem to ramble on?
3. Redundant sentences are boring.
4. Sentences that are longer than necessary may confuse your reader.
5. A sentence with too many subordinate clauses becomes a mental maze for the inattentive reader.

Chapter 10
Sentence Combining

p. 336   *QUICK CHECK* 1

(Answers may vary.)

1. Ancient peoples believed that dreams carried important messages about the future.
2. Today, dreams still fascinate people all over the world.
3. For instance, Sigmund Freud, the great psychoanalyst, believed that dreams illustrated conflicts in a person's inner life.
4. Following in Freud's footsteps, his student Carl Jung was particularly interested in dreams.
5. Nevertheless, other people believe that dreams are simply the brain's meaningless, random activity, perhaps resulting from eating too much spicy food.

p. 338   *QUICK CHECK* 2

(Answers may vary.)

1. William Least Heat-Moon's first name comes from an English ancestor, and his last name was given to him by his Sioux father.
2. In 1977, Least Heat-Moon left his Missouri home and began traveling across the country on back roads.
3. The title of his book *Blue Highways* doesn't refer to the actual color of roads; it refers to the blue lines that marked the back roads on his highway map.

4. Least Heat-Moon's trip began in the middle of the nation, and his route was shaped like a jagged, sideways heart.
5. Small, oddly named towns and friendly, helpful people made his journey memorable.

p. 342 *QUICK CHECK* 3

(*Answers may vary.*)

1. Space medicine, which deals with the physical effects of space travel, is one of the most important areas of space study.
2. Doctors learned much about the human body's reactions to space travel as they collected medical data during early space missions.
3. Engineers must consider how the spacecraft's acceleration will affect the astronauts' bodies.
4. A space shuttle is designed to protect the astronauts against the high-intensity radiation that they encounter in space.
5. Because a person's heart and muscles weaken in a weightless condition, astronauts must exercise regularly in space.

Chapter 11
Capitalization

p. 360 *QUICK CHECK* 1

1. the Far West
2. a city north of Louisville
3. Lock the door!
4. Mary McLeod Bethune
5. Mexican gold
6. She said, "It was not I!"
7. the Utah Salt Flats

8. C
9. III. History of China
10. 210 Thirty-eighth Avenue North

p. 365 *QUICK CHECK* 2

1. St. Patrick's Cathedral
2. *City of New Orleans*
3. the Federal Reserve Bank
4. the Normandy Invasion
5. C
6. Cherokee history
7. Jones and Drake, Inc.
8. on Labor Day
9. C
10. Gold Medal flour

p. 370 *QUICK CHECK* 3

1. the *Washington Post*
2. ex-Senator Margaret Chase Smith
3. *I'll Fly Away*
4. C
5. Emancipation Proclamation
6. the first chapter in *The Grapes of Wrath*
7. the teachings of Islam
8. C
9. Come with me, Dad.
10. the New Testament

Chapter 12
Punctuation

p. 382 *QUICK CHECK* 1

1. Wow! liftoff?
2. Hurry!"
3. Mrs. W. St., Pa.?
4. Co. P.M.
5. yet"?

p. 388 *QUICK CHECK* 2

1. happy,
2. picnic,
3. C
4. White River Bridge,

resurfacing,
5. C

p. 392 *QUICK CHECK 3*

1. Well, fact,
2. aloof,
3. ruins, empire,
4. fall,
5. ringing, Suzanne,

p. 397 *QUICK CHECK 4*

1. Address inquiries to Manager, Able Industries, Inc., 6235 South Main Street, Salt Lake City, Utah.
2. This technique has been technically possible for the last fifty years.
3. C
4. All the coins I had, had been lost.
5. From the hilltop we could see the stars; below, the town was dark.

p. 399 *QUICK CHECK 5*

1. heritage;   4. 1893;
2. Oklahoma;   5. popular;
3. tricks;

p. 402 *QUICK CHECK 6*

1. Major leaders in the women's suffrage movement included the following women: Carrie Chapman Catt, Susan B. Anthony, Lucretia Mott, and Elizabeth Cady Stanton.
2. I think I'll entitle my autobiography *Into the Fire: The Life of Sam Kettle.*
3. My task was simple: Locate the whereabouts of the Lost Dutchman Mine.
4. By 5:00 that afternoon, I had memorized twelve verses,

beginning with Genesis 1:1.
5. Medal of Honor winners include Sergeants José Mendoza López and Macarío García.

Chapter 13
Punctuation

p. 411 *QUICK CHECK 1*

1. Does the library have a copy of <u>Ashanti to Zulu: African Traditions</u>?
2. There was an article in <u>Omni</u> about Arthur C. Clarke's <u>2001: A Space Odyssey</u> and the similarities to our own space flights; the article also reviewed Clarke's <u>2010: Odyssey Two.</u>
3. Can you tell me the name of the symbol over the second <u>n</u> in the Spanish word <u>niño</u>?
4. While reading a history book called <u>The Rise and Fall of Nazi Germany</u>, I used my dictionary to look up the definitions of the following terms: <u>Anschluss</u> and <u>Luftwaffe</u>.
5. I don't like that karate game; <u>Super Mario Brothers</u> is still my favorite.

p. 419 *QUICK CHECK 2*

[1] "I think 'The Weeping Woman' would be a good title for my new song," Tomás told Jim. "Can you guess what it's about?"

[2] "Well, I once read a magazine article titled 'La Llorona, the Weeping Woman' about a popular Mexican American legend," Jim replied.

[3] "That's the legend I'm talking about!" Tomás exclaimed. "I first heard it when I was a little boy growing up in southern California."

[4] "I think," Jim commented, "people in the music business would call the song a 'tear-jerker' because it tells a sad story about a poor, wronged woman who goes crazy, drowns her children, and kills herself; then she returns as a ghost to look for them forever."

[5] "Didn't your mother ever say, 'Don't believe those horrible stories,'?" Tomás asked Jim.

p. 426 *QUICK CHECK 3*

1. Haven't you and your sister ever visited your sister and brother-in-law's ranch?
2. No, not yet; it's something we've been wanting to do for a long time.
3. I'll bet; I'd be saying so long to this town's city streets and be out there in a flash.
4. Well, it's not all fun and games; their day does start at four o'clock in the morning, so a visit isn't just a week's vacation.
5. Yikes! I'm just fixin' to get to sleep by then; maybe Texas's wilds are better left to you and yours.

p. 435 *QUICK CHECK 4*

1. Les Brown—be sure to watch his show—is a tremendous motivational speaker who encourages people to make positive

changes in their lives.
2. The citizen who spoke before the town's planning committee stated, "The project under proposal (the halfway house) will provide benefits both to the residents of the house and to society."
3. Providing visuals—pictures, charts, maps, or graphs—can often help an audience understand technical information more easily.
4. Use two-thirds cup of wheat germ, a quarter of a cup of raisins—currants may be substituted for raisins—and/or a cup of nuts.
5. You can give me a call at (504) 555–7232 or reach me at the Lion Building; the ZIP Code is 10102-2354.

Chapter 14
Spelling and Vocabulary

p. 450 *QUICK CHECK 1*

1. finally
2. mischief
3. wryness
4. proceed
5. receive

p. 453 *QUICK CHECK 2*

1. mileage
2. grazing
3. vied
4. freezable
5. truly
6. dirtiest
7. surveyor
8. paid
9. dimmer
10. cowed

p. 458 *QUICK CHECK 3*

1. scarves
2. dishes
3. agencies
4. radios
5. 500s *or* 500's
6. feet
7. bass *or* basses [the fish]
8. bases
9. z's
10. points of honor

Index

INDEX

Acknowledgments

For permission to reprint copyrighted material, grateful acknowledgment is made to the following sources:

A.M.E. Church: From "I Sit and Sew" by Alice Dunbar-Nelson from *The A.M.E. Church Review.* Copyright 1920 by The A.M.E. Church.

American Documentaries and Shelby Foote: From "Men at War: An Interview With Shelby Foote" from *The Civil War: An Illustrated History* by Geoffrey C. Ward. Copyright © 1990 by American Documentaries.

The Asia Society: From "Thoughts of Hanoi" by Nguyen Thi Vinh, translated by Nguyen Ngoc Bich. Copyright © 1975 by The Asia Society.

Bantam Books, a division of Bantam, Doubleday, Dell Publishing Group, Inc.: From *Yeager: An Autobiography* by General Chuck Yeager and Leo Janos. Copyright © 1985 by Yeager, Inc. All rights reserved.

Clarion Books/Houghton Mifflin Co.: From *From Top Hats to Baseball Caps, From Bustles to Blue Jeans* by Lila Perl. Text copyright © 1990 by Lila Perl. All rights reserved.

The Continuum Publishing Company: From "The Sixth Sally" from *The Cyberiad: Fables for the Cybernetic Age* by Stanislaw Lem, translated by Michael Kandel. English translation copyright © 1974 by The Seabury Press, Inc.

John Daniel & Co. Publishers: From "The Old Cherry Tree" from *Brief Cherishing: A Napa Valley Harvest* by Hildegarde Flanner. Copyright © 1985 by Hildegarde Flanner.

Joan Daves Agency as agent for the proprietor of The Heirs to the Estate of Martin Luther King, Jr.: From "Letter from Birmingham Jail" from *Why We Can't Wait* by Martin Luther King, Jr. Copyright © 1963 by Martin Luther King, Jr.; copyright renewed © 1991 by Coretta Scott King.

Discover Syndication: From "Language Watch" section titled "Clever Kanzi" by Frederic Golden from *Discover,* vol. 12, no. 3, March 1991. Copyright © 1991 by Discover Magazine.

Edward Dolnick: From "The Ghost's Vocabulary" by Edward Dolnick. Originally published in *The Atlantic Monthly,* vol. 268, no. 4, October 1991. Copyright © 1991 by Edward Dolnick.

Doubleday, a division of Bantam, Doubleday, Dell Publishing Group, Inc.: From "Animal Senses" from *The Living World* by Tony Seddon and Jill Bailey. Copyright © 1986 by BLA Publishing, Ltd.

Farrar, Straus & Giroux, Inc.: From "First Death in Nova Scotia" and from "One Art" from *The Complete Poems 1927-1979* by Elizabeth Bishop. Copyright © 1979, 1983 by Alice Helen Methfessel. From "West With the Night" from *West With the Night* by Beryl Markham. Copyright © 1942, 1983 by Beryl Markham. Published by North Point Press.

Shelby Foote and American Documentaries: From "Men at War: An Interview With Shelby Foote" from *The Civil War: An Illustrated History* by Geoffrey C. Ward. Copyright © 1990 by American Documentaries.

Gibbs Smith Publisher: From "A Flight of Geese" from *The Girl From Cardigan* by Leslie Norris. Copyright © 1988 by Leslie Norris.

Harmony Books, a division of Random House, Inc.: From *Life, the Universe and Everything* by Douglas Adams. Copyright © 1982 by Douglas Adams. From page 55 of *Labyrinth: Solving the Riddle of the Maze* by Adrian Fisher and Georg Gerster. Text copyright © 1990 by Adrian Fisher, compilation copyright © 1990 by Adrian Fisher and Georg Gerster.

HarperCollins Publishers, Inc.: From *Jonah's Gourd Vine* by Zora Neale Hurston. Copyright 1934 by Zora Neale Hurston; copyright renewed © 1962 by John C. Hurston. From *Seven Arrows* by Hyemeyohsts Storm. Copyright © 1972 by Hyemeyohsts Storm.

Houghton Mifflin Co.: From *Tough Trip Through Paradise* by Andrew García. Copyright © 1967 by the Rock Foundation. All rights reserved. From *The Heart is a Lonely Hunter* by Carson McCullers. Copyright 1940 by Carson Smith McCullers, copyright renewed © 1967 by Carson McCullers.

J.C.A. Literary Agency, Inc.: From "The Land and the Water" from *The Wind Shifting West* by Shirley Ann Grau. Copyright © 1973 by Shirley Ann Grau.

Alfred A. Knopf, Inc.: From pp. 24-25 from *Alistair Cooke's America* by Alistair Cooke. Copyright © 1973 by Alistair Cooke. From "The Negro Speaks of Rivers" from *Selected Poems* by Langston Hughes. Copyright 1926 by Alfred A. Knopf, Inc., copyright renewed 1954 by Langston Hughes.

Life Picture Sales and John Neary: From "Eliot Porter" from *Life,* vol. 14, no. 2, p. 80, February 1991.

Lothrop, Lee and Shepard Books, a division of William Morrow & Co., Inc.: From pp. 34-35 from *Dogs: All About Them* by Alvin and Virginia Silverstein. Copyright © 1986 by Alvin and Virginia Silverstein.

William Morrow & Company, Inc.: From "Primitive Blues and Primitive Jazz" from *Blues People: Negro Music in White America* by LeRoi Jones. Copyright © 1963 by LeRoi Jones.

National Geographic Society: From "Whatzat? An Odd Bird With a Cow's Stomach" from the "Geographica" section and from "Emeralds" by Fred Ward from *National Geographic,* vol. 178, no. 1, July, 1990. Copyright © 1990 by the National Geographic Society.

John Neary and Life Picture Sales: From "Eliot Porter" from *Life,* vol. 14, no. 2, p. 80, February 1991.

New World Dictionaries, a division of Simon & Schuster, New York: From the entry "obscure" from *Webster's New World Dictionary of American English,* Third College Edition. Copyright © 1988 by Simon & Schuster, Inc.

The New York Review of Books: From "In Sorrow's Kitchen" by Darryl Pinckney from *The New York Review of Books,* vol. XXV, no. 20, December 21, 1978.

Copyright © 1978 by *The New York Review of Books.*

The New York Times Company: From "Nurses Get a Taste of an Elderly Patient's Life" by Andrew H. Malcolm from "Suburban Journal" section of *The New York Times,* October 20, 1992, p. 20. Copyright © 1992 by The New York Times Company.

Newsweek: From "I Won't Be Celebrating Columbus Day" by Susan Shown Harjo from *Newsweek,* Columbus Special Issue, Fall/Winter 1991. Copyright © 1991 by Newsweek, Inc. All rights reserved. From "Classrooms of Babel" by Connie Leslie, Daniel Glick, and Jeanne Gordon from *Newsweek,* vol. CXVII, no. 6, February 11, 1991. Copyright © 1991 by Newsweek, Inc. All rights reserved.

Random House, Inc.: From *I Know Why the Caged Bird Sings* by Maya Angelou. Copyright © 1969 by Maya Angelou. From *The Woman Warrior: Memoirs of a Girlhood Among Ghosts* by Maxine Hong Kingston. Copyright © 1975, 1976 by Maxine Hong Kingston.

David Roberts: From "The Decipherment of Ancient Maya" by David Roberts. First appeared in *The Atlantic Monthly,* vol. 268, no. 3, September 1991.

Charles Scribner's Sons, an imprint of Macmillan Publishing Company: From *In Our Time* by Ernest Hemingway. Copyright 1925 by Charles Scribner's Sons; copyright renewed 1953 by Ernest Hemingway.

Tribune Media Services: From "Car-Buying: The Compleat Guide" from "Wit's End" by Dave Barry from *The Washington Post Magazine,* January 21, 1990, p. 36. Copyright © 1990 by *The Washington Post.*

Viking Penguin, a division of Penguin Books USA Inc.: From *Reading the Numbers* by Mary Blocksma. Copyright © 1989 by Mary Blocksma. From "Flight" from *The Long Valley* by John Steinbeck. Copyright 1938, copyright renewed © 1966 by John Steinbeck.

H.W. Wilson Company: From entries from "Moize, Elizabeth A." through "Molecular Beams" from *Readers' Guide to Periodical Literature, 1990.* Copyright © 1990, 1991 by the H.W. Wilson Company.

Workman Publishing Company, Inc.: From "Three Great Homemade Props" from

Be A Clown! by Turk Pipkin. Copyright © 1989 by Turk Pipkin. All rights reserved.

The following excerpts also appear in *Holt High School Handbook 2.*

From *Dinosaur Days in Texas* by Tom and Jane D. Allen with Savannah Waring Walker. Copyright © 1989 by Hendrick-Long Publishing Company. Published by Hendrick-Long Publishing Company.

From *The Negro Novel in America* by Robert Bone. Copyright © 1958 by Yale University Press, Inc. Published by Yale University Press, Inc.

From "A Wagner Matinée" by Willa Cather.

Quote about prepositions attributed to Winston Churchill.

From "The Rime of the Ancient Mariner" by Samuel Taylor Coleridge.

From "Marigolds" by Eugenia Collier from *Negro Digest*, November 1969. Copyright © 1969 by Johnson Publishing Company, Inc. Published by Johnson Publishing Company, Inc.

From "The Moustache" from *Eight Plus One* by Robert Cormier. Copyright © 1975 by Robert Cormier. Published by Pantheon Books, a division of Random House, Inc.

From a letter by Emily Dickinson from "The Vision and Veto of Emily Dickinson" by Thomas H. Johnson in *Final Harvest: Emily Dickinson's* Poems, selected and introduced by Thomas H. Johnson.

From "On the Mall" from *The White Album* by Joan Didion. Copyright © 1979 by Joan Didion. Published by Simon & Schuster, Inc.

From *Pilgrim at Tinker Creek* by Annie Dillard. Copyright © 1974 by Annie Dillard. Published by HarperCollins Publishers, Inc.

From *Meditation 17* by John Donne.

From *Essays: First Series, History* by Ralph Waldo Emerson, 1841.

From *Poor Richard's Almanack* by Benjamin Franklin.

From *Barrio Boy* by Ernesto Galarza. Copyright © 1971 by University of Notre Dame Press. Published by University of Notre Dame Press.

Three excerpts from *Zora Neale Hurston: A Literary Biography* by Robert E. Hemenway. Copyright © 1977 by the Board of Trustees of the University of Illinois. Published by University of Illinois Press.

From "Speech in Virginia Convention, Richmond, March 23, 1775" by Patrick Henry.

From "Zora Neale Hurston" by Lillie P. Howard from *Dictionary of Literary Biography, Volume Fifty-one: Afro-American Writers from the Harlem Renaissance to 1940*, edited by Trudier Harris. Copyright © 1987 by Gale Research Company. Published by Gale Research Company.

From "Zora Neale Hurston: Just Being Herself" by Lillie P. Howard from *Essence*, November 1980. Published by Essence Communications, Inc.

Three excerpts from *Dust Tracks on a Road* by Zora Neale Hurston. Copyright 1942 by Zora Neale Hurston, copyright renewed © 1970 by John C. Hurston. Published by J.B. Lippincott Company.

From "How It Feels to Be Colored Me" from *I Love Myself When I Am Laughing* by Zora Neale Hurston, edited by Alice Walker.

From *Mules and Men* by Zora Neale Hurston. Copyright 1935 by Zora Neale Hurston. Published by J.B. Lippincott Company.

Quote by Zora Neale Hurston from "Book of the Times" by John Chamberlain from *The New York Times*, November 7, 1942. Copyright 1942 by The New York Times Company. Published by The New York Times Company.

From "The Tom-Tom Cries and Laughs" from *From Du Bois to Van Vechten: The Early New Negro Literature, 1903-1926* by Chidi Ikonné. Copyright © 1981 by Congressional Information Service, Inc. Published by Greenwood Press.

From a Speech by Chief Joseph delivered in Washington, D.C.

Two excerpts from "Speech of Surrender" by Chief Joseph, 1877.

From "Araby" in *Dubliners* by James Joyce.

From "New African" from *Sarah Phillips* by Andrea Lee. Copyright © 1984 by Andrea Lee. Published by Random House, Inc.

From "The Magic Barrel" from *The Magic Barrel* by Bernard Malamud. Copyright © 1954, 1958 by Bernard Malamud. Published by Farrar, Straus and Giroux, Inc.

From "To Da-duh, in Memoriam" from *Reena and Other Stories* by Paule Marshall. Copyright © 1983 by The Feminist Press at The City University of New York. Published by The Feminist Press.

Three excerpts from *Blue Highways: A Journey into America* by William Least Heat Moon. Copyright © 1982 by William Least Heat Moon. Published by Little, Brown and Company, in association with The Atlantic Monthly.

From *The Road to Wigan Pier* by George Orwell. Published by Harcourt Brace & Company.

Two excerpts from *1984* by George Orwell. Published by Harcourt Brace & Company.

From *The Masque of the Red Death* by Edgar Allen Poe.

From "The Jilting of Granny Weatherall" from *Flowering Judas and Other Stories* by Katherine Anne Porter. Copyright 1930, renewed © 1958 by Katherine Anne Porter. Published by Harcourt Brace & Company.

From "The Wheelbarrow" from *Selected Stories* by V. S. Pritchett. Copyright © 1978 by V. S. Pritchett. Published by Literistic, Ltd. and Random House, Inc.

From "Gentleman of Río en Medio" by Juan A. A. Sedillo from *We Are Chicanos,* edited by Philip D. Ortego.

From *MacBeth* by William Shakespeare.

From "The Jacket" from *Small Faces* by Gary Soto. Copyright © 1986 by Gary Soto. Published by Arte Público Press.

From *The Red Pony* by John Steinbeck. Copyright 1933, 1937, 1938 and renewed © 1961, 1965, 1966 by John Steinbeck. Published by Viking, a division of Penguin Books USA, Inc.

From "Book of the Times" by Ralph Thompson from *The New York Times,* October 6, 1937. Copyright 1937 by The New York Times Company. Published by The New York Times Company.

From card catalog information for *Action-Getting Resumes for Today's Jobs* by Gary Turbak from the Library of Congress.

From *Life on the Mississippi* by Mark Twain.

From "Vol. I. Pudd'nhead Wilson's New Calendar," ch. 18, from *Following the Equator* by Mark Twain/Samuel Clemens, 1897.

From *The United States Constitution.*

From *The Analects of Confucious* translated by Arthur Waley. Copyright 1938 by George Allen & Unwin, Ltd. Published by Macmillan Publishing Company.

From "In Search of Zora Neale Hurston" by Alice Walker from *Ms.,* vol. III, no. 9, March 1975. Published by Ms. Magazine Corp.

From "Zora Neal Hurston: Author and Folklorist" by Margaret F. Wilson from *Negro History Bulletin,* October/November/December 1982. Published by Negro History Bulletin.

From *American Hunger* by Richard Wright. Copyright 1944 by Richard Wright, copyright © 1977 by Ellen Wright. Published by HarperCollins Publishers, Inc.

From *Black Writers of the Thirties* by James O. Young. Copyright © 1973 by Louisiana State University Press. Published by Louisiana State University Press.

ILLUSTRATION CREDITS

Rich Lo—78, 188, 369, 381, 469, 527

Martin Kornick—96, 158, 314, 457

Tom Gianni—106, 245, 338, 461